CLYMER®

HONDA

CR250R & CR500R • 1988-1996

The world's finest publisher of mechanical how-to manuals

INTERTEC PUBLISHING

P.O. Box 12901, Overland Park, Kansas 66282-2901

Copyright ©1992 Intertec Publishing

FIRST EDITION
First Printing May, 1992
Second Printing December, 1993

SECOND EDITION
First Printing October, 1996
Second Printing August, 1998
Third Printing February, 2000

Printed in U.S.A.

CLYMER and colophon are registered trademarks of Intertec Publishing.

ISBN: 0-89287-682-4

Library of Congress: 96-77870

Technical photography by David Harter.

Technical illustrations by Steve Amos and Robert Caldwell.

COVER: Photographed by Mark Clifford, Mark Clifford Photography, Los Angeles California. Motorcycle courtesy of Rice Honda of La Puente, La Puente, California.

Intertec Book Division

President Raymond E. Maloney
Vice President, Book Division Ted Marcus

The following books and guides are published by Intertec Publishing.

CLYMER SHOP MANUALS
Boat Motors and Drives
Motorcycles and ATVs
Snowmobiles
Personal Watercraft

ABOS/INTERTEC/CLYMER BLUE BOOKS AND TRADE-IN GUIDES
Recreational Vehicles
Outdoor Power Equipment
Agricultural Tractors
Lawn and Garden Tractors
Motorcycles and ATVs
Snowmobiles and Personal Watercraft
Boats and Motors

AIRCRAFT BLUEBOOK-PRICE DIGEST
Airplanes
Helicopters

AC-U-KWIK DIRECTORIES
The Corporate Pilot's Airport/FBO Directory
International Manager's Edition
Jet Book

I&T SHOP SERVICE MANUALS
Tractors

INTERTEC SERVICE MANUALS
Snowmobiles
Outdoor Power Equipment
Personal Watercraft
Gasoline and Diesel Engines
Recreational Vehicles
Boat Motors and Drives
Motorcycles
Lawn and Garden Tractors

CONTENTS

QUICK REFERENCE DATA

TIRE INFLATION PRESSURE (COLD)

Size	Air pressure		
	psi		kg/cm^2
CR250R			
Front			
80/100-21 (51M)	15		1.0
Rear			
110/100-18 (64M)	15		1.0
CR500R			
Front			
80/100-21 (51M)	15		1.0
Rear			
110/100-18 (64M)	15		1.0

RECOMMENDED TRANSMISSION OIL

All models	Honda 4-stroke oil SAE 10W-40 or equivalent API classification SF or SG

APPROXIMATE CLUTCH/TRANSMISSION OIL CAPACITIES

Model	Liters	U.S. qt.	Imp. qt.
CR250R			
1988-1989	550 cc		
At oil change	0.55	0.58	0.48
After disassembly	0.6	0.63	0.53
1990-1991			
At oil change	0.63	0.67	0.55
After disassembly	0.7	0.74	0.62
CR500R			
1988-1989			
At oil change	0.65	0.68	0.57
After disassembly	0.7	0.74	0.62
1990-1996			
At oil change	0.68	0.71	0.60
After disassembly	0.75	0.79	0.66

FRONT FORK AIR PRESSURE

	Standard		Maximum	
	psi	kg/cm^2	psi	kg/cm^2
All models	0	0	6	0.4

FUEL/OIL PREMIX RATIO

Model	Premix ratio
CR250R	20:1
CR500R	
1988-1991	20:1
1992-1996	32:1

FRONT FORK OIL CAPACITY

	ml	U.S. oz.	Imp. oz
CR250R			
1988			
Standard	564	19.1	19.9
Minimum	516	17.5	18.2
Maximum	573	19.4	20.2
1989			
Standard	657	22.2	23.1
Minimum	636	21.5	22.4
Maximum	671	22.7	23.7
1990			
Standard	640	21.6	22.5
Minimum	617	20.8	21.7
Maximum	650	22.0	22.9
1991			
Standard	651	22.0	22.9
Minimum	631	21.3	22.7
Maximum	665	22.5	23.4
CR500R			
1988			
Standard	575	19.4	20.2
Minimum	527	17.8	18.5
Maximum	584	19.8	20.5
1989			
Standard	641	21.7	22.6
Minimum	620	21.0	21.9
Maximum	655	22.1	23.0
1990			
Standard	612	20.7	21.6
Minimum	605	20.5	21.4
Maximum	639	21.6	22.5
1991			
Standard	657	22.2	23.1
Minimum	631	21.3	22.2
Maximum	665	22.5	23.4
1992			
Standard	582	19.7	20.5
Minimum	552	18.7	19.5
Maximum	584	19.8	20.6
1993			
Standard	572	19.3	20.1
Minimum	541	18.3	19.1
Maximum	584	19.8	20.6
1994			
Standard	567	19.2	20.0
Minimum	534	18.1	18.9
Maximum	576	19.5	20.3

(continued)

FRONT FORK OIL CAPACITY (continued)

	ml	U.S. oz.	Imp. oz
CR500R (continued)			
1995			
Standard	525	17.8	18.5
Minimum	499	16.9	17.6
Maximum	539	18.2	19.0
1996			
Standard	636	21.5	22.4
Minimum	613	20.7	21.6
Maximum	658	22.3	23.2

FRONT FORK OIL LEVEL

	mm	in.
CR250R		
1988		
Standard	124	4.88
Maximum	115	4.53
Minimum	170	6.69
1989		
Standard	115	4.53
Maximum	105	4.13
Minimum	132	5.20
1990		
Standard	124	4.88
Maximum	114	5.67
Minimum	144	5.67
1991		
Standard	107	4.21
Maximum	95	3.74
Minimum	124	4.88
CR500R		
1988		
Standard	123	4.84
Maximum	114	4.49
Minimum	169	6.65
1989		
Standard	127	4.99
Maximum	116	4.6
Minimum	146	5.8
1990		
Standard	158	6.22
Maximum	133	5.2
Minimum	164	6.5
1991		
Standard	102	4.02
Maximum	95	3.74
Minimum	124	4.88
1992		
Standard	95	3.74
Maximum	93	3.66
Minimum	124	4.88
1993		
Standard	105	4.13
Maximum	93	3.66
Minimum	136	5.35

(continued)

FRONT FORK OIL LEVEL (continued)

	mm	in.
CR500R (continued)		
1994		
Standard	110	4.33
Maximum	101	3.98
Minimum	143	5.63
1995		
Standard	98	3.86
Maximum	84	3.31
Minimum	124	4.88
1996		
Standard	92	3.62
Maximum	73	2.87
Minimum	112	4.41

DRIVE CHAIN SLACK

	mm	in.
CR250R	35-40	1 3/8-1 9/16
CR500R		
1988-1991	35-40	1 3/8- 1 9/16
1992-on	35-45	1 3/8-1 49/64

CLUTCH LEVER FREE PLAY

	mm	in.
All models	10-20	3/8-3/4

THROTTLE ROTATIONAL FREE PLAY

	mm	in.
All models	3-5	1/8-1/4

TUNE-UP SPECIFICATIONS

Spark plug	
CR250R	
1988	
Type	Champion QN-84 or QN59G, NGK BR9EG or BR9EV, ND W27ESR-V or W27ESR-G
Gap	0.5-0.6 mm (0.020-0.024)
1989-1991	
Type	Champion QN-86 or QN-2G, NGK BR8EG or BR8EV, ND W24ESR-V or W24ESR-G
Gap	0.5-0.6 mm (0.020-0.024)
CR500R	
Type	Champion QN-86 or QN-2G, NGK BR8EG or BR8EV, ND W24ESR-V or W24ESR-G
Gap	0.5-0.6 mm (0.020-0.024)
Ignition timing	
CR250R	"F" mark @ 5,000 ±100 rpm
CR500R	"F" mark @ 4,000 ±100 rpm

(continued)

TUNE-UP SPECIFICATIONS (continued)

Carburetor air screw setting	
CR250	2 turns*
CR500R	
1988	1-1 1/2 turns*
1989-1990	2 turns*
1991-1996	1-1 1/2 turns*

* Number of turns out from a lightly seated position.

COOLING SYSTEM SPECIFICATIONS

	Liters	U.S. quart	Imp. quart
Capacity			
CR250R			
At coolant change	0.81	0.856	0.71
After disassembly	0.84	0.888	0.74
CR500R			
At coolant change	1.08	1.1	0.95
After disassembly	1.22	1.3	1.07
Freezing point			
(hydrometer test)			
Water-to-antifreeze ratio			
55:45	−32 ° C (−25 ° F)		
50:50	−37 ° C (−34 ° F)		
45:55	−44.5 ° C (−48 ° F)		

CHAPTER ONE

NOTE: If you own a 1992 CR500R or later model, first check the Supplement at the back of this book for any new service information.

GENERAL INFORMATION

This comprehensive manual provides service and maintenance procedures for the 1988-1991 Honda CR250R and the 1988-1996 Honda CR500R motorcycles. The easy-to-use text gives information on maintenance, tune-up, repair and overhaul. With hundreds of photos and drawings that correspond to and support the detailed steps, you will find everything needed to keep your Honda operating in peak condition.

A shop manual is a reference designed to help you find information fast. As in all Clymer books, this one was planned with you in mind. All chapters are thumb-tabbed for locating major topics. The *Index* at the rear of the book lists maintenance tasks by subject and paragraph heading. All procedures, tables, photos, etc., are presented in plain terms for the reader who may be working on the bike or using this manual for the first time. At the same time, the text is complete enough to meet the needs and purposes of the experienced mechanic.

Consider this book as a valuable tool and keep it near your work area. It will help lower repair and maintenance costs and improve your understanding of the bike. It will also contribute to making your work on the bike safe, enjoyable and rewarding.

To save yourself time, energy and confusion, read this entire chapter and become acquainted with the special features and organization of this manual.

The most frequently used maintenance specifications and capacities are located on the *Quick Reference Data* pages at the front the book.

Table 1 lists model coverage with engine and chassis serial numbers.

Metric and U.S. standards are used throughout this manual. U.S. to metric conversion is given in **Table 2**.

General torque specifications are given in **Table 3**.

Table 4 is a listing of the (initial) basic tools needed.

MANUAL ORGANIZATION

This chapter provides general information and discusses tools and equipment useful for maintenance, troubleshooting and repair. Chapter Two, *Troubleshooting*, contains methods and suggestions for quick, accurate diagnosis and repair of problems. Troubleshooting procedures discuss typical symptoms and logical methods to pinpoint the trouble.

Chapter Three, *Lubrication, Maintenance and Tune-up*, explains all normal periodic lubrication and preventive maintenance tasks necessary to keep the CR running well. Chapter Three also includes recommended tune-up procedures, eliminating the constant need to refer to other chapters on the various assemblies.

Subsequent chapters describe specific systems such as the engine, clutch and transmission, fuel and exhaust, liquid cooling system, suspension and brakes. Each chapter provides complete disassembly, repair and assembly procedures in easy-to-follow step-by-step form. If a repair is impractical for a home mechanic, it is so indicated. Usually, those repairs listed as impractical are more economically done by a dealer or competent repair shop. Specifications concerning a particular system are included at the end of the appropriate chapter.

Special tools are specified for some of the procedures in this manual. In most cases, the tool is illustrated by a photo or drawing and a number of them show the tool in actual use. Well-equipped mechanics may find they can substitute similar tools already on hand or can fabricate their own.

NOTES, CAUTIONS AND WARNINGS

The terms NOTE, CAUTION and WARNING appear throughout this manual and have specific meanings. A NOTE provides additional or special information to make a step or procedure easier or clearer. Disregarding a NOTE might cause inconvenience, but would not cause equipment damage or personal injury.

A CAUTION is provided in a procedure wherever equipment damage could result. Disregarding a CAUTION could cause permanent mechanical damage; however, personal injury is unlikely.

A WARNING is the most serious and emphasizes areas where personal injury or even death could result from negligence. Mechanical damage is also highly probable. WARNINGS *are to be taken seriously*. In some cases, serious injury or death has resulted from disregarding similar warnings.

REFERENCE TO LOCATIONS

To maintain consistency in locating components, keep in mind this manual's reference to locations. "Front" refers to the front of the bike. The front of any component, such as the engine, is the end which faces toward the front of the bike. The "left-" and "right-hand" sides refer to the position of the parts as viewed by a rider sitting on the seat facing forward. For example, the throttle control is on the

right-hand side and the clutch lever is on the left-hand side. These rules are simple, but they make identification and related instructions easier to follow.

SERVICE HINTS

Most of the service procedures covered are straightforward and can be performed by anyone reasonably handy with tools. It is suggested, however, that you consider your own capabilities carefully before attempting any operation involving major disassembly of the engine or transmission.

1. Some operations, such as spherical bearing replacement of the Pro-Link suspension pivot arm, require the use of special disassembly/assembly tools. It would be wiser to have these performed by a shop equipped for such work, rather than trying to do the job yourself with makeshift equipment. Other procedures require precise measurements with a good understanding of how the measuring tool works. Unless you have the skills and equipment required, it would be better to have a qualified shop make the measurements for you.

2. When servicing the engine, clutch or suspension components, the bike should be secured in a safe manner. A wooden box made of 3/4 in. plywood or a metal stand are excellent supports and can be transported easily.

3. There are many items available that can be used on your hands before and after working on your bike. Pro-Tek is a product that is applied to your hands prior to working on your bike and makes clean-up a lot easier. Waterless hand soaps such as Sta-Lube and powdered soaps such as Boraxo also work well for cleaning grease and dirt from the hands.

4. Repairs go much faster and easier if the bike is clean before you begin work. In some instances an important punch mark, arrow or line may go unnoticed due to grease or dirt. There are special cleaners, such as Gunk or Bel-Ray Degreaser (**Figure 1**) for washing the engine and related parts. For the best results, follow the manufacturer's directions on the container. Clean all oily or greasy parts with cleaning solvent as you remove them.

> *WARNING*
> *Gasoline presents an extreme fire hazard. Never use gasoline as a cleaning agent. Be sure to work in a well-venti-*

lated area when using cleaning solvent. Keep a fire extinguisher, rated for gasoline fires, in the work area.

5. Special tools are required for some repair procedures. Most of the special tools necessary are referenced by a Honda part number and can be ordered from an authorized dealer. Many times a tool can be rented from a rental shop or fabricated by a mechanic or machinist (often at considerable savings).

6. Much of the labor charged by mechanics is for removal, disassembly, assembly and reinstallation of other parts to reach the defective unit. It is usually possible to perform much of the preliminary work yourself and then take the defective unit in to the dealer for repair.

7. If you decide to tackle the job yourself, read the entire section in this manual which pertains to it, noting any special procedures. Study the illustrations and text until you have a *thorough* understanding of what is involved in completing the job satisfactorily.

8. If special tools are required, be sure that they are or will be available before you start. It is frustrating and time-consuming to get partly into a job and then be unable to complete it.

9. Protect finished surfaces from physical and corrosion damage due to gasoline, battery acid or brake fluid.

10. Simple wiring checks can be easily made at home, but knowledge of electronics is almost a necessity for performing tests with complicated electronic testing gear. Remember to disconnect the battery ground cable before working near electrical connections or disconnecting wires.

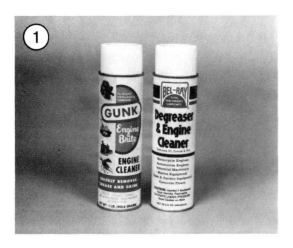

11. During disassembly of parts, keep a few general cautions in mind. Force is rarely needed to get things apart. If parts are a tight fit, such as a bearing in a case, there is usually a tool designed to separate them. Never use a screwdriver to pry apart parts with machined surfaces such as crankcase halves. This mars the flat surfaces and creates leaks.

12. Make diagrams (or take a Polaroid picture) wherever similar-appearing parts are found. For instance, crankcase bolts are often not the same length. You may think you can remember where everything came from, but mistakes are costly. There is also the possibility you may be sidetracked and not return to work for days or even weeks, at which time carefully laid out parts may become disturbed.

13. Tag all similar internal parts for location and mark all mating parts for position. Record the number and thickness of any shims as they are removed. Small parts can be identified by placing them in plastic sandwich bags. Seal and label the bags with masking tape. The spaces in egg cartons and cupcake tins are excellent for nuts and bolts and can be labeled by the order of disassembly.

14. Wiring should be tagged with masking tape and marked as each wire is removed.

15. Frozen or very tight bolts and screws can often be loosened by soaking with penetrating oil, such as WD-40 or Liquid Wrench, then sharply striking the bolt head a few times with a hammer and punch (or screwdriver for screws). Avoid heat unless absolutely necessary, since it may melt, warp or remove the temper from many parts.

16. No parts, except those assembled with a press fit, require unusual force during assembly. If a part is hard to remove or install, find out why before proceeding.

17. Cover all openings after removing parts to keep dirt, small tools, etc., from falling in.

18. In the procedural steps, the term "replace" means to discard a defective or non-reusable part and replace it. "Overhaul" means to remove, disassemble, inspect, measure, repair or replace defective parts, then reassemble and install the systems or parts.

19. Wiring connections and brake components should be kept clean and free of grease and oil.

20. Whenever a rotating part butts against a stationary part, look for a shim or washer. Use new gaskets if there is any doubt about the condition of the old ones.

21. Heavy grease can be used to hold small parts in place if they tend to fall out during assembly. However, keep grease and oil away from electrical and brake components.

22. Carbon can be removed from the cylinder head, the piston crown and the exhaust port with a dull screwdriver. *Do not* scratch either surface. Wipe off the surface with a clean cloth when finished.

23. Carburetors are best cleaned by disassembling them and soaking the parts in a commercial carburetor cleaner. All gaskets and rubber parts should be removed first. Never soak gaskets and rubber parts in these cleaners. Never use wire to clean out jets and air passages; they are easily damaged. Use compressed air to blow out the carburetor *after* the float has been removed.

24. A baby bottle makes a good measuring device for adding oil to the front forks. Get one that is graduated in fluid ounces and cubic centimeters. Paint or mark the bottle and seal it after use to avoid the possibility of accidental poisoning. Remember that oils and fluids leave residues that can be harmful.

25. Take your time and do the job right. A rebuilt engine must be broken-in using the same precautions as a new engine. Refer to the owner's manual for the rpm limits and maintenance requirements during break-in.

SPECIAL TIPS

Due to the extreme stress and demands placed on a motorcycle of this type, several points should be kept in mind when performing service and repair. The following items are general suggestions that may contribute to the overall life and safety of the machine while helping to avoid costly failures.

1. Use a locking compound such as Loctite No. 242 (blue Loctite) on all bolts and nuts, even if they are secured with lockwashers. This type of Loctite does not harden completely and allows easy removal of the bolt or nut. A screw or bolt lost from an engine cover or bearing retainer could easily cause serious and expensive damage before its loss is noticed. When applying Loctite, use a small amount. If too much is used, it can work its way down the threads and stick to other parts. Keep a tube of Loctite in your tool box; when used properly it is cheap insurance.

2. Use a hammer-driven impact tool to help remove bolts that are very tight. This tool helps prevent the rounding off of bolt heads and ensures a tight installation.

3. When straightening out the "fold-over" type lockwasher (as used on the clutch nut), use a wide-blade chisel such as an old and dull wood chisel. Such a tool provides a better purchase on the folded tab, making straightening out easier.

4. When installing the "fold-over" type lockwasher, always use a new washer if possible. If a new washer is not available, always fold over a part of the washer that has not been previously folded. Reusing the same fold may cause the washer to split and break, resulting in the loss of its locking ability and a loose piece of metal adrift in the engine. When folding the washer over, start the fold with a screwdriver and finish it with a pair of pliers. Try not to make the fold too sharp or the chances of it breaking under stress are increased. Keep several washers of each size in your tool box for field repairs.

5. When replacing missing or damaged fasteners, especially on the engine or frame components, always use Honda replacement parts. They are specially hardened for each application. The wrong 25-cent bolt could easily cause serious and expensive damage, not to mention rider injury.

6. When installing gaskets in the engine, always use Honda replacement gaskets *without* sealer, unless designated. These gaskets are designed to swell when they come in contact with oil. Gasket sealer will prevent the gaskets from swelling as intended, resulting in oil leaks. Honda gaskets are cut from material to the precise thickness needed. Installation

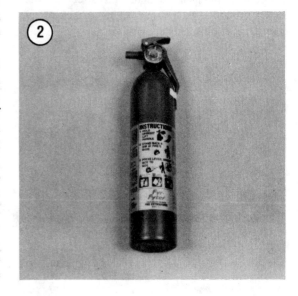

of a too-thick or too-thin gasket in a critical area could cause engine damage.

SAFETY FIRST

A safe mechanic, whether amateur or professional, can work for years and never sustain a serious injury. By observing a few rules of common sense and safety, you can enjoy many hours servicing your own motorcycle. Ignoring these rules can result in serious injuries to yourself and damage to the motorcycle.

1. Never use gasoline as a cleaning solvent.

2. Never smoke or use a torch in the vicinity of flammable liquids such as cleaning solvents, spray lubricants or oil and grease in open containers. .

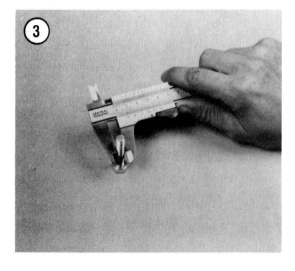

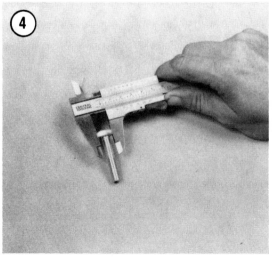

3. If welding or brazing is required on the machine, remove the fuel tank and the shock absorber (containing highly pressurized nitrogen) to a safe distance, at least 50 feet away.

4. Never smoke or use a torch in areas where battery charging is being performed. Hydrogen gas is formed during the charging process and is highly explosive.

5. Always use wrenches of the correct sizes to avoid damage to nuts and injury to yourself.

6. When loosening a tight or stuck nut, think about the direction you are turning it and what would happen if the wrench should slip.

7. Keep your work area clean and uncluttered.

8. Wear safety goggles when drilling, grinding or using a cold chisel. Safety goggles should also be worn when using compressed air. Dirt, metal filings and small parts can ricochet and be blown into your eyes.

9. Never use worn tools. Wipe grease and oil from tools before and after using them.

10. Keep a fire extinguisher (**Figure 2**) near the work area and be sure it is rated for both Class B (flammable liquids—gasoline, oil, paint, etc.) and Class C (electrical—wiring, etc.) type fires.

TORQUE SPECIFICATIONS

Torque specifications throughout this manual are given in Newton-meters (N•m) and foot-pounds (ft.-lb.).

General torque specifications for nuts and bolts that are not listed in the respective chapters are listed in **Table 3**. To use the table, first determine the size of the nut or bolt by measuring it with a vernier caliper. **Figure 3** and **Figure 4** show how this is done.

PARTS REPLACEMENT

Honda makes frequent changes during a model year. Some are minor, others are relatively major. When you order parts from the dealer or other parts distributor, always order by engine and frame number. The frame serial number is stamped on the right-hand side of the steering head (**Figure 5**). The engine serial number is located on the lower side of the crankcase below the drive sprocket (**Figure 6**). The carburetor identification number is located on the left-hand side of the carburetor body above the float bowl as shown in **Figure 7**. Write the numbers down and carry them with you. Compare the new parts to the old ones before purchasing them. If they are not alike, have the parts manager explain the difference to you.

Table 1 lists model coverage with engine and serial chassis numbers.

LUBRICANTS

Periodic lubrication is a major part of preventive maintenance and long life for any type of equipment. The *type* of lubricant used is just as important as the lubrication service itself, although in an emergency the wrong type of lubricant is better than none at all. The following paragraphs describe the types of lubricants most often used on motorcycle equipment. Be sure to follow the manufacturer's recommendations for lubricant types.

Generally, all liquid lubricants are called "oil." They may be mineral-based (including petroleum bases), natural-based (vegetable and animal bases), synthetic-based or emulsions (mixtures). "Grease" is an oil to which a thickening base has been added so that the end product is semi-solid. Grease is often classified by the type of thickener added. Lithium soap is a very common thickener.

Transmission Oil

The transmission is lubricated by a four-stroke engine oil. Four-stroke oil for motorcycle and automotive engines is graded by the American Petroleum Institute (API) and the Society of Automotive Engineers (SAE) in several categories. Oil containers display these ratings on the top or label.

API oil grade is indicated by letters; oils for gasoline engines are identified by an "S." The transmission in the Honda models described in this manual requires SG or SF graded oil (**Figure 8**).

Viscosity is an indication of the oil's thickness. The SAE uses numbers to indicate viscosity; thin oils have low numbers while thick oils have high numbers. A "W" after the number indicates that the viscosity testing was performed at a low temperature to simulate cold-weather operation. Oils fall into the 5W-30 and 20W-50 range.

Multi-grade oils (for example 10W-40) are less viscous (thinner) at low temperatures and more viscous at high temperatures. This allows the oil to

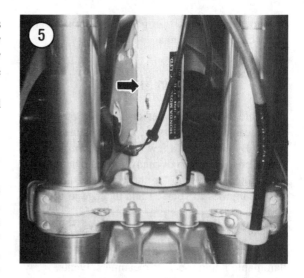

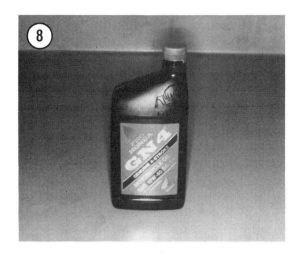

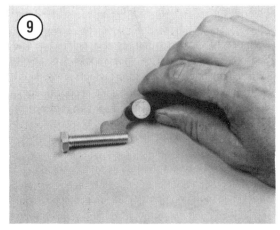

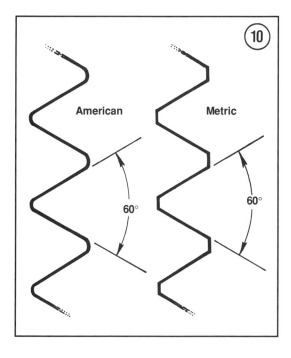

perform efficiently across a wide range of operating conditions. The lower the number, the easier the component will rotate in cold climates. Higher numbers are usually recommended for operation in hot weather conditions.

Grease

Greases are graded by the National Lubricating Grease Institute (NLGI). Greases are graded by number according to the consistency of the grease; these range form No. 000 to No. 6, with No. 6 being the most solid. A typical multipurpose grease is NLGI No. 2. For specific applications, equipment manufacturers may require grease with an additive such as molybdenum disulfide (MOS2).

FASTENERS

Motorcycles are manufactured with fasteners of various designs and materials. Fastener design determines the type of tool required to work the fastener. Fastener material is carefully selected to decrease the possibility of physical failure.

Nuts, bolts and screws are manufactured in a wide range of thread patterns. To join a nut and bolt, the diameters and threads of both must be clean and properly matched.

If the threads on 2 fasteners match, only a small amount of force should be needed to turn the nut on the bolt (or bolt into a threaded hole). If much force is required, check the thread condition on each fastener. If the thread condition is good but the fasteners jam, the threads are not compatible. A screw pitch gauge (**Figure 9**) is commonly used to determine thread pitch and will be discussed later in this chapter.

Honda motorcycles are manufactured with ISO (International Organization for Standardization) metric fasteners. The threads are cut differently than those of American fasteners (**Figure 10**). Fasteners in which the threads are cut so that the fastener must be turned *clockwise* to tighten it are the most common and are called right-hand threads. Some fasteners have left-hand threads and must be turned *counterclockwise* to be tightened. Left-hand threads are used in locations where normal rotation of the equipment would tend to loosen a right-hand threaded fastener.

ISO Metric Screw Threads

ISO metric threads come in 3 standard thread sizes: coarse, fine and constant pitch. The ISO coarse pitch is used for most common fastener applications. The fine pitch thread is used on certain precision tools and instruments. The constant pitch thread is used mainly on machine parts and not for fasteners. The constant pitch thread, however, is used on all metric thread spark plugs. ISO metric threads are specified by the capital letter M followed by the diameter in millimeters and the pitch (or distance between each thread) in millimeters separated by the sign ×. For example a M8 × 1.25 bolt is one that has a diameter of 8 millimeters with a distance of 1.25 millimeters between each thread. The measurement across 2 flats on the head of the bolt indicates the proper wrench size to be used. **Figure 3** shows how to determine bolt diameter.

NOTE
*When purchasing a bolt from a dealer or parts store, you must specify the bolt length. The correct way to measure bolt length is by measuring the length starting from underneath the bolt head to the end of the bolt (**Figure 11**). Always measure bolt length in this manner to prevent the purchase of bolts that are too long.*

Machine Screws

There are many different types of machine screws. **Figure 12** shows a number of screw heads requiring different types of turning tools. Heads are also de-signed to protrude above the metal (round) or to be slightly recessed in the metal (flat). See **Figure 13**.

Bolts

Commonly called bolts, the technical name for these fasteners is cap screw. Metric bolts are described by the diameter and pitch (the distance between each thread).

Nuts

Nuts are manufactured in a variety of types and sizes. Most are hexagonal (6-sided) and mate to bolts, screws and studs with the same diameter and pitch.

Figure 14 shows several types of nuts. The common nut is generally used with a lockwasher. Self-locking nuts have a nylon insert which prevents the nut from loosening, eliminating the need for a lockwasher. Wing nuts are designed for fast removal by

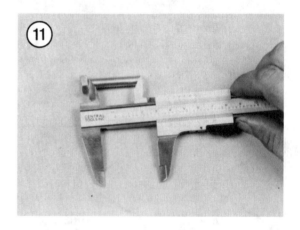

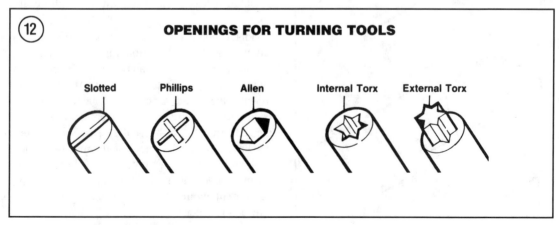

OPENINGS FOR TURNING TOOLS

Slotted   Phillips   Allen   Internal Torx   External Torx

hand and are used for convenience in non-critical locations.

The size of a metric nut is specified by the diameter of the opening and the thread pitch. This is similar to bolt specifications, but without the length dimension. The measurement across 2 flats on the nut indicates the proper wrench size to be used.

Prevailing Torque Fasteners

Several types of bolts, screws and nuts incorporate a system that develops an interference between the bolt, screw, nut or tapped hole threads. Interference is achieved in various ways: by distorting threads, coating threads with dry adhesive or nylon, distort-

ing the top of an all-metal nut, using a nylon insert in the center or at the top of a nut, etc.

Prevailing torque fasteners offer greater holding strength and better vibration resistance. Some prevailing torque fasteners can be reused if in good condition. Others, like the nylon insert nut, form an initial locking condition when the nut is first installed; the nylon forms closely to the bolt thread pattern, thus reducing any tendency for the nut to loosen. When the nut is removed, the locking efficiency is greatly reduced. For greatest safety, it is recommended that you install new prevailing torque fasteners whenever they are removed.

Washers

Flat washers and lockwashers are the basic and most commonly used washers. Flat washers are simple discs with a hole to fit a screw or bolt. Lockwashers are designed to prevent a fastener from working loose due to vibration, expansion and contraction. Washers are used in the following applications:

    a. As spacers.

    b. To prevent galling or damage of equipment by the fastener.

    c. To help distribute fastener load during torquing.

    d. As seals.

Flat washers are often used between a lockwasher and fastener to provide a smooth bearing surface and allow the fastener to be easily turned with a tool. **Figure 15** shows several types of washers.

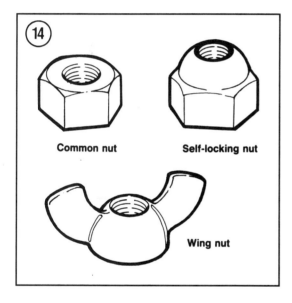

(14)

Common nut   **Self-locking nut**

Wing nut

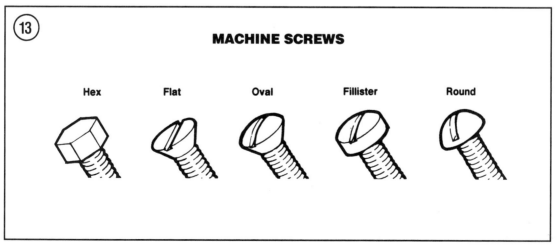

(13)

MACHINE SCREWS

Hex   **Flat**   **Oval**   **Fillister**   **Round**

Cotter Pins

Cotter pins (**Figure 16**) are used to secure special kinds of fasteners. The threaded stud must have a hole through which the cotter pin will pass. The cotter pin then wraps around castellations on the nut or nut lock piece. Cotter pins should not be reused after removal.

Circlips

Circlips are used to retain items on shafts (external type) or within tubes (internal type). Circlips are available in external or internal design. In some applications, circlips of varying thicknesses are used to control the end play of parts assemblies. These are often called selective circlips. Circlips should be replaced during installation, as removal weakens and deforms them.

Circlips are available in two basic styles, machined or stamped circlips. Machined circlips (**Figure 17**) can be installed in either direction (shaft or housing) because both faces are machined, thus creating two sharp edges. Stamped circlips (**Figure 18**) are manufactured with one sharp edge and one rounded edge. When installing stamped circlips in a thrust situation (transmission shafts, fork tubes, etc.), the sharp edge must face away from the part producing the thrust. When installing circlips, observe the following:

    a. Compress or expand circlips only enough to install them.

    b. After the circlip is installed, make sure it is completely seated in its groove.

BASIC HAND TOOLS

An assortment of common hand tools are required to maintain and service your bike successfully. You may already have some of these tools for home or car repairs. Due to the fact that some tools are made specifically for bike repairs, you will have to purchase these. Remember that a wide variety of quality tools will make bike repairs much easier and faster.

Top-quality tools are not only essential, they are also more economical in the long run. When purchasing tools for your collection, stay away from the "advertised specials" featured at some parts houses, discount stores and chain drug stores. These are usually a poor grade tool that can be sold cheaply.

They are usually made of inferior (softer) materials and are thick, heavy and clumsy. Their rough finish makes them difficult to clean and they usually don't last very long. Quality tools are made of alloy steel and are heat treated for greater strength. They are lighter, more comfortable, better balanced and easy to clean. The initial cost of good-quality tools is

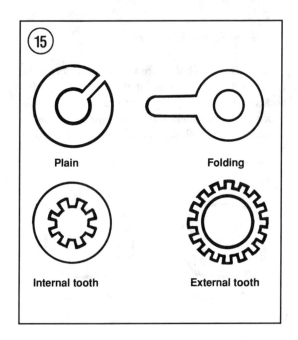

Plain   Folding

Internal tooth   External tooth

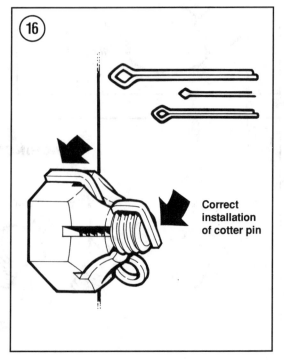

Correct installation of cotter pin

higher, but tool replacement trips can be costly in time and fuel. Every tool in every size is not necessary in the beginning so collect a little at a time and soon you will have a carefully "chosen" collection of the necessary tools.

Keep your tools clean and in a tool box. Have them organized in a logical manner with the sockets and related drives together, the open-end and box-end wrenches together, etc. Wipe off dirt and grease with a clean cloth and occasionally oil ratchet drives to prevent rust and seizure. Always return your tools to a designated storage place. Make sure that tools "borrowed" from you are promptly returned.

The following are tools required to perform virtually any repair job on a bike. Each tool is described

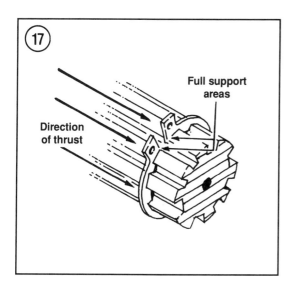

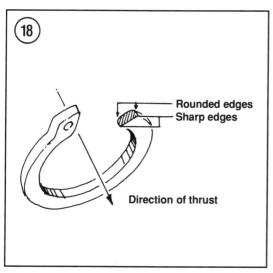

and the recommended size given for starting a tool collection. **Table 1** includes the tools that should be on hand for both simple home repairs or a major bike overhaul. Additional and special tools, along with duplicates of some may be added as you do more in-depth and complex service procedures on the bike. Nearly all motorcycles (except the U.S.-built Harley and some English bikes) use metric size bolts and nuts. If you are starting your collection now, you may want to buy accordingly.

Screwdrivers

The screwdriver is a very basic tool, but if used improperly it will do more damage than good. The slot on a screw has a definite dimension and shape. A screwdriver must be selected to conform with that shape. Use a small screwdriver for small screws and a large one for large screws or the screw head will be damaged.

Two basic types of screwdrivers are required to repair the bike—a common (flat-blade) screwdriver and the Phillips screwdriver.

Screwdrivers are available in sets which often include an assortment of common and Phillips blades. If you buy them individually, buy at least the following:

    a. Common screwdriver—5/16 × 6 in. blade.

    b. Common screwdriver—3/8 × 12 in. blade.

    c. Phillips screwdriver—size 2 tip, 6 in. blade.

Use screwdrivers only for driving screws. Never use a screwdriver for prying or chiseling. Do not try to remove a Phillips or Allen head screw with a common screwdriver; you can damage the head so that the proper tool will be unable to remove it.

Keep screwdrivers in the proper condition and they will last longer and perform better. Always keep the tip of a common screwdriver in good condition. **Figure 19** shows how to grind the tip to the proper shape if it becomes damaged. Note the symmetrical sides of the tip.

Pliers

Pliers come in a wide range of types and sizes. Pliers are useful for cutting, bending and crimping. They should never be used to cut hardened objects or to turn bolts or nuts. **Figure 20** shows several pliers commonly used in bike repairs.

Each type of pliers has a specialized function. Gas pliers are general purpose pliers and are used mainly for holding things and for bending. Vise-grip pliers are used to hold objects very tight like a vise. Needle-nose pliers are used to hold or bend small objects. Channel-lock pliers can be adjusted to hold various sizes of objects; the jaws remain parallel to grip around objects such as pipe or tubing. There are many more types of pliers.

Vise-grip Pliers

Vise-grip pliers (**Figure 21**) are used as pliers or to hold objects very tightly while another task is performed on the work. Vise-grip pliers are available in many types and sizes for more specific tasks.

Box-end and Open-end Wrenches

Box-end and open-end (**Figure 22**) wrenches are available in sets or separately in a variety of sizes. The number stamped near the end refers to the distance between 2 parallel flats on the hex-head bolt or nut.

Box-end wrenches are usually superior to open-end wrenches. An open-end wrench grips the nut on only 2 flats. Unless it fits well, it may slip and round off the points on the nut. The box-end wrench grips all 6 flats. Both 6-point and 12-point openings on box-end wrenches are available. The 6-point provides superior holding power; the 12-point allows a shorter swing.

Combination wrenches which are open on one side and boxed on the other are also available (**Figure 23**). Both ends are the same size.

Adjustable (Crescent) Wrenches

An adjustable wrench (also called Crescent wrench) can be adjusted to fit nearly any nut or bolt head. See **Figure 24**. However, it can loosen and slip, causing damage to the nut and maybe to your knuckles. Use an adjustable wrench only when other wrenches are not available.

Crescent wrenches come in sizes ranging from 4-18 in. overall. A 6 or 8 in. wrench is recommended as an all-purpose wrench.

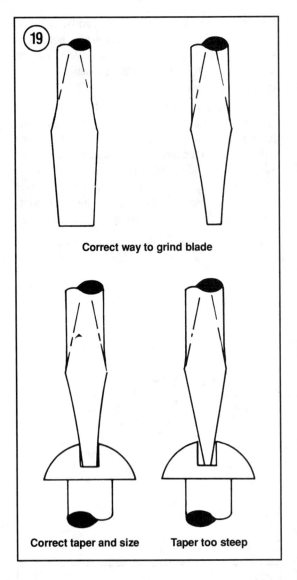

Correct way to grind blade

Correct taper and size   Taper too steep

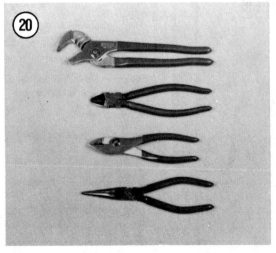

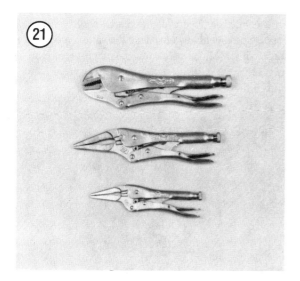

Socket Wrenches

This type of wrench is undoubtedly the fastest, safest and most convenient to use. Sockets which attach to a ratchet handle (**Figure 25**) are available with 6-point or 12-point openings and 1/4, 3/8, 1/2 and 3/4 inch drives (**Figure 26**). The drive size indicates the size of the square hole which mates with the ratchet handle.

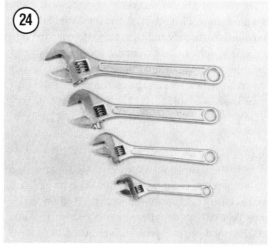

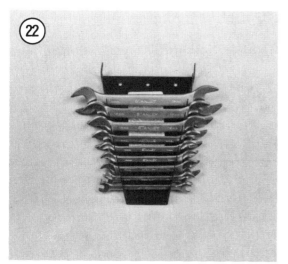

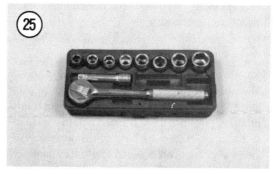

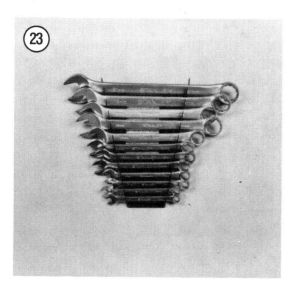

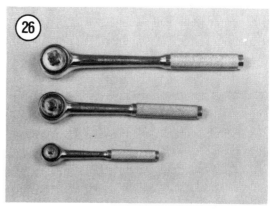

Torque Wrench

A torque wrench (**Figure 27**) is used with a socket to measure how tightly a nut or bolt is installed. They come in a wide price range and with either 3/8 or 1/2 in. square drive. The drive size indicates the size of the square drive which mates with the socket.

Impact Driver

This tool is invaluable when working with bolts that are extremely tight. It makes removal of engine and clutch parts easy and eliminates damage to bolts and screw slots. Sockets that are specially designed for impact use can also be used with a hand impact driver. Impact drivers and interchangeable bits (**Figure 28**) are available at most large hardware, motorcycle or auto parts stores.

Circlip Pliers

Circlip pliers (commonly called snap ring pliers) are necessary to remove the circlips used on shafts or within engine or suspension housings (**Figure 29**). External pliers (spreading) are used to remove circlips that fit on the outside of a shaft. Internal pliers (squeezing) are used to remove circlips which fit inside a gear or housing.

Hammer

The correct hammer is necessary for bike repairs (**Figure 30**). Use only a hammer with a face (or head) of rubber or plastic or the soft-faced type that is filled with buckshot. These are sometimes necessary in engine tear-downs. *Never* use a metal-faced hammer

on the bike as severe damage will result in most cases. You can always produce the same amount of force with a soft-faced hammer. A metal-faced hammer, however, will be required when using a hand impact driver.

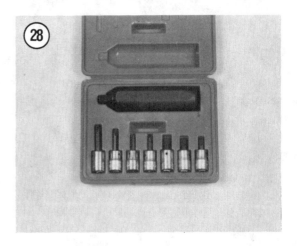

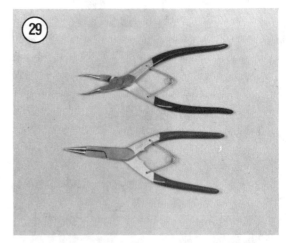

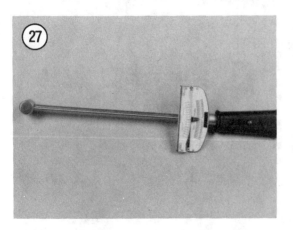

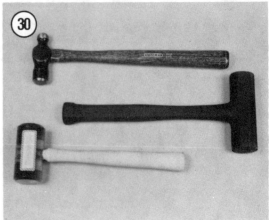

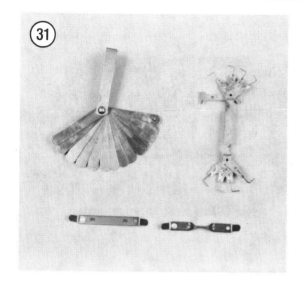

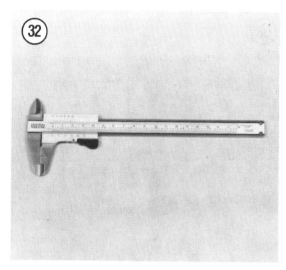

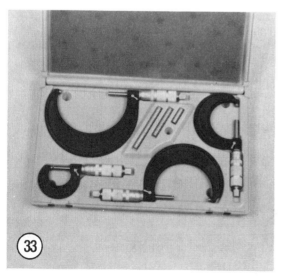

PRECISION MEASURING TOOLS

Precision measuring is an important part of motorcycle service. When performing many of the service procedures in this manual, you will be required to make a number of measurements. These include basic checks such as engine compression and spark plug gap. As you progress into engine disassembly and service, measurements will be required to determine the condition of the piston and cylinder bore, crankshaft runout, clutch plate thickness and so on. The degree of accuracy required will dictate which tool is necessary. Precision measuring tools are expensive. Depending on your experience with engine or suspension service, it may be advisable to have these measurements made at a dealer. However, as your skill and confidence increase, you may want to begin purchasing some of these specialized tools. The following is a description of the measuring tools required during engine, transmission and suspension overhaul.

Feeler Gauge

The feeler gauge consists of flat or round hardened steel blades and machined to various thicknesses (**Figure 31**). Wire gauges are used to measure spark plug gap. Flat gauges are used for all other measurements. A few styles of feeler gauges are available for specialized uses. On this style, the gauge end is small and angled to permit measurements in limited spaces.

Vernier Caliper

This tool is designed to take inside, outside and depth measurements with close precision. It can be used to measure clutch spring length, clutch plate thickness, shims and thrust washers. See **Figure 32**.

Outside Micrometer

The outside micrometer is one of the most reliable tools for precision measurement (**Figure 33**). Outside micrometers will be required for measuring piston diameter and will be used with a cylinder bore gauge to measure the cylinder bore. They can be purchased individually or in a set.

Dial Indicator

Dial indicators (**Figure 34**) are precision tools used to check dimension variations on machined parts such as transmission shafts and axles. Dial indicators are also used to check the end play on crankshafts and axle shafts. Various dial types are available for different measuring requirements. For motorcycle repair, select a dial indicator with a continuous dial.

Cylinder Bore Gauge

The cylinder bore gauge is a very specialized precision tool. The gauge set in **Figure 35** is comprised of a dial indicator, handle and a number of length adapters to adapt the gauge to different bore sizes. The bore gauge can be used to make cylinder bore measurements such as bore size, taper and out-of-round. Some bore gauges can be used to measure brake caliper and master cylinder bore sizes. An outside micrometer must be used with the bore gauge to determine bore dimensions.

Small Hole Gauges

A set of small hole gauges (**Figure 36**) allows you to measure a hole, groove or slot up to 13 mm (0.500 in.) in size. A small hole gauge will be required to measure brake caliper and brake master cylinder bore diameters. An outside micrometer must be used with the small hole gauge to determine bore dimensions.

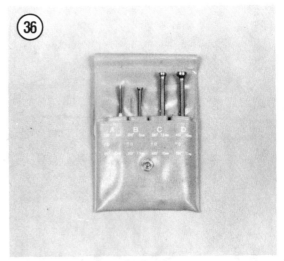

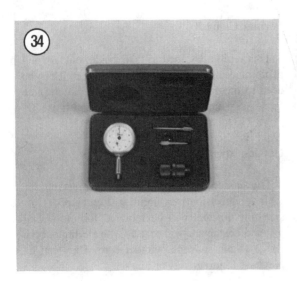

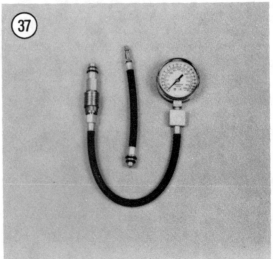

Compression Gauge

An engine with low compression cannot be properly tuned and will not develop full power. A compression gauge measures engine compression. The gauge shown in **Figure 37** has a flexible stem with an extension that can allow you to hold it while kicking the engine over.

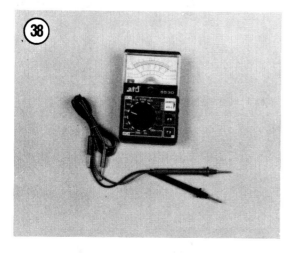

Multimeter or Volt-ohm Meter (VOM)

This instrument (**Figure 38**) is invaluable for electrical system troubleshooting and service. A few of its functions may be duplicated by homemade test equipment, but for the serious mechanic it is a must. Its uses are described in the applicable sections of the book.

Strobe Timing Light

This instrument is necessary for tuning. By flashing a light at the precise instant the spark plug fires, the position of the timing mark can be seen. Marks on the alternator flywheel line up with the stationary mark on the crankcase while the engine is running.

Suitable lights range from inexpensive neon bulb types to powerful xenon strobe timing lights. See **Figure 39**. Neon timing lights are difficult to see and must be used in dimly lit areas. Xenon strobe timing lights can be used outside in bright sunlight.

Portable Tachometer

A portable tachometer is necessary for reading engine rpm. Ignition timing and carburetor adjustments are performed at specified rpm limits. See **Figure 40**.

Battery Hydrometer

A hydrometer (**Figure 41**) is the best way to check a battery's state of charge. A hydrometer measures the weight or density (specific gravity) of the sulfuric acid in the battery's electrolyte. The models within this publication are not equipped with a battery.

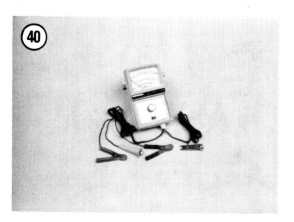

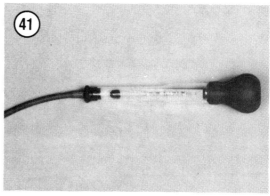

Screw Pitch Gauge

A screw pitch gauge (**Figure 42**) determines the thread pitch of bolts, screws, studs, etc. The gauge is made of a number of thin plates. Each plate has a thread shape cut on one edge to match one thread pitch. When using a screw pitch gauge to determine a thread pitch size, try to fit different blade sizes onto the bolt thread until both threads match (**Figure 43**).

Plastigage

Plastigage (**Figure 44**) is a wax-like material sold in a flat color-coded envelope. The outside of the envelope is marked in both millimeters and thousandths of an inch. The color of the envelope specifies the specific clearance range of the Plastigage. Plastigage is used to measure crankshaft and connecting rod bearing clearances. Although Plastigage will not be needed for any of the procedures covered in this manual, it is a measuring device that you may use in the future as your skills and experience increase.

Magnetic Stand

A magnetic stand (**Figure 45**) is used to hold a dial indicator securely when checking the runout of a round object or when checking the end play of a shaft.

V-blocks

V-blocks (**Figure 46**) are precision ground blocks used to hold a round object when checking its runout or condition. On models covered in this manual,

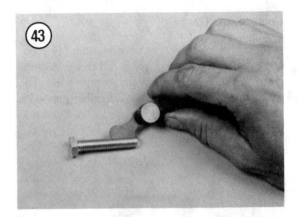

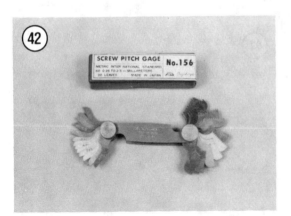

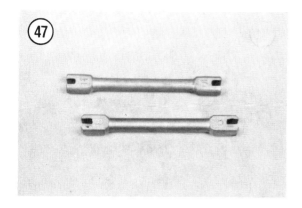

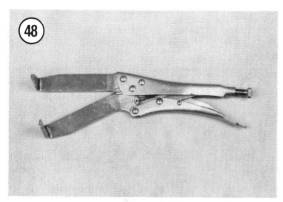

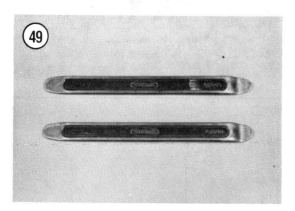

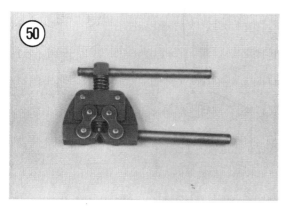

V-blocks can be used when checking the runout of the crankshaft, wheel axles and fork tubes.

SPECIAL TOOLS

The following are some special tools unique to motorcycle service and a few of these may be required for major repairs. These are described in the appropriate chapters and are available from your Honda dealer or other manufacturers as indicated.

Spoke Wrench

This wrench is specifically designed to tighten wheel spokes (**Figure 47**). Use the correct size to prevent rounding out and damaging the spoke nipple.

The Grabbit

The Grabbit (**Figure 48**) is a special tool used to hold the clutch boss when removing the clutch nut. It is also used to secure the drive sprocket when removing the drive sprocket nut.

Tire Levers

Changing tires is a frequent operation on a competition or off-road motorcycle. To prevent pinching tubes during tire changing, purchase a good set of tire levers (**Figure 49**). Never use a screwdriver in place of a tire lever. Prior to using a tire lever, check the working end for burrs and remove them. Don't use tire levers for prying objects other than tires.

Flywheel Puller

A flywheel puller will be required to remove the rotor and service the stator plate assembly or when adjusting the ignition timing. The rotor must also be removed prior to splitting crankcase halves. There is no substitute for a flywheel puller and makeshift removal is almost certain to damage the rotor or crankshaft.

Chain Breaker

A chain breaker (**Figure 50**) is a useful tool for cutting the drive chain to size.

Fork Oil Level Gauge

The specifications for changing fork oil are listed in both fork oil capacity and fork oil level. Front fork oil capacity is given in cubic centimeters (cc) while front fork oil level is expressed in millimeters (mm). To obtain maximum performance from your front forks, a fork oil level gauge (**Figure 51**) should be used to measure the fork oil level after pouring in the pre-measured amount of fork oil. On the models covered in this manual, accurate fork oil measurements are necessary and a fork oil level gauge is recommended for service and maintenance.

EXPENDABLE SUPPLIES

Certain expendable supplies are also required during maintenance and repair work. These include grease, oil, gasket cement, wiping rags, cleaning solvent and distilled water. Ask your dealer for special locking compounds, silicone and assembly lubricants, and other available products (**Figure 52**). Cleaning solvents can be found at most automotive parts stores and kerosene is available at some service stations.

MECHANIC'S TIPS

Removing Frozen Nuts and Screws

When a fastener rusts and cannot be removed, several methods may be used to loosen it. First, apply penetrating oil such as Liquid Wrench or WD-40 (available at any hardware or auto supply store). Apply it liberally and let it penetrate for 10-15 minutes. Tap the fastener lightly several times with a small hammer. Reapply the penetrating oil if necessary.

For frozen screws, apply penetrating oil as described then insert a screwdriver in the slot and tap the top of the screwdriver with a hammer. This loosens the rust so the screw can be removed in the normal way. If the screw head is too chewed up to use a screwdriver, grip the head with Vise-grip pliers and twist the screw out.

Remedying Stripped Threads

Occasionally, threads are stripped through carelessness or impact damage. Often the threads can be

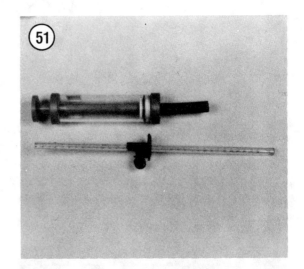

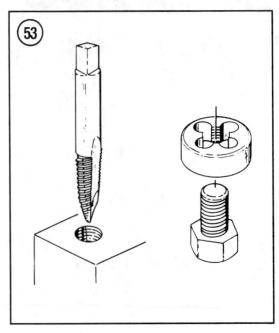

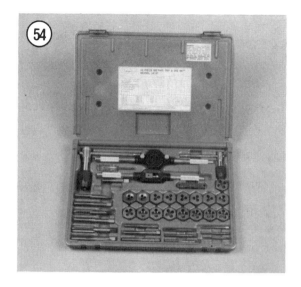

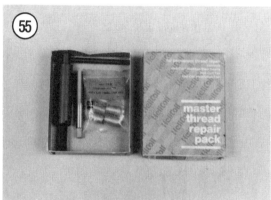

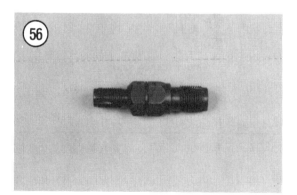

cleaned up by running a tap (for internal threads on nuts) or die (for external threads on bolts) through the threads (**Figure 53**). Taps and dies can be purchased individually or in a set (**Figure 54**). If an internal thread is damaged, a thread insert or Helicoil (**Figure 55**) can be installed. Follow the manufactures directions for the insert.

Spark plug threads can be cleaned or repaired with a spark plug tap (**Figure 56**).

Removing Broken Screws or Bolts

When the head breaks off a screw or bolt, several methods are available for removing the remaining portion.

If a large portion of the remainder projects out, try gripping it with Vise-grip pliers. If the projecting portion is too small, file it to fit a wrench or cut a slot in it to fit a screwdriver. See **Figure 57**.

If the head breaks off flush, use a screw extractor. To do this, centerpunch the remaining portion of the screw or bolt. Drill a small hole in the screw and tap the extractor into the hole. Back the screw out with a wrench on the extractor. See **Figure 58**.

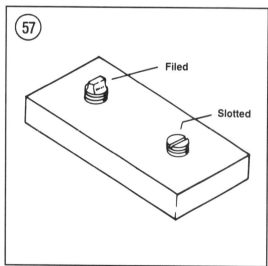

Figure 58 and Tables 1-4 are on the following pages.

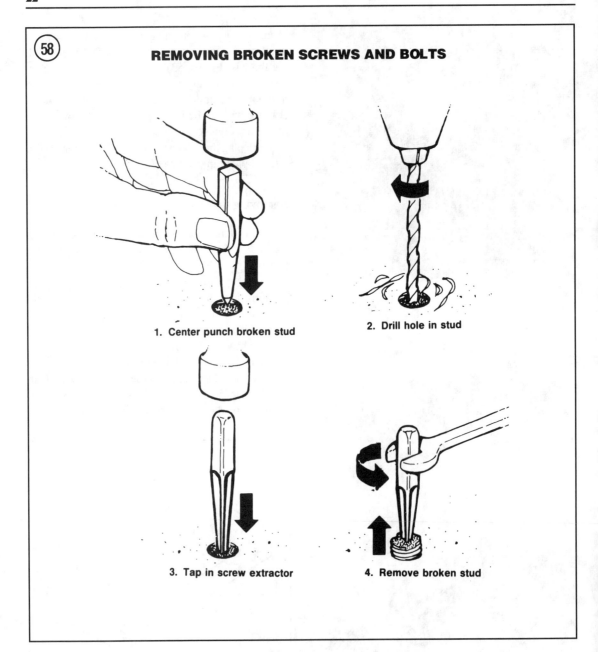

58 REMOVING BROKEN SCREWS AND BOLTS

1. Center punch broken stud

2. Drill hole in stud

3. Tap in screw extractor

4. Remove broken stud

Table 1 ENGINE AND CHASSIS NUMBERS

Model	Year	Engine Serial no. start to end	Frame Serial no. start to end
CR250R	1988	ME03E-5000001 to 5009970	ME030-JM000001 to JM004826
	1989	ME03E-5100001-on	ME030-KM100001-on
	1990	ME03E-5200023 to 5208362	ME030-LM200013 to LM203598
	1991	ME03E-5300007-on	ME030-MM300005-on
CR500R	1988	PE02E-5700008 to 5703132	PE020-JM700005 to JM702250
	1989	PE02E-5800018-on	PE020-KM800010-on
	1990	PE02E-5900010 to 5904044	PE020-LM900005 to LM902547
	1991	PE02E-5000009 to 5003006	PE020-MM000006 to MM001974

Table 2 DECIMAL AND METRIC EQUIVALENTS

Fractions	Decimal in.	Metric mm	Fractions	Decimal in.	Metric mm
1/64	0.015625	0.39688	33/64	0.515625	13.09687
1/32	0.03125	0.79375	17/32	0.53125	13.49375
3/64	0.046875	1.19062	35/64	0.546875	13.89062
1/16	0.0625	1.58750	9/16	0.5625	14.28750
5/64	0.078125	1.98437	37/64	0.578125	14.68437
3/32	0.09375	2.38125	19/32	0.59375	15.08125
7/64	0.109375	2.77812	39/64	0.609375	15.47812
1/8	0.125	3.1750	5/8	0.625	15.87500
9/64	0.140625	3.57187	41/64	0.640625	16.27187
5/32	0.15625	3.96875	21/32	0.65625	16.66875
11/64	0.171875	4.36562	43/64	0.671875	17.06562
3/16	0.1875	4.76250	11/16	0.6875	17.46250
13/64	0.203125	5.15937	45/64	0.703125	17.85937
7/32	0.21875	5.55625	23/32	0.71875	18.25625
15/64	0.234375	5.95312	47/64	0.734375	18.65312
1/4	0.250	6.35000	3/4	0.750	19.05000
17/64	0.265625	6.74687	49/64	0.765625	19.44687
9/32	0.28125	7.14375	25/32	0.78125	19.84375
19/64	0.296875	7.54062	51/64	0.796875	20.24062
5/16	0.3125	7.93750	13/16	0.8125	20.63750
21/64	0.328125	8.33437	53/64	0.828125	21.03437
11/32	0.34375	8.73125	27/32	0.84375	21.43125
23/64	0.359375	9.12812	55/64	0.859375	21.82812
3/8	0.375	9.52500	7/8	0.875	22.22500
25/64	0.390625	9.92187	57/64	0.890625	22.62187
13/32	0.40625	10.31875	29/32	0.90625	23.01875
27/64	0.421875	10.71562	59/64	0.921875	23.41562
7/16	0.4375	11.11250	15/16	0.9375	23.81250
29/64	0.453125	11.50937	61/64	0.953125	24.20937
15/32	0.46875	11.90625	31/32	0.96875	24.60625
31/64	0.484375	12.30312	63/64	0.984375	25.00312
1/2	0.500	12.70000	1	1.00	25.40000

Table 3 GENERAL TORQUE SPECIFICATIONS*

Thread size	N·m	ft.-lb.	in.-lb.
Bolt			
5 mm	4.5-6	–	40-53
6 mm	8-12	6-9	
8 mm	18-25	13-18	
10 mm	30-40	22-29	
12 mm	50-60	36-44	
Nut			
5 mm	4.5-6	–	40-53
6 mm	8-12	6-9	
8 mm	18-25	13-18	
10 mm	30-40	22-29	
12 mm	50-60	36-44	
Screw			
5 mm	3.5-5	–	31-44
6 mm and SH type bolt			
with 8 mm head	7-11	–	61-97
6 mm flange bolt/nut	10-14	7-10	
8 mm flange bolt/nut	24-30	17-22	
10 mm flange bolt/nut	35-45	25-33	

* Use these torque values for fasteners not individually listed.

Table 4 RECOMMENDED (INITIAL) BASIC TOOLS

Tools	Size or Specification
Screwdrivers	
Slot	5/16 × 8 in. blade
Slot	3/8 × 12 in. blade
Phillips	Size 2 tip, 6 in. blade
Pliers	
Slip-joint	6 in. overall
Locking pliers	10 in. overall
Needlenose	6 in. overall
Groove-joint	12 in. overall
Circlip pliers	—
Wrenches	
Box-end set	10-17, 20, 32 mm
Open-end set	10-17, 20, 32 mm
Adjustable	6 and 12 in. overall
Socket set	1/2 in. drive ratchet with 10-17, 20, 32 mm sockets
Allen wrench set	2-10 mm
Spoke wrench	—
Special tools	
Impact driver	1/2 in. drive with assorted tips
Torque wrench	1/2 drive—0-140 N·m (0-100 ft.-lb.)
Hammers	Steel faced. Rubber or plastic faced (lead shot filled)
Feeler/wire gauge	Flat feeler type and wire gauge
Tire levers	For motorcycle tires

CHAPTER TWO

TROUBLESHOOTING

Diagnosing mechanical problems is relatively simple if you use orderly procedures and keep a few basic principles in mind. Begin by defining the symptoms as accurately as possible and localizing the problem. Then follow up by testing and analyzing those areas which could cause the symptoms. An impulsive approach may eventually solve the problem, but it can be very costly in terms of wasted time and unnecessary parts replacement.

Preventive maintenance such as proper lubrication and periodic tune-ups, as discussed in Chapter Three, will reduce the necessity for troubleshooting. Remember though, even with the best of care, a competition or off-road motorcycle is prone to problems which will require the troubleshooting process.

Start with the simple process of eliminating the obvious and assume nothing. If you are riding along and the engine suddenly quits, check the easiest, most accessible problems first. Is there fuel mixture in the tank? Is the fuel shutoff valve in the ON position? Has the spark plug wire fallen off?

If nothing obvious turns up in a quick check, look a little further. Learning to recognize and describe symptoms will make repairs easier for you or a mechanic at the shop. Describe problems accurately and fully. Saying "it won't run" isn't the same as saying "it quit while climbing a hill and won't start" or "it sat in my garage for 3 months and wouldn't start."

Gather as many symptoms together as possible to aid in diagnosis. Note whether the engine lost power gradually or all at once, was there an excess of smoke? and if so, what color was it. Remember that the more complicated a machine is, the easier it is to troubleshoot because symptoms point to specific problems.

After the symptoms are defined, areas which could cause the problems can be tested and analyzed.

Guessing at the cause of a problem may provide the solution, but it can easily lead to frustration, wasted time and a series of expensive, unnecessary parts replacements.

Fancy equipment or complicated test gear is not necessary for determining whether repairs can be attempted at home. A few simple checks could save a large repair bill and time lost while the bike sits in a dealer's service department. On the other hand, be realistic and don't attempt repairs beyond your abilities. Service departments tend to charge considerably for putting together a disassembled engine that may have been abused. Some dealers won't even take on such a job—so use common sense and don't get in over your head.

OPERATING REQUIREMENTS

An engine needs 3 basics to run properly: correct fuel-air mixture, compression and a spark at the correct time. If one or more are missing, the engine just won't run. Of the 3 basics, the electrical system is the weakest link. More problems result from electrical breakdowns than from any other source. Keep that in mind before you begin tampering with carburetor adjustments and the like.

If the bike has been sitting for any length of time and refuses to start, check and clean the spark plug and then proceed to the gasoline delivery system. This includes the fuel tank, fuel tank vent line, fuel shutoff valve and the fuel line to the carburetor. Gasoline deposits may have formed and gummed up the carburetor jets and air passages. Gasoline tends to lose its potency after standing for long periods. Condensation may contaminate the fuel with water. Drain the old fuel-oil mixture and try starting with a fresh tankful.

TROUBLESHOOTING INSTRUMENTS

Chapter One lists the instruments needed and instruction on their use.

STARTING THE ENGINE

When your engine refuses to start, frustration can cause you to forget basic starting principles and procedures. The following is a guide to help you through the basic starting procedures.

Starting a Cold Engine

1. Turn the fuel valve ON.
2. Shift the transmission into neutral.
3. Pull the choke/idle speed knob up.
4. With the throttle closed, kick the engine over with a full, continuous, quick stroke of the kickstarter.
5. When the engine starts, push down the choke/idle speed knob as soon as possible to prevent fouling the spark plug.
6. Warm the engine for at least 2 minutes or until the side of the engine is very warm. Slowly increase rpm without "blipping" the throttle.

Starting a Warm Engine

1. Turn the fuel valve ON.
2. Shift the transmission into neutral.
3. Make sure the choke/idle speed knob is down.

4. Open the throttle 1/8 to 1/4 of a turn and kick the engine over with a full, quick, continuous stroke.

Stopping the Engine

1. Shift transmission into neutral.

2. Turn the fuel valve to the OFF position. Failure to close the valve may cause the carburetor to overflow, fill the crankcase with fuel, and result in hard starting.

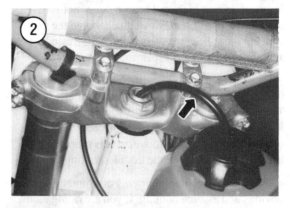

3. Open the throttle lightly 2 or 3 times and then close it.

4. Depress the kill button and hold it until the engine stops.

EMERGENCY TROUBLESHOOTING

When the bike is difficult to start or won't start at all, it does not help to wear out your leg on the kickstarter. Check the obvious problems first by going down the following list step by step. If it still

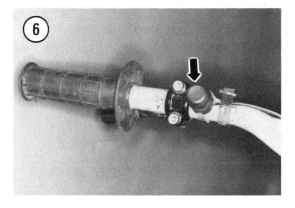

will not start, refer to the appropriate troubleshooting procedure which follows in this chapter.

1. Is the choke/idle speed knob in the right position? The valve should be moved *up* for a cold engine and *down* for a warm engine (**Figure 1**).

2. Is there fuel in the tank? Open the filler cap and rock the bike. Listen for fuel sloshing around. Is the gasoline-oil mixture correct? Has the bike been sitting long enough for the fuel mixture to deteriorate? If in doubt, drain the fuel and fill with a fresh, correctly mixed gas-oil mixture. Check that the vent tube (**Figure 2**) is not clogged. Remove the tube from the filler cap and blow it out.

NOTE
On all models covered in this manual, mix the fuel in a ratio of 20 parts gasoline to 1 part oil (20:1). Too little oil will cause premature wear and engine damage. Too much oil will cause excessive smoking and spark plug fouling.

WARNING
Do not use an open flame to check in the tank. A serious explosion is certain to result.

3. If you suspect that the cylinder is flooded, or the smell of fuel is strong, open the throttle all the way and kick the engine over several times. If the cylinder is severely flooded (fouled or wet spark plug), remove the plug and dry the base and electrode thoroughly with a soft cloth. Replace the plug and attempt to start the engine.

4. Is the fuel shutoff valve (**Figure 3**) in the ON position?

5. If the tank has fuel and the mixture is good, pull off the fuel line at the carburetor. Turn the fuel valve to ON and observe if fuel is flowing. If fuel does not flow out, the valve should be checked for dirt or foreign matter, then cleaned or replaced.

6. Check the carburetor overflow hose on the bottom of the float bowl. If fuel is running out of the hose, the float may be stuck. Check the vent hose (**Figure 4**) to make sure it is clear.

7. Is the spark plug wire (**Figure 5**) on tight? Push it on and slightly rotate it to clean the electrical connection between the plug and the connector.

8. Make sure the kill button (**Figure 6**) is not stuck or the wiring is not frayed and shorting out.

TROUBLESHOOTING

An engine that refuses to start or is difficult to start is very frustrating. More often than not, the problem is very minor and can be found with a simple and logical troubleshooting approach.

The following items show a beginning point from which to isolate engine starting problems. Malfunctions in various individual components, such as the CDI unit or alternator exciter coil, can also contribute to some of the following symptoms. See Chapter Seven for troubleshooting and testing procedures regarding specific electronic components.

Engine Fails to Start

Perform the following spark test to determine if the ignition system is operating properly.
1. Remove the spark plug from the cylinder.
2. Connect the spark plug wire and connector to the spark plug and touch the spark plug's base to a good ground such as the engine cylinder head. Position the spark plug so you can see the electrodes.
3. Crank the engine over with the kickstarter. A fat blue spark should be evident across the spark plug electrodes.

> *WARNING*
> *If it is necessary to hold the high voltage lead, do so with an insulated pair of pliers. The high voltage generated by the CDI could produce serious or fatal shocks.*

4. If the spark is good, check for one or more of the following possible malfunctions:
   a. Obstructed fuel line.
   b. Leaking head or cylinder base gasket.
5. If spark is not good, check for one or more of the following:
   a. Fouled or wet spark plug.
   b. Faulty spark plug.
   c. Broken or shorted high tension lead to the spark plug.
   d. Faulty ignition coil.
   e. Faulty pulse generator.
   f. Dirty pulse generator air gap.
   g. Loose electrical connections.
   h. Loose or broken ignition coil ground wire.
   i. Improperly adjusted pulse generator air gap (1988 CR500R).

Engine is Difficult to Start

Check for one or more of the following possible malfunctions:
   a. Fouled spark plug.
   b. Improperly adjusted choke.
   c. Contaminated fuel system.
   d. Improperly adjusted carburetor.
   e. Faulty ignition coil.
   f. Faulty pulse generator.
   g. Dirty pulse generator air gap.
   h. Improperly adjusted pulse generator air gap (1988 CR500R).

Engine Will Not Turn Over

Check for one or more of the following possible malfunctions:
   a. Defective kickstarter.
   b. Seized piston.
   c. Seized crankshaft bearings.
   d. Broken connecting rod.
   e. Locked-up transmission or clutch assembly.

ENGINE PERFORMANCE

In the following checklist, it is assumed that the engine runs, but is not operating at peak performance. The following is a list of possible causes that can be used as a starting point for isolating engine performance problems. Malfunctions in various individual components, such as the CDI unit or alternator exciter coil, can also contribute to some of the following symptoms. See Chapter Seven for troubleshooting and testing procedures regarding specific electronic components.

Engine Will Not Idle

   a. Choke/idle speed knob incorrectly adjusted.

> *NOTE*
> *For a stable idle speed, the choke/idle speed knob must be turned at least 6 turns (36 clicks) counterclockwise from the fully seated position.*

   b. Fouled or improperly gapped spark plug.
   c. Leaking head gasket.
   d. Obstructed fuel line or fuel shutoff valve.
   e. Ignition timing incorrect.

f. Faulty alternator.

g. Faulty ignition coil.

Engine Misses at High Speed

a. Fouled or improperly gapped spark plug.

b. Ignition timing incorrect.

c. Contaminants in fuel.

d. Clogged air filter.

e. Improper carburetor main jet selection.

f. Clogged jets in the carburetor.

g. Obstructed fuel line or fuel shutoff valve.

h. Faulty alternator.

i. Faulty pulse generator.

j. Improperly adjusted pulse generator air gap (1988 CR500R).

k. HPP valves not fully open. Both valves must be fully open at high speeds.

Engine Overheating

a. Coolant level low.

b. Faulty radiator cap.

c. Passages blocked in the radiator, hoses or water jackets in the engine.

d. Too lean fuel/oil mixture.

e. Incorrect carburetor adjustment or jet selection.

f. Improper ignition timing.

g. Improper spark plug heat range.

h. Crankcase air leak.

Smoky Exhaust and Engine Runs Roughly

a. Carburetor mixture too rich.

b. Improperly adjusted choke.

c. Water or other contaminants in fuel.

d. Clogged fuel line.

e. Clogged air filter element.

f. HPP valves not operating correctly.

Engine Loses Power

a. Carburetor incorrectly adjusted.

b. Engine overheating.

c. Improper ignition timing.

d. Weak ignition coil.

e. Incorrectly gapped plug.

f. Obstructed muffler.

g. Dragging brake(s).

h. HPP valves not operating correctly. Both valves must be fully open at high speeds.

Engine Will Not Accelerate

a. Carburetor mixture too lean.

b. Clogged fuel line.

c. Improper ignition timing.

d. Dragging brake(s).

e. Clogged air filter element.

f. HPP valves not operating correctly. Both valves must be fully open at high speeds.

ENGINE NOISES

1. *Knocking or pinging during acceleration*—Caused by using poor fuel or a fuel with a lower octane rating than recommended. Pinging can also be caused by spark plugs of the wrong heat range. Refer to *Spark Plug Selection* in Chapter Three.

2. *Slapping or rattling noises at low speed or during acceleration*—May be caused by piston slap (excessive piston to cylinder wall clearance).

3. *Knocking or rapping while decelerating*—Usually caused by excessive rod bearing clearance.

4. *Persistent knocking and vibration*—Usually caused by excessive main bearing clearance.

5. *Rapid on-off squeal*—Compression leak around cylinder head gasket or spark plug.

EXCESSIVE VIBRATION

This can be difficult to find without disassembling the engine. Usually this is caused by loose engine mounting hardware.

2-STROKE PRESSURE TESTING

Many owners of 2-stroke engines are plagued by hard starting and generally poor running for which there seems to be no cause. Carburetion and ignition may show that all is well.

The crankcase in a 2-stroke engine must be alternately under pressure and vacuum. After the piston closes the intake port, further downward movement of the piston causes the entrapped mixture to be pressurized so that it can rush quickly into the cylinder when the scavenging ports are opened. Upward piston movement creates a slight vacuum in the crankcase, enabling fuel-air mixture to be drawn in from the cylinder.

If crankcase seals or cylinder gaskets leak, the crankcase cannot hold pressure or vacuum and proper engine operation becomes impossible. Any other source of leakage such as a defective cylinder base gasket or porous or cracked crankcase castings will result in the same conditions.

It is possible to test for and isolate engine pressure leaks. The test is simple but does require elaborate equipment. Briefly, what is done is to seal off all natural engine openings, then apply air pressure. If the engine does not hold air, a leak or leaks are indicated. Then it is necessary to locate and repair all leaks.

The following procedure describes a typical pressure test.

1. Remove the carburetor.
2. Install the pressure adapter and its gasket in place of the carburetor.
3. Block off the exhaust port, using suitable adapters and fittings. Remove the HPP valves and valve

guides. Block the HPP valve guide openings in the cylinder head with suitable fittings.
4. Connect the pressurizing bulb and gauge to the pressure fitting installed where the carburetor was, then squeeze the bulb until the gauge indicates approximately 9 psi.
5. Observe the pressure gauge. If the engine is in good condition, pressure should not drop more than 1 psi in several minutes. Any pressure loss of more than 1 psi in 1 minute indicates serious sealing problems.

Before condemning the engine, first be sure that there are no leaks in the test equipment itself. Then go over the entire engine carefully. Large leaks can be heard; smaller ones can be found by going over every possible leakage source with a small brush and liquid soap solution. The following are possible leakage points:

a. Crankshaft seals.
b. Spark plug.
c. Cylinder head joint.
d. Cylinder base joint.
e. Reed valve assembly joint.

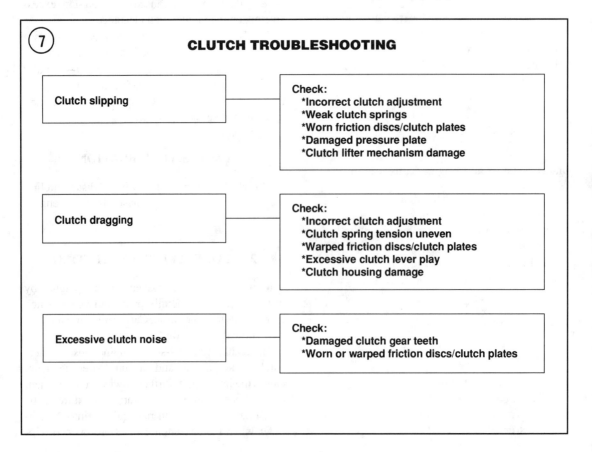

f. Carburetor base joint.

g. Crankcase joint.

CLUTCH

The three basic clutch troubles are:

a. Clutch noise.

b. Clutch slipping.

c. Improper clutch disengagement.

All clutch troubles, except adjustments, require partial engine disassembly to identify and cure the problem. Refer to Chapter Five for the procedures.

The troubleshooting procedures outlined in **Figure 7** will help you systematically solve the majority of clutch problems.

TRANSMISSION

The basic transmission troubles are:

a. Excessive gear noise.

b. Difficult shifting.

c. Gears pop out of mesh.

d. Incorrect shift lever operation.

Transmission symptoms are often hard to distinguish from clutch symptoms. Verify the symptoms to make sure they are not clutch related before working on the transmission.

Figure 8 outlines troubleshooting procedures that will help you in solving the majority of transmission troubles.

IGNITION SYSTEM

1988 and later CR250R and CR500R models are equipped with a capacitor discharge ignition (CDI) system. This system is solid state and uses no contact breaker points or other moving parts. Due to the solid state design, problems with the capacitor discharge system are relatively few. When problems do arise, they generally stem from one of the following:

a. Weak spark.

b. No spark.

It is possible to check CDI systems that:

a. Do not have spark.

b. Have a weak spark.

c. Have damaged or broken wires.

It is difficult to diagnose malfunctions in CDI systems that are due to:

a. Vibration.

b. Components that malfunction only when the engine is hot or under a load.

1. Check the kill button and its wiring to the CDI unit.

2. Determine if any connections are loose or wires are shorting out between:

a. The alternator and CDI unit.

b. The CDI unit and ignition coil.

c. The ignition coil and plug.

3. Check the stator/stator setting plate screws for tightness. If the screws are loose, check the ignition timing.

4. Remove the fuel tank and check all taped electrical connectors. If necessary, clean the connectors with electrical contact cleaner.

5. If the problem cannot be located, refer to Chapter Seven for further information.

FRONT SUSPENSION AND STEERING

Poor handling may be caused by improper tire pressure, a damaged or bent frame or steering components, bent wheel rims, a loose or worn swing arm pivot bolt, worn wheel bearings, loose axles or dragging brake(s). Refer to the appropriate chapters regarding maintenance and service.

BRAKE PROBLEMS

A sticking disc brake may be caused by a stuck piston(s) in the caliper assembly, a warped pad or improper brake lever clearance. The troubleshooting procedures in **Figure 9** will help you to isolate the majority of disc brake problems. See Chapter Eleven for information on front and rear disc brake service.

Figures 8-9 are on the following pages.

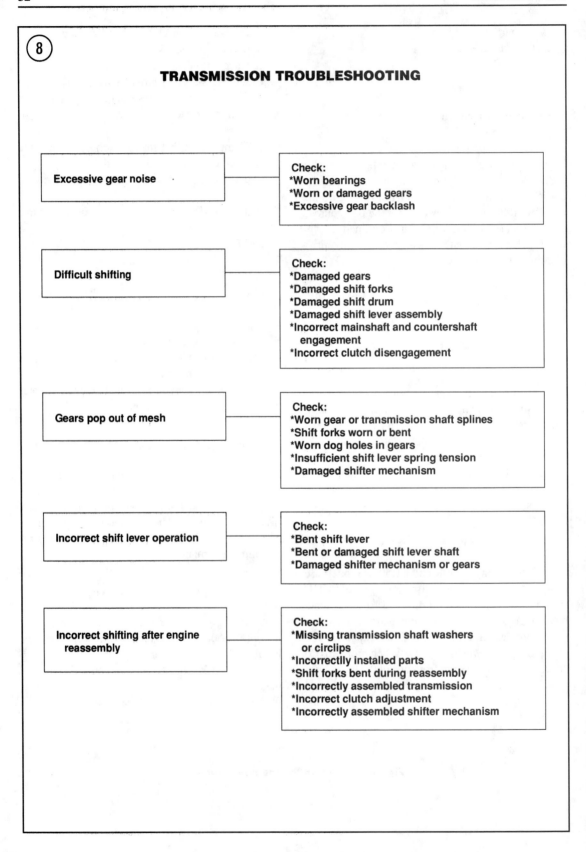

(8)

TRANSMISSION TROUBLESHOOTING

Excessive gear noise

Check:
*Worn bearings
*Worn or damaged gears
*Excessive gear backlash

Difficult shifting

Check:
*Damaged gears
*Damaged shift forks
*Damaged shift drum
*Damaged shift lever assembly
*Incorrect mainshaft and countershaft
  engagement
*Incorrect clutch disengagement

Gears pop out of mesh

Check:
*Worn gear or transmission shaft splines
*Shift forks worn or bent
*Worn dog holes in gears
*Insufficient shift lever spring tension
*Damaged shifter mechanism

Incorrect shift lever operation

Check:
*Bent shift lever
*Bent or damaged shift lever shaft
*Damaged shifter mechanism or gears

Incorrect shifting after engine reassembly

Check:
*Missing transmission shaft washers
  or circlips
*Incorrectly installed parts
*Shift forks bent during reassembly
*Incorrectly assembled transmission
*Incorrect clutch adjustment
*Incorrectly assembled shifter mechanism

⑨

DISC BRAKE TROUBLESHOOTING

2

Disc brake fluid leakage

Check:
*Loose or damaged line fittings
*Worn caliper piston seals
*Scored caliper piston or bore
*Loose banjo bolts
*Damaged oil line washers
*Leaking master cylinder diaphragm
*Leaking master cylinder secondary seal
*Cracked master cylinder housing
*Too high brake fluid level
*Loose or damaged master cylinder cover

Brake overheating

Check:
*Warped brake disc
*Incorrect brake fluid
*Caliper piston and/or brake pads hanging up
*Riding brakes during riding

Brake chatter

Check:
*Warped brake disc
*Incorrect caliper alignment
*Loose caliper mounting bolt
*Loose front axle nut and/or clamps
*Worn wheel bearings
*Damaged hub
*Restricted brake hydraulic line
*Contaminated brake pads

Brake locking

Check:
*Incorrect brake fluid
*Plugged passages in master cylinder
*Caliper piston and/or brake pads hanging up
*Warped brake disc

Insufficient brakes

Check:
*Air in brake lines
*Worn brake pads
*Low brake fluid
*Incorrect brake fluid
*Worn brake disc
*Worn caliper piston seals
*Glazed brake pads
*Leaking primary cup seal in master cylinder
*Contaminated brake pads and/or disc

Brake squeal

Check:
*Contaminated brake pads and/or disc
*Dust or dirt collected behind brake pads
*Loose parts

NOTE: If you own a 1992 CR500R or later model, first check the Supplement at the back of this book for any new service information.

CHAPTER THREE

LUBRICATION, MAINTENANCE AND TUNE-UP

Motorcycles designed for off-road or racing events are subjected to tremendous heat, stress and vibration. Although many years of experience and design have produced one of the best motorcycles of its kind, the Honda CR is still subject to problems resulting from poor maintenance procedures. When corrective and preventive maintenance is neglected, the bike cannot perform to its full potential, and can become unreliable and actually dangerous to ride.

To obtain the maximum in performance, safety and overall life from the Honda CR, it is necessary to make periodic inspections and adjustments. Frequently, minor problems are found during these inspections that are simple and inexpensive to correct. It is very frustrating to find that a major repair and expense could have been avoided by recognizing and correcting a small problem. Familiarize yourself with the motorcycle by doing simple tune-up, lubrication and maintenance procedures. Then, as you become more knowledgeable and self-confident, you can tackle more involved jobs, such as disassembly and inspection of components. This chapter explains lubrication, maintenance and tune-up procedures required for the Honda CR. **Table 1** is a suggested factory maintenance schedule. **Tables 1-12** at the end of this chapter provide various specifications.

ROUTINE CHECKS

Pre-practice Inspection Items

The following checks should be performed prior to the first ride of the day.

1. Inspect all fuel lines and fittings for wetness indicating a poor connection or deteriorating fuel line.

2. Make sure the fuel tank is full with the correct 20:1 fuel/oil mixture.

3. Make sure the transmission and clutch oil level is correct. Add oil if necessary.

4. Inspect the coolant level. With the engine cool, the coolant must be up to the bottom of the radiator filler neck.

5. Make sure all coolant hose clamps are tight. Inspect the hoses for leakage or abrasion; replace as necessary.

6. Make sure the air cleaner element is clean.

7. Make sure the spark plug heat range is correct and the plug is not carbon fouled. Inspect the spark plug lead for tightness at both the spark plug and the ignition coil.

8. Check the operation of the clutch and adjust if necessary.

9. Check the throttle and the brake levers. Make sure they operate properly with no binding.

10. Inspect the front and rear suspension. Make sure it has a good solid feel with no looseness.

11. Check the steering head for looseness and proper adjustment.

12. Inspect the drive chain for wear, correct tension and proper lubrication.

13. Inspect all drive chain guides and tension rollers for wear or damage; replace if necessary.

14. Check for tire damage and correct tire pressure. Refer to **Table 2**.

15. Check all spokes for looseness; tighten if necessary.

16. Make sure the rim locks are tight; tighten if necessary.

17. Check the air pressure in the front forks. Refer to **Table 3**.

18. Check the exhaust expansion chamber spring(s) for damage and tightness; replace if necessary.

19. Check the tightness of all fasteners, especially engine mounting hardware.

Pre-race Items

The following checks should be performed before the first race of the day.

1. Perform all items listed under *Pre-practice Inspections Items*.

2. Check the clutch for slippage or drag; adjust if necessary.

3. Inspect the air cleaner element for dirt or breakage; replace if necessary.

4. Check the cylinder head and piston for carbon buildup; clean off as necessary.

5. Check all control cables for proper lubrication. Lubricate cables if necessary.

6. Inspect the drive and driven sprockets for wear and damage; replace if necessary.

7. Check the fuel system for contamination; drain and refill if necessary.

8. Check the exhaust expansion chamber for dents and damage; repair or replace if necessary.

9. Inspect the brake pads for wear and proper contact with the disc; adjust or replace as necessary.

SERVICE INTERVALS

The services and intervals shown in **Table 1** are recommended by the factory. Strict adherence to

these recommendations will ensure long service from the Honda. If the bike is run in an area of high humidity, the lubrication services must be done more frequently to prevent rust.

For convenience when maintaining your motorcycle, most of the services shown in the table are described in this chapter. However, some procedures which require more than minor disassembly or adjustment are covered elsewhere in the appropriate chapter.

PERIODIC LUBRICATION

Oil

Oil is graded according to its viscosity, which is an indication of how thick it is. The Society of Automotive Engineers (SAE) system distinguishes oil viscosity by numbers. Thick oils have higher viscosity numbers than thin oils. For example, an SAE 5 oil is a thin oil while an SAE 90 oil is relatively thick.

Grease

A good-quality grease, preferably waterproof, should be used. Water does not wash grease off parts as easily as it washes oil off. In addition, grease maintains it lubricating qualities better than oil on long and strenuous rides. In a pinch though, the wrong lubricant is better than none at all. Correct the situation as soon as possible.

Engine Lubrication

The CR engine is a 2-stroke type that requires a combination gasoline/oil mixture to lubricate internal engine components. Proper fuel mixing is therefore very important to the life and efficiency of the engine.

Always mix fuel in the exact proportions specified. Too little oil can cause serious and expensive engine damage. Too much oil can cause poor performance and a fouled spark plug.

Use a premium grade of leaded gasoline with a Research octane rating between 92 and 100. Use a good grade of 2-stroke oil in a 20:1 mixture. Mix the gasoline in a separate container or tank, not the bike's fuel tank. Use a container with a larger volume than the gasoline to allow room to agitate and mix the fuel completely.

Once the container of 2-stroke oil has been opened, it should be used within one month or the oil may start to oxidize. Also, mix only the amount that will be used for that day's ride. Gasoline loses its potency after sitting for a period of time. The oil also loses some of its lubricating ability when mixed with gasoline and then not used for a period of time.
1. Pour half of the required gasoline into a clean sealable container.
2. Add the required amount of 2-stroke oil (for the total amount of the fuel to be mixed) and mix thoroughly.
3. Add the remainder of the gasoline and mix the entire contents thoroughly.
4. Always use a funnel equipped with a fine screen when adding the fuel mixture to the bike's fuel tank.

Transmission/Clutch Oil Level Check

1. Start the engine and ride the bike for approximately 5-10 minutes to allow the oil to circulate throughout the transmission and clutch assemblies. Shut off the engine and let the oil settle.
2. Place the bike on a level surface. Place a metal or wood stand under the frame to support the bike securely in a vertical position.
3. Perform the following:
   a. Unscrew the oil level check bolt (A, **Figure 1**) located in the right-hand crankcase cover just in front of the brake lever.
   b. A small amount of oil should run out. The bike must be level for a correct reading. If oil does run out, reinstall the oil level check bolt.
   c. If oil does not run out, the oil level is low. Remove the oil filler cap (B, **Figure 1**) and add SAE 10W-40 engine oil until oil starts to run out of the oil level check bolt hole.
4. Reinstall the oil level check bolt. Install the filler cap and tighten it securely.

Transmission/Clutch Oil Change

Regular oil changes will contribute greatly to transmission and clutch longevity. Change the oil at the intervals indicated in **Table 1**.

This interval assumes that the bike is operated in moderate climates. If it is operated under dusty or racing conditions, the oil will get dirty more quickly

and should be changed more frequently than recommended.

Use only a high-quality detergent motor oil with an API rating of SF or SG. The quality rating is stamped or printed on the container (**Figure 2**). Try to use the same brand of oil at each oil change. The correct viscosity is SAE 10W-40.

> *CAUTION*
> *Do not add any friction-reducing additives to the oil as it will cause clutch slippage. Also do not use an oil with graphite added. The use of graphite oil will void any applicable Honda warranty.*

To change the transmission/clutch oil you will need the following:
   a. Drain pan.

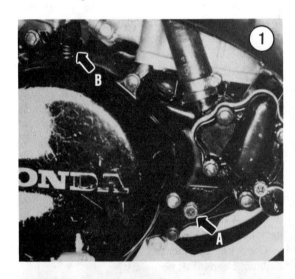

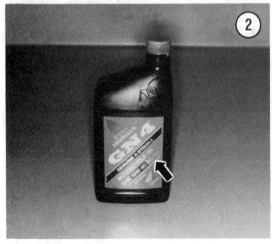

b. Funnel.

c. Can opener or pour spout.

d. 12 mm socket and socket wrench.

e. 1 quart of oil.

There are several ways to discard the old oil safely. Put it into a plastic gallon milk or bleach container. Most service stations and oil retailers will accept your used oil for recycling; some may even give you money for it. Never drain the oil onto the ground.

1. Start the engine and allow it to reach operating temperature.

2. Shut the engine off and place a drain pan under the drain plug.

3. Remove the drain plug and washer (**Figure 3**). Remove the oil filler cap. This will speed up the flow of oil.

4. Let the oil drain for at least 15-20 minutes.

5. Install the drain plug and washer and tighten securely. Honda specifications recommend tightening the drain plug to 25-35 N•m (18-25 ft.-lb.).

6. Insert a funnel into the oil fill hole and fill the transmission and clutch portion of the crankcase with the correct viscosity and quantity of oil. The approximate capacity at oil change intervals are listed in **Table 4**. If the engine has been disassembled, the oil capacity is greater. See **Table 4** for approximate capacities.

7. Install the oil filler cap.

8. Start the engine. Let the engine run at moderate speed and check for leaks.

9. Ride the bike for 5-10 minutes and turn the engine off. Check for correct oil level; adjust as necessary.

Front Fork Oil Change (1988 Models)

The recommended fork oil for 1988 models is Pro Honda Suspension Fluid SS-7 or equivalent. See **Table 5** and **Table 6** for recommended fork oil levels and capacities. The fork assembly must be partially disassembled for this procedure. Due to the number of procedures and components, it is recommended that you work on one fork leg at a time.

WARNING
If fork air pressure is released too quickly in Step 1, fork oil may spurt out with the air. Protect your eyes and clothing when performing this step.

1. Remove each air valve bleeder cap (**Figure 4**) and depress the valve stem to release air pressure from the fork.

2. Remove the drain bolt and sealing washer on the bottom of the fork leg (**Figure 5**) and drain the fork oil into a suitable container.

3. Remove the fork as described under *Front Fork Removal/Installation (1988-1990 Models)* in Chapter Nine.

4. Remove the clamping screws and clamps (**Figure 6**) at the top and bottom of the rubber boot. Remove the rubber boot from the groove in the slider and slide it off of the fork tube.

5. The fork cap/air valve assembly should have been loosened in the removal steps. If not, clamp the slider portion of the fork in a vise with soft jaws and loosen, but do not remove, the fork cap/air valve.

> *WARNING*
> *Be careful when loosening the fork cap/air valve assembly as the spring is under pressure.*

6. Remove the fork cap/air valve assembly, by hand, from the fork tube.

7. Remove the fork cap/air valve assembly from the piston rod, by performing the following:

    a. Hold (compress) the spring back to gain access to the fork cap locknut.

    b. Place a wrench on the fork cap locknut (A, **Figure 7**).

    c. Place a wrench on the fork cap/air valve assembly (C, **Figure 7**). Loosen and remove the fork cap/air valve assembly from the piston rod.

    d. Remove the spring seat and the fork spring.

    e. Remove the fork from the vise.

8. While holding the fork leg over a suitable container, pour the remainder of the fork oil out of the tube. Pump the fork leg and piston rod several times, by hand, to flush out the oil.

9. Install the sealing washer and oil drain bolt (**Figure 5**) into the fork slider. Tighten the bolt securely.

10. Hold the fork upright and pour the recommended fork oil into the piston rod until a small amount can be seen flowing from the side breather hole (**Figure 8**). Wipe off any oil that escapes from the hole.

11. Pour the recommended fork oil into the fork tube to the proper level listed in **Table 5**, while pumping the piston rod slowly.

12. Pump the fork tube slowly at least five times. Pump the piston rod at least 10 times, then collapse the fork tube to its full bottomed position.

13. Allow the oil to settle, then measure the fork oil level from the top of the tube. Refer to **Figure 8**.

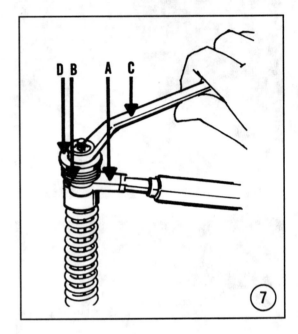

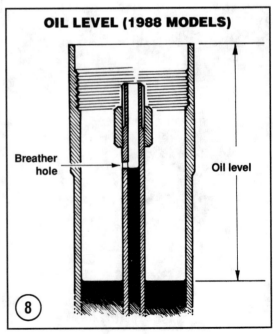

OIL LEVEL (1988 MODELS)

Breather hole

Oil level

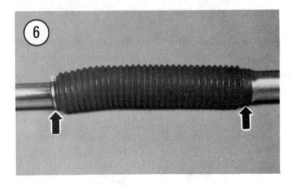

Adjust if necessary. Refer to **Table 6** for the correct oil level.

NOTE
Make a note of the fork oil level, so the opposite fork leg can be refilled to the same capacity.

14. Clean the fork spring thoroughly and install the fork spring and spring seat.

15. Slightly compress the fork and thread the fork cap/air valve onto the piston rod.

16. To tighten the fork cap/air valve assembly, perform the following:
   a. Hold the spring back to allow access to the locknut on the piston rod.
   b. Place a wrench on the locknut (A, **Figure 7**).
   c. Place a wrench (C, **Figure 7**) on the fork cap/air valve assembly (D, **Figure 7**).
   d. Tighten the fork cap/air valve assembly against the locknut to 17.5-22.5 N•m (12.7-16.3 ft.-lb.).

17. Thread the fork cap into the fork tube, but do not tighten completely. It will be tightened to specifications during installation.

18. Slide the rubber boot (**Figure 6**) and clamps onto the fork tube. Install the rubber boot into the groove in the top of the slider.

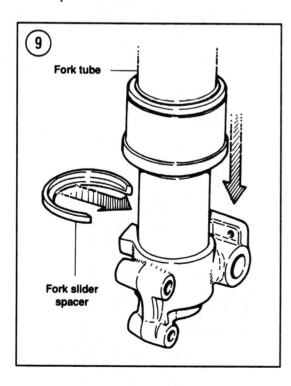

19. Install the fork assembly as described in Chapter Nine.

20. After the fork assembly has been installed, rotate the rubber boot so the breather holes are facing toward the rear. Push the boot up until it contacts the lower fork bridge and tighten the clamp screws.

21. Perform the same procedure for the opposite fork leg.

Fork Oil Change (1989-1990 Models)

The procedure for changing the fork oil varies slightly between the 1989 and 1990 models. However, the special fork slider spacer (Honda part No. 07KMZ-KZ30101), is necessary for obtaining an accurate oil level measurement on both models. The slider spacer is a relatively inexpensive tool and should be available at your dealer. Read the procedures carefully and make sure to perform the specific procedures for your model. The factory recommended fork oil for 1989 models is Pro Honda Suspension Fluid SS-7 or equivalent. The factory recommended fork oil for 1990 models is Pro Honda Suspension Fluid SS-7M or equivalent. See **Table 5** and **Table 6** at the end of the chapter for the recommended fork oil levels and capacities.

WARNING
If air pressure is released too quickly in Step 1, oil may spurt out with the air. Protect your eyes and clothing when performing this step.

1. Remove the air valve cap (**Figure 4**) and press the valve stem to release the air pressure from the fork.

2. Remove the fork legs as described under *Front Fork Removal/Installation (1988-1990 Models)* in Chapter Nine.

3. The fork cap should have been loosened in the removal steps. If not, clamp the slider portion in a vise with soft jaws and loosen, but do not remove, the fork cap assembly.

WARNING
Be careful when loosening the fork cap/air valve assembly as the spring is under pressure.

4. Install the special slider spacer (**Figure 9**) onto the lower end of the slider and gently lower the fork tube onto the spacer.

5. Remove the fork cap from the piston rod by performing the following:

   a. Place a wrench on the fork cap locknut (B, **Figure 10**).

   b. Place a wrench on the fork cap/air valve assembly (A, **Figure 10**) and loosen and remove the fork cap/air valve assembly.

6A. On 1989 models, push the spring collar downward (C, **Figure 10**) and remove the spring seat (D, **Figure 10**). Then remove the spring collar, locknut and spring.

6B. On 1990 models, push the spring collar downward (C, **Figure 10**) and remove the locknut (B, **Figure 10**). Then remove the spring seat (D, **Figure 10**) and spring collar (C, **Figure 10**) and spring.

7. Remove the special slider spacer from the slider.

CAUTION
Following removal of the fork cap from the piston rod, you will note that the tube can move up and down freely in the slider. Hold both the fork tube and slider with your hand to keep them from damaging the dust seal and guide bushing. If damage occurs, fork oil may leak from the slider.

8. Hold the fork leg over a suitable container with one hand. With the other hand, hold the piston rod and pump the rod in and out to expel the fork oil. Do this about 8-10 times to expel all of the oil.

9. Reinstall the special fork slider spacer (**Figure 9**) to the end of the slider.

10A. On 1989 models, secure the fork leg in a vertical position and perform the following:

   a. Pour the fork oil into the piston rod until a small amount can be seen flowing from the side breather hole (**Figure 11**).

   b. Pump the piston rod 8-10 times, then place the piston rod at its full bottomed out position.

   c. Measure the fork oil from the top of the fork tube with the leg vertical (**Figure 11**). Adjust if necessary. See **Table 5** and **Table 6** for oil levels and capacities.

NOTE
Make a note of the oil level, so the opposite fork leg can be filled to the same capacity.

10B. On 1990 models, secure the fork leg in a vertical position and perform the following:

a. Install the locknut to the piston rod with the cutout facing upward. This is temporary, so the piston rod will not be able to drop into the cylinder. Thread the locknut, by hand, as far as it will go.

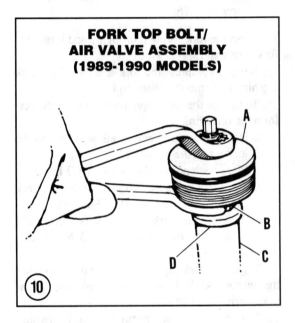

FORK TOP BOLT/ AIR VALVE ASSEMBLY (1989-1990 MODELS)

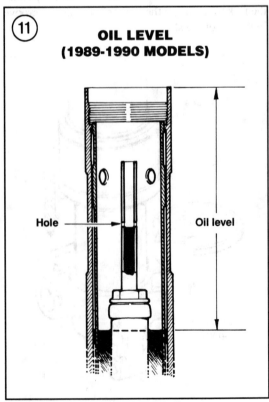

OIL LEVEL (1989-1990 MODELS)

Hole — Oil level

b. Pour half the recommended amount of fork oil into the fork tube.

c. With the piston rod at its fully bottomed out position, pour fork oil into the piston rod until a small amount can be seen flowing from the side breather hole (**Figure 11**).

d. Slowly pump the piston rod and fork tube, about 8-10 times, then fully compress the fork leg.

e. Measure the fork oil from the top of the fork tube with the leg vertical (**Figure 11**). Adjust if necessary. See **Table 5** and **Table 6** for oil levels and capacities.

NOTE
Make a note of the oil level, so the opposite fork leg can be filled to the same capacity.

11A. On 1989 models, install the fork cap/air valve assembly by performing the following:

a. Install the fork cap locknut (B, **Figure 12**) so the inner threads (A, **Figure 12**) are facing upward and thread it down, by hand, until it seats. Measure the distance between the locknut and the top of the piston rod. It should measure at least 14 mm (0.55 in.). Adjust if necessary.

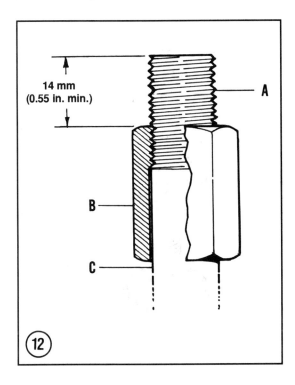

14 mm
(0.55 in. min.)

A

B

C

⑫

b. Install the fork spring into the fork tube.

c. Cut a piece of stiff wire to 12 inches.

d. Wrap one end of the wire around the piston rod, below the locknut.

e. Feed the other end through the spring collar and pull the piston rod up through it. Remove the wire.

f. While pushing the collar down against the spring tension, install the spring seat (D, **Figure 10**) between the locknut (B, **Figure 10**) and collar (C, **Figure 10**).

11B. On 1990 models, install the fork cap assembly by performing the following:

a. Install the spring with the tapered side facing upward. Only the tapered end will fit into the fork cap, so use the cap as a guide.

b. Cut a piece of stiff wire to 24 inches.

c. Wrap one end of the wire around the piston rod, below the locknut.

d. Feed the other end through the spring collar.

e. While pulling the wire, rock the collar until it slides down onto the piston rod.

f. Remove the wire and the locknut.

g. While pushing the collar down (C, **Figure 13**) against the spring tension, install the spring seat (B, **Figure 13**) and locknut with the cutouts facing upward (A, **Figure 13**). Make sure the spring seat is seated in the collar correctly.

h. Screw the locknut on, by hand, until it stops. The distance between the locknut and the top of the piston rod must be 14 mm (0.55 in.). See D, **Figure 13**. Adjust if necessary.

12. Lubricate the O-ring on the fork cap. Replace the O-ring, if worn or damaged.

13. Thread the fork cap/air valve onto the piston rod until it makes contact with the locknut.

14. Using a wrench to hold the fork cap/air valve (A, **Figure 10**), place a wrench on the locknut (B, **Figure 10**). Tighten the fork cap/air valve against the locknut to 17.5-22.5 N•m (12.7-16.3 ft.-lb.).

15. Thread the fork cap into the fork tube, but do not tighten. It will be tightened to specifications during installation.

16. Remove the special slider spacer from the slider.

17. Perform the same procedures on the opposite fork leg.

18. Install the fork assembly as described under *Front Fork Removal/Installation* in Chapter Nine.

Fork Oil Change (1991 Models)

A special fork slider spacer (Honda part No. 07KMZ-KZ30101) is necessary for obtaining the correct oil level measurement on 1991 models. This tool is relatively inexpensive and should be available at your dealer. The recommended fork oil for 1991 models is Pro Honda Suspension Fluid SS-7M or equivalent. See **Table 5** and **Table 6** for the recommended fork oil levels and capacities.

1. Remove the fork assembly as described under *Front Fork Removal/Installation (1991 Models)* in Chapter Nine.

2. Install the special slider spacer (**Figure 9**) to the lower end of the slider.

3. The fork cap should have been loosened during the removal steps. If not, clamp the slider portion in a vise with soft jaws and loosen, but do not remove, the fork cap.

> *CAUTION*
> *Be careful when loosening the fork cap assembly as the spring is under pressure.*

4. Gently lower the fork tube down onto the special slider spacer.

5. Hold the fork cap bolt with a wrench (A, **Figure 14**). Insert a wrench onto the piston rod locknut (B, **Figure 14**), then loosen and remove the fork cap bolt from the piston rod.

> *NOTE*
> *After the fork cap is removed, you will notice that the fork slider can move up*

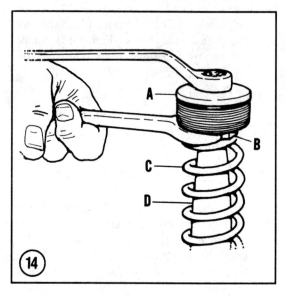

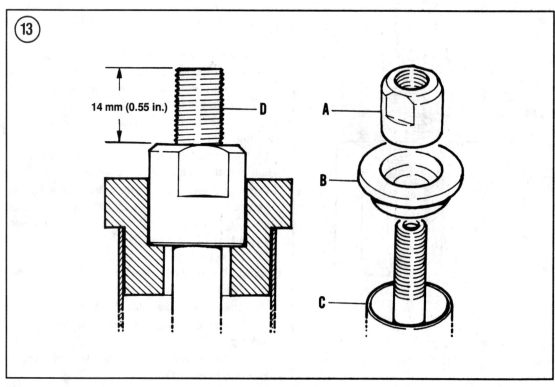

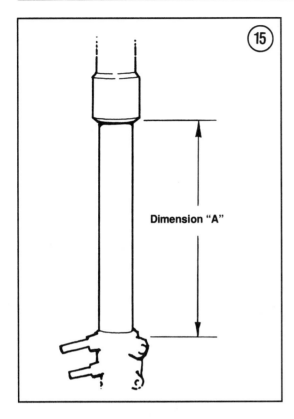

Dimension "A"

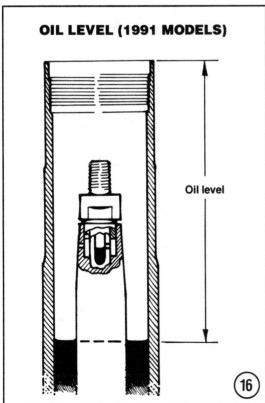

OIL LEVEL (1991 MODELS)

Oil level

and down freely within the fork tube. Hold both the fork tube and slider with your hand to prevent the guide and slide bushings from being damaged. If damage occurs, oil may leak from the fork slider.

6. Remove the spring seat from the fork cap and remove the spring (C, **Figure 14**). Do *not* remove the locknut.

7. Inspect the spring guide (D, **Figure 14**) for damage or wear, but it is not necessary to remove it from the piston rod. If damage or wear is present and removal is necessary, make sure it is reinstalled with the oil hole at the top.

8. Hold the fork leg over an approved container and pour until all the oil appears to have been expelled.

9. Pump the piston rod 8-10 times to expel oil from the damper rod assembly.

10. Make sure the special slider spacer is in place and pour half of the recommended amount of fork oil into the fork tube.

11. Bleed the air from the fork leg by performing the following:

NOTE
*Refer to **Figure 15**. In the next step, on CR250R models, do not extend the fork tube more than 300 mm (11.8 in.) at dimension "A." On CR500R models, do not extend the fork tube more than 250 mm (9.8 in.) at dimension "A." Extending the fork tube past these dimensions will cause fork oil to spill from the oil hole in the slider.*

  a. Extend the fork tube and, while covering the tube with your hand, compress the leg slowly.

  b. Perform this procedure several times.

12. With the piston rod at its bottomed out position, pour the oil into the piston rod until a small amount can be seen flowing out of the piston rod end. See **Figure 16**.

13. Slowly pump the piston rod and fork tube, 8-10 times.

14. Pour fork oil into the tube, to the recommended capacity. Measure the oil level from the top, with the tube vertical (**Figure 16**). Repeat Step 13 and adjust, if necessary.

15. Compress the fork leg fully and allow the air bubbles to escape for 5 minutes. Measure the oil level again.

NOTE
Make a note of the oil level, so the opposite fork leg can be filled to the same capacity.

16. Install the spring and fork cap by performing the following:

    a. Cut a piece of stiff wire to 24 inches.

    b. Attach one end around the piston rod, below the locknut.

    c. Hold the fork spring with the tapered end up. The tapered end is the only end that will fit into the fork cap.

    d. Feed the wire through the fork spring and pull up on the piston, while holding the oil lock valve (at lower end of piston rod). Remove the wire.

17. Lubricate the fork cap O-ring. Replace the O-ring if it is worn or damaged.

18. Install the spring seat onto the fork spring and thread the fork cap (A, **Figure 14**) onto the piston rod. Make sure the spring seat is seated correctly between the fork cap and spring.

19. While holding the locknut (B, **Figure 14**) with a wrench, tighten the fork cap bolt against the locknut to 20-24 N•m (14-17 ft.-lb.).

20. Thread the fork cap into the fork tube, but do not tighten. It will be tightened to specifications during installation.

21. Remove the special slider spacer.

22. Perform the same procedures on the opposite fork leg.

23. Install the front fork as described under *Front Fork Removal/Installation* in Chapter Nine.

Drive Chain Lubrication

Oil the drive chain as indicated in **Table 1** or sooner if it becomes dry. A properly maintained drive chain will provide maximum service life and reliability.

1. Place a metal or wood stand under the frame to support the bike securely with the rear wheel off the ground.

2. Shift the transmission into NEUTRAL.

3. Oil the bottom run of the chain with a commercial chain lubricant or SAE 10W-40 engine oil. Concentrate on getting the lubricant down between the side plates of each chain link.

4. Rotate the rear wheel to bring the unoiled portion of the chain within reach. Continue until all of the chain is lubricated.

Control Cable Lubrication

The control cables should be lubricated at the interval indicated in **Table 1**. They should also be inspected at this time for fraying and the cable sheath should be checked for chafing. Cables are relatively inexpensive and should be replaced when found to be faulty.

The control cables can be lubricated either with oil or with any of the popular cable lubricants and a cable lubricator. The first method requires more time and complete lubrication of the entire cable is less certain.

Examine the exposed end of the inner cable. If it is dirty or the cable feels gritty when moved up and down in its housing, first spray it with a solvent such as LPS-25 or WD-40. Let this solvent drain out, then proceed with the following steps.

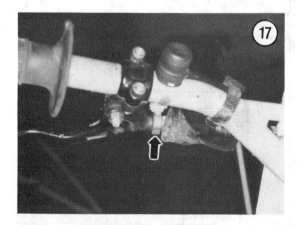

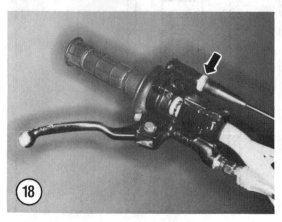

Lubricating with oil

1. Disconnect the cables from the clutch lever (**Figure 17**) and the throttle grip assembly (**Figure 18**).

2. Make a cone of stiff paper and tape it to the end of the cable sheath (**Figure 19**).

3. To avoid a mess, place a shop cloth at the end of each cable to catch the oil as it runs out.

4. Hold the cable upright and pour a small amount of thin oil (SAE 10W-30) into the cone. Work the cable in and out of the sheath for several minutes to help the oil work its way down to the end of the cable.

5. Remove the cone. Reconnect and adjust the cables as described in this chapter.

Lubricating with cable lubricator

1. Disconnect the cables from the clutch lever (**Figure 17**) and the throttle grip assembly (**Figure 18**).

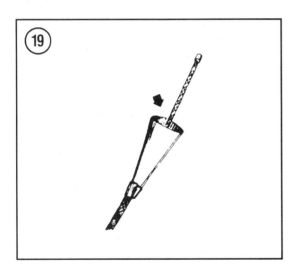

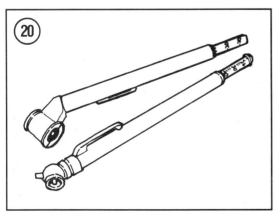

2. Place a shop cloth at the end of each cable to catch all excess lubricant that will flow out.

3. Attach a lubricator following the manufacturer's instructions.

4. Insert the nozzle of the lubricant can in the lubricator, press the button on the can and hold it down until the lubricant begins to flow out of the other end of the cable.

5. Remove the lubricator. Reconnect and adjust the cables as described in this chapter.

Swing Arm Bushing and Needle Bearing Lubrication

The swing arm needle bearings and bushings should be lubricated at the intervals indicated in **Table 1**. The swing arm must be removed and disassembled to lubricate the bushings and bearings. There are no grease fittings. Refer to Chapter Ten for complete details.

Pro-Link Suspension Lubrication

The Pro-Link suspension bearings should be lubricated at the intervals indicated in **Table 1**. The Pro-Link suspension components must be removed and disassembled to lubricate the bearings. There are no grease fittings. Refer to Chapter Ten for complete details.

PERIODIC MAINTENANCE

Tire Pressure

Tire pressure should be checked and adjusted to maintain the smoothness of the tire, good traction and handling and to get the maximum life out of the tire. A simple, accurate gauge (**Figure 20**) can be purchased for a few dollars and should be carried in your motorcycle tool kit. The appropriate tire pressures are shown in **Table 2**.

Tire Inspection

The tires take a lot of punishment so inspect them periodically for excessive wear, cuts, abrasions, etc. If you find a nail or other object in the tire, mark its location with a light crayon before removing it. This will help locate the hole for repair. Refer to Chapter Nine for tire changing and repair information.

Rim Inspection

Frequently inspect the wheel rims. If a rim has been damaged, it may have been knocked out of alignment. Improper wheel alignment can cause severe vibration and result in an unsafe riding condition. Also make sure the rim locks (**Figure 21**) are tight.

Wheel Spoke Tension

Tap each spoke with a wrench. The higher the pitch of sound it makes, the tighter the spoke. The lower the sound frequency, the looser the spoke. A "ping" is good; a "klunk" says the spoke is too loose.

If one or more spokes are loose, tighten them as described in Chapter Nine.

Drive Chain Adjustment

The drive chain adjustment should be checked at the interval indicated in **Table 1**.

1. Place a metal or wood stand under the frame to support the bike securely with the rear wheel off the ground.

2. Shift the transmission into NEUTRAL.

3. When the drive chain is pushed up midway between the sprockets on the upper chain run (**Figure 22**), the correct amount of free play should be as specified in **Table 6**. If adjustment is necessary, continue to Step 4.

4. Loosen the rear axle nut.

5. Loosen the locknut (A, **Figure 23**) and turn the adjuster bolt (B, **Figure 23**) on each side in or out to increase or decrease chain slack.

6. Make sure that the adjustment plate (A, **Figure 24**) aligns with the same mark (B, **Figure 24**) on each side of the swing arm.

7. Rotate the rear wheel to move the chain to another position and recheck the adjustment. Chains rarely wear or stretch evenly and, as a result, the free play will not remain constant over the entire chain. If the chain cannot be adjusted within these limits, it is excessively worn or stretched and should be replaced. If the sprockets are worn, replace the sprockets as well. Never install a new chain over worn sprockets.

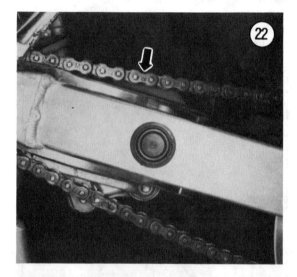

WARNING
Excess free play can result in chain
breakage which could cause a serious
accident.

8. When adjustment is correct, sight along the chain from the rear sprocket to see that it is correctly aligned. The chain should leave the rear sprocket in a straight line (A, **Figure 25**). If it is cocked to one side or another (B and C, **Figure 25**), the rear wheel is incorrectly aligned and must be corrected. Turn the adjuster bolts or nuts in opposite directions until the chain and sprockets are correctly aligned. When the alignment is correct, readjust the free play as described in Step 5. Tighten the adjuster locknuts.

9. Tighten the rear axle nut to the torque specification listed in **Table 8**.

Drive Chain Cleaning, Inspection and Lubrication

Remove, thoroughly clean and lubricate the drive chain at the intervals specified in **Table 1**.

1. Remove the drive chain as described in Chapter Ten.

CAUTION
Use only kerosene to clean O-ring chains. Do not use solvent or any other type of solution as the O-rings may swell, permanently damaging the chain.

2. Immerse the chain in a pan of kerosene or non-flammable solvent and let it soak for about half an hour. Move it around and flex it during this period so that dirt between the pins and rollers may work its way out.

3. Carefully scrub the rollers and side plates with a medium-soft brush and rinse away loosened grit. Rinse it a couple of times to make sure all dirt is washed out. Dry the chain with a shop cloth, then hang it up and allow the chain to dry thoroughly.

4. After cleaning the chain, examine it carefully for wear or damage. If any signs are visible, replace the chain.

5. Lay the drive chain alongside a ruler (**Figure 26**) and compress the links together. Then stretch them apart. If more than 6 mm (1/4 in.) of movement within 300 mm (12 in.) of chain length is possible, replace the drive chain.

CAUTION
*Always check both sprockets (**Figure 27**) every time the drive chain is removed. If any wear is visible on the teeth, replace the sprocket. Never install a new chain over worn sprockets or a worn chain over new sprockets.*

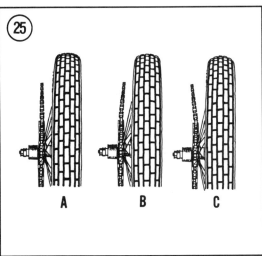

A   B   C

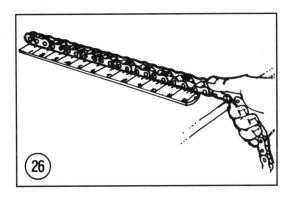

6. Check the inner faces of the inner plates (**Figure 28**). They should be lightly polished on both sides. If they show considerable wear on both sides, the sprockets are not aligned. Align them as described under *Drive Chain Adjustment* in this chapter.

7. Lubricate the chain with a good grade of chain lubricant following the manufacturer's instructions.

8. Reinstall the chain as described in Chapter Ten.

9. Adjust chain free play as described under *Drive Chain Adjustment* in this chapter.

Drive Chain Slider, Rollers and Guides

Although the drive chain slider and the drive chain rollers are of the same design for the models covered in this manual, there are slightly different configurations of drive chain guides between 1988-1989 and 1990-on models.

1. The drive chain slider is located on the drive chain side of the swing arm. There is no visible wear limit line on the slider, but if a deep groove is worn down into the top surface of the slider (**Figure 29**) or to the dimension listed in **Table 9**, the slider must be replaced. Replace the slider as described in Chapter Ten.

2. The drive chain guide is attached to the swing arm close to the driven sprocket. If the drive chain is visible through the wear inspection window, the guide must be replaced. Refer to **Figure 30** for

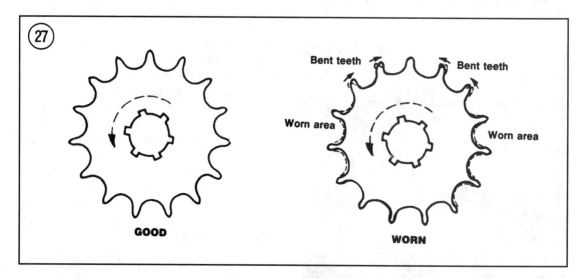

(27)

Bent teeth   Bent teeth

Worn area   Worn area

GOOD   WORN

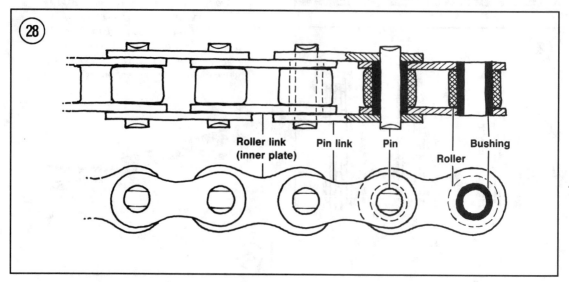

(28)

Roller link (inner plate)   Pin link   Pin   Bushing   Roller

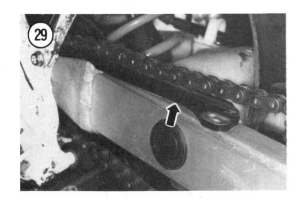

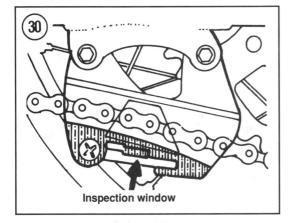

Inspection window

1988-1989 models or A, **Figure 31** for 1990-on models.

3. To replace the drive chain guide, loosen and remove the bolts (B, **Figure 31**) securing the guide to the swing arm. Install a new guide and tighten the bolts securely.

4. On 1988 and 1989 models, the chain guide is adjustable to allow the use of various sprocket sizes (**Figure 32**). Position the guide rear mounting bolt in the lower hole for 53 tooth sprockets. Position the guide rear mounting bolt in the upper hole for 49 or 51 tooth sprockets.

5. The rollers are attached to the frame directly above and below the drive chain where the drive chain reaches its maximum up and down movement. Inspect the drive chain rollers as follows:

    a. Remove the bolt securing the upper roller (**Figure 33**) and the bolt securing the lower roller (**Figure 34**) and remove each roller from the frame.

    b. Measure the outside diameter (OD) of each roller with a vernier caliper and compare to the dimension listed in **Table 9**. If worn to the

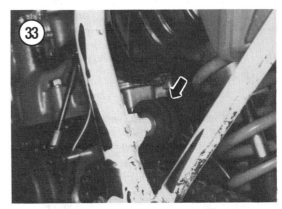

service limit dimension or less, replace the
roller(s).

c. Install a new roller(s) and tighten the bolt
securely.

Front Disc Brake Fluid Level

Hydraulic brake fluid in the reservoir should be to
the upper casting ledge inside the reservoir body.
The upper ledge is only visible when the master
cylinder top cover is removed (**Figure 35**). If the
brake fluid reaches the lower level mark, visible
through the viewing port on the reservoir (**Figure
36**), the fluid level must be corrected by adding fresh
brake fluid.

To add fluid to the front master cylinder:

1. Place the bike on level ground and position the
handlebar so the master cylinder reservoir is level.

2. Clean any dirt from the area around the cover
before removing the cover.

3. Remove the cover and diaphragm (**Figure 37**).

> *WARNING*
> *Use only brake fluid clearly marked
> DOT 4 and specified for disc brakes.
> Others may vaporize and cause brake
> failure. Dispose of fluid according to
> local EPA regulations—never reuse
> brake fluid.*

> *CAUTION*
> *Be careful when adding brake fluid. Do
> not spill it on painted or plated surfaces
> as it will destroy the finish. Wash off the
> area immediately with soapy water and
> thoroughly rinse it off with clean water.*

4. Reinstall the diaphragm and cover (**Figure 37**).
Tighten the screws securely.

Rear Disc Brake Fluid Level

Hydraulic brake fluid must be between the upper
and lower marks on the rear master cylinder. See
Figure 38.

To add fluid to the rear master cylinder reservoir:

1. Place the bike on level ground.

2. Clean any dirt from the area around the cover
before removing the cover.

3. Remove the cover.

> *WARNING*
> *Use only brake fluid clearly marked
> DOT 4 and specified for disc brakes.
> Others may vaporize and cause brake
> failure. Dispose of any unused fluid ac-
> cording to local EPA regulations. Never
> reuse brake fluid. Contaminated brake
> fluid can cause brake failure.*

> *CAUTION*
> *Be careful when adding brake fluid. Do
> not spill it on painted or plated surfaces*

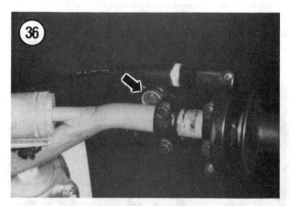

as it will destroy the finish. Wash off the area immediately with soapy water and thoroughly rinse off with clean water.

4. Install the cover.

Disc Brake Lines

Check the brake lines between the master cylinder and the brake caliper assembly. If there is any leak-

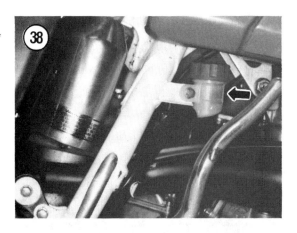

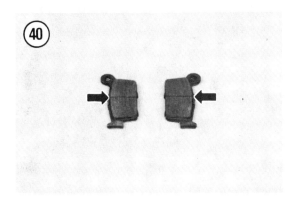

age, tighten the connections and bleed the brakes as described in Chapter Eleven. If tightening the connection does not stop the leak or if the brake line is obviously damaged, cracked or chafed, replace the brake line and bleed the system as described under *Bleeding the System* in Chapter Eleven.

Disc Brake Pad Wear

Inspect the brake pads (**Figure 39**) for excessive or uneven wear or scoring of the disc. If the pads are worn to the bottom of the wear limit groove (**Figure 40**), the pads must be replaced. The wear limit groove is also visible with the pads installed by sighting at the mid-point where the pad makes contact with the disc. If pad replacement is necessary, refer to Chapter Eleven.

> *WARNING*
> *Always replace both pads at the same time to maintain even pressure on the brake disc.*

Disc Brake Fluid Change

Every time the reservoir cap is removed, a small amount of dirt and moisture enters the brake fluid system. The same thing happens if a leak occurs or any part of the hydraulic brake system is loosened or disconnected. Dirt can clog the system and cause unnecessary wear. Water in the brake fluid vaporizes at high temperature, impairing the hydraulic action and reducing the brake's stopping ability.

To maintain peak braking efficiency, change the brake fluid every year. To change brake fluid, see *Bleeding the System* in Chapter Eleven. Continue adding new brake fluid to the master cylinder and bleeding the fluid out at the caliper until the brake fluid leaving the caliper is clean and free of contaminants.

> *WARNING*
> *Use only brake fluid clearly marked DOT 4 and specified for disc brakes. Others may vaporize and cause brake failure. Dispose of any unused fluid according to local EPA regulations— never reuse brake fluid. Contaminated brake fluid can cause brake failure.*

Front Disc Brake Lever Free Play

The front disc brake lever should be adjusted for proper clearance between the piston and the adjuster bolt. Refer to **Figure 41**. If adjustment is necessary, perform the following:

1. Slide back the rubber protective boot.

2. At the hand lever, loosen the locknut (A, **Figure 42**) and turn the adjuster (B, **Figure 42**) to achieve the correct amount of clearance (**Figure 41**). Tighten the locknut.

3. Measure the free play at the end of the lever. If the amount of free play (B, **Figure 41**) exceeds 30 mm (1.25 in.), there is air in the brake line and the brake must be bled. See *Bleeding the System* in Chapter Eleven.

4. Slide the protective boot back in place.

Rear Brake Pedal Height Adjustment

The rear brake pedal should be adjusted to your own personal preference.

1. Place a metal or wood stand under the frame to support the bike securely.

2. Check that the brake pedal is in the at-rest position.

3. Loosen the locknut on the pivot link (between the brake arm and master cylinder) and turn the adjuster nut (**Figure 43**) until the desired height is obtained.

4. Tighten the locknut.

Clutch Adjustment

The clutch adjustment takes up slack caused by cable stretching. There is no provision for adjusting the clutch mechanism.

If the proper amount of free play cannot be achieved by using this adjustment procedure, either the cable has stretched to the point that it needs to be replaced or the clutch friction discs are worn and need replacing. Refer to Chapter Five for cable and disc replacement.

1. Loosen the locknut on the hand lever (**Figure 44**). Screw in the adjuster barrel until 10-20 mm (3/8-3/4 in.) of free play is obtained at the tip of the lever (**Figure 45**). Tighten the locknut.

2. If the adjuster barrel is too far out or if the proper amount of free play cannot be achieved at the hand lever, additional adjustment can be made at the inte-

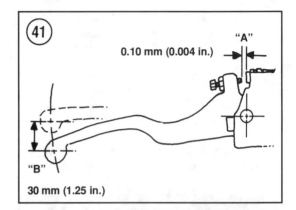

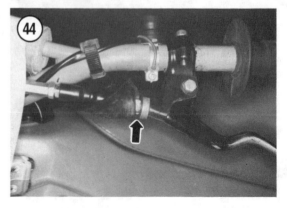

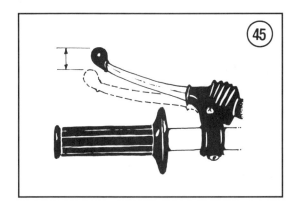

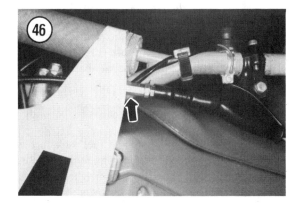

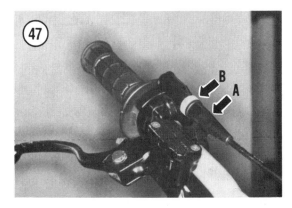

gral cable adjuster near the front number plate (**Figure 46**).

3. At the hand lever, loosen the locknut and turn the adjuster barrel all the way in toward the hand lever. Then back it out one full turn. Tighten the locknut.

4. If necessary, remove the bolt securing the front number plate and move the plate out of the way.

5. At the cable adjuster, loosen the locknut and turn the adjuster (**Figure 46**) until the correct amount of lever free play is obtained. Tighten the locknut.

6. If necessary, repeat Step 1 for fine adjustment.

7. After adjustment is completed, check that the locknuts are tight on the hand lever and the cable adjuster.

8. Test ride the bike and make sure the clutch is operating correctly.

Throttle Adjustment and Operation

The throttle lever should move smoothly from the fully closed to the fully open position. The throttle grip should have the amount of rotational free play listed in **Table 10**.

Minor adjustments can be made at the throttle grip. Major adjustments can be made where the throttle cable attaches to the carburetor top cap.

1. If adjustment is necessary, slide back the rubber boot (A, **Figure 47**), loosen the locknut (B, **Figure 47**) and turn the adjuster at the throttle grip in or out to achieve proper free play rotation. Tighten the locknut.

2. If the proper amount of free play cannot be achieved at the throttle grip, there is an additional adjustment point at the top of the carburetor. Slide the rubber cap (**Figure 48**) up the throttle cable and off the carburetor top cap. Loosen the locknut and turn the adjuster to achieve the proper amount of free play at the hand lever. Tighten the locknut.

3. Check the throttle cable from grip to carburetor. Make sure it is not kinked or chafed. Replace as necessary.

4. Make sure the throttle grip rotates freely from a fully closed to fully open position. Check with the handlebar at center, at full right and at full left. If necessary, remove the throttle grip and apply a lithium-based grease to it.

5. If the proper amount of free play cannot be attained, the throttle cable has stretched and must be replaced as described in Chapter Six.

HPP System Inspection

The exhaust valves in the HPP system should be decarbonized at the interval listed in **Table 1**, or whenever engine performance decreases at either end of the rpm range.

Refer to Chapter Six for all service procedures.

Air Cleaner Element

The air cleaner removes dust and abrasive particles from the air before the air enters the carburetor and engine. Without the air cleaner, very fine particles could enter into the engine and cause rapid wear of the piston rings, cylinder and bearings. Small passages in the carburetor could become clogged. Never run the bike without the air cleaner element installed.

Proper air cleaner servicing can do more to ensure long service from your engine than almost any other single item. Service the air filter element before every race.

1. Remove the seat.

2. Remove the bolt securing the air cleaner element assembly (**Figure 49**) and remove the assembly (**Figure 50**).

3. Wipe out the interior of the air box with a shop rag dampened with cleaning solvent. Remove any foreign matter that may have passed through a broken element.

4. Remove the element from the element holder by carefully pulling the foam off the holder.

5. Clean the element gently in cleaning solvent until all dirt is removed. Thoroughly dry each element in a clean shop cloth until all solvent residue is removed. Let it dry for about one hour.

NOTE
Inspect the element. If it is torn or broken in any area, it should be replaced. Do not run with a damaged element as it may allow dirt to enter the engine.

6. Pour a small amount of SAE 80 gear oil or foam air filter oil onto the air cleaner element and work it into the porous foam material. Do not oversaturate the element as too much oil will restrict air flow. The element will be discolored by the oil and should have an even color indicating that the oil is distributed evenly. If foam air filter oil was used, let the element dry for another hour before installation. If installed too soon, the chemical carrier in the foam air filter oil will be drawn into the engine and may cause damage.

7A. On 1988 models, align the pin on the element holder (B, **Figure 51**A) with the hole in the foam (C, **Figure 51**A) and install the air cleaner element onto the element holder.

7B. On 1989-on models, install the air cleaner element onto the element holder.

8. Apply multipurpose grease on the element sealing surface (A, **Figure 51A**).

9A. On 1988 models, install the air cleaner assembly with the UP mark on the element holder facing up.

9B. On 1989-on models, install the air cleaner assembly by aligning the tab on the element with the triangle mark on the element case (**Figure 51B**).

10. Install and tighten the air cleaner bolt.

11. Install the seat.

Fuel Line Inspection

Inspect the fuel line from the fuel tank to the carburetor. If it is cracked or starting to deteriorate, it must be replaced. Make sure the small hose clamps are in place and holding the hoses securely.

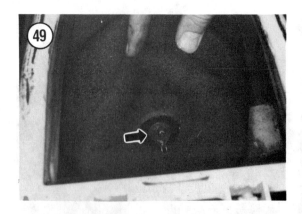

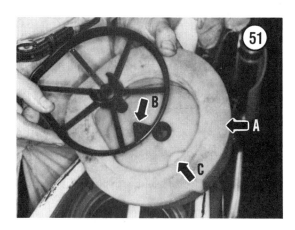

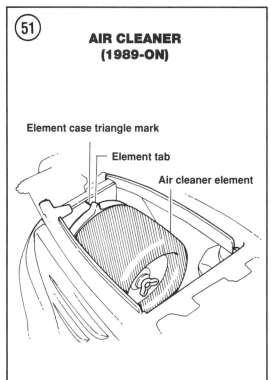

**AIR CLEANER
(1989-ON)**

Element case triangle mark

Element tab

Air cleaner element

*WARNING
A damaged or deteriorating fuel line presents a very dangerous fire hazard to both the rider and the bike if fuel should spill onto a hot engine.*

Cooling System Inspection

Perform the following inspection at the intervals indicated in **Table 1**.

1. Test the specific gravity of the coolant with an antifreeze tester to ensure adequate temperature and corrosion protection. The system must have at least a 50:50 mixture of antifreeze and distilled water. Never let the mixture become less than 40 percent antifreeze or corrosion will occur. Do not exceed the maximum percentages recommended in **Table 11**.

2. Check all cooling system hoses for damage or deterioration. Replace any hose that is questionable. Make sure all hose clamps are tight.

3. Carefully clean any road dirt, bugs, mud, etc., from the radiator core(s). Use a whisk broom, compressed air or low-pressure water. If the radiator(s) has been hit by a small rock or other item, carefully straighten out the fins with a screwdriver. If the radiator(s) has been damaged across approximately 20 percent or more of the frontal area, the radiator(s) should be recored or replaced.

Coolant Change

The cooling system should be completely drained and refilled at the interval indicated in **Table 1**.

*CAUTION
Use only a high-quality ethylene glycol antifreeze specifically labeled for use with aluminum engines. Do not use an alcohol-based antifreeze.*

*WARNING
Antifreeze is classified as an environmental toxic waste by the EPA and cannot be legally disposed of by flushing down a drain or pouring it onto the ground. Place antifreeze in a suitable container and dispose of it according to local EPA regulations. Do not store coolant where it is accessible to children or animals.*

In areas where freezing temperatures occur, add a higher percentage of antifreeze to protect the system from temperatures far below those likely to occur. **Table 11** lists the recommended amount of antifreeze for protection at various ambient temperatures.

> *CAUTION*
> *Do not use a higher percentage of anti-freeze-to-water than recommended for the ambient temperature. A higher concentration of antifreeze will decrease the performance of the cooling system.*

The following procedure must be performed when the engine is cool.

1. Place a metal or wood stand under the frame to hold the bike securely.

2. Remove the right side cover, if necessary, and remove the radiator cap (**Figure 52**). This will speed up the draining process.

> *CAUTION*
> *Be careful not to spill antifreeze on painted surfaces as it will destroy the surface. Wash immediately with soapy water and rinse thoroughly with clean water.*

> *NOTE*
> *In the next step, the engine is shown removed for clarification only. It is not necessary to remove the engine for these procedures.*

3. Place a drain pan under the right-hand side of the engine. Remove the drain screw on the cylinder (**Figure 53**) and on the water pump (**Figure 54**).

4. Take the bike off the stand and tip the bike from side to side to drain any residual coolant from the cooling system. Place the bike back onto the stand.

5. Inspect the sealing washers on the drain screws; replace if necessary. Install both drain screws.

6. Place a funnel into the radiator filler neck and refill the radiator. Slowly add the coolant through the radiator filler neck. Use the recommended mixture of antifreeze and distilled water. See **Table 10**. Do not install the radiator cap at this time.

7. Take the bike off the stand and lean it about 20° to the left and then to the right. This will help bleed air from the cooling system. If necessary, add additional coolant to the system.

8. Install the radiator cap securely.

> *CAUTION*
> *If the radiator cap is not installed correctly, coolant loss and engine damage may occur.*

> *NOTE*
> *It is normal for a small amount of coolant to be lost through the overflow tube after the engine is warmed up.*

Exhaust System

Before every race, inspect the exhaust system for cracks or dents which could alter performance. See *Exhaust System* in Chapter Six for repair methods. Also check for broken or weak springs.

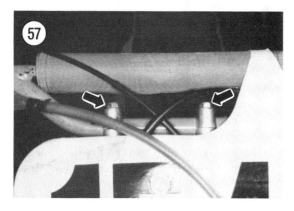

The muffler should be repacked with new glass wool if the old glass wool has deteriorated. See *Repacking the Muffler* in Chapter Six for this procedure.

Wheel Bearings

There is no factory-recommended interval for cleaning and repacking the wheel bearings. They should be serviced whenever they are removed from the wheel hub or whenever there is the likelihood of water contamination. Service procedures are covered in Chapter Nine and Chapter Ten.

Steering Head Adjustment Check

The steering head is fitted with tapered roller bearings. It should be checked as indicated in **Table 1**. Place a metal or wood stand under the frame to support the bike securely with the front wheel off the ground. Hold onto the front fork tubes and gently rock the fork assembly back and forth. If it feels loose, exceptionally tight or sounds gritty, the steering stem must be disassembled and inspected. Refer to Chapter Nine.

Front Suspension Check

1. Apply the front brake and pump the forks up and down as vigorously as possible. Check for smooth operation and look for any oil leaks.
2. Make sure the upper fork bridge bolts (**Figure 55**) and lower (**Figure 56**) fork bridge bolts are tight.
3. Make sure the bolts securing the handlebar holders (**Figure 57**) are tight and that the handlebar is secure.
4. Check that all nuts securing the front axle holders are tight (**Figure 58**).

> *CAUTION*
> *If any of the previously mentioned bolts and nuts are loose, refer to Chapter Nine for correct procedures and torque specifications.*

Rear Suspension Check

1. Place the bike on a metal or wood stand with the rear wheel off the ground.
2. Push hard on the rear wheel (sideways) to check for side play in the swing arm bushings.
3. Check the tightness of the upper and lower shock absorber mounting bolts and nuts.
4. Make sure the rear axle nut (**Figure 59**) is tight.

CAUTION
If any of the previously mentioned bolts and nuts are loose, refer to Chapter Ten for correct procedures and torque specifications.

Nuts, Bolts and Other Fasteners

Constant vibration can loosen many of the fasteners on the motorcycle. Check the tightness of all fasteners, especially those on:

a. Engine mounting hardware.
b. Engine crankcase covers.
c. Handlebar and front forks.
d. Gearshift lever.
e. Brake pedal and lever.
f. Exhaust system.

TUNE-UP

A complete tune-up should be performed at the interval indicated in **Table 1** for normal riding and racing. The purpose of the tune-up is to restore the performance lost due to normal wear and deterioration of parts. **Table 12** summarizes tune-up specifications.

The spark plug should be routinely replaced at every other tune-up or if the electrodes show signs of erosion. Have the new parts on hand before you begin.

Because different systems in an engine interact, the procedure should be done in the following order:

a. Clean or replace the air cleaner element.
b. Check or replace the spark plug.
c. Check the ignition timing.
d. Adjust the carburetor idle speed.
e. Decarbonize the engine and exhaust system.

To perform a tune-up on your Honda, you will need the following tools:

a. 18 mm spark plug wrench.
b. Socket wrench and assorted sockets.
c. Spark plug wire feeler gauge and gapper tool.
d. Ignition timing light.
e. Tune-up tachometer.

Spark Plug Selection

Spark plugs are available in various heat ranges. Plugs that are hotter and colder than the original plug are available.

Select a plug of a heat range designed for the loads and temperature conditions under which the bike will be run. The use of an incorrect heat range can cause a seized piston, scored cylinder wall or damaged piston crown. The use of a non-resistor spark plug may cause ignition problems or damage.

In general, use a hot plug for low speeds, low engine loads and low temperatures. Use a cold plug for high speeds, high engine loads and high temperatures. The plug should operate hot enough to burn off unwanted deposits, but not so hot that it is damaged or causes preignition. A spark plug of the correct heat range will show a light tan color on the portion of the insulator within the cylinder after the plug has been in service.

The reach (length) of a plug is also important. A longer than normal plug could interfere with the piston, causing permanent and severe damage. Refer to **Figure 60**. The recommended spark plugs are listed in **Table 12**.

Spark Plug Removal/Cleaning

1. Grasp the spark plug lead (**Figure 61**) as near to the plug as possible and pull it off the plug. If the

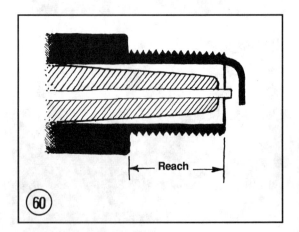

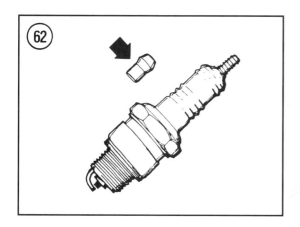

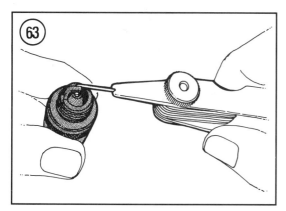

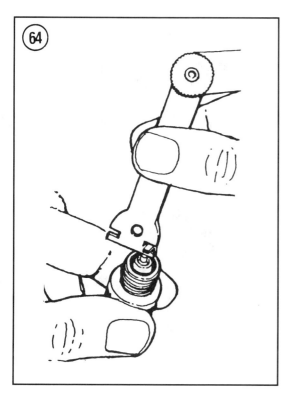

boot is stuck to the plug, twist it slightly to break it loose.

2. Blow away any dirt that has accumulated in the spark plug well.

CAUTION
Dirt can fall into the cylinder when the plug is removed, causing serious engine damage. Use a strip of masking tape to cover the opening if the spark plug is not going to be reinstalled right away.

3. Remove the spark plug with an 18 mm spark plug wrench.

NOTE
If the plug is difficult to remove, apply penetrating oil around the base of the plug and let it soak in about 10-20 minutes.

4. Inspect the spark plug carefully. Look for a plug with broken center porcelain, excessively eroded electrodes and excessive carbon or oil fouling. Replace the plug if necessary. If deposits are light, the plug may be cleaned in solvent with a wire brush or in a special spark plug sandblast cleaner. Regap the plug as explained in this chapter.

Spark Plug Gapping and Installation

A new plug should be carefully gapped to ensure a reliable, consistent spark. You must use a special spark plug gapping tool with a wire feeler gauge.

1. Remove the new plug from the box and screw on the loose end piece (**Figure 62**).

2. Insert a wire feeler gauge between the center and the side electrode of each plug (**Figure 63**). The correct gap is listed in **Table 12**. If the gap is correct, you will feel a slight drag as you pull the wire through. If there is no drag or the gauge won't pass through, bend the side electrode with the gapping tool (**Figure 64**) to set the proper gap.

3. Put a small drop of oil or aluminum anti-seize compound on the threads of the spark plug.

4. Screw the spark plug in by hand until it seats. Very little effort is required. If force is necessary, you have a plug cross-threaded; unscrew it and try again.

5. Tighten the spark plug an additional 1/2 turn after the gasket has made contact with the head. If you are reinstalling an old, regapped plug and are reusing the old gasket, only tighten an additional 1/4 turn.

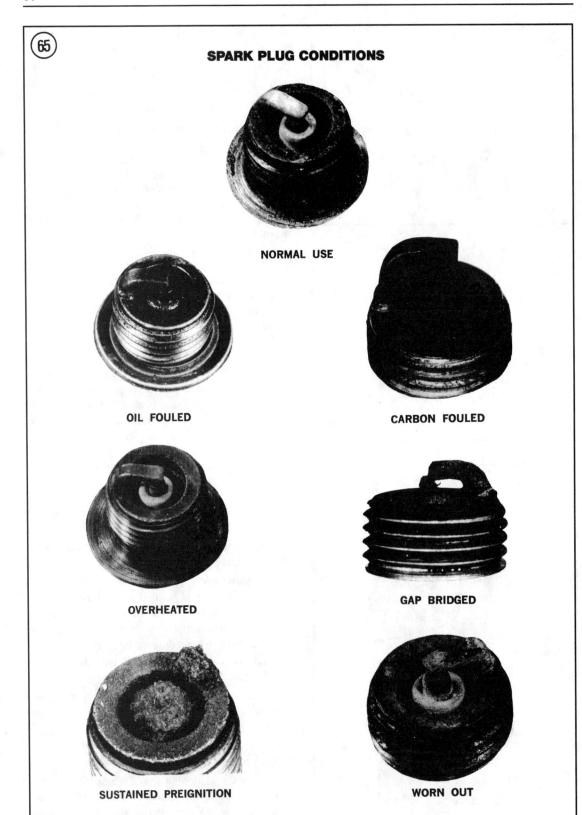

65

SPARK PLUG CONDITIONS

NORMAL USE

OIL FOULED

CARBON FOULED

OVERHEATED

GAP BRIDGED

SUSTAINED PREIGNITION

WORN OUT

CAUTION
Do not overtighten. This will only squash the gasket and destroy its sealing ability. It can also change the plug gap.

6. Install the spark plug lead. Make sure the lead is on tight.

Reading Spark Plugs

Much information about engine and spark plug performance can be determined by careful examination of the spark plug. This information is valid only after performing the following steps.

1. Ride the bike a short distance at full throttle in any gear.

2. Push the engine kill switch to OFF before closing the throttle and simultaneously pull in the clutch or shift to NEUTRAL. Coast and brake to a stop.

3. Remove the spark plug and examine it. Compare it to **Figure 65**.

4. If the plug is defective, replace it. If its condition indicates other engine problems, the bike cannot be properly tuned until repairs are made.

Ignition Timing

The Honda CR is equipped with a capacitor discharge ignition (CDI) system. This system uses no breaker points and is essentially non-adjustable, but the timing can be checked to make sure all ignition components are operating correctly. Incorrect ignition timing can cause a drastic loss of engine performance and efficiency. It may also cause overheating.

If both the alternator rotor and stator assembly are replaced as a matched set, the ignition timing will be okay. If only one of the components is replaced, there is a special procedure required to match the components to each other. Refer to *Timing Adjustment* in Chapter Seven for ignition timing. Refer to Chapter Seven for individual component testing procedures.

Carburetor Adjustment

Turning the air screw in enriches the fuel mixture and turning it out leans the mixture.

1. Turn the air screw (A, **Figure 66**) in until it lightly seats then back it out the number of turns indicated in **Table 12**.

2. Start the engine and let it reach normal operating temperature. The engine must be able to run without the choke.

3. Turn the air screw in or out until the engine revs up smoothly without hesitation.

4. If desired, turn the choke/idle speed knob (B, **Figure 66**) to adjust the idle speed. Initial adjustment is 6 turns or 36 clicks out (counterclockwise) from a lightly seated position. There is no specification for idle speed; it's strictly personal preference.

5. Test the adjustment by accelerating away from a slow corner on a track. Acceleration should be smooth without hesitation or stumbling. Repeat Step 3 if necessary.

Carbon Removal

Carbon buildup should be removed from the engine and exhaust system at the intervals indicated in **Table 1**.

On a 2-stroke engine, carbon builds up quickly in the combustion chamber, on the piston crown, in the cylinder's exhaust port and in the exhaust system. The carbon deposits will increase the compression ratio and decrease engine performance. Overheating and preignition from carbon deposits can cause engine damage.

If the carbon is removed at the specified times and a good grade of 2-stroke oil is used, the carbon buildup will rarely amount to more than a thick film which can be removed with a soft cloth soaked in solvent. If the deposits are left too long, they will have to be scraped off with a soft-metal scraper.

1. Remove the exhaust system, cylinder head, cylinder and piston as described in Chapter Four and Chapter Six.

2. Gently scrape off carbon deposits from the piston crown (**Figure 67**) and the cylinder head (**Figure 68**) with a dull screwdriver or the end of a hacksaw blade (**Figure 69**). Do not scratch the surface as this can cause hot spots.

3. Wipe the surfaces clean with a shop cloth dipped in solvent.

CAUTION
Be careful not to damage the HPP valves within the exhaust ports.

4. Scrape off the carbon deposits in the exhaust port (**Figure 70**) with a dull screwdriver or the end of a hacksaw blade. Do not scratch the surface.

NOTE
Figure 70 *is shown with the engine removed for clarity. It is not necessary to remove it to perform this procedure.*

5. Remove carbon from the HPP system. Refer to Chapter Six.

6. Install the piston, cylinder and cylinder head.

7. Gently scrape off carbon deposits from the interior of the head pipe where it attaches to the cylinder.

8. Remove the muffler from the expansion chamber.

9. Clean out the rest of the expansion chamber by running a piece of used motorcycle drive chain around in it. Another way is to chuck a length of wire cable, with the loose end frayed, in an electric drill. Use the drill to run the frayed cable around in the expansion chamber a couple of times. Also tap on the exterior of the chamber with a rubber mallet to break any additional carbon loose.

10. Blow out the interior with compressed air.

11. Clean out the interior of the muffler with the same methods used on the expansion chamber.

12. Visually inspect the entire exhaust system assembly especially in the areas of welds, for cracks or other damage. Repair or replace any faulty component.

13. Install the exhaust system.

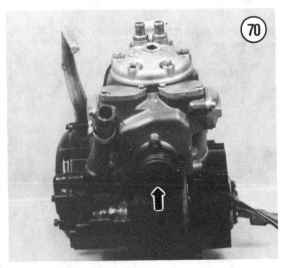

Table 1 COMPETITION MAINTENANCE SCHEDULE*

Every race or **60 miles (100 km)**	Inspect and lubricate all control cables Lubricate and adjust drive chain Clean air cleaner element Check and adjust wheel spoke tension Decarbonize the HPP exhaust valves (models so equipped) Inspect exhaust system
Every 3 races or **180 miles (300 km)**	Complete engine tune-up Replace piston Replace piston ring(s) Replace spark plug Replace front fork oil Change clutch/transmission oil Replace drive chain Replace driven sprocket
Every 6 races or **400 miles (600 km)**	Replace all control cables Replace drive chain tensioner upper and lower rollers
Every 9 races or **600 miles (900 km)**	Replace piston pin Replace connecting rod small end bearing Replace drive sprocket Disassemble Pro-Link linkage and lubricate Remove swing arm and lubricate bushings Inspect steering head bearings
Every year	Inspect cooling system; drain and replace engine coolant (liquid-cooled models) Drain and replace hydraulic brake fluid (models so equipped)

*This Honda factory competition maintenance schedule should be considered as a guide to general maintenance and lubrication intervals. Harder than normal use and exposure to mud, water, sand, high humidity, etc., will naturally dictate more frequent attention to most maintenance items.

Table 2 TIRE INFLATION PRESSURE (COLD)

Size	Air pressure
CR250R Front 80/100-21 (51M)	15 psi (1.0 kg/cm^2)
Rear 110/100-18 (64M)	15 psi (1.0 kg/cm^2)
CR500R Front 80/100-21 (51M)	15 psi (1.0 kg/cm^2)
Rear 110/100-18 (64M)	15 psi (1.0 kg/cm^2)

Table 3 FRONT FORK AIR PRESSURE

| | Standard | | Maximum | |
	psi	kg/cm^2	psi	kg/cm^2
All models	0	0	6	0.4

Table 4 APPROXIMATE CLUTCH/TRANSMISSION OIL CAPACITIES

Model	liters	U.S. qt.	Imp. qt.
CR250R			
1988-1989			
At oil change	0.55	0.58	0.48
After disassembly	0.6	0.63	0.53
1990-1991			
At oil change	0.63	0.67	0.55
After disassembly	0.7	0.74	0.62
CR500R			
1988-1989			
At oil change	0.65	0.68	0.57
After disassembly	0.7	0.74	0.62
1990-1991			
At oil change	0.68	0.71	0.60
After disassembly	0.75	0.79	0.66

Table 5 FRONT FORK OIL CAPACITY

	ml	U.S. oz.	Imp. oz
CR250R			
1988			
Standard	564	19.1	19.9
Minimum	516	17.5	18.2
Maximum	573	19.4	20.2
1989			
Standard	657	22.2	23.1
Minimum	636	21.5	22.4
Maximum	671	22.7	23.7
1990			
Standard	640	21.6	22.5
Minimum	617	20.8	21.7
Maximum	650	22.0	22.9
1991			
Standard	651	22.0	22.9
Minimum	631	21.3	22.7
Maximum	665	22.5	23.4
CR500R			
1988			
Standard	575	19.4	20.2
Minimum	527	17.8	18.5
Maximum	584	19.8	20.5
1989			
Standard	641	21.7	22.6
Minimum	620	21.0	21.9
Maximum	655	22.1	23.0

(continued)

Table 5 FRONT FORK OIL CAPACITY (continued)

CR500R (continued)			
1990			
Standard	612	20.7	21.6
Minimum	605	20.5	21.4
Maximum	639	21.6	22.5
1991			
Standard	657	22.2	23.1
Minimum	631	21.3	22.2
Maximum	665	22.5	23.4

3

Table 6 FRONT FORK OIL LEVEL

	mm	in.
CR250R		
1988		
Standard	124	4.88
Maximum	115	4.53
Minimum	170	6.69
1989		
Standard	115	4.53
Maximum	105	4.13
Minimum	132	5.20
1990		
Standard	124	4.88
Maximum	114	5.67
Minimum	144	5.67
1991		
Standard	107	4.21
Maximum	95	3.74
Minimum	124	4.88
CR500R		
1988		
Standard	123	4.84
Maximum	114	4.49
Minimum	169	6.65
1989		
Standard	127	4.99
Maximum	116	4.6
Minimum	146	5.8
1990		
Standard	158	6.22
Maximum	133	5.2
Minimum	164	6.5
1991		
Standard	102	4.02
Maximum	95	3.74
Minimum	124	4.88

Table 7 DRIVE CHAIN SLACK

	mm	in.
All models	35-40	1 3/8-1 9/16

Table 8 REAR AXLE NUT TORQUE SPECIFICATIONS

	N·m	ft.-lb.
All models	85-105	62-77

Table 9 DRIVE CHAIN SLIDER AND ROLLER WEAR LIMIT

	Slider	Roller
All models	5.0 mm (0.19 in.)	25.0 mm (0.98 in.)

Table 10 THROTTLE ROTATIONAL FREE PLAY

	mm	in.
All models	3-5	1/8-1/4

Table 11 ANTIFREEZE PROTECTION

Freezing point (hydrometer test) Water-to-antifreeze ratio	
55:45	-32° C (-25° F)
50:50	-37° C (-34° F)
45:55	-44.5° C (-48° F)

Table 12 TUNE-UP SPECIFICATIONS

Spark plug	
CR250R	
1988	
Type	Champion QN-84, NGK BR9EG, ND W27ESR-V
Gap	0.5-0.6 mm (0.020-0.024 in.)
1989-1991	
Type	Champion QN-86, NGK BR8EG, ND W24ESR-V
Gap	0.5-0.6 mm (0.020-0.024 in.)
CR500R	
1988-1991	
Type	Champion QN-86, NGK BR8EG, ND W24ESR-V
Gap	0.5-0.6 mm (0.020-0.024 in.)

(continued)

Table 12 TUNE-UP SPECIFICATIONS (continued)

Ignition timing	
CR250R	"F" mark @ 5,000 ±100 rpm
CR500R	"F" mark @ 4,000 ±100 rpm
Carburetor air screw setting*	
CR250	2 turns
CR500R	
1988	1-1 1/2 turns
1989-1990	2 turns
1991	1-1 1/2 turns

* Number of turns out from the lightly seated position.

3

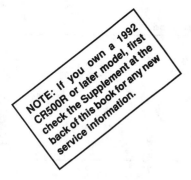
NOTE: If you own a 1992 CR500R or later model, first check the Supplement at the back of this book for any new service information.

CHAPTER FOUR

ENGINE

This chapter explains removal, inspection, service and reassembly procedures for the liquid-cooled engines used on the Honda CR250R and CR500R from 1988 to 1991.

Although the clutch and transmission are located within the engine they are covered in Chapter Five to simplify this material. Alternator service is covered in Chapter Seven and cooling system service procedures are detailed in Chapter Eight.

Prior to starting any engine work, it is recommended that you reread Chapter One. The service hints, special tips and the information on fasteners and tools are relevant to the procedures in this chapter and will help you do a better job.

Engine specifications for the CR250R and CR500R are located in **Table 1** and **Table 2** at the end of the chapter. **Table 3** provides tightening torque values.

ENGINE OPERATING PRINCIPLES

Figure 1 explains how the engine works. This will be helpful when troubleshooting or repairing the engine.

ENGINE LUBRICATION

Lubrication for the engine is provided by the fuel/oil mixture used to power the engine. There is no oil supply in the crankcase as it would be drawn into the cylinder and foul the spark plug. There is sufficient oil in the mixture to lubricate both the crankshaft bearings and the cylinder. The clutch and transmission have their own oil supply.

SERVICING ENGINE IN FRAME

The motorcycle frame is a good holding fixture for servicing or removing the following components. Also, many stubborn bolts and nuts can be loosened while the engine is still in the frame and removed later when the engine is on the bench.

a. Cylinder head.
b. Cylinder.
c. Piston.
d. Alternator.
e. Carburetor.
f. Clutch.
g. External shift mechanism.
h. Water pump.
i. Drive sprocket.

2-STROKE OPERATING PRINCIPLES

The crankshaft in this discussion is rotating in a clockwise direction.

As the piston travels downward, it uncovers the exhaust port (A) allowing the exhaust gases, which are under pressure, to leave the cylinder. A fresh fuel/air charge, which has been compressed slightly, travels from the crankcase into the cylinder through the transfer port (B). Since this charge enters under pressure, it also helps to push out the exhaust gases.

While the crankshaft continues to rotate, the piston moves upward, covering the transfer port (B) and exhaust port (A). The piston is now compressing the new fuel/air mixture and creating a low pressure area in the crankcase at the same time. As the piston continues to travel, it uncovers the intake port (C). A fresh fuel/air charge, from the carburetor (D), is drawn into the crankcase through the intake port, because of the low pressure within it.

Now, as the piston's travel nears the top, the spark plug fires, thus igniting the compressed fuel/air mixture. The piston continues to top dead center (TDC) and is pushed downward by the expanding gases.

As the piston travels down, the exhaust gases leave the cylinder and the complete cycle starts all over again.

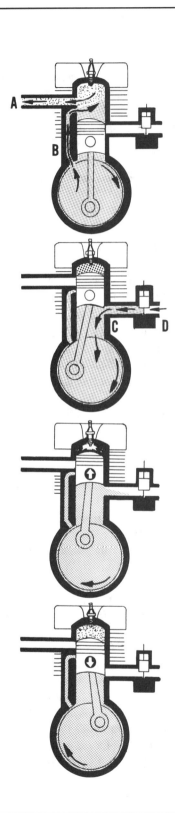

ENGINE REMOVAL/INSTALLATION

1. Thoroughly clean the exterior of the motorcycle. Take particular care to remove all dirt and grease from tiny crevices on the outside of the engine. If water is used to flush away dirt and solvent, blow or wipe the engine dry.

2. Drain the transmission and clutch oil as described under *Transmission/Clutch Oil Change* in Chapter Three.

3. Place a metal or wood stand under the frame in a way that will support the bike securely, but will allow the rear wheel to turn.

4. Remove the seat.

5. Remove the fuel tank as described under *Fuel Tank Removal/Installation* in Chapter Six.

6. Remove the expansion chamber as described in Chapter Six.

7. Drain the radiator coolant.

8. Disconnect the coolant hoses from the cylinder head and water pump (top right crankcase cover) as described in Chapter Eight.

9. Remove the radiators as described in Chapter Eight.

10. Disconnect the high tension lead from the spark plug (**Figure 2**).

11. Remove the carburetor as described in Chapter Six.

12. Remove the rear brake lever as described in Chapter Ten.

13. Disconnect the alternator and pulse generator connections (**Figure 3**). You may need to loosen the plastic bands slightly that secure the wires to the frame. On 1989-on models, two bands exist for holding the wires.

14. Rotate the rear wheel to bring the drive chain master link to the top of front sprocket. Remove the drive chain as described under *Drive Chain Removal/Installation* in Chapter Ten.

15. The frame can serve as a holding device for removing the drive sprocket at this time. If this is preferred, follow the steps for removing the sprocket under *Drive Sprocket Removal/Installation* in this chapter. If you prefer to leave the drive sprocket on the engine assembly, proceed to Step 16.

16. Slide back the protective boot on the clutch hand lever and loosen the clutch cable locknut (**Figure 4**). Turn the adjuster all the way in toward the cable sheath to allow maximum slack in the clutch cable.

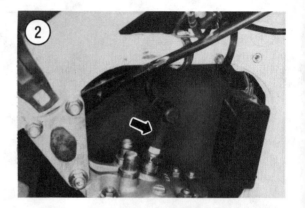

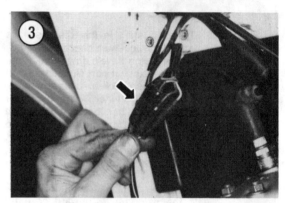

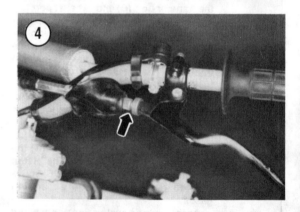

17. Remove the screws securing the alternator cover and remove the cover and gasket.

18. Disconnect the clutch cable from the clutch lifter lever by sliding the end out (A, **Figure 5**) and pulling the cable up through the top of the crankcase (B, **Figure 5**).

19. If the engine is going to be totally disassembled, the following components can be removed at this time, as described in their respective chapters.

    a. Cylinder head (this chapter).
    b. Cylinder (this chapter).
    c. Piston (this chapter).
    d. Alternator (Chapter Seven).
    e. Clutch (Chapter Five).
    f. External shift mechanism (Chapter Five).
    g. Water pump (Chapter Eight).

20. If the alternator was removed in Step 19 and the engine is to be totally disassembled, the crankcase bolts can be loosened while the engine is still in the frame. Refer to *Crankcase and Crankshaft Disassembly* in this chapter for crankcase bolt locations.

21. Remove the rubber cap from the left engine hanger plate.

22. Remove the bolts securing the engine to the hanger plates and remove the hanger plates (**Figure 6**).

23. Remove the front engine mounting bolt and nut (**Figure 7**).

24. Remove the middle engine mounting bolt and nut (**Figure 8**).

25. Remove the shock absorber lower mounting bolt (**Figure 9**).

26. Remove the swing arm pivot nut and slide the pivot bolt through the frame, swing arm and engine. On 1988 CR500R models, the pivot nut is on the left side and the pivot bolt slides out from the right. On all other models, the pivot bolt is removed from the left-hand side (**Figure 10**).

27. Remove the engine from the left side of the frame (**Figure 11**).

NOTE
After the engine has been removed, re-install the swing arm pivot bolt through the frame and into the swing arm. This will keep the swing arm in position.

28. Install the engine by reversing these steps.

29. Make sure the engine mounting rear bushing and swing arm dust caps are in place at the points where the swing arm pivot bolt passes through. On 1988 CR500R models, the pivot bolt is installed through the right-hand side. On all other models, the pivot bolt is installed from the left-hand side.

30. Tighten all mounting bolts and nuts to the torque specifications listed in **Table 3**.

31. Before starting the engine, be sure to check the following items as described in Chapter Three:

    a. Transmission oil level.
    b. Coolant level.
    c. Clutch adjustment.
    d. Throttle adjustment.
    e. Drive chain adjustment.

CYLINDER HEAD

Removal

The cylinder head, cylinder and the piston may be removed without removing the engine from the frame. Allow the engine to cool to room temperature before removing the head to avoid possible distortion.

1. Drain the radiator coolant as described under *Coolant Change* in Chapter Three.

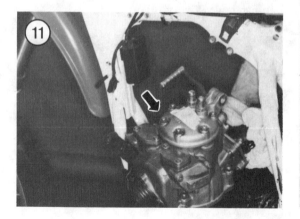

2. On CR250R models, remove the seat and fuel tank as described in Chapter Six.

3. On CR500R models, remove the seat, right side cover and the expansion chamber as described in Chapter Six.

4. Disconnect the spark plug lead.

5. Loosen the radiator hose clamps and disconnect the radiator hoses from the cylinder head (A, **Figure 12**).

6. Remove the rubber cap from the left hanger plate (B, **Figure 12**).

7. Remove the upper engine mounting bolts and hanger plates.

8. Remove the spark plug.

9. Remove the cylinder head nuts (C, **Figure 12**). CR250R models have six cylinder head nuts. CR500R models have seven cylinder head nuts.

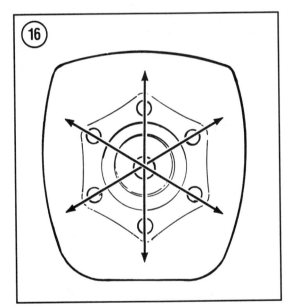

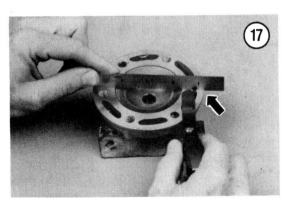

Loosen the cylinder head nuts in a crisscross pattern, turning each nut 1/4 turn until all the nuts have been loosened. Then remove the nuts.

10. Lift off the cylinder head (A, **Figure 13**). If the head does not come off easily, use a soft-faced mallet to tap it lightly around the circumference of the head. Don't attempt to pry it off. You could damage the sealing surface.

11. Remove the cylinder head gasket (B, **Figure 13**) and discard it.

Inspection

1. Remove all traces of gasket material from the cylinder head mating surface (**Figure 14**).

2. Clean the cylinder head as described under *Engine Decarbonization* in this chapter.

3. Check for cracks in the combustion chamber. A cracked head must be replaced.

4. Make sure the coolant passageways are clear. Apply compressed air to each opening in the head.

5. Check the coolant fittings (**Figure 15**) for damage or corrosion; replace if necessary.

6. Place a straightedge across the cylinder head/cylinder gasket surface at several points (**Figure 16**). Measure the warpage by inserting a flat feeler gauge between the straightedge and the cylinder head at each location (**Figure 17**). If a small amount of warpage exists, the head can be taken to a dealer or machine shop for resurfacing. If warpage exceeds the service limit of 0.05 mm (0.002 in.), it should be replaced.

7. Inspect the cylinder head mounting bolts and threads (A, **Figure 18**). These bolts are subject to hydrolysis (due to dissimilar metals) which can lead to thread corrosion. Clean the bolt threads thor-

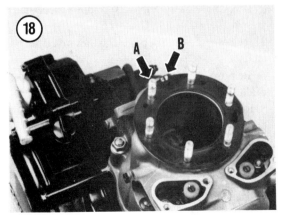

oughly with contact cleaner and coat the threads with Honda Anaerobic thread lock or equivalent.

Installation

1. Install a new head gasket. On 1988-CR250R and all CR500R models, position the gasket tab toward the rear. On 1989 and later CR250R models, install the gasket with the "UP" mark facing up (B, **Figure 18**).

2. Install the cylinder head and the nuts. The CR250R models have six nuts. The CR500R models have seven nuts. Tighten the nuts, using a torque wrench (**Figure 19**). Tighten the nuts in several stages, using a crisscross pattern, to the torque specification listed in **Table 3**.

3. Install the spark plug and spark plug lead.

4. Install the engine upper holding plates, bolts and nuts. Tighten to the torque specifications listed in **Table 3**.

5. Install the rubber cap to the left hanger plate.

6. Connect all radiator hoses to the cylinder head and tighten the hose clamps.

7. On CR250R models, install the fuel tank, side covers and the seat, as described in Chapter Six.

8. On CR500R models, install the expansion chamber, right side cover and the seat.

9. Fill the radiator with coolant as described in Chapter Three.

CYLINDER

Removal

1. Remove the carburetor as described in Chapter Six.

2. If not previously removed, remove the exhaust system as described in Chapter Six.

3. Remove the cylinder head as described in this chapter.

4. Remove the radiators as described in Chapter Eight.

5. Remove the exhaust manifold and gasket by removing the three bolts surrounding the manifold (**Figure 20**). It may be necessary to remove the spring prior to removing the lower right-hand bolt.

6. On CR250R models, remove the HPP exhaust valve upper covers (A, **Figure 21**) and side covers (B, **Figure 21**).

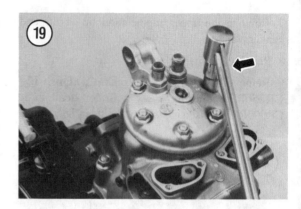

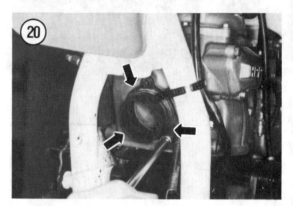

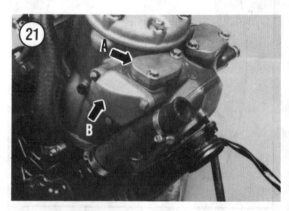

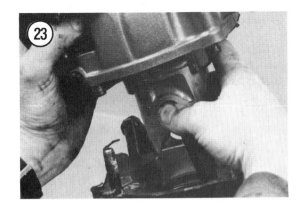

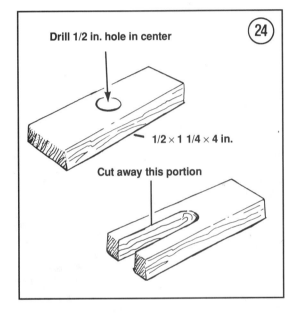

Drill 1/2 in. hole in center

1/2 × 1 1/4 × 4 in.

Cut away this portion

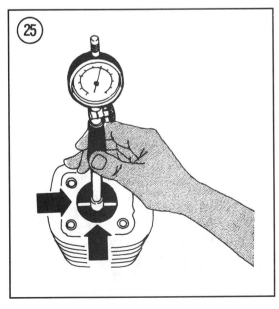

7. Remove the reed valve assembly as described in this chapter.

8. Remove the four flange nuts (**Figure 22**) securing the cylinder to the crankcase.

CAUTION
Do not twist the cylinder on the piston during Step 9 or you may snag a ring on a transfer port.

9. Use a soft-faced mallet to tap the cylinder lightly around the lower sealing area to free it from the crankcase. Pull the cylinder straight up and off of the crankcase studs (**Figure 23**).

10. Remove the base gasket and locating dowels. Discard the gasket.

11. Install a piston holding fixture, such as the home-made version in **Figure 24**, under the piston to hold it in position.

12. Stuff clean rags into the top of the crankcase around the connecting rod to prevent the entry of dirt and foreign matter.

Inspection

The following procedure requires the use of highly specialized and expensive measuring instruments. If such equipment is not readily available, have the measurements performed by a dealer or qualified machine shop.

1. Using solvent, soak the remaining old cylinder head or base gasket material to help ease its removal. Use a broad-tipped *dull* chisel and gently scrape off all gasket residue. Do not gouge the sealing surfaces as an air leak will result.

NOTE
On all CR250R models covered in this manual, the Nikasil-plated cylinder cannot be rebored. No oversize pistons are available for these models. If the cylinder is worn to the service limit, it must be replaced. References to cylinder boring apply to the CR500R models only.

2. Measure the cylinder bore with a cylinder gauge (**Figure 25**) or inside micrometer at 3 depths within the cylinder (**Figure 26**). Measure in 2 axes, in line with the piston pin and at 90° to the pin. If taper or out-of-round exceeds the service limits listed in **Table 1** (CR250R) or **Table 2** (CR500R) or if any

single measurement is in excess of the service limit shown in **Table 1**, the cylinder must be rebored to the next oversize and a new piston installed. The new piston should be obtained before the cylinder is rebored so that the piston can be measured. Slight manufacturing tolerances must be taken into account to determine the actual size and working clearance. Piston-to-cylinder clearance is listed in **Table 1** (CR250R) and **Table 2** (CR500R).

3. Check the cylinder wall (A, **Figure 27**) for scratches. If scratched, the cylinder should be rebored. The maximum wear limit on the cylinder is listed in **Table 1** (CR250R) and **Table 2** (CR500R). If the cylinder is worn to this limit, it must be replaced. Never rebore a cylinder if the finished rebore diameter will be this dimension or greater.

4. Check the cylinder wall near the intake (B, **Figure 27**) and exhaust port of the cylinder. Make sure there are no rough or cracked areas. Turn the cylinder over and inspect the fins within the transfer ports. Make sure there are no cracks. If any are present, have them repaired by a shop specializing in precision aluminum castings or replace the cylinder.

5. On CR250R models, inspect the HPP system located in the cylinder. See Chapter Six.

Installation

1. Check the cylinder base studs for tightness. If any are loose, remove them and clean the threads with contact cleaner. Electrolysis can take place due to the differences in metals and the bolts may be corroded. Carefully check and reinstall the studs with Honda Anaerobic Thread Lock, or equivalent.

2. Clean, if necessary, the dowel pins (on the 2 left-side base studs) and install (C, **Figure 28**).

3. Install a new cylinder base gasket (A, **Figure 28**) on the crankcase.

4. On CR250R models, perform the following:

    a. Lightly oil the piston, piston rings and cylinder bore with clean 2-stroke oil.

    b. Rotate the crankshaft to bring the piston in contact with the piston holding fixture.

    c. Position the HPP spindle cam (B, **Figure 28**) so that it is facing toward the front of the bike as shown in **Figure 29**. If the cam is not facing

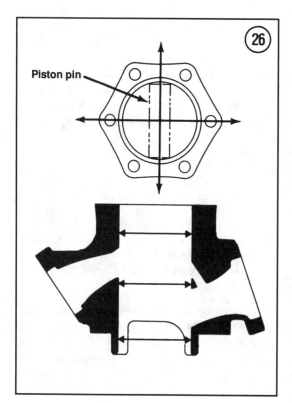

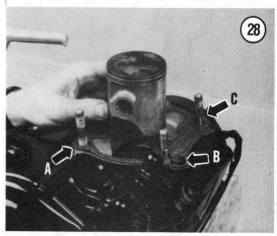

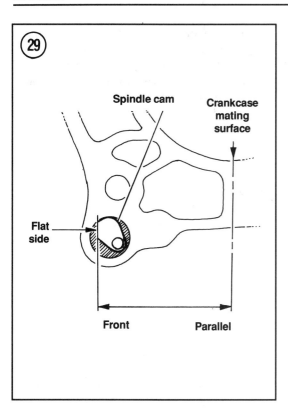

as shown, remove the spring retainer shaft cap
and insert a flat blade screwdriver. Turn the
retainer shaft 90° *counterclockwise*. See **Figure 30**. This will disengage the governor
mechanism from the cam and allow you to
position the cam.

d. If the piston was removed and reinstalled,
make sure the marks on the rings are facing up
and the "IN" mark on the piston is facing the
intake side.

e. Compress the top ring and start the chamfered
edge of the cylinder over it.

f. Holding both exhaust valves fully closed with
your fingers (so the E-clips are touching the
valve guides), slide the cylinder down over the
piston (**Figure 31**).

NOTE
Do not rotate the cylinder as the piston
rings can snag on a cylinder port and
break.

g. Compress each ring and lower the cylinder
completely over the piston while aligning the

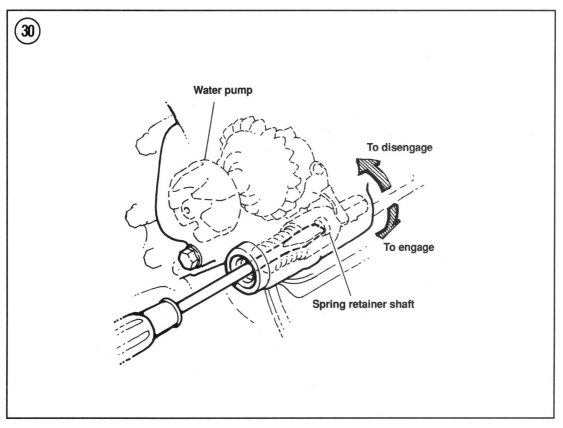

pin (A, **Figure 31**) of the spindle cam with the cut-out (B, **Figure 31**) of the rack.

h. Remove the piston holding fixture and lower the cylinder until it is resting on the crankcase.

> *NOTE*
> *At this point the cylinder will not seat completely against the crankcase because the HPP actuating mechanism is not yet engaged.*

i. Pull open the right exhaust valve. When the valve is near fully open, the cylinder will drop down onto the crankcase. The cutout on the rack and the cam spindle pin are now engaged. Push the exhaust valve fully closed.

> *NOTE*
> *Make sure the gap between the cylinder and crankcase mating surface has been closed up. If the cylinder and crankcase are not mating properly, repeat sub-step i.*

j. Install the four cylinder flange nuts and tighten to 35-45 N•m (25-33 ft.-lb.).

k. Insert a flat-blade screwdriver (**Figure 32**) into the slot in the top of the right pinion shaft (**Figure 32**) and turn it counterclockwise 1/8 to 1/4 of a turn past where spring tension is felt. This will ensure that the valve is fully closed and slack is removed from the system.

> *NOTE*
> *Be sure the exhaust valves are fully closed. If they are not, adjust the HPP as described in Chapter Six.*

l. While holding tension on the pinion shaft with one screwdriver (**Figure 32**), engage the spring retainer shaft (**Figure 30**) by turning it *clockwise* 90° with another screwdriver. The retainer shaft should engage easily and you will feel the slight detent when the shaft reaches the 90° detent.

m. Confirm engagement by turning the pinion shaft clockwise. A slight spring resistance will be felt. If it turns freely, the shaft is not engaged and sub-steps k and l will have to be repeated.

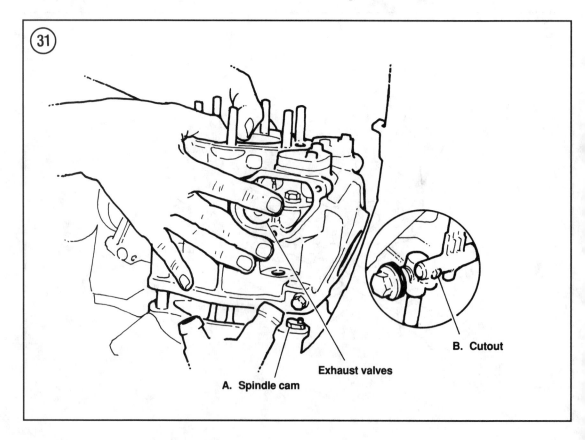

(31)

B. Cutout

Exhaust valves

A. Spindle cam

n. Install gaskets on the left and right exhaust valve covers and tighten to specified torque.

o. Install the left and right cylinder upper covers.

NOTE
Check the exhaust valves for smooth operation by turning the pinion shaft. Inspect the assembly of the retainer shaft and follower cam if the exhaust valves fail to operate smoothly.

p. Adjust the exhaust valves as described in Chapter Six.

5. On CR500R models, perform the following:

a. Lightly oil the piston, piston rings and cylinder bore.

b. Rotate the crankshaft to bring the piston in contact with the piston holding fixture.

c. If the piston was removed and reinstalled, make sure the marks on the piston rings are facing up and the "IN" mark on the piston is facing the intake side.

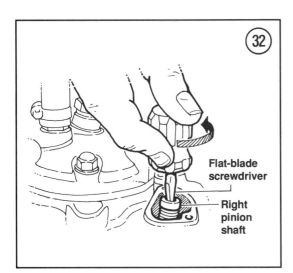

Flat-blade screwdriver

Right pinion shaft

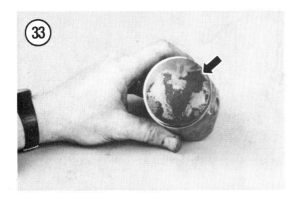

d. Locate the piston ring end gaps on the pins in the ring grooves.

e. Start the cylinder down over the piston.

f. Compress the top ring and start the chamfered edge of the cylinder over it.

g. Compress the second ring and slide the cylinder down over it. Slide the cylinder down until it completely covers both rings.

NOTE
Do not rotate the cylinder as the piston rings may snag a cylinder port and break.

4

h. Compress each ring as the piston passes by the intake port.

i. Install the four cylinder flange nuts and tighten to specifications listed in **Table 3**.

6. Reverse removal Steps 1-7 for installing the remainder of the components.

ENGINE DECARBONIZING

CAUTION
Be careful not to damage the exhaust port or the HPP components.

Much of the carbon build-up in the cylinder head, on the piston crown (**Figure 33**) and in the exhaust port of the cylinder can be wiped away with solvent and a shop cloth. Hard carbon deposits can be scraped from the combustion chamber with a dull screwdriver or the end of a hacksaw blade (**Figure 34**). Be careful not to scar the surface of the head, either in the combustion chamber or along the seal-

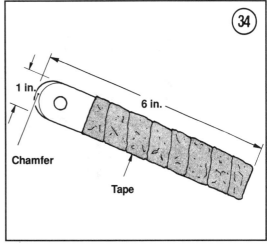

1 in.

6 in.

Chamfer

Tape

ing surface. Small burrs resulting from gouges on the surface of the chamber will create hot spots which can cause preignition and heat erosion. Gouges on the sealing surface can result in combustion chamber leaks.

After scraping, clean the cylinder head and cylinder in solvent. Carefully clean the spark plug bore with a fine wire brush and blow out all carbon particles with compressed air.

EXHAUST VALVE DECARBONIZATION

Exhaust valve decarbonization is covered in Chapter Six.

REED VALVE ASSEMBLY

The engine is equipped with a power reed valve assembly that is installed in the intake port of the cylinder head (**Figure 35**). Particular care must be taken when handling and repairing the reed valve assembly. A malfunctioning reed valve will cause severe performance loss as well as contributing to early engine failure due to a too-lean fuel mixture.

Removal/Installation

1. Remove the carburetor as described in Chapter Six.

2. Remove the six insulator bolts (**Figure 36**) securing the reed valve assembly to the cylinder and remove the assembly. If the assembly is difficult to remove, use a drift or broad-tipped screwdriver and gently tap on the side of the assembly to help break it loose from the gasket and cylinder.

3. Remove the insulator and reed valve assembly from the cylinder.

4. Inspect the assembly as described in this chapter.

5. Install the reed valve assembly and insulator and tighten the six insulator mounting bolts securely.

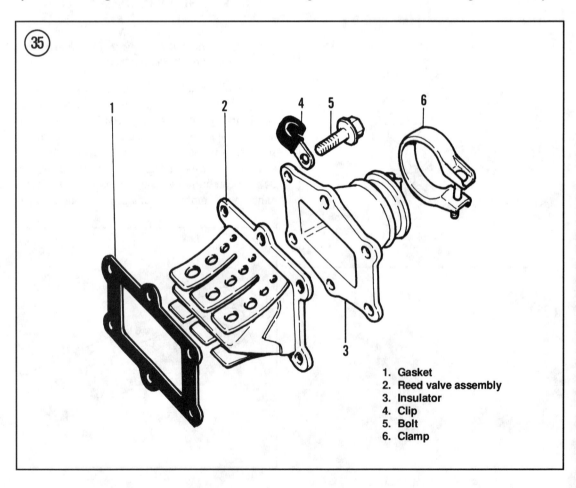

35

1. Gasket
2. Reed valve assembly
3. Insulator
4. Clip
5. Bolt
6. Clamp

Inspection

Refer to **Figure 37** for basic reed valve construction. Fiberglass reeds (A) open and close the inlet port in response to crankcase pressure changes, allowing the fuel/air mixture to enter. They then close off to allow the crankcase to pressurize. The reed stops (D) prevent the reeds from opening too far.

1. Carefully examine the reed valve assembly for visible signs of wear, distortion or damage. The use of a feeler gauge and a straightedge (**Figure 38**) will help in determining if distortion is present.

2. Do not disassemble the reed valve assembly. Carefully examine the reed plate, reed stop and gasket. Check for signs of cracks, fiberglass fatigue, distortion or foreign matter damage. Pay particular attention to the rubber gasket seal. If any of these components are damaged in any way, the entire

assembly will have to be replaced. Replacement parts are not available for the stock reed valve assembly.

NOTE
Make sure all parts are clean and free of any small dirt particles or lint as they may cause a small amount of distortion in the reed plate.

PISTON, PISTON PIN AND PISTON RINGS

The piston is made of an aluminum alloy. The piston pin is made of steel and is held in place by a clip at each end. Honda recommends replacing the piston and rings after 7.5 hours of operation under racing conditions. The piston pin and connecting rod small end bearing should be replaced after 22.5 hours of operation under racing conditions.

Piston Removal

1. Remove the cylinder head and the cylinder as described in this chapter.

2. Cover the crankcase opening with a clean shop cloth to prevent parts or foreign matter from entering. Set the piston on a piston holding fixture.

WARNING
The edges of both piston rings are very sharp. Be careful when handling them to avoid cut fingers.

3. Remove the top ring from the piston by spreading the ends at the gap with your thumbs and sliding the

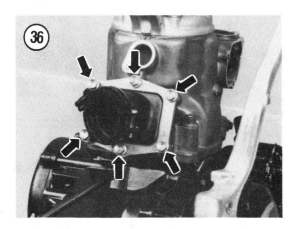

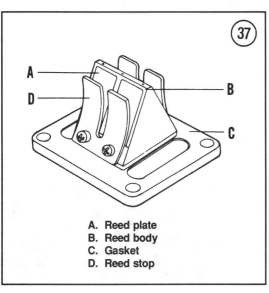

A. Reed plate
B. Reed body
C. Gasket
D. Reed stop

opposite side of the ring up over the piston (**Figure 39**). Repeat for the lower ring.

4. Remove the piston ring clips (**Figure 40**) from each side of the piston with a pair of needle-nose pliers or a suitable tool. Hold your thumb over one edge of the clip during removal to prevent it from springing out.

5. Hold the piston firmly in one hand and press the pin out with a drift or deep socket that is slightly smaller in diameter than the pin.

> *CAUTION*
> *Don't apply sideways force to the connecting rod. Do not hammer the pin out. The pin (**Figure 41**) is installed with a snug press fit.*

6. If the pin is difficult to remove, wrap a rag heated with hot water around the piston and leave it in place for a couple of minutes. If the pin is still difficult to push out, use a homemade tool as shown in **Figure 42**.

7. Lift the piston off the connecting rod and remove the needle bearing assembly (**Figure 43**) from the connecting rod small end.

8. If the piston is going to be left off for some time, place a piece of foam insulation tube over the end of the rod to protect it.

9. Thoroughly clean all parts in solvent and dry with compressed air.

Connecting Rod, Bearing and Piston Inspection

1. Examine the bearing cage for cracks at the corners of the needle slots (**Figure 44**) and inspect the needles themselves for cracking. If any cracks are found, the bearing must be replaced.

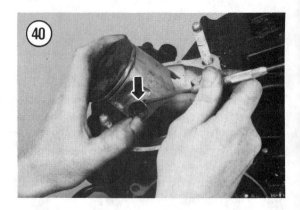

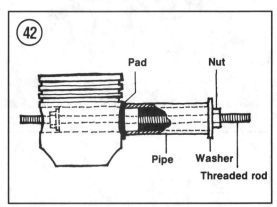

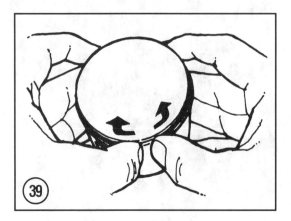

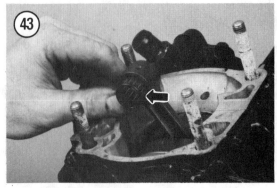

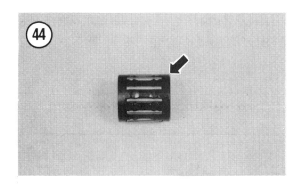

44

2. Wipe the bore in the connecting rod with a clean rag and check it for galling, scratches or any other signs of damage. If any of these conditions exist, replace the connecting rod as described under *Crankshaft and Crankcase* in this chapter.

3. Install the needle bearing into the connecting rod. Oil the piston pin and install it in the connecting rod bearing. Slowly rotate the piston pin and check for play (**Figure 45**). If there is play, remove the piston pin and bearing and measure the connecting rod ID On the CR250R, the service limit for the connecting rod ID is 22.03 mm (0.867 in.). On the CR500R, the service limit for the connecting rod ID is 25.025 mm (0.9852 in.). If the ID is not over the service limit, replace the bearing and piston pin. If the ID is over the service limit, the crankshaft assembly should be replaced.

4. Measure the inside diameter of the piston pin bore with a snap gauge (**Figure 46**) and measure the outside diameter of the piston pin with a micrometer (**Figure 47**). Compare with dimensions (piston pin-to-piston clearance) given in **Table 1** (CR250R) or **Table 2** (CR500R). Replace the piston and piston pin as a set if either or both are worn.

5. Carefully check the piston for cracks at the top edges of the transfer cutaways (**Figure 48**) and replace it if any are found. Check the piston skirt for brown varnish buildup. More than a very slight amount is an indication of worn or sticking rings. The piston rings should be replaced.

CAUTION
Do not wire brush the piston skirts.

6. On the CR250R, measure the outside diameter of the piston across the skirt at right angles to the piston pin. Measure at a distance of 25-30 mm (0.98-1.18 in.) from the bottom of the exhaust side skirt. Refer

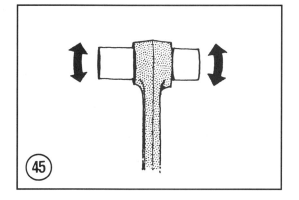

45

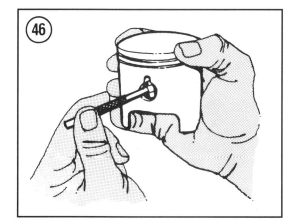

46

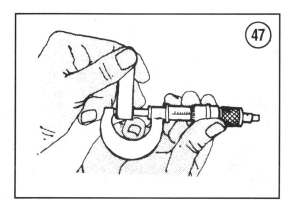

47

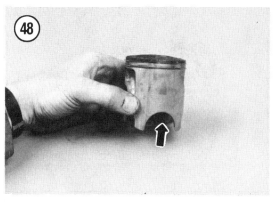

48

to dimensions given in **Table 1** and replace the piston if it is worn to the service limit.

7. On the CR500R, measure the outside diameter of the piston across the skirt at right angles to the piston pin. Measure at a distance of 10-25 mm (0.39-0.98 in.) from the bottom of the skirt (**Figure 49**). Refer to the dimensions given in **Table 2** and replace the piston if it is worn to the service limit.

8. Measure piston-to-cylinder clearance as described under *Piston Clearance Measurement* in this chapter.

Piston Clearance Measurement

1. Make sure the piston and cylinder walls are clean and dry.

2. Measure the inside diameter of the cylinder bore at a point 13 mm (1/2 in.) from the upper edge with a bore gauge (**Figure 50**).

3. Measure the outside diameter of the piston across the skirt at right angles to the piston pin hole. On the CR250R, measure at a distance of 25-30 mm (0.98-1.18 in.) from the bottom of the *exhaust side skirt*. On the CR500R, measure at a distance of 10-25 mm (0.39-0.98 in.) from the bottom of the skirt.

4. Piston clearance is the difference between the maximum piston diameter and the minimum cylinder diameter. Subtract the dimension of the piston from the cylinder dimension. If the clearance exceeds the service limit dimensions in **Table 1** (CR250R) or **Table 2** (CR500R), the cylinder should

be replaced (CR250R) or rebored (CR500R) to the next oversize and a new piston installed.

NOTE
On CR250R models, the nikasil-plated cylinder cannot be rebored. No oversize

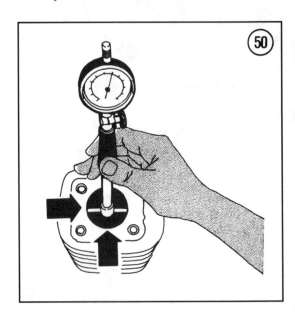

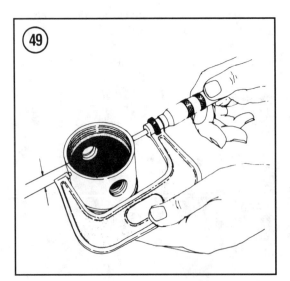

pistons are available. If the cylinder is worn to the service limit, it must be replaced. On CR500R models, two oversize pistons and rings are available.

5. To establish a final overbore dimension with a new piston, add the piston skirt measurement to the specified clearance. This will determine the dimension for the cylinder overbore size. Remember, do not exceed

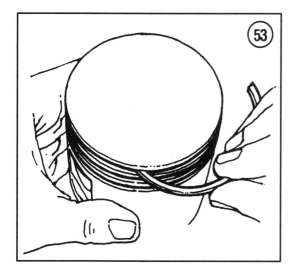

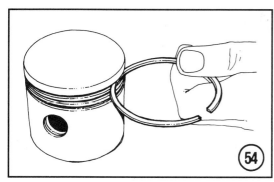

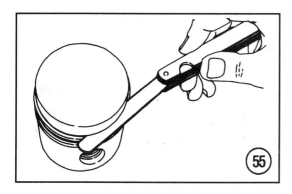

the cylinder maximum service limit inside diameter indicated in **Table 1** (CR250R) or **Table 2** (CR500R).

Piston Installation

1. Lightly oil the needle bearing assembly and install it in the connecting rod (**Figure 43**).
2. Oil the pin and install it in the piston (**Figure 41**) until the end of it extends slightly beyond the inside of the boss.
3. Place the piston over the connecting rod with the "IN" mark on the piston crown (**Figure 51**) toward the rear (intake side). Line up the pin with the bearing and push the pin into the piston until it is even with the piston pin lip grooves.
4. Install new piston pin clips (**Figure 52**) in the ends of the pin bosses. Make sure that they are seated in the grooves and that the ends are away from the removal notch.

CAUTION
Never reuse old piston pin clips as serious engine damage can result.

5. Install the piston rings as described in this chapter.
6. Install the cylinder and cylinder head as described in this chapter.

Piston Ring Removal/Inspection/Installation

WARNING
The edges of all piston rings are very sharp. Be careful when handling them to avoid cut fingers.

1. Remove the top ring by spreading the end gap with your thumbs just enough to slide the ring up from the opposite side and over the piston (**Figure 39**). Repeat this step for the other ring.
2. Carefully remove all carbon buildup from the ring grooves with a broken piston ring (**Figure 53**).
3. Inspect the grooves carefully for burrs, nicks or broken lands. Recondition or replace the piston if necessary.
4. Roll each ring around in its piston groove as shown in **Figure 54** to check for binding. Minor binding may be cleaned up with a fine-cut file.
5A. *CR250R*—Measure the side clearance (piston ring-to-groove clearance) of each ring in its groove with a flat feeler gauge (**Figure 55**), and compare to

dimensions listed in **Table 1**. If the clearance is greater than specified, the rings must be replaced. If the clearance is still excessive with the new rings, the piston must also be replaced.

5B. *CR500R*—Honda does not provide piston ring-to-groove clearance specifications.

6. Measure each of the rings for end gap wear as shown in **Figure 56**. Place each ring, one at a time, into the cylinder and push it in about 20 mm (3/4 in.). Use the crown of the piston to ensure that the ring is square in the cylinder. Measure the gap with a flat feeler gauge. Refer to dimensions given in **Table 1** (CR250R) or **Table 2** (CR500). If the gap is greater than the wear limit, the rings should be replaced.

7. When installing new rings, measure their end gap in the same manner as for the old ones. If the gap is less than the minimum specified, carefully file the ends of the rings with a fine file until the gap is correct.

8. Install the piston rings with their markings facing up.

9. Install the piston rings—first the bottom one, then the top one—by carefully spreading the ends of the ring with your thumbs and slipping the ring over the top of the piston. Remember that the marks on the piston rings are toward the top of the piston.

10. Make sure the rings are completely seated in their grooves all the way around the piston and that the end gap is aligned with the locating pin in the ring groove.

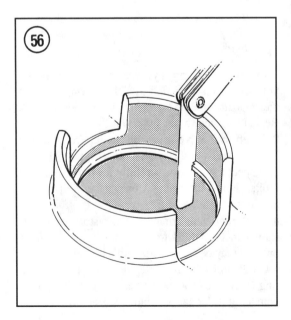

RIGHT CRANKCASE COVER

Removal

This procedure is necessary to service the clutch, primary drive gear, kickstarter and as part of a total crankcase disassembly.

1. Drain the clutch/transmission oil as described under *Transmission/Clutch Oil Change* in Chapter Three.

2. Loosen and remove the drain bolts and drain the coolant.

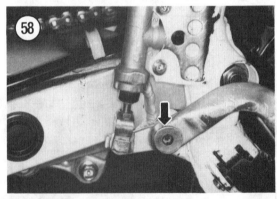

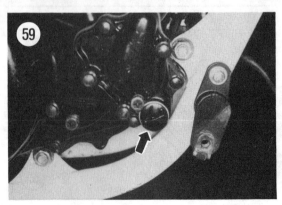

3. Remove the expansion chamber as described in Chapter Six.

4. Disconnect the radiator hoses from the right crankcase cover (water pump).

5. Remove the bolt securing the kickstarter lever and remove the lever (**Figure 57**).

6. Remove the brake pedal pivot bolt and brake return spring and remove the brake pedal (**Figure 58**).

7. On the CR250R, perform the following:

    a. Remove the spring retainer shaft cap at the front right-hand side of the engine (**Figure 59**).

    b. Turn the spring retainer shaft counterclockwise 90° to disengage (**Figure 60**).

8. Remove the bolts from the crankcase cover and remove the cover (**Figure 61**).

9. Remove the cover gasket and two locating dowel pins.

10. If the primary drive gear is going to be removed, loosen the bolt securing it to the crankshaft (A, **Figure 62**). Place a copper washer or copper penny into mesh with the primary drive gear and the clutch outer housing. This will keep the clutch outer housing from turning while loosening the bolt. Remove the copper washer after the bolt has been loosened.

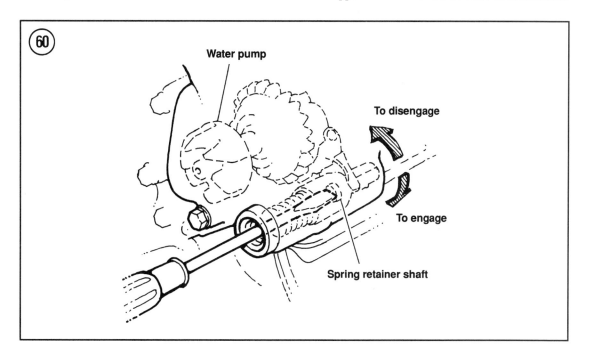

60

Water pump

To disengage

To engage

Spring retainer shaft

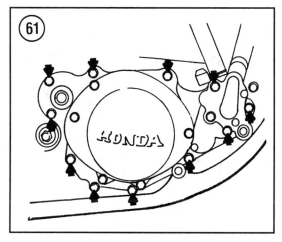

61

HONDA

62

B

A

B

Installation

1. On CR250R models, perform the following:

    a. If removed, install the primary drive gear and tighten to specifications in **Table 3**.

    b. Install the two locating dowel pins (B, **Figure 62**) and a new cover gasket.

    c. Before installing the right hand cover, push the follower cam in completely.

    d. Make sure the spring retainer shaft is positioned with the cut-outs on the shaft aligned with the governor rocker arm small end.

    e. Install the right crankcase cover while engaging the water pump gear with the primary gear on the case. You may have to slide the kick-starter lever on its shaft and crank the engine to align the gears properly.

    f. Install the cover completely and tighten the cover mounting bolts to 8-12 N•m (6-9 ft.-lb.). On 1989 and later models, the water pump cover bolts have a larger flange than the SH type bolts. Tighten the water pump cover bolts to 10-14 N•m (7-10 ft.-lb.).

    g. Engage the spring retainer shaft by turning it *clockwise* 90° with a flat-blade screwdriver (**Figure 63**). The retainer shaft should engage easily and you should feel a slight detent when the shaft reaches the 90° detent.

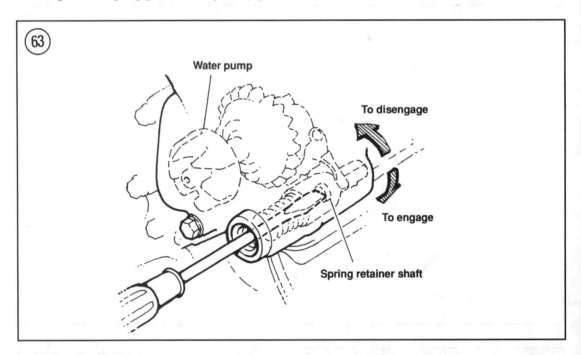

h. Apply grease to the brake lever pivot bolt.

i. Reverse Steps 1-6 for installation of the remainder of components.

2. On CR500R models, perform the following:

a. If removed, install and tighten the primary drive gear to specification shown in **Table 3**.

b. Install the two locating dowel pins and a new cover gasket.

c. Install the right crankcase cover while engaging the water pump gear with the primary

drive gear. Tighten the right crankcase cover bolts to 8-12 N•m (6-9 ft.-lb.).

d. Apply grease to the brake lever pivot bolt.

e. Reverse removal Steps 1-6 for the remainder of the components.

PRIMARY DRIVE GEAR

Removal/Installation

Prior to removal of the drive gear, reread Step 10 under *Right Crankcase Cover Removal*.

1. Remove the clutch as described in Chapter Five.

2. Perform the following:

a. Remove the bolt securing the primary drive gear. Refer to A, **Figure 62**.

b. Remove the conical spring washer.

c. Remove the primary drive gear (**Figure 64**).

d. Remove the collar.

3. Install by reversing these steps while noting the following.

4. Install the conical spring washer with the "OUT" mark (**Figure 65**) facing outward.

5. Tighten the bolt to the torque specification listed in **Table 3**.

DRIVE SPROCKET

Removal/Installation

1. Place a metal or wood stand under the frame to support the bike securely with the rear wheel off the ground.

2. Remove the bolts (**Figure 66**) securing the drive chain guard and remove the drive chain guard.

3. Shift the transmission into gear and have an assistant apply the rear brake. This will keep the drive sprocket from turning while the following steps are performed.

4. On all models, perform the following:

a. Remove the drive sprocket bolt (**Figure 67**) and cone spring washer (A, **Figure 68**) securing the drive sprocket.

b. Loosen the rear axle nut and loosen the drive chain adjust nuts. Push the rear wheel forward to produce slack in the drive chain.

c. Remove the drive chain from the sprocket.

d. Slide the drive sprocket off of the countershaft splines and remove it (B, **Figure 68**).

5. Install by reversing these removal steps while noting the following.

6. If the crankcase was disassembled, coat the collar and O-ring with grease (**Figure 69**) and push the O-ring into the collar until it is seated. Then slide the O-ring and collar onto the countershaft until it seats (**Figure 70**).

7. Install the drive sprocket with the raised shoulder toward the outside (**Figure 71**).

8. Install the cone spring washer with the "OUT-SIDE" mark facing toward the outside (A, **Figure 68**).

9. Tighten the sprocket bolt(s) securely.

CRANKCASE AND CRANKSHAFT

When disassembly of the crankcase, splitting the cases or removal of the crankshaft assembly is required, the engine must be removed from the frame. The crankcase is made in 2 halves of precision diecast aluminum alloy and is of the "thin-walled" type. To avoid damage, do not hammer or pry on any of the interior or exterior projected walls. The cases are assembled with a gasket between the 2 halves and locating dowel pins that align the halves when they are bolted together.

Crankcase separation requires the use of a special tool, Honda part No. 07937-4300000 or equivalent.

The crankshaft assembly is made up of 2 full-circle flywheels pressed together on a hollow crankpin. The connecting rod big-end bearing on the crankpin is a needle bearing assembly. The crankshaft assembly is supported in 2 ball-type bearings in the crankcase. Service to the crankshaft assembly is limited to removal and replacement.

The procedure which follows is presented as a complete, step-by-step major lower-end rebuild that should be followed if an engine is to be completely reconditioned. However, if you're replacing a known failed part, the disassembly should be carried out only until the failed part is accessible. There is no need to disassemble the engine beyond that point so long as you know the remaining components are in good condition and that they were not affected by the failed part.

Disassembly

1. Before removing the clutch, loosen the bolt (A, **Figure 72**) securing the primary drive gear to the end of the crankshaft.

NOTE
Wedge a soft copper washer (or penny) between the primary drive gear and the

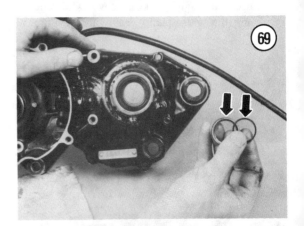

gear on the clutch outer housing (B, Figure 72) to keep the primary drive gear from rotating during removal and installation of the bolt.

2. Remove all exterior engine assemblies as described in this chapter and other related chapters.

   a. Cylinder head (this chapter).

   b. Cylinder (this chapter).

   c. Piston and piston pin (this chapter).

   d. Kickstarter (this chapter).

   e. Alternator (Chapter Seven).

   f. Clutch (Chapter Five).

   g. External shift mechanism (Chapter Five).

   h. Primary drive gear and sprocket (this chapter).

   i. Crankshaft and countershaft collars (this chapter).

3. Loosen all crankcase bolts while the engine is still in the frame.

4. Remove the engine from the frame as described in this chapter.

5. Loosen the crankcase screws in a crisscross pattern until they are all loose. Completely remove all screws. Refer to **Figure 73** for crankcase screw locations.

6. Install the crankcase separator (puller) to the left crankcase. Refer to **Figure 74**.

CAUTION
*While tightening the puller in Step 7, make sure the puller body is kept parallel to the crankcase surface (**Figure 75**). Otherwise it will put an uneven stress on the case halves and damage them.*

7. Turn the tool handle clockwise to separate the cases. Using a soft-faced mallet, frequently tap around the perimeter of the crankcase half that the separator tool is attached to and on the end of the transmission shafts while tightening the separator tool.

8. Separate and remove the left crankcase half completely.

9. Pull out the shift fork shafts (A, **Figure 76**) and separate and remove the shift forks (B, **Figure 76**) and gearshift drum (C, **Figure 76**).

10. While holding as shown in the following figures, remove the mainshaft (A, **Figure 77**) and countershaft (B, **Figure 77**) assemblies together from the other crankcase half.

11. The crankshaft may have an interference fit between the crankcase bearing and the bearing surface on the crankshaft. This results from variations in manufacturing tolerances. A hydraulic press is recommended for removing the crankshaft, but you may be able to pull the crankshaft straight up and out of the crankcase. If the crankshaft will not come out by hand, try tapping on the left-hand end of the crankshaft with a soft-faced mallet and remove the

crankshaft assembly from the left-hand crankcase half.

CAUTION
Use only a soft-faced mallet. Otherwise, the splines may be damaged.

CAUTION
If you cannot remove the crankshaft with either of these 2 methods, take the crankcase assembly to a dealer and have it disassembled. Do not pound the crankshaft out of the crankcase.

Inspection

1. Clean both crankcase halves inside and out with cleaning solvent. Dry thoroughly with compressed air and wipe with a clean shop cloth. Be sure to

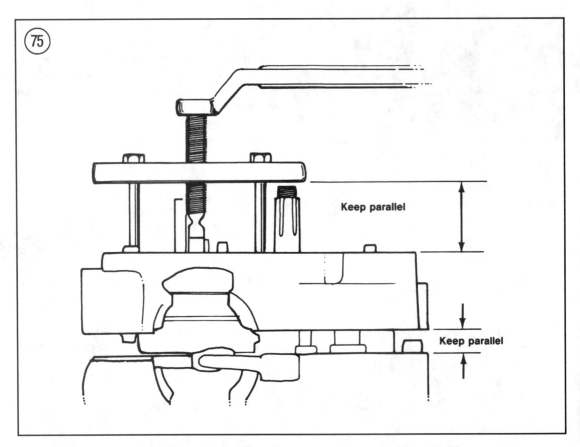

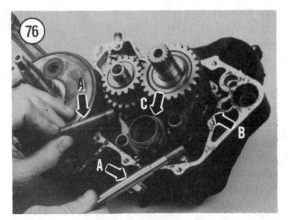

remove all traces of the old gasket material from the mating surfaces.

2. Check the crankshaft main bearings and the transmission bearings in both halves (**Figure 78**) for roughness and play by rotating them slowly by hand. If any roughness or play can be felt in a bearing, it must be replaced. Refer to *Bearing and Oil Seal Replacement* in this chapter for the correct procedure.

3. Carefully examine the cases for cracks and fractures. Check the areas around the stiffening ribs (A, **Figure 79**), bearing bosses and threaded holes. If any are found, have them repaired by a shop specializing in the repair of precision aluminum castings or replace the crankcase halves as a set.

4. Make sure the crankcase studs (B, **Figure 79**) are secure in the crankcase; tighten if necessary.

5. Check the condition of the connecting rod big-end bearing by grasping the rod in one hand and lifting up on it. With the help of your other hand, rap sharply on the top of the rod. A sharp metallic sound, such as a click, is an indication that the bearing or crankpin or both are worn and must be replaced.

6. Discard the crankcase gaskets and transmission seals. They should be replaced with new ones each time the lower end is disassembled.

7. Check the tapered end of the crankshaft (A, **Figure 80**) on the alternator side and the splines (B, **Figure 80**) on the clutch side of the crankshaft. If either is damaged, the crankshaft must be replaced.

8. Check the connecting rod-to-crankshaft side clearance with a flat feeler gauge (**Figure 81**). Compare to dimensions given in **Table 1** (CR250R) or **Table 2** (CR500R). If the clearance is greater than specified, the crankshaft assembly must be replaced.

9. Other inspections of the crankshaft assembly involve accurate measuring equipment and should be entrusted to a dealer or competent machine shop. The crankshaft assembly operates under severe stress, and dimensional tolerances are critical. These dimensions are given in **Table 1** (CR250R) and **Table 2** (CR500R). If any are off by the slightest amount, severe damage or destruction of the engine may occur. The crankshaft should be replaced as a

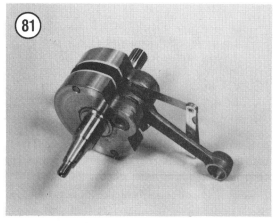

unit as it cannot be serviced without the aid of a 9,000-11,000 kilogram (10-12 ton) capacity press, holding fixture and crankshaft jig.

10. Inspect the oil seals (**Figure 82**). They should be replaced every other time the crankcase is disassembled. Refer to *Bearing and Oil Seal Replacement* in this chapter.

Bearing and Oil Seal Replacement

1. Pry out old seals (**Figure 82**) with a small screwdriver, taking care not to damage the crankcase bore. If the seals are old and difficult to remove, heat the cases as described in Step 3 and use an awl to punch a small hole in the steel backing of the seal. Install a small sheet metal screw partway into the seal and pull the seal out with a pair of pliers.

CAUTION
Do not install the screw too deeply or it may contact and damage the bearing behind it.

2. Remove the bolts securing the countershaft bearing retainer (**Figure 83**) and remove the bearing retainer.

3. The bearings are installed with a slight interference fit. If the bearings remained on the crankshaft when it was removed, they can be removed with a bearing puller (Honda part No. 07631-0010000 or equivalent). If the bearings remained in the crankcase halves, the following method can be used. Heat the crankcase in an oven to about 100° C (212° F). An easy way to check the proper temperature is to drop tiny drops of water on the case; if they sizzle and evaporate immediately, the temperature is correct. Heat only one case at a time.

CAUTION
Do not heat the cases with a torch (propane or acetylene). Never bring a flame into contact with the bearing or case. The direct heat will destroy the case hardening of the bearing and will likely cause warpage of the case.

4. Remove the heated case from the oven and hold onto the 2 crankcase studs with a kitchen potholder, heavy gloves or heavy shop cloths.

5. Remove the oil seals if not already removed (see Step 1).

6. Hold the case with the bearing side down and tap it squarely on a piece of soft wood. Continue to tap until the bearing(s) falls out. Repeat for the other half.

CAUTION
Be sure to tap the crankcase squarely on the piece of wood. Avoid damaging the sealing surfaces of the crankcase.

7. If the bearings are difficult to remove, they can be gently tapped out with a socket or piece of pipe the same size as the bearing outer race.

CAUTION
If the bearings or seals are difficult to remove or install, don't take a chance on expensive damage. Have the work performed by a dealer or competent machine shop.

8. While heating the crankcase halves, place new bearings in a freezer if possible. Chilling them will slightly reduce their overall diameter while the hot crankcase is slightly larger due to heat expansion. This will make installation easier.

9. Install the new bearing(s) in the heated cases. Press each bearing in by hand until it is completely seated. Do not hammer it in. If a bearing will not seat, remove it and cool it. Reheat the case and install the bearing again.

10. Oil seals are best installed with a special driver available at a Honda dealer or motorcycle supply store. However, a proper size socket or piece of pipe can be substituted. Make sure that the bearing and seals are not cocked in the hole and that they are seated properly.

NOTE
When installing a new crankshaft seal, grease both crankshaft and the seal. Stretch the seal to make it flexible.

11. Install a thread locking agent to the countershaft bearing retainer bolts (**Figure 83**) and tighten to 8-12 N•m (6-9 ft.-lb.).

Assembly

NOTE
On all models covered in this manual, the left-hand end of the crankshaft (tapered end with Woodruff key) is the alternator side.

1. Lightly oil the inner race of the right-hand main bearing and the right-hand end of the crankshaft with

clean 2-stroke oil. Carefully press the crankshaft straight into the right-hand crankcase half, turning the crankshaft while pushing.

2. Refer to Chapter Five and reinstall the transmission shaft assemblies and the internal shift mechanism.

3. Install the alignment dowels and install a new crankcase gasket (**Figure 84**).

4. Install the crankcase breather tube, if removed.

5. Crankcase assembly tools (Honda part No. 07965-1660100), Assembly collar (Honda part No. 07965-1660301) and Threaded adapter (Honda part No. 07965-KA30000) are recommended for assembly of the crankcase halves. If these tools are not available, the following steps can be used, but proceed cautiously.

6. Set the opposite case in place over the assembled crankcase on your workbench. Push it down squarely into place until it reaches the crankshaft bearing. This is usually about 13 mm (1/2 in.).

CAUTION
Crankcase halves should fit together without force; in the next step, do not attempt to pull them together with the crankcase screws. If the halves are difficult to assemble, separate them and investigate the cause of the interference. If the transmission shafts were disassembled, recheck to make sure that a gear is not installed backwards.

7. Lightly tap the case halves together with a plastic or rubber mallet until they seat.

8. Rotate the crankshaft and transmission shafts by hand to make sure they rotate freely.

9. Install the crankcase screws. Refer to **Figure 73** for crankcase screw locations. On CR500R models, install the two crankcase breather hose clamps to the rear screws. Tighten all crankcase screws in a crisscross pattern in 2 or 3 steps until they are firmly hand-tight.

10. After the crankcase halves are completely assembled, once again rotate the crankshaft and transmission shafts by hand to make sure they rotate freely and that there is not binding. If binding is present, disassemble the crankcase halves and correct the problem.

11. After a new crankcase gasket is installed, it must be trimmed. Carefully trim off all excess crankcase gasket material at the mating seams (**Figure 85**), so

the cylinder base has a flat surface and the cylinder base gasket can seat and seal completely.

12. Install the crankcase assembly into the bike's frame.

13. Install all exterior engine assemblies as described in this chapter and other related chapters.

    a. Cylinder head (this chapter).

    b. Cylinder (this chapter).

    c. Piston and piston pin (this chapter).

    d. Kickstarter (this chapter).

    e. Alternator (Chapter Seven).

    f. Clutch (Chapter Five).

    g. External shift mechanism (Chapter Five).

14. If removed, install the rear engine mounting bushing into the crankcase (**Figure 86**).

15. Install the primary drive gear as described in this chapter and tighten the bolt to the torque specification listed in **Table 3**.

> *NOTE*
> *Wedge a soft copper washer (or penny) between the primary drive gear and the gear on the clutch outer housing to keep the primary drive gear from rotating during installation.*

16. Coat the inside of the countershaft collar and O-ring with grease and install to the countershaft (**Figure 87**).

17. Install the drive sprocket as described in this chapter.

18. Fill the transmission with oil as described under *Transmission/Clutch Oil Change* in Chapter Three.

KICKSTARTER/IDLER GEAR

Removal

1. Remove the right crankcase cover as described in this chapter.

2. Remove the clutch as described in Chapter Five.

3. Perform the following:

    a. Unhook the return spring from the hole in the crankcase (**Figure 88**) and withdraw the kickstarter shaft assembly from the crankcase half (**Figure 89**).

    b. Remove the kickstarter idler gear (A, **Figure 90**) and bushing (B, **Figure 90**).

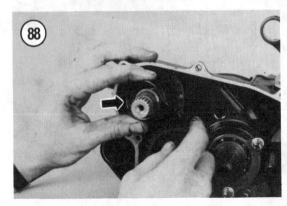

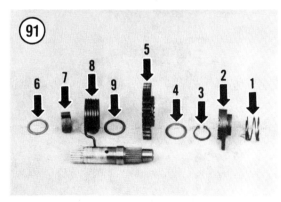

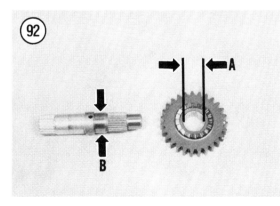

Disassembly/Inspection/Assembly

Refer to **Figure 91** for this procedure.

1. Clean the assembled shaft in solvent and dry with compressed air.

2. Remove the ratchet spring (1) and the kickstarter ratchet (2).

3. Remove the circlip (3) and slide off the thrust washer (4) and kickstarter pinion gear (5).

4. From the other end of the shaft, remove the first thrust washer (6), collar (7), return spring (8) and second thrust washer (9).

5. Measure the inside diameter of the kickstarter pinion gear (A, **Figure 92**). If the dimension exceeds the service limit dimensions listed in **Table 1** (CR250R) or **Table 2** (CR500R), the gear must be replaced.

6. Measure the outside diameter of the kickstarter shaft (B, **Figure 92**) where the kickstarter pinion gear rides. If the dimension is to the service limit listed in **Table 1** (CR250R) or **Table 2** (CR500R) or less, the shaft must be replaced.

7. Measure the inside diameter of the idler gear (A, **Figure 90**) and the inside and outside diameters of the idler gear bushing (B, **Figure 90**). If the bushing is to the service limits, replace it and check for play between the idler gear bushing and idler gear. If play exists, the inside diameter of the idler gear is to the service limit and must be replaced also.

8. Measure the outside diameter of the countershaft on which the idler gear and bushing ride.

9. Check for chipped, broken or missing teeth on the gears; replace as necessary.

10. Make sure the ratchet gear operates smoothly on the shaft.

11. Check all parts for uneven wear. Replace any that are questionable.

12. Apply assembly oil to all sliding surfaces of all parts before assembly.

13. Refer to **Figure 91** for the following procedures:

  a. Install the kickstarter pinion gear (5) onto the shaft.

  b. Install the thrust washer (4) and the circlip (3). Make sure the circlip is correctly seated in the groove in the kickstarter shaft.

  c. Align the punch marks on the kickstarter ratchet and the punch mark on the shaft (**Figure 93**). Slide on the ratchet.

  d. Install the ratchet spring (1).

14. On the other side of the shaft, install the second thrust washer (9) and the return spring (8) and place the hook into the hole in the shaft (**Figure 94**).

15. Slide on the collar (7) and push the collar into place within the return spring.

16. Install the first thrust washer (6).

Installation

1. Install the assembled shaft (drive ratchet facing crankcase) into the crankcase.

2. Rotate the assembly clockwise and hook the return spring into the hole in the crankcase (A, **Figure 95**).

3. Install the idle gear bushing (B, **Figure 90**) onto the transmission countershaft.

4. Install the kickstarter idle gear (B, **Figure 95**) with the larger of the raised shoulders facing the crankcase.

5. Install the clutch assembly as described in Chapter Five.

6. Install the right crankcase cover as described in this chapter.

BREAK-IN PROCEDURE

If the rings were replaced, a new piston installed, the cylinder rebored or honed (CR500R models only) or major lower end work performed, the engine should be broken in just as though it were new. The performance and service life of the engine depend greatly on a careful and sensible break-in.

For the first 5-10 hours of operation, no more than one-third throttle should be used and speed should be varied as much as possible within the one-third throttle limit. Prolonged steady running at one speed, no matter how moderate, is to be avoided as well as hard acceleration.

Table 1 ENGINE SPECIFICATIONS, CR250R

Item	Specification	Wear limit
Engine type	Water-cooled, 2-stroke, single	
Bore/stroke	66.4 × 72.0 mm (2.61 × 2.83 in.)	
Displacement	249.3 cc (15.2 cu. in.)	
Compression ratio		
1988	9.0 to 1	
1989	8.8 to 1	
1990-1991	8.5 to 1	
Lubrication	Fuel-oil mixture	
Air filtration	Foam element	
Cylinder head warpage	—	0.05 mm (0.002 in.)
Cylinder bore	66.390-66.405 mm (2.6138-2.6144 in.)	66.44 mm (2.616 in.)
Cylinder out-of-round	—	0.05 mm (0.002 in.)
Piston/cylinder clearance	0.04-0.075 mm (0.0016-0.0030 in.)	0.1 mm (0.04 in.)
Piston diameter	66.330-66.350 mm (2.6114-2.6122 in.)	66.28 mm (2.609 in.)
Piston pin bore		
1988	18.007-18.013 mm (0.7089-0.7092 in.)	18.03 mm (0.710 in.)
1989-1991	18.002-18.008 mm (0.7087-0.7090 in.)	18.02 mm (0.709 in.)
Piston pin diameter	17.994-18.000 mm (0.7084-0.7087 in.)	17.98 mm (0.708 in.)
Piston/pin clearance		
1988	0.007-0.019 mm (0.0003-0.0008 in.)	0.03 mm (0.001 in.)
1989-1991	0.002-0.014 mm (0.0001-0.0006 in.)	0.02 mm (0.001 in.)
Piston rings		
Number	2	
Ring end gap		
1988-1989	0.3-0.5 mm (0.01-0.02 in.)	0.6 mm (0.024 in.)
1990-1991	0.40-0.55 mm (0.016-0.022 in.)	0.65 mm (0.026 in.)
Ring side clearance		
1988-1989		
Top	0.045-0.075 mm (0.0018-0.0030 in.)	0.095 mm (0.0037 in.)
Second	0.025-0.055 mm (0.0010-0.0022 in.)	0.075 mm (0.0030 in.)
1990-1991		
Top	0.060-0.100 mm (0.0024-0.0039 in.)	0.120 mm (0.0047 in.)
Second	0.050-0.080 mm (0.0020-0.0031 in.)	0.095 mm (0.0037 in.)
Connecting rod		
Small end ID	22.002-22.014 mm (0.8662-0.8667 in.)	22.03 mm (0.867 in.)
Big end radial clearance	0.010-0.022 mm (0.0004-0.0009 in.)	0.03 mm (0.001 in.)
Big end side clearance	0.2-0.6 mm (0.01-0.02 in.)	0.7 mm (0.03 in.)
Crankshaft journal runout	—	0.05 mm (0.002 in.)

(continued)

Table 1 ENGINE SPECIFICATIONS, CR250R (continued)

Item	Specification	Wear limit
Cylinder head warpage	—	0.05 mm (0.002 in.)
Kickstarter shaft diameter	21.959-21.980 mm (0.8645-0.8654 in.)	21.95 mm (0.864 in.)
Kickstarter pinion inner diameter	22.020-22.041 mm (0.8669-0.8678 in.)	22.06 mm (0.869 in.)
Kickstarter idler gear		
Countershaft diameter	16.966-16.984 mm (0.6680-0.6687 in.)	16.95 mm (0.667 in.)
Gear inner diameter	20.020-20.041 mm (0.7882-0.7890 in.)	20.07 mm (0.790 in.)
Kickstart idler gear bushing		
Inner diameter	17.000-17.018 mm (0.6693-0.6700 in.)	17.04 mm (0.671 in.)
Outer diameter	19.979-20.000 mm (0.7866-0.7874 in.)	19.96 mm (0.786 in.)

Table 2 ENGINE SPECIFICATIONS, CR500R

Item	Specification	Wear limit
Engine type	Water-cooled 2-stroke, single	
Bore/stroke	89.0 × 79.0 mm (3.5 × 3.1 in.)	
Displacement	491.4 cc (29.9 cu. in.)	
Compression ratio	6.8 to 1	
Lubrication	Fuel/oil mixture	
Air filtration	Foam element	
Cylinder head warpage	—	0.05 (0.002 in.)
Cylinder bore	89.020-89.035 mm (3.5047-3.5053 in.)	89.07 mm (3.507 in.)
Cylinder out-of-round	—	0.05 mm (0.002 in.)
Piston/cylinder clearance	0.070-0.105 mm (0.0027-0.0041 in.)	0.12 mm (0.0047 in.)
Piston diameter	88.93-88.95 mm (3.501-3.502 in.)	88.88 mm (3.499 in.)
Piston pin bore		
1988	20.007-20.013 mm (0.7876-0.7879 in.)	20.03 mm (0.789 in.)
1989-1991	20.002-20.008 mm (0.7875-0.7877 in.)	20.02 mm (0.788 in.)
Piston pin diameter		
1988	19.994-20.000 mm (0.7871-0.7874 in.)	19.98 mm (0.787 in.)
1989-1991	19.994-20.000 mm (0.7871-0.7874 in.)	19.992 mm (0.7871 in.)
Piston/pin clearance		
1988	0.007-0.019 mm (0.0003-0.0008 in.)	0.03 mm (0.001 in.)
1989-1991	0.002-0.014 mm (0.0001-0.0006 in.	0.02 mm (0.0008 in.)
Piston rings		
Number	2	
Ring end gap	0.3-0.5 mm (0.012-0.020 in.)	0.6 mm (0.02 in.)

(continued)

Table 2 ENGINE SPECIFICATIONS, CR500R (continued)

Item	Specification	Wear limit
Connecting rod		
Small end inner diameter	25.002-25.014 mm	25.025 mm
	(0.9846-0.9848 in.)	(0.9852 in.)
Big end side clearance		
1988-1989	0.2-0.6 mm	0.7 mm
	(0.008-0.024 in.)	(0.03 in.)
1990-1991	0.4-0.8 mm	0.9 mm
	(0.016-0.031 in.)	(0.04 in.)
Big end radial clearance	0.008-0.020 mm	0.03 mm
	(0.0003-0.0008 in.)	(0.001 in.)
Crankshaft journal runout	0.03 mm	0.05 mm
	(0.001 in.)	(0.002 in.)
Kickstarter shaft outer diameter	21.959-21.980 mm	21.95 mm
	(0.8645-0.8654 in.)	(0.864 in.)
Kickstarter pinion inner diameter	20.020-20.041 mm	20.06 mm
	(0.7882-0.7890 in.)	(0.790 in.)
Kickstarter idler gear		
Countershaft outer diameter	16.966-16.984 mm	16.95 mm
	(0.6680-0.6687 in.)	(0.667 in.)
Bushing inner diameter	17.000-17.018 mm	17.04 mm
	(0.6693-0.6700 in.)	(0.671 in.)
Bushing outer diameter	19.979-20.000 mm	19.96 mm
	(0.7866-0.7874 in.)	(0.786 in.)
Gear inner diameter	20.020-20.041 mm	20.07 mm
	(0.7882-0.7890 in.)	(0.790 in.)

4

Table 3 ENGINE TORQUE SPECIFICATIONS

Item	N·m	ft.-lb.
Engine hanger bolts		
8 mm	24-29	17-21
10 mm		
1988-1991 CR250R	38-48	28-35
1988-1989 CR500R	38-48	28-35
1990-1991 CR500R	60-70	44-51
Engine mounting bolts (lower)		
1988-1989	38-48	28-35
1990-1991	60-70	44-51
Shock absorber lower bolt	38-48	28-35
Brake arm pivot bolt	24-28	17-20
Swing arm pivot bolt	80-100	59-73
Cylinder head	24-29	17-21
Cylinder		
CR250R		
1988	38-48	28-35
1989-1991	35-45	25-33
CR500R		
1988	38-48	28-35
1989-1991	35-45	25-33
Alternator rotor	50-60	36-44
Primary drive gear nut or bolt	40-50	29-36

NOTE: If you own a 1992 CR500R or later model, first check the Supplement at the back of this book for any new service information.

CHAPTER FIVE

CLUTCH AND TRANSMISSION

The clutch is a wet multi-plate unit which operates immersed in an oil supply it shares with the transmission. The clutch center is splined to the transmission mainshaft and the clutch outer housing can rotate freely on the mainshaft. The clutch outer housing is geared via the primary drive gear to the crankshaft. The clutch release mechanism is operated by the clutch cable through the hand lever mounted on the handlebar.

Clutch and transmission specifications are listed in **Tables 1-4** at the end of the chapter.

CLUTCH

Refer to **Figure 1** for the following procedures.

Removal/Disassembly

The clutch assembly can be removed with the engine in the frame, and without removing the right crankcase cover.

> *NOTE*
> *For clarification purposes, the engine is shown removed from the frame and in some cases other components are*
> *shown partially disassembled. It is not necessary to disassemble other components unless noted in the related procedure.*

1. Drain the clutch/transmission oil as described under *Transmission/Clutch Oil Change* in Chapter Three.

2. Disconnect the rear brake pedal return spring.

3. Remove the rear brake pedal pivot bolt (**Figure 2**) and spring.

4. Remove the six clutch cover screws and remove the cover (**Figure 3**).

> *NOTE*
> *It is not necessary to remove the right crankcase cover to service the clutch. It will be necessary only if the primary drive gear or other internal parts require inspection or service. The right crankcase cover is shown removed in some parts of this procedure for clarity.*

5. Loosen the clutch spring bolts and clutch springs using a crisscross pattern in 2 or 3 progressive steps (**Figure 4**).

6. Remove the clutch pressure plate (**Figure 5**).

CLUTCH

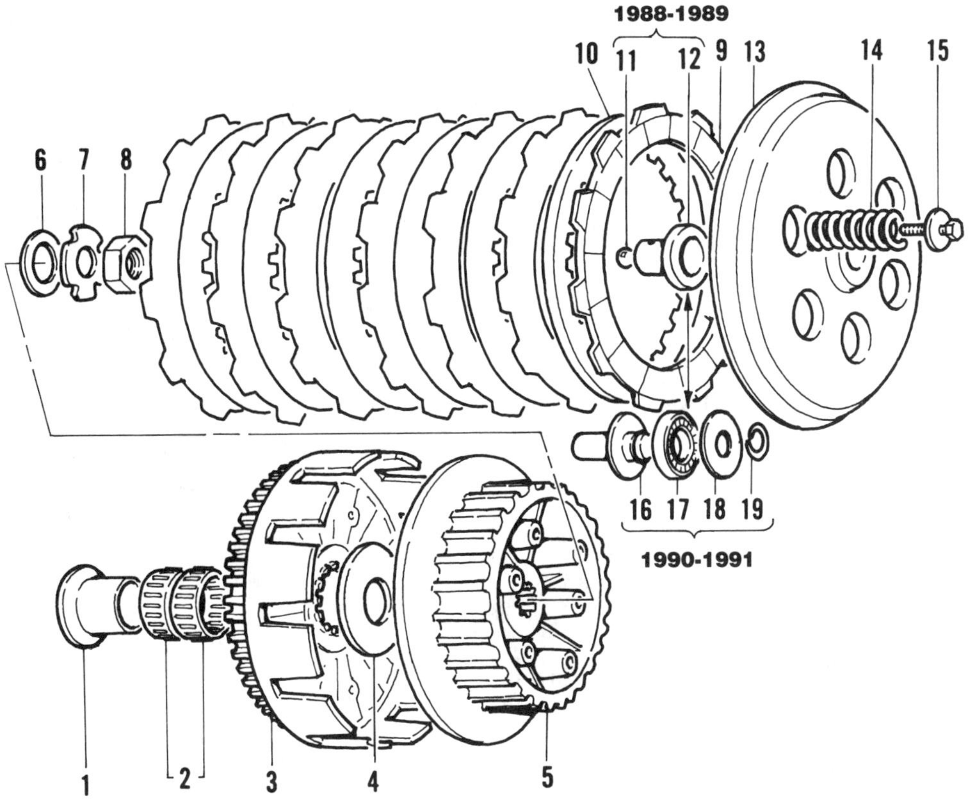

1. Clutch outer guide
2. Needle bearings
3. Clutch outer housing
4. Thrust washer
5. Clutch center
6. Thrust washer
7. Lockwasher
8. Locknut
9. Clutch friction plates
10. Clutch plates
11. Steel ball
12. Clutch lifter
13. Pressure plate
14. Clutch spring
15. Clutch bolt
16. Clutch lifter
17. Needle bearing
18. Washer
19. Stopper ring

7A. On 1988-1989 models, perform the following:

   a. Remove the 7 clutch friction discs and 6 clutch plates (**Figure 6**).

   b. Remove the clutch lifter, steel ball and clutch lifter rod. Refer to **Figure 1**. Be careful not to lose the steel ball.

7B. On 1990-1991 models, perform the following:

   a. Remove the 8 clutch friction discs and 7 clutch plates (**Figure 6**).

   b. Remove the clutch lifter (**Figure 7**) and lifter rod (**Figure 8**).

8. Straighten the locking tabs on the lockwasher.

9. To prevent the clutch outer housing from turning when performing Step 12, hold it with a special tool such as the "Grabbit" (**Figure 9**).

> *NOTE*
> *The "Grabbit" tool can be obtained by order through Precision Manufacturing Sales Co., Inc., P.O. Box 149, Clearwater, Florida 34617.*

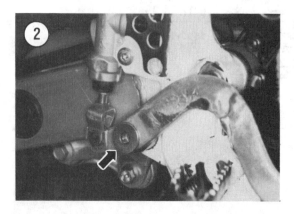

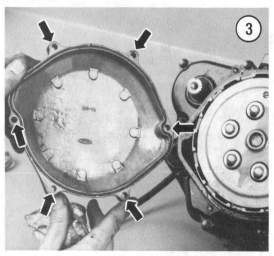

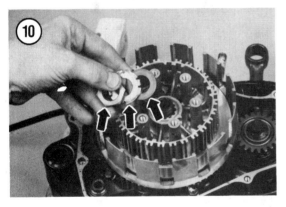

10. Remove the locknut, lockwasher and thrust washer securing the clutch center in place (**Figure 10**).

11. Remove the clutch center.

12. Remove the retainer washer, clutch outer housing and needle bearings (A, **Figure 11**) from the shaft.

13. Remove the clutch outer guide (B, **Figure 11**) from the shaft.

14. Inspect the clutch parts as described in this chapter.

Assembly/Installation

1. Coat the surfaces of any new friction discs and clutch plates with engine oil before assembly to avoid having the clutch lock up when used for the first time.

2. Install the clutch outer guide (B, **Figure 11**) and needle bearing (A, **Figure 11**) onto the shaft.

3. Install the clutch outer housing (**Figure 12**).

4. Install the retainer washer (A, **Figure 13**) onto the shaft and install the clutch center (B, **Figure 13**).

5

5. Install the thrust washer (A, **Figure 14**) and a new lockwasher (B, **Figure 14**) onto the shaft and align the lockwasher tab with the groove of the clutch center.

6. Install the locknut (C, **Figure 14**) and tighten by holding the clutch outer drum with the "Grabbit" or other tool. Tighten the locknut (**Figure 15**) to the torque specifications in **Table 4**.

7. Bend down the tab(s) of the new lockwasher onto the flats of the locknut.

8A. On 1988-1989 models, perform the following:

    a. Install the 7 friction discs and 6 clutch plates alternately, beginning with a friction disc (**Figure 16**), then a clutch plate.

    b. Apply grease to the steel ball and clutch lifter rod.

    c. Insert the clutch lifter rod (**Figure 8**) into the mainshaft.

    d. Insert the steel ball into the clutch lifter and install the clutch lifter

8B. On 1990-1991 models, perform the following:

    a. Install the 8 friction discs and 7 clutch plates alternately, beginning with a friction disc (**Figure 16**), then a clutch plate.

    b. Apply grease to the clutch lifter rod (**Figure 8**) and insert it into the mainshaft.

    c. Install the clutch lifter onto the rod (**Figure 7**).

9. Install the clutch pressure plate (**Figure 17**), the clutch springs and clutch bolts (**Figure 18**). Tighten the bolts securely in a crisscross pattern in 2 or 3 stages.

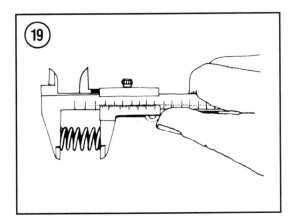

10. Install the clutch cover. Tighten the screws securely in a crisscross pattern.

11. Install the rear brake pivot bolt and spring. Connect the return spring.

12. Refill the clutch/transmission oil with the recommended type and quantity of oil. See *Transmission/Clutch Oil Change* in Chapter Three.

CLUTCH INSPECTION

1. Clean all parts in a petroleum-based solvent such as kerosene and dry thoroughly with compressed air.

2. Measure the free length of each clutch spring as shown in **Figure 19**. If any one of the springs is worn to the service limit listed in **Table 1**, they should be replaced as a set.

3. Measure the thickness of each friction disc at several places around the disc as shown in **Figure 20**. Replace any disc that is worn to the service limit listed in **Table 1**.

4. Check the clutch plates for warpage on a flat surface plate such as a piece of plate glass (**Figure 21**). Replace any that are warped to the service limit listed in **Table 1**.

> *NOTE*
> *If any of the clutch springs, friction discs or clutch plates require replacement, you should replace all of them as a set to retain maximum clutch performance.*

5. Inspect the grooves and studs in the pressure plate (**Figure 22**). If either shows signs of wear or galling, the pressure plate should be replaced.

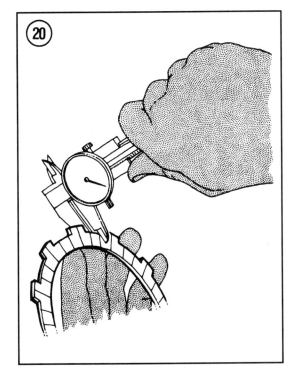

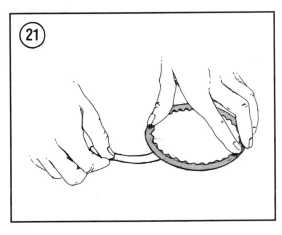

6. Inspect the inner splines (A, **Figure 23**) and outer grooves (B, **Figure 23**) in the clutch center. If damaged, the clutch center should be replaced.

7. Inspect the teeth on the clutch outer housing (**Figure 24**). Remove any small nicks on the gear teeth with an oilstone. If damage is severe, the clutch housing should be replaced.

8. Inspect the slots in the clutch outer housing (**Figure 25**) for cracks, nicks or galling where it comes in contact with the friction disc tabs. If any severe damage is evident, the clutch housing must be replaced.

9. *1988-1989 models*—Inspect the steel ball and the clutch lifter for wear (**Figure 26**); replace as a set if necessary. Inspect the lifter rod for bends or excessive wear; replace if necessary.

10. *1990-1991 models*—Inspect the clutch lifter assembly by turning the lifter plate (A, **Figure 27**) with your finger. If the needle bearing is binding, replace the bearing, washer and stop ring as a set. Also inspect the lifter rod (B, **Figure 27**) for bends or excessive wear; replace if necessary.

11. Measure the inside diameter (**Figure 28**) of the clutch outer housing where the clutch outer guide and needle bearings ride. Compare to the dimension listed in **Table 1**. If worn to the service limit, the housing must be replaced.

12. Measure the outside diameter of the clutch outer housing guide (**Figure 29**). Compare to the dimension listed in **Table 1**. If worn to the service limit, the clutch outer housing guide must be replaced.

13. Inspect the needle bearings. Make sure they rotate smoothly with no signs of wear; replace if necessary.

14. Inspect the retainer washer for wear or damage; replace if necessary.

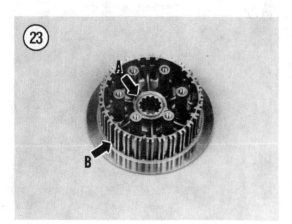

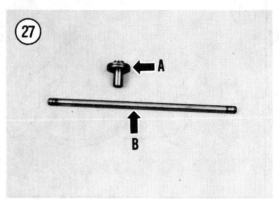

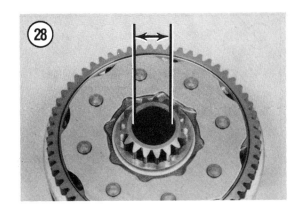

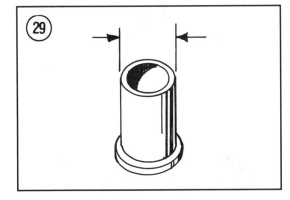

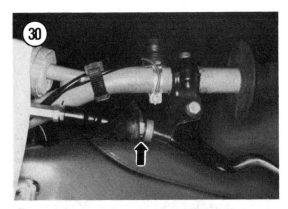

CLUTCH CABLE

Removal/Installation

The clutch cable will wear and stretch at different intervals under various riding conditions, but it will eventually stretch to the point where replacement becomes necessary.

1. At the clutch lever, pull back the rubber protective boot covering the cable adjuster.

2. Loosen the locknut and turn the adjuster barrel (**Figure 30**) all the way toward the cable sheath. Slip the cable end out of the hand lever.

3. Remove the screws securing the alternator cover and remove the cover and gasket. Remove the cable end from the clutch lever (A, **Figure 31**) by pulling outward and withdraw the cable from the hole in the top of the crankcase (B, **Figure 31**).

4. Tie a piece of heavy string or cord (approximately 2-3 m/6-8 ft. long) to the clutch mechanism end of the cable. Wrap the knot with duct tape to prevent snagging. Tie the other end of the string to the footpeg.

5. At the handlebar end of the cable, carefully pull the cable and attached string out through the frame and from behind the steering head area.

6. Remove the tape and untie the string from the old cable. The string will be used to pull the new cable into exactly the same place the old one occupied.

7. Lubricate the new cable as described under *Control Cable Lubrication* in Chapter Three.

8. Tie the string to the clutch mechanism end of the new clutch cable and wrap it with tape.

9. Carefully pull the string back through the frame, routing the new cable through the same path as the old cable.

10. Remove the tape and untie the string from the cable and the footpeg.

11. Connect the clutch end of the cable to the clutch arm (A, **Figure 31**) and install the alternator cover. Use a new gasket if necessary.

12. Connect the other end of the cable to the clutch lever on the handlebar.

13. Adjust the clutch cable as described in Chapter Three.

EXTERNAL SHIFT MECHANISM

On a competition or off-road motorcycle, the gearshift lever is subject to considerable abuse. If the

5

gearshift lever gets bent during a hard spill, the shift lever shaft may also be bent. It is very difficult to straighten the gearshift spindle (shift shaft) without subjecting the crankcase to high stress at the point where the shaft enters it. Examine the damage carefully as it may be cheaper to replace the shaft than to risk further damage trying to straighten it. The gearshift spindle (shift shaft) runs through the crankcase but is removed and serviced from the same side of the crankcase as the clutch assembly. This can be accomplished with the engine in the frame.

Removal

Refer to **Figure 32** for the following procedure.

1. Drain the transmission/clutch oil as described under *Transmission/Clutch Oil Change* in Chapter Three.

2. Remove the gearshift lever by loosening the bolt and sliding it off the spline (**Figure 33**).

3. Remove right crankcase cover as described in *Right Crankcase Cover Removal/Installation* in Chapter Four.

4. Remove the clutch assembly as described in this chapter.

5. Withdraw the gearshift spindle assembly (**Figure 34**). Don't lose the small thrust washer on the inside of the assembly.

6. Remove the small collar on the drum shifter (A, **Figure 35**).

7. Remove the bolts (B, **Figure 35**) securing the guide plate and remove the plate and the drum shifter assembly. Don't let the ratchet pawls fall when removing the drum shifter.

8. Remove the bolt (A, **Figure 36**) securing the stopper arm and remove the arm, return spring and thrust washer.

9. Remove the center bolt (B, **Figure 36**) securing the shift drum center and remove the shift drum center (**Figure 37**).

Inspection

1. Inspect the return spring on the gearshift spindle assembly (A, **Figure 38**). If it is broken or weak, it must be replaced.

2. Inspect the gearshift spindle assembly shaft (B, **Figure 38**) for bending, wear or other damage; replace if necessary.

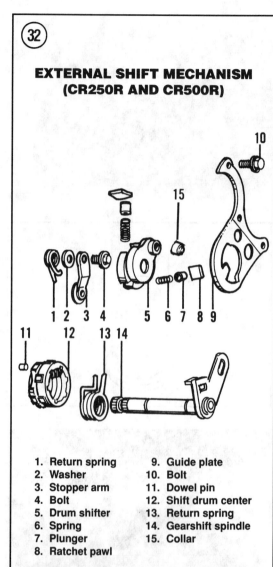

32

EXTERNAL SHIFT MECHANISM (CR250R AND CR500R)

1. Return spring
2. Washer
3. Stopper arm
4. Bolt
5. Drum shifter
6. Spring
7. Plunger
8. Ratchet pawl
9. Guide plate
10. Bolt
11. Dowel pin
12. Shift drum center
13. Return spring
14. Gearshift spindle
15. Collar

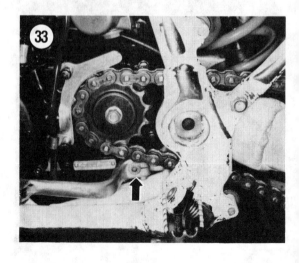

33

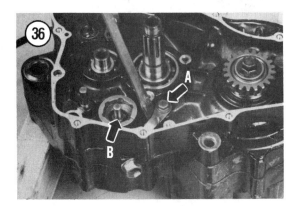

3. Inspect the ratchet pawls, plungers and springs (**Figure 39**) for wear or damage; replace as necessary.

4. Inspect the roller on the stopper arm. It must roll freely with no binding; replace if necessary.

Installation

1. Install the spring and washer onto the stopper arm. Install the bolt. Tighten the bolt securely.

2. Using a screwdriver, move the stopper arm back (**Figure 36**).

3. Align the dowel pin in the backside of the shift drum center with the hole in the shift drum (**Figure 40**) and install the shift drum center.

5

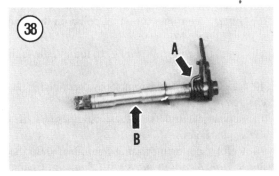

4. Apply a thread locking agent to the center bolt and tighten the bolt securely.

5. Position the roller on the stopper arm into one of the detents on the back portion of the drum shifter.

6. Apply clean transmission oil to the plungers, springs and ratchet pawls. Install these items into the drum shifter as shown in **Figure 41**. Then install this assembly into the backside of the guide plate (**Figure 42**).

7. Install the guide plate/drum shifter assembly and tighten the bolts securely.

8. Install the small collar (A, **Figure 35**) on the drum shifter.

9. Make sure the small thrust washer (**Figure 43**) is installed on the inside of the gearshift spindle assembly.

10. Install the gearshift spindle assembly and align the shifter finger onto the small collar on the drum shifter (**Figure 44**).

11. Install the gearshift lever onto the spindle (shift shaft).

12. Install the clutch assembly as described in this chapter.

13. Replace the right crankcase cover as described in Chapter Four.

14. Refill the clutch/transmission oil as described under *Transmission/Clutch Oil Change* in Chapter Three.

15. Adjust the clutch as described in Chapter Three.

5-SPEED TRANSMISSION AND INTERNAL SHIFT MECHANISM

For access to the transmission and internal shift mechanism it will be necessary to remove the engine and split the crankcase as described in Chapter Four. Once the crankcase has been split, removal of the transmission and shift drum is a simple task of pulling the assemblies up and out of the crankcase. Installation is more complicated and is covered more completely than the removal sequence.

Refer to **Table 2** for specifications on the internal shift mechanism and **Table 3** for transmission specifications.

If disassembling a used, well run-in engine, pay particular attention to any additional shims that may have been added by a previous owner. These may have been added to take up the tolerances of worn components and must be reinstalled in the same position since the shims have developed a wear

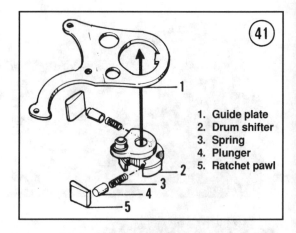

1. Guide plate
2. Drum shifter
3. Spring
4. Plunger
5. Ratchet pawl

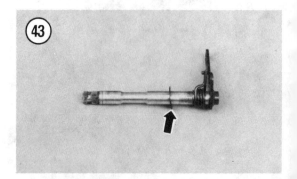

pattern. If new parts are going to be installed, these shims may be eliminated. This is something you will have to determine upon reassembly.

Removal/Installation

1. Remove the engine and split the crankcase as described in Chapter Four. Position the engine so that the transmission components can be removed by pulling up and out (**Figure 45**).

2. Pull each shift fork shaft out of the crankcase (**Figure 46**).

3. Pivot the forks away from the drum to allow access to the shift drum and remove the drum (**Figure 47**).

4. Remove the shift forks.

5. Remove the transmission assemblies (mainshaft and countershaft) each as a set (**Figure 48**).

6. Inspect the assemblies as described under *Preliminary Inspection* before disassembling them.

7. Inspect the shift fork shafts, shift forks and shift drum as described under *Internal Shift Mechanism Inspection* toward the end of this chapter.

8. Disassemble the mainshaft and countershaft assemblies and inspect as described in this section.

9. Install the 2 transmission assemblies by engaging them together in their proper relationship to each other. Install them in the right-hand crankcase. While installing each assembly, hold the thrust washer in place with your fingers (**Figure 48**). Make sure the thrust washer is still positioned correctly after the assemblies are installed. Tap the end of both shafts (**Figure 49**) with a plastic or rubber mallet to make sure they are seated completely.

NOTE
If the thrust washer on the end of the countershaft is not seated correctly, it

will prevent the crankcase halves from mating completely.

10. Each shift fork is marked with a letter. One fork is marked with a "R." One is marked with a "L," and one is marked with a "C."

11. On CR250R models, the shift forks are installed with the "R" and "L" shift forks facing "up" toward the left crankcase and the "C" shift fork facing "down" toward the right crankcase.

12. On 1988 CR500R models, the shift forks are installed with their marks facing "down" toward the right crankcase.

13. On 1989 and later CR500R models, the shift forks are installed with their marks facing "up" toward the left crankcase.

14. Install the center shift fork into the groove in the gear and install the shift fork shaft (**Figure 50**).

15. Install the right-hand shift fork (**Figure 51**) and the left-hand shift fork (**Figure 52**). Engage the shift forks into the grooves in the gears, but do not insert the shift fork shaft.

16. Coat all bearing and sliding surfaces of the shift drum with assembly oil and install the shift drum.

17. Pivot the right-hand and left-hand shift forks to mesh them with the shift drum and install the shift fork shaft (A, **Figure 53**). Make sure the shift fork shaft is installed with the tapered end toward the right crankcase half. See **Figure 46**.

18. Spin the transmission shafts and use the shift drum to shift through the gears. Make sure that by shifting, you can engage all the gears. Do this until you are satisfied that the transmission is working correctly. It is very time-consuming and frustrating to assemble and then disassemble the crankcase to correct errors.

NOTE
This procedure is much easier with the aid of a helper. Since the transmission assemblies are loose, they won't spin very easily. Have another person spin the transmission shaft while you turn the shift drum and engage all the gears.

19. Check to make sure the thrust washers (B, **Figure 53**) are installed on both shaft assemblies.

Preliminary Inspection

Following the removal of the transmission shaft assemblies, but prior to disassembly, they should be cleaned and inspected.

1. Remove the mainshaft and countershaft assemblies as described in this chapter (**Figure 54**).

2. Thoroughly clean the assembled shafts with solvent and a stiff brush. Dry with compressed air or let each assembly sit on rags to dry.

3. Visually inspect the components of each assembly for excessive wear. Any burrs, pitting or roughness on the teeth of a gear will cause wear on the mating gear. Minor roughness can be cleaned up with an oilstone but components with deep scars should be replaced.

CAUTION
Defective gears should be replaced. Replacement of the mating gear on the other shaft is recommended even though it may not show the same amount of damage or wear.

4. Carefully examine the engagement dogs. If any are chipped, worn, rounded or missing, the affected gear must be replaced.

5. Have a dealer or machine shop check the runout of each transmission shaft. If you have the equipment, perform the following. Mount the shaft in a lathe, on V-blocks or on a suitable centering device.

Place a dial indicator so that its plunger contacts a constant surface nearest the center of the shaft. Rotate the shaft and record the extremes of the dial readings. Replace the shaft if the runout reading exceeds 0.04 mm (0.0016 in.).

6. Rotate the transmission and shift drum bearings with your fingers (**Figure 55**). Check the bearing and race for roughness, noise and radial play. Replace any bearing that is questionable. Refer to *Bearing and Oil Seal Replacement* in Chapter Four.

7. If the transmission shafts appear satisfactory (**Figure 54**) and will not be disassembled, apply engine oil to all components and reinstall them in the crankcase as described in this chapter.

Mainshaft Disassembly/Assembly

Mainshaft disassembly is the same for CR250R and CR500R models manufactured from 1988 to 1991. Use **Figure 56** and **Figure 57** for mainshaft component breakdown. Note that the figures are labeled from left to right. **Figure 56** lists the components by name, while **Figure 57** uses letters to guide you through the disassembly/assembly steps. Note the position of the mainshaft and lay the assembly out as shown when following the disassembly/assembly procedures.

NOTE
A large egg flat (the type restaurants get their eggs in) is an excellent tool for disassembly of transmission components. The individual depressions allow you to remove parts and set them in positions relative to the order of disassembly. This is very helpful when reinstalling these components.

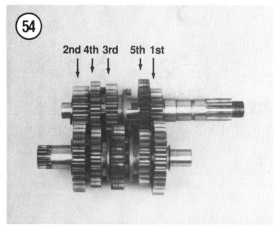

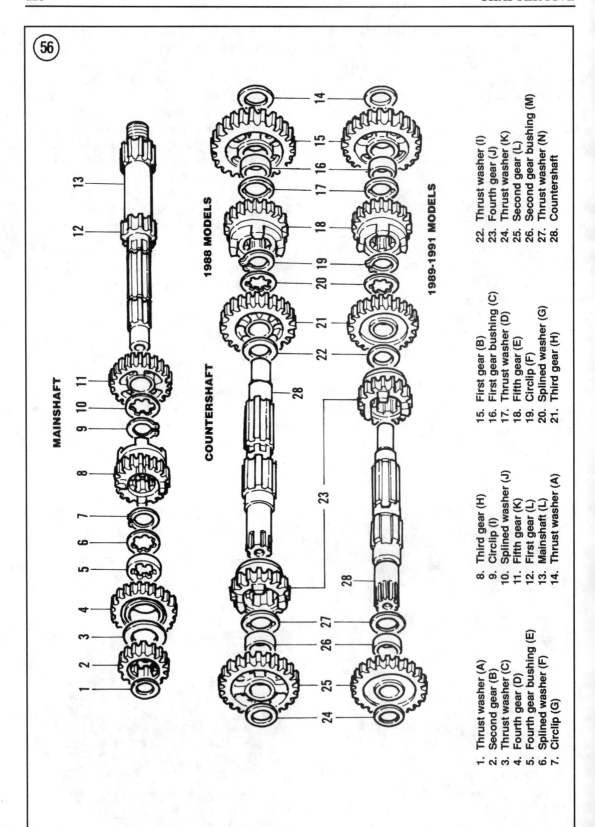

MAINSHAFT

1988 MODELS

COUNTERSHAFT

1989-1991 MODELS

1. Thrust washer (A)
2. Second gear (B)
3. Thrust washer (C)
4. Fourth gear (D)
5. Fourth gear bushing (E)
6. Splined washer (F)
7. Circlip (G)

8. Third gear (H)
9. Circlip (I)
10. Splined washer (J)
11. Fifth gear (K)
12. First gear (L)
13. Mainshaft (L)
14. Thrust washer (A)

15. First gear (B)
16. First gear bushing (C)
17. Thrust washer (D)
18. Fifth gear (E)
19. Circlip (F)
20. Splined washer (G)
21. Third gear (H)

22. Thrust washer (I)
23. Fourth gear (J)
24. Thrust washer (K)
25. Second gear (L)
26. Second gear bushing (M)
27. Thrust washer (N)
28. Countershaft

1. If not cleaned in the *Preliminary Inspection* procedure, use solvent and a stiff brush to clean the mainshaft and countershaft thoroughly.

2. Slide off the thrust washer (A) followed by 2nd gear (B) and the thrust washer (C).

3. Slide off the 4th gear (D) followed by the 4th gear bushing (E).

4. Remove the splined washer (F), then the circlip (G).

5. Slide off the 3rd gear (H).

6. Remove the circlip (I) followed by the splined washer (J).

7. Slide off 5th gear (K).

8. Check each gear for excessive wear, burrs, pitting or chipped or missing teeth. Check the condition of the lugs on the gears.

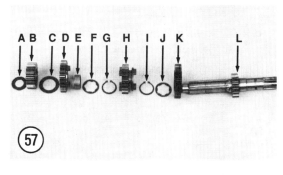

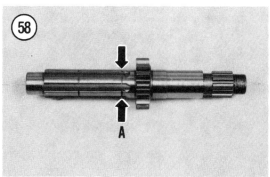

CAUTION
Defective gears should be replaced. It is a recommended procedure to replace the mating gears on the countershaft, even if the wear or damage is not as extensive.

NOTE
1st gear (L) is part of the mainshaft. If the gear is defective, the mainshaft must be replaced.

9. Make sure all the gears slide smoothly on the mainshaft splines.

10. Measure the outside diameter of the raised portion of the splines at location A, **Figure 58**. Refer to the dimensions listed in **Table 3**. If the shaft is worn to the service limit, the shaft must be replaced.

11. Measure the inside diameter of the 4th and 5th gears. Refer to the dimensions listed in **Table 3**. If the gear(s) is worn to the service limit (or greater) the gear(s) must be replaced.

NOTE
It is recommended that all circlips be replaced at every disassembly to ensure proper gear alignment.

Refer to **Figure 57** for the following procedure.

12. Slide on the 5th gear (K) and follow with the splined washer (J) and circlip (I).

13. Slide on the 3rd gear (H) followed by the circlip (G), then the splined washer (F).

14. Slide on the 4th gear bushing (E) followed by 4th gear (D) and thrust washer (C).

15. Slide on the 2nd gear (B) and follow with the thrust washer (A).

16. Following assembly, refer to **Figure 54** for the correct placement of all gears. Make sure the circlips are seated correctly in the grooves of the mainshaft.

Countershaft Disassembly/Assembly

The disassembly/assembly procedures for the countershaft components are essentially the same for CR250R and CR500R models. However, design differences do exist between 1988 and 1989 through 1991 models. Refer to **Figure 56** and **Figure 59** for this procedure. Note that **Figure 59** is labeled from right to left. **Figure 56** lists the components by name, while **Figure 59** is lettered to guide you through the disassembly/assembly steps.

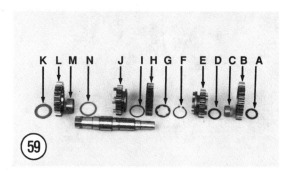

Refer to the illustrations and position the countershaft as shown when disassembling and assembling the components.

NOTE
Use the same large egg flat that was used for mainshaft disassembly. This is a much easier way to keep the relationship of parts in order.

1. If not cleaned in the *Preliminary Inspection* procedure, thoroughly clean the countershaft with solvent and a stiff brush. Dry with compressed air or let sit on rags to drip dry.

2. Slide off the thrust washer (A), followed by 1st gear (B), then the first gear bushing (C).

3. Slide off the thrust washer (D) followed by the 5th gear (E).

4. Remove the circlip (F), then the splined washer (G).

5. Slide off the 3rd gear (H), then the thrust washer (I).

6. On 1989 and later models, remove the 4th gear (J) from this side.

7. From the other side of the shaft, remove the thrust washer (K).

8. Slide off the 2nd gear (L), followed by the 2nd gear bushing (M), then the thrust washer (N).

9. On 1988 models, remove the 4th gear (J) from this side.

10. Check each gear for excessive wear, burrs, pitting or chipped or missing teeth. Check the condition of the lugs on the gears.

CAUTION
Defective gears should be replaced. It is recommended that mating gears on the mainshaft be replaced even though damage or wear may not be as extensive.

11. Make sure all gears slide smoothly on the countershaft splines.

12. Measure the outside diameter of the countershaft at locations B, C and D as shown in **Figure 60**. Refer to the dimensions given in **Table 3**. If the shaft is worn to the service limit, the shaft must be replaced.

13. Measure the inside diameter of the 1st, 2nd and 3rd gears (**Figure 61**). Refer to the dimensions given in **Table 3**. If the gear(s) is worn to the service limit, the gear(s) must be replaced.

NOTE
It is recommended that you replace the circlip every time the transmission is disassembled to ensure proper gear alignment.

14. On 1988 models, perform the following on the left-hand side of the countershaft:

   a. Slide on the 4th gear (J) followed by the thrust washer (N), then the 2nd gear bushing (M).

   b. Slide on the 2nd gear (L) followed by the thrust washer (K).

Perform the following to the right-hand side of the countershaft:

   a. Slide on the thrust bearing (I) followed by the 3rd gear (H), then the splined washer (G).

   b. Install the circlip (F), followed by the 5th gear (E) and thrust washer (D).

   c. Slide on 1st gear bushing (C), followed by 1st gear (B), then the thrust washer (A).

15. On 1989 and later models, perform the following to the left-hand side of the countershaft:

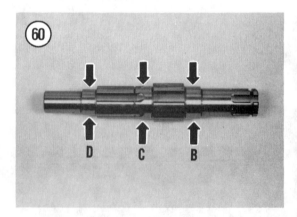

a. Slide on the thrust washer (N), followed by the 2nd gear bushing (M).

b. Slide on the 2nd gear (L), then the thrust washer (K).

16. From the right-hand side of the shaft, perform the following:

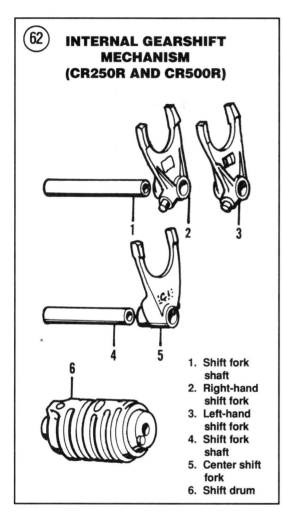

INTERNAL GEARSHIFT MECHANISM (CR250R AND CR500R)

1. Shift fork shaft
2. Right-hand shift fork
3. Left-hand shift fork
4. Shift fork shaft
5. Center shift fork
6. Shift drum

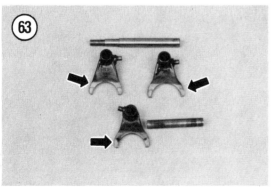

a. Slide on the 4th gear (J) and follow with the thrust bearing (I), then the 3rd gear (H) and splined washer (G).

b. Install the circlip (F), followed by 5th gear (E), then the thrust washer (D).

c. Install the 1st gear bushing (C), and follow with the 1st gear (B), then the thrust washer (A).

17. Following assembly, check the circlip to make sure it is seated correctly in the groove of the countershaft.

NOTE
After the mainshaft and countershaft components are assembled, engage (mesh) the 2 assemblies together in the correct position and placement of all gears (Figure 54). Check to make sure all the gears are installed correctly. This is the last opportunity for checking the assemblies before installing them into the crankcase.

INTERNAL SHIFT MECHANISM INSPECTION

The internal shift mechanism involves essentially the same components for the CR250R and CR500R, but shift fork installation procedures vary between the model and year manufactured. The internal shift mechanism is made up of the shift fork shafts, the shift forks and the shift drum.

NOTE
It is recommended that prior to disassembly of the following components, a diagram or trace drawing be made of parts and locations. Write down any identifying numbers and letters next to the items to help you when reassembling the components.

Refer to **Figure 62**.

1. Remove the internal shift mechanism assemblies as described under *5-Speed Transmission and Internal Shift Mechanism* in this chapter.

2. Inspect each of the shift forks (**Figure 63**) for signs of wear or cracking. Check for areas that are bent and slide the forks along the shift shaft to check for smoothness. Replace any fork that is worn or damaged.

3. Check for any arc-shaped wear or burn marks, which indicate the shift fork has contacted a gear. Check the fork fingers for wear and replace the fork if necessary.

4. Measure the inside diameter of each shift fork with an inside micrometer or snap gauge (**Figure 64**). If any parts are worn to their service limit given in **Table 2**, they must be replaced.

5. Using a micrometer, measure the width of the fork fingers (shift pawls) as shown in **Figure 65**. Replace the fork if the fingers are worn to the service limit. See **Table 2**.

6. Check the cam pin followers (A, **Figure 66**) on each shift fork for wear or damage and replace if necessary.

7. Check the shift fork shafts (B, **Figure 66**) for bends by rolling each shaft on a piece of plate glass. If the shaft is bent, it must be replaced.

8. Using a micrometer, measure the outside diameter of each shift fork shaft. Compare to the dimensions listed in **Table 2** and replace if worn to the service limit.

9. Inspect the grooves in the shift drum (**Figure 67**) for nicks, wear or roughness. If any of the groove profiles have excessive wear or damage, replace the shift drum.

10. Apply a light coat of transmission oil to the inside bores of the shift forks and on the outside of the shift fork shafts prior to installation.

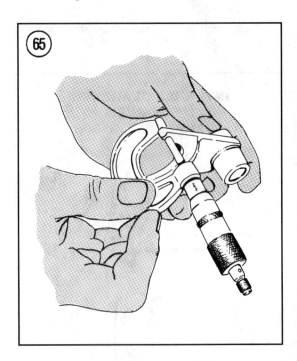

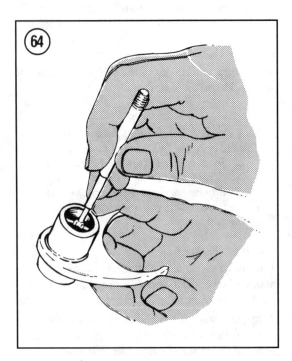

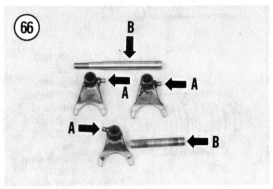

Table 1 CLUTCH SPECIFICATIONS

Item	Standard	Wear limit
Friction disc thickness	2.92-3.08 mm (0.115-0.121 in.)	2.85 mm (0.112 in.)
Clutch plate warpage	—	0.20 mm (0.008 in.)
Clutch spring free length		
CR250R		
1988	43.1 mm (1.70 in.)	41.3 mm (1.63 in.)
1989	44.8 mm (1.76 in.)	43.0 mm (1.69 in.)
1990-1991	44.2 mm (1.74 in.)	42.4 mm (1.67 in.)
CR500R		
1988-1989	44.50 mm (1.752 in.)	42.5 mm (1.67 in.)
1990-1991	44.20 mm (1.740 in.)	42.2 mm (1.66 in.)
Clutch outer housing ID	32.009-32.034 mm (1.2602-1.2612 in.)	32.054 mm (1.262 in.)
Clutch outer housing guide outside diameter	27.987-28.000 mm (1.1019-1.1024 in.)	27.973 mm (1.1013 in.)

Table 2 SHIFT FORK AND SHAFT SPECIFICATIONS

Item	Specifications	Wear limit
Shift fork ID		
Center	11.003-11.021 mm (0.4332-0.4339 in.)	11.04 mm (0.435 in.)
Right- and left-hand	12.041-12.056 mm (0.4740-0.4746 in.)	12.07 mm (0.475 in.)
Shift fork shaft OD		
Center	10.977-10.984 mm (0.4322-0.4324 in.)	10.95 mm (0.431 in.)
Right- and left-hand	11.983-11.994 mm (0.4718-0.4722 in.)	11.98 mm (0.472 in.)
Shift fork fingers	4.93-5.00 mm (0.194-0.197 in.)	4.8 mm (0.19 in.)

Table 3 TRANSMISSION SPECIFICATIONS

Item	Wear limit
CR250R	
Gear ID mainshaft	
4th	28.05 mm (1.104 in.)
5th	25.07 mm (0.987 in.)
Gear ID countershaft	
1st	22.07 mm (0.869 in.)
2nd	30.07 mm (1.184 in.)
3rd	25.07 mm (0.987 in.)
Mainshaft OD	
At location A	24.94 mm (0.982 in.)

(continued)

Table 3 TRANSMISSION SPECIFICATIONS (continued)

Item	Wear limit
CR250R (continued)	
Countershaft OD	
At location B	26.94 mm (1.061 in.)
At location C	24.96 mm (0.983 in.)
At location D	18.94 mm (0.746 in.)
CR500R	
Gear ID mainshaft	
4th	28.05 mm (1.104 in.)
5th	25.05 mm (0.986 in.)
Gear ID countershaft	
1st	22.05 mm (0.868 in.)
2nd	30.05 mm (1.183 in.)
3rd	25.05 mm (0.986 in.)
Mainshaft	
Mainshaft 5th gear bushing OD	24.94 mm (0.982 in.)
Countershaft	
1st gear bushing	
OD	21.95 mm (0.864 in.)
ID	19.04 mm (0.750 in.)
2nd gear bushing	
OD	29.95 mm (1.179 in.)
ID	27.04 mm (1.065 in.)
Mainshaft OD	
At location A	24.94 mm (0.982 in.)
Countershaft OD	
At location B	26.94 mm (1.061 in.)
At location C	24.94 mm (0.982 in.)
At location D	18.94 mm (0.746 in.)

Table 4 CLUTCH TORQUE SPECIFICATIONS

Item	N·m	ft.-lb.
Clutch center nut		
CR250R		
1988-1990	55-65	40-47
1991	80-84	58-61
CR500R	77-87	56-63

NOTE: If you own a 1992 CR500R or later model, first check the Supplement at the back of this book for any new service information.

FUEL AND EXHAUST SYSTEMS

6

The fuel system consists of the fuel tank, fuel shutoff valve and a single Keihin carburetor. Although the carburetor's function remains essentially unchanged, some changes have occurred and vary from model and year manufactured.

The exhaust system consists of an expansion chamber and a muffler. The CR250R models are equipped with a special system to vary the effective expansion chamber volume to broaden the power band. This system is called HPP (Honda Power Port).

This chapter includes service procedures for all parts of the fuel and exhaust systems. **Tables 1-3** at the end of the chapter provide specifications and tightening torque recommendations.

CARBURETOR OPERATION

For troubleshooting of the fuel system, an understanding of the function of each of the carburetor components and their relation to one another is a valuable aid. The carburetor supplies the proper mix of atomized fuel and air to the engine. At idle, incoming air metered by the air screw siphons a small amount of fuel through the slow jet. This mixture enters the carburetor through the slow jet circuit outlet and the bypass area. At larger throttle openings, the air stream siphons fuel through the main jet and needle jet. The tapered needle increases the effective flow capacity of the needle jet as it is lifted in that it occupies progressively less of the area of the jet.

At full throttle, the carburetor venturi is fully open and the needle position permits full fuel flow through the main jet.

CARBURETOR SERVICE

Carburetor service (removal and cleaning) should be performed when poor engine performance or hesitation is observed. Alterations in jet size, etc., should be attempted only if you're experienced in this type of "tuning" work; a bad guess could result in costly engine damage or, at the very least, poor performance. If, after servicing the carburetor and making the adjustments described in this chapter, the motorcycle does not perform correctly (and assuming that other factors affecting performance are correct), the motorcycle should be checked by a dealer or other qualified performance tuning specialist.

Removal/Installation

1. Place the bike on a metal or wood stand that will support it securely.

2. Remove the fuel tank as described under *Fuel Tank Removal/Installation* in this chapter. It is not absolutely necessary to remove the fuel tank for carburetor removal, but it does make it easier.

3. Turn the handlebar fully to the left to allow maximum slack in the throttle cable.

4. Turn the fuel shutoff valve to the "OFF" position and disconnect the fuel line at the carburetor by removing the tension spring (A, **Figure 1**).

5. Loosen the insulator and air cleaner connecting tube clamps (**Figure 2**).

6. Loosen the main jet cover at the bottom of the carburetor (B, **Figure 1**) and drain the fuel into a safe container.

> **WARNING**
> *Gasoline presents an extreme fire hazard. Work only in a well-ventilated area and keep a fire extinguisher, rated for gasoline fires, available at all times.*

> **NOTE**
> *Before removing the top cap in Step 7, thoroughly clean the area around it so no dirt will fall into the carburetor.*

7. Tilt the carburetor to the left side and unscrew the top of the carburetor.

8. Pull the throttle valve assembly up and out of the carburetor (**Figure 3**).

9. If the top cap and throttle valve assembly are not going to be removed from the throttle cable, wrap a clean shop rag around them to keep them clean.

10. Loosen the insulator (A, **Figure 4**) and air cleaner connecting tube clamps (**Figure 2**) completely and slide them away from the carburetor.

11. Note the routing of the carburetor left vent tube (B, **Figure 4**), right vent tube and overflow tube (on bottom), then carefully pull them free. Leave them attached to the carburetor.

12. Gently work the carburetor free from the rubber boots and take it to the workbench for disassembly and cleaning.

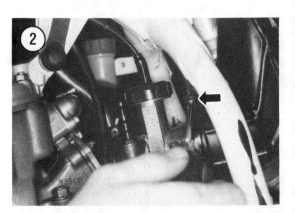

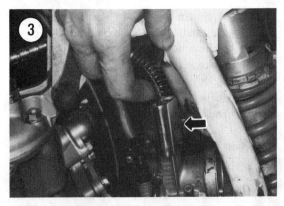

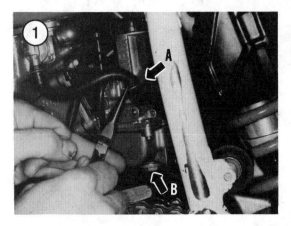

13. Install by reversing these steps while noting the following.

   a. Position the cutaway in the slide (**Figure 5**) toward the air box and install the slide into the carburetor (**Figure 6**).

   b. Align the raised lug on top of the front carburetor throat with the groove on the carburetor insulator band.

14. Adjust the throttle and air screw as described in Chapter Three.

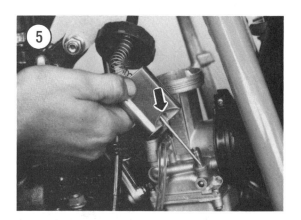

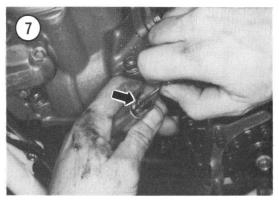

Throttle Valve Assembly
Disassembly/Assembly

1. Remove the throttle cable from the cable holder by compressing the throttle valve spring into the cap and sliding the cable out of the groove (**Figure 7**). Remove the spring and top cap.

2. Push the cable holder slightly with a 6 mm socket or Phillips screwdriver and rotate it 90° counter-clockwise (**Figure 8**).

3. Remove the cable holder, set collar, set spring and jet needle from the slide (**Figure 9**).

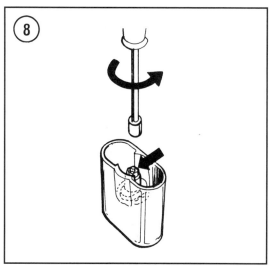

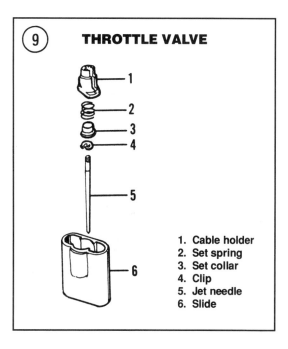

THROTTLE VALVE

1. Cable holder
2. Set spring
3. Set collar
4. Clip
5. Jet needle
6. Slide

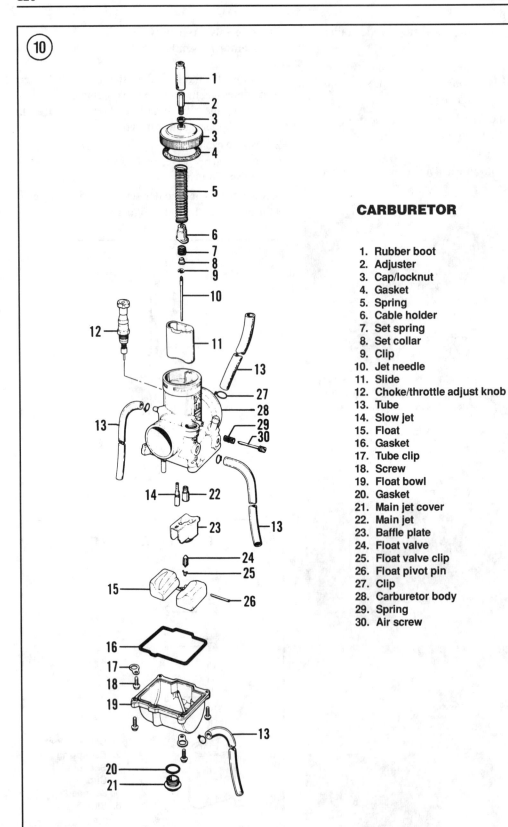

CARBURETOR

1. Rubber boot
2. Adjuster
3. Cap/locknut
4. Gasket
5. Spring
6. Cable holder
7. Set spring
8. Set collar
9. Clip
10. Jet needle
11. Slide
12. Choke/throttle adjust knob
13. Tube
14. Slow jet
15. Float
16. Gasket
17. Tube clip
18. Screw
19. Float bowl
20. Gasket
21. Main jet cover
22. Main jet
23. Baffle plate
24. Float valve
25. Float valve clip
26. Float pivot pin
27. Clip
28. Carburetor body
29. Spring
30. Air screw

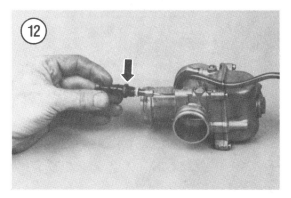

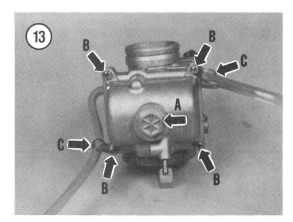

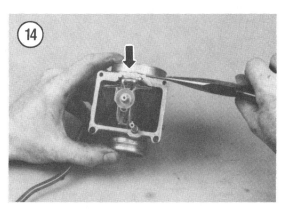

4. If the needle jet clip is going to be removed, record the clip position before removal. The standard clip position is listed in **Table 1**.

5. Install by reversing these steps while noting the following.

    a. Install the cable holder, set spring, and set collar over the jet needle clip and jet needle (**Figure 9**).

    b. Rotate the cable holder 90° clockwise.

CARBURETOR BODY

Disassembly/Assembly

Refer to **Figure 10** for this procedure.

NOTE
Before removing the air screw, carefully screw it in until it lightly seats. Count and record the number of turns so it can be reinstalled in the same position.

1. Unscrew the air screw (**Figure 11**) and remove the spring and the air screw.

2. Loosen the locknut and remove the choke/idle adjust knob assembly (**Figure 12**) from the carburetor body.

3. Unscrew the main jet cover and O-ring seal (A, **Figure 13**).

4. Remove the screws (B, **Figure 13**) securing the float bowl and remove the float bowl. Note the location of the vent and overflow tube clamps (C, **Figure 13**) as they must be reinstalled in the same location.

5. Remove the float pin (**Figure 14**) and remove the float and float needle valve (A, **Figure 15**).

6. Remove the baffle plate (B, **Figure 15**).

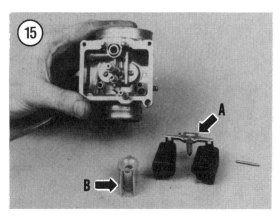

7. Remove the main jet (**Figure 16**) and the slow jet (**Figure 17**).

8. Do not try to remove the jet block from the carburetor.

9. Remove the gasket (**Figure 18**) from the float bowl.

NOTE
Further disassembly is neither necessary nor recommended.

10. Clean all parts, except rubber or plastic parts, in a good grade of carburetor cleaner. This solution is available at most motorcycle or automotive supply stores in a small, resealable tank with a dip basket for just a few dollars. If it is tightly sealed when not in use, the solution will last for several cleanings. Follow the manufacturer's instructions for correct soak time.

11. Remove all parts from the cleaner and blow dry with compressed air. Blow out the jets (**Figure 19**) with compressed air. Do not use a piece of wire to clean them as minor gouges in the jet can alter flow rate and upset the fuel/air mixture. Blow out all passages in the carburetor with compressed air.

12. Be sure to clean out the overflow tube in the float bowl from both ends (**Figure 20**).

13. Inspect the float valve seat in the body (**Figure 21**) and the end of the float valve needle (**Figure 22**) for wear or damage. If either is damaged, replace them as a set.

14. Unscrew the locknut (2, **Figure 23**) and remove the choke/idle adjust knob. Check the valve (3, **Figure 23**) for wear or damage. If any parts are worn, the entire assembly must be replaced. If okay, reassemble and tighten the locknut.

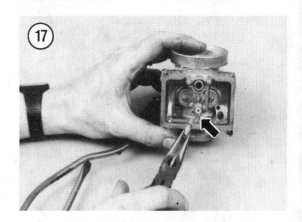

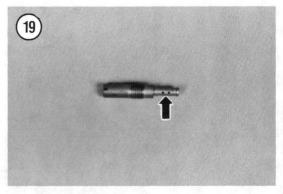

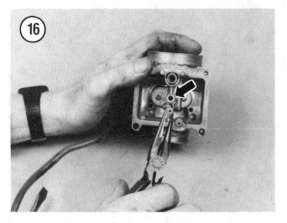

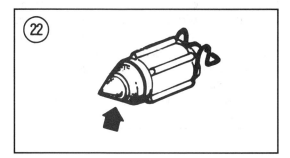

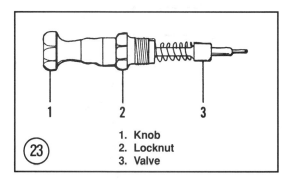

1. Knob
2. Locknut
3. Valve

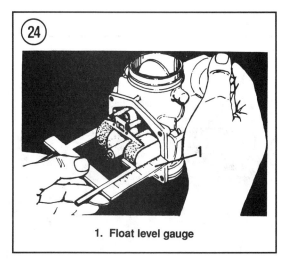

1. Float level gauge

15. Inspect all O-ring seals. O-rings tend to become hardened after prolonged use and heat and therefore lose their ability to seal properly.

16. Assembly is the reverse of these disassembly steps. Note the following.

17. Screw the air screw in the same number of turns as noted during disassembly.

18. Check the float height and adjust, if necessary.

19. After the carburetor has been assembled, it should be adjusted as described in Chapter Three.

CARBURETOR ADJUSTMENTS

Float Adjustment

The carburetor assembly has to be removed and partially disassembled for this adjustment.

1. Remove the carburetor as described in this chapter.

2. Remove the float bowl from the main body.

3. Hold the carburetor so the float arm is just touching the float needle, not pushing it down. Use a float level gauge (**Figure 24**), vernier caliper or small ruler and measure the distance from the carburetor body to the float. The correct height is listed in **Table 1**.

4. Adjust by carefully bending the tang on the float arm (**Figure 25**). If the float level is set too high, the result will be a rich fuel/air mixture. If it is set too low, the mixture will be too lean. Both float chambers must be at the same height.

Jet Needle Adjustment

The position of the jet needle can be adjusted to affect the fuel/air mixture for medium throttle open-

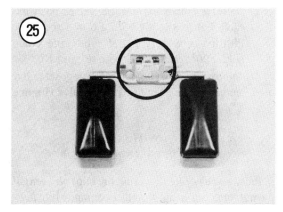

ings (1/4 to 3/4 open). The straight portion of the needle regulates fuel flow at low throttle openings and the tapered portion regulates fuel flow at mid-throttle.

There are 5 grooves in the upper portion of the needle for the needle clip to fit. Refer to **Figure 26**. Raising the needle position (lowering the needle clip) enriches the fuel mixture. Lowering the needle position (raising the needle clip) leans the fuel mixture.

The top of the carburetor must be removed for this adjustment. It is not necessary to remove the carburetor, but removing the fuel tank will make it a lot easier.

1. Place a metal or wood stand under the frame to support the bike securely.

2. Remove the fuel tank as described in this chapter.

NOTE
Before removing the top cap, thoroughly clean the area around it so no dirt will fall into the carburetor.

3. Perform the following:
   a. Turn the handlebars fully to the left to obtain maximum amount of slack in the throttle cable.
   b. Loosen the rubber insulator and air box connecting tube clamps and lean the carburetor to the left (outward).
   c. Unscrew the top cap (**Figure 3**) and pull the throttle valve assembly up and out of the carburetor.
   d. To remove the throttle valve from the throttle cable, compress the throttle valve spring into the top cap and remove the throttle cable from the cable holder in the throttle valve (**Figure 7**).
   e. To disassemble the throttle valve, push the cable holder slightly with a 6 mm socket or Phillips screwdriver and rotate the cable holder 90° counterclockwise (**Figure 8**).
   f. Remove the cable holder, set spring, set collar and jet needle from the throttle valve (**Figure 27**).

NOTE
Record the clip position before removal.

4. Raising the needle (lowering the clip) will enrich the mixture during mid-throttle opening, while low-

ering the needle (raising the clip) will lean the mixture. Refer to **Figure 28**.

5. Refer to **Table 1** for standard clip position.

6. Reassemble and install the top cap.

7. When installing the throttle valve into the carburetor, position the cut-out in the throttle slide so that it is facing the air box assembly.

High-elevation and Temperature Adjustment

High-elevation and ambient temperature adjustment consists of 3 different changes to the carburetor: main jet size change, a different location of the clip on the jet needle and a different air screw setting.

If the bike is going to be ridden for any sustained period at high elevations (above 1,500 m/5,000 ft.), the main jet should be changed to a one-step smaller jet. Never change the jet by more than one size at a time without test riding the bike and running a spark

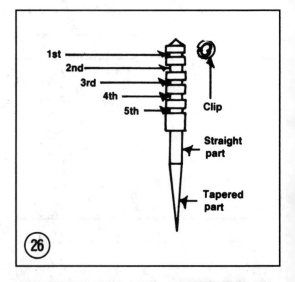

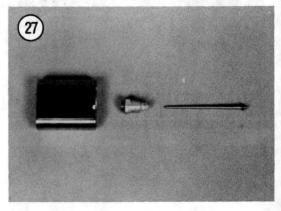

plug test. Refer to *Reading Spark Plugs* in Chapter Three.

CAUTION
If the carburetor has been adjusted for high-elevation operation (smaller jet, needle jet clip location and air jet setting), it must be changed back to standard settings when ridden at elevations below 1,500 m (5,000 ft.). Engine overheating and piston seizure will occur if the engine runs too lean with the smaller jet, changed needle jet clip location and different air screw setting.

1. Remove the carburetor as described in this chapter.

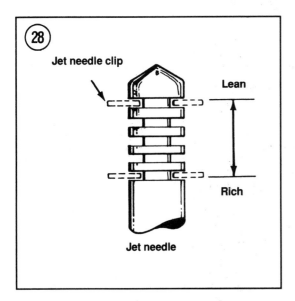

Jet needle clip

Lean

Rich

Jet needle

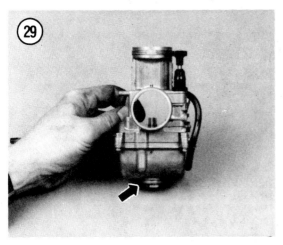

2. Unscrew the main jet cover on the float bowl (**Figure 29**).
3. Unscrew the main jet (**Figure 30**) and replace it with the factory recommended size as indicated in **Table 2**.
4. Install the main jet cover onto the float bowl and tighten securely.
5. Perform the following:
   a. Unscrew the top cap and pull the throttle valve assembly up and out of the carburetor (**Figure 3**).
   b. To remove the throttle valve from the throttle cable, compress the throttle valve spring into the top cap and slide the throttle cable from the groove in the cable holder (**Figure 7**).
   c. To disassemble the throttle valve, push the cable holder slightly with a 6 mm socket or Phillips screwdriver and rotate the cable holder 90° counterclockwise (**Figure 8**).
   d. Remove the cable holder, set spring, set collar and jet needle from the throttle valve slide (**Figure 27**).
6. Remove the clip from the jet needle. The standard position is listed in **Table 1**.
7. Reposition the clip according to the specifications listed in **Table 2**.
8. Reassemble the throttle valve assembly and install it into the carburetor.
9. Install the carburetor assembly as described in this chapter.
10. The air screw opening should be changed according to the factory information listed in **Table 2**.
11. Start the engine and adjust the idle speed as described in Chapter Three.
12. Test ride the bike and perform a spark plug test; refer to *Reading Spark Plugs* in Chapter Three.

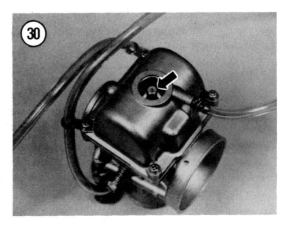

OPTIONAL HONDA CARBURETOR
COMPONENTS

Honda offers many factory components for the various Honda CR carburetors. These components allow you to tune the carburetor for any specific race track, elevation, humidity condition, etc.

Included are various main jet sizes, different jet needle sizes and profiles, throttle valve cutaways with different dimensions and throttle valve springs with different spring rates.

Due to the multitude of combinations available with the different components, consult a tuning specialist or knowledgeable Honda dealer as to which combination of components best suits your specific condition or problem.

Remember, when tuning a carburetor there is always the possibility of running with a too-lean mixture which could lead to costly engine damage. Always change main jets and other components one size at a time to help avoid this problem. After changing any one component on the carburetor, test ride the bike and perform a spark plug test as described in Chapter Three.

THROTTLE CABLE

Removal/Installation

1. Place the bike on a metal or wood stand that will support it securely.

2. Remove the fuel tank and seat as described in this chapter. Fuel tank and seat removal is not absolutely necessary, but it does make the following procedure easier.

NOTE
Before removing the top cap, thoroughly clean the area around it so no dirt will fall into the carburetor.

3. Perform the following:

   a. Unscrew the top cap and pull the throttle valve assembly up and out of the carburetor (**Figure 3**).

   b. To remove the throttle valve from the throttle cable, compress the throttle valve spring into the top cap and slide the throttle cable out from the groove in the cable holder (**Figure 7**). Remove the spring and cap from the cable.

NOTE
Place a clean shop rag over the top of the carburetor to keep any foreign matter from falling into the throttle slide area.

4. At the handlebar, loosen the locknut on the throttle grip and turn the adjuster (**Figure 31**) all the way in to allow slack in the cable.

5. Remove the 2 screws (**Figure 32**) securing the throttle and separate the 2 halves of the assembly. Remove the assembly from the handlebar.

6. Remove the throttle cable end from the throttle grip.

7. Remove the bolt securing the front number plate and remove the strap hook that secures the plate to the handlebars.

8. Tie a piece of heavy string or cord (approximately 2-3 m/6-8 ft. long) to the carburetor end of the throttle cable. Wrap this end with tape to prevent snagging. Tie the other end of the string to the frame.

9. At the throttle lever end of the cable, carefully pull the cable and attached string out through any loops

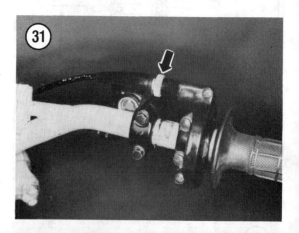

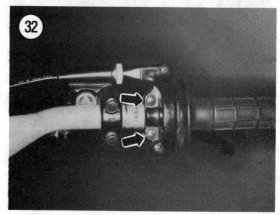

on the frame. Make sure the attached string follows the same path as the cable through the frame and behind the number plate.

10. Remove the tape and untie the string from the old cable.

11. Lubricate the new cable as described in Chapter Three.

12. Tie the string to the new throttle cable and wrap it with tape.

13. Carefully pull the string back through the frame, routing the new cable through the same path as the old cable.

14. Remove the tape and untie the string from the cable and the frame.

15. Attach the cable to the throttle housing and install the throttle housing. Tighten the screws securely.

16. Install the cable through the carburetor top cap and slide the throttle spring into place. Slide the cable end into the groove in the cable holder.

17. Install the slide into the carburetor with the cutaway positioned toward the air box.

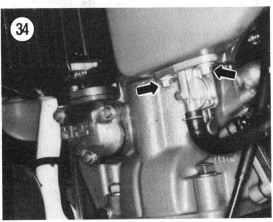

18. Check the throttle for smooth operation. Turn the front forks from full left to full right and make sure the throttle closes automatically from all steering positions.

19. Adjust the throttle cable at both the carburetor top cap and throttle grip as described in Chapter Three.

FUEL SHUTOFF VALVE AND FILTER

Removal/Installation

The integral fuel filter in the fuel shutoff valve removes particles in the fuel which might otherwise enter the carburetor. This could cause the float needle to stay in the open position or clog one of the jets.

1. Turn the fuel shutoff valve (facing engine) to the "OFF" position (A, **Figure 33**) and remove the fuel line from the valve (B, **Figure 33**).

> *NOTE*
> *The fuel tank can either be removed or left in place. Drain all fuel from it in either case.*

2. Install a longer piece of clean fuel line to the valve and place the loose end into a clean, sealable metal container. If the fuel is kept clean, it can be reused.

3. Turn the fuel shutoff valve to the "ON" position and open the fuel filler cap. This will speed up the flow of fuel. Drain the tank completely.

4. Remove the screws (**Figure 34**) securing the fuel shutoff valve to the fuel tank. Remove the small collars that surround the screws and remove the valve.

5. After removing the valve, insert a corner of a clean shop rag into the opening in the tank to stop the dribbling of fuel onto the engine and frame.

6. Remove the fuel filter from the shutoff valve. Clean it with a medium soft toothbrush and blow out with compressed air; replace if defective.

7. Install by reversing these removal steps while noting the following.

8. Be sure to install the O-ring seal onto the filter.

9. Do not forget to install the small collars that surround the screws.

10. Check for fuel leakage after installation is complete.

FUEL TANK

Removal/Installation

1. Place a metal or wood stand under the frame to support the bike securely.

2. Remove the seat by removing the bolts on the left and right side at the top of the rear side covers (**Figure 35**).

3. Turn the fuel shutoff valve to the "OFF" position (A, **Figure 33**) and remove the fuel line to the carburetor (B, **Figure 33**).

> *NOTE*
> *It is possible to remove the fuel tank with or without the front side covers attached to it.*

4. If you would prefer to remove the fuel tank and front side covers as one assembly, perform the following:

    a. Remove the bolt and washer on the lower front section of the front side covers (**Figure 36**). This bolt secures the side cover to the side of the radiator.

    b. At the upper opening in each of the side covers, locate the bolt (**Figure 37**) that secures the fuel tank to the motorcycle frame. Remove the bolt and washer from both the left and right side.

    c. Unhook the rubber retaining strap at the rear of the tank (**Figure 38**).

5. To remove the side covers prior to removing the fuel tank, perform the following:

    a. Remove the upper (**Figure 39**) and lower bolts and washers securing the side covers to the fuel tank.

    b. Remove the bolts and washers on the lower front section of the front side cover (**Figure 36**). These bolts secure the side covers to the side of the radiator.

    c. Remove the side covers.

    d. Remove the bolt and washer securing the fuel tank to the frame (**Figure 40**).

    e. Unhook the rubber retaining strap (**Figure 38**) at the rear of the tank.

6. Remove the vent line from the receptacle in the steering head.

7. Pull the tank up and toward the rear and remove the tank.

8. Inspect the rubber cushions on the frame where the fuel tank is held in place. Replace as a set if either is damaged or starting to deteriorate.

9. Install by reversing these removal steps.

FUEL TANK REPAIR

Sealing (Pin-hole Size)

A pin-hole size leak can be sealed with the use of a product called Theroxite Gas Tank Sealer Stick or equivalent. Follow the manufacturer's instructions.

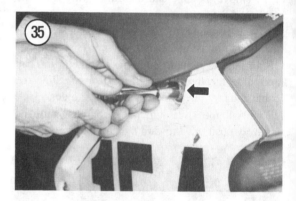

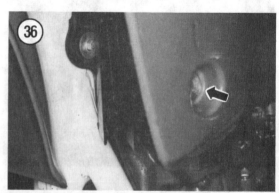

Sealing (Small-hole Size)

This procedure requires the use of a non-petroleum, non-flammable solvent.

If you feel unqualified to do it, take the tank to a dealer and have the tank sealed.

WARNING
Before attempting any service on the fuel tank, be sure to have a fire extinguisher rated for gasoline or chemical fires within reach. Do not smoke or allow anyone to smoke or work where there are any open flames (i.e., water heater or clothes drier gas pilot). The work area must be well ventilated.

1. Remove the fuel tank as described in this chapter.

2. Mark the spot on the tank where the leak is visible with a grease pencil.

3. Remove the fuel filler cap and turn the fuel shutoff valve to "ON". Use compressed air and direct the air nozzle into the fuel filler neck. Blow the interior of the tank dry.

4. Turn the fuel shutoff valve "OFF" and pour about 1 quart (1 liter) of non-petroleum solvent into the tank; install the fuel filler cap and shake the tank vigorously 1 or 2 minutes. This is to remove all residue.

5. Drain the non-petroleum based solution into a safe storable container. This solution may be reused. Let the tank air out overnight before using the sealant.

6. Remove the fuel shutoff valve from the tank. If necessary, plug the tank opening with a cork or tape it closed with duct tape. Thoroughly clean the surrounding area with ignition contact cleaner so the tape will hold securely.

7. Again blow the tank interior completely dry with compressed air.

8. The following step is best done outdoors as the fumes are very strong and flammable. Pour a sealant (formulated for plastic tanks) into the tank (a silicone rubber base sealer such as Pro-Tech, Kreem Super Sealer or equivalent). These are available at most motorcycle supply stores.

9. Position the tank so that the point of the leak is at the lowest part of the tank. This will allow the sealant to accumulate at the point of the leak.

10. Let the tank sit in this position for at least 48 hours.

11. After the sealant has dried, install the fuel shutoff valve, turn it to "OFF" and refill the tank with fuel.

12. After the tank has been filled, let it sit for at least 2 hours and recheck the leak area.

13. Install the tank.

FUEL FILTER

The bike is fitted with a small fuel filter screen in the shutoff valve. Considering the dirt and residue that is often found in today's gasoline, it is a good

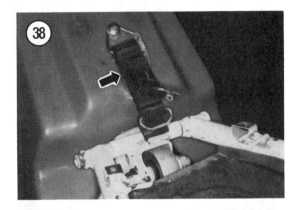

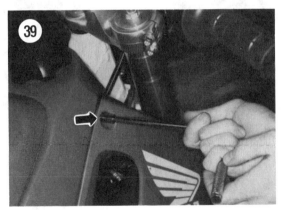

idea to install an inline fuel filter to help keep the carburetor clean.

Your local Honda dealer should be able to suggest a good quality inline fuel filter. Just cut the flexible fuel line from the fuel tank to the carburetor and install the filter. Cut out a section of the fuel line the length of the filter so the fuel line does not kink and restrict fuel flow.

EXHAUST SYSTEM

Removal/Installation

1. Place a metal or wood stand under the frame to support the bike securely.
2. Remove the seat by removing the upper rear side cover bolts on each side.
3. Remove the right rear side cover.
4. Perform the following:
   a. Remove the 2 bolts (**Figure 41**) securing the muffler to the frame. Remove the muffler by pulling toward the rear and separating from the expansion chamber.
   b. Remove the 2 springs securing the expansion chamber to the cylinder using needle-nose pliers or Vise-grip pliers.

On 1988 models, both springs hook over the top of the expansion chamber. On 1989 and later models, there is an upper and lower spring (**Figure 42**).

5. Remove the bolt (**Figure 43**) securing the expansion chamber to the mid-section of the frame.
6. Remove the bolt securing the expansion chamber to the lower front of the frame (**Figure 44**).
7. Remove the expansion chamber and gasket.
8. Inspect the entire exhaust system for damage and repair, if necessary, as described in this chapter.
9. Inspect the rubber isolated mounting brackets; replace any that are starting to deteriorate.
10. Inspect the expansion chamber springs for damage or weakness, replace if necessary.
11. Make sure the cylinder exhaust port sealing flange (**Figure 45**) is in place and in good condition.
12. Install the exhaust system by reversing these removal steps while noting the following.

> *WARNING*
> *Be careful not to hurt your fingers or hands while installing the springs from the cylinder to the expansion chamber. Be sure to use Vise-grip pliers or another suitable tool (**Figure 46**). Do **not***

try to install the springs with a screwdriver and your fingers.

13. Make sure the rubber seal between the expansion chamber and the muffler is in good condition and sealing correctly.
14. Tighten all bolts securely.
15. After installation is complete, start the engine and make sure there are no exhaust leaks.

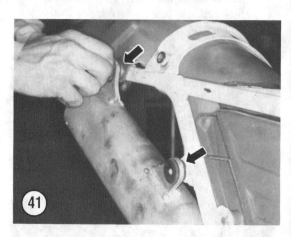
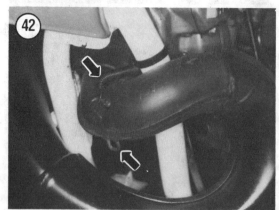

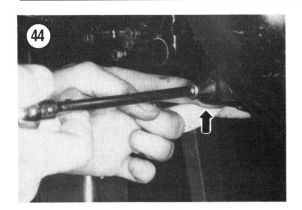

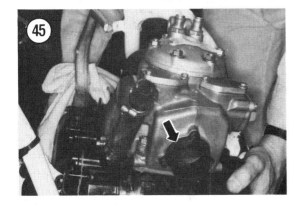

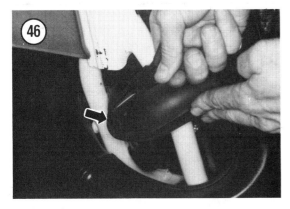

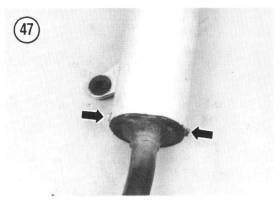

Small Dent Repair

Even small dents in the expansion chamber can alter system flow characteristics enough to degrade performance. Minor damage can be easily repaired if you have welding equipment, some simple body tools and a body shop slide hammer.

1. Remove the expansion chamber as described in this chapter.

2. Drill a small hole in the center of the dent.

3. Screw the end of the slide hammer into the hole.

4. Heat the area around the dent with an acetylene torch. When the dent is heated to a uniform orange-red color, operate the slide hammer to raise the dent.

5. When the dent is removed, unscrew the slide hammer and weld or braze the drilled hole closed.

Large Dent Repair

Large dents that are not crimped can be removed with heat and a slide hammer as described under *Small Dent Repair* in this chapter. However, several holes must be drilled along the center of the dent so that it can be pulled out evenly.

If the dent is sharply crimped along the edges, the damaged section must be removed and repaired.

1. Before cutting out the damaged section, scribe alignment marks over the area where the cuts will be made. This will aid when reassembling the section back into the main body.

2. Use a hacksaw and cut out the damaged section.

3. Straighten the section with a body dolly and hammer.

4. Weld the section back into place.

5. After the welding is completed, wire brush and clean up all welds. Paint the entire exhaust chamber with a high-temperature paint to prevent it from rusting.

Repacking The Muffler

On both CR250R and CR500R motorcycles, the glass wool in the silencer can be replaced.

1. Remove the muffler mounting bolts and slide the rubber seal between the muffler and expansion chamber to one side.

2. Remove the muffler (**Figure 41**).

3. Remove the silencer case bolts (**Figure 47**).

4. Hold the end of the silencer case in a vise using a cloth or rag to avoid damaging or denting the case.

5. Pull the muffler apart as shown in **Figure 48**.

6. Pull the glass wool packing off the inner pipe.

7. Using a wire brush, clean the carbon deposits from the inner pipe.

8. Install the new glass wool packing onto the inner pipe. Use muffler sealant (available from a dealer) and apply it to the 2 points shown in **Figure 49**.

9. Slide the inner pipe assembly into the silencer case and secure the case with the bolts (**Figure 47**).

10. Wipe off any excess sealant.

11. Connect the muffler and expansion chamber by bringing the rubber seals together and install the muffler mounting bolts.

HPP SYSTEM (CR250R)

The HPP (Honda Power Port) system used on the CR250R is an extension of the race track experience gained with the ATAC system used on prior models.

The HPP system broadens the engine's power band throughout the rpm range without sacrificing peak power. This system varies the height of the exhaust port with 2 sliding valves at the top of the exhaust port. The exhaust port timing is changed as engine speed increases or decreases. At low engine rpm, the exhaust valves are closed and as engine speed increases, the exhaust valves begin to open until they are completely open at high engine rpm. This allows the engine to produce maximum efficiency and power.

As engine speed increases, steel balls within the governor move out from centrifugal force. As the balls move out so does the face of the governor, which opens the exhaust valves within the exhaust port. When engine speed decreases, the exhaust valves begin to close. The overall effect provides the best exhaust valve timing for power and torque throughout the rpm range rather than just at one extreme.

Exhaust Valve Decarbonizing

CAUTION
The exhaust valve system consists of a considerable number of precision parts. Before beginning decarbonizing, study the illustrations and procedures carefully. Mismatching or improper assembly will affect engine performance and may lead to expensive engine damage.

The exhaust valve should be decarbonized after every race or after every 2 1/2 hours of operation, whichever comes first.

To prevent intermixing parts, work on one exhaust valve at a time. This also permits you to use the assembled valve as a reference if you get confused during reassembly of the other.

NOTE
The cylinder is shown removed in some of the following steps for clarity only. It is not necessary to remove the cylinder when performing these procedures.

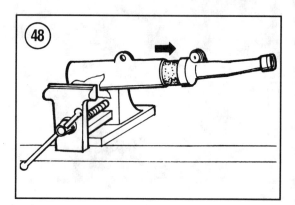

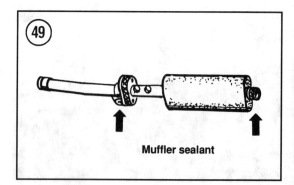

Muffler sealant

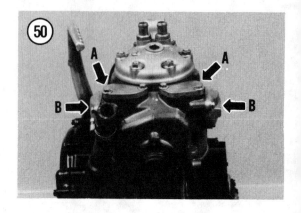

1. Remove the expansion chamber as described in this chapter.

2. Remove the bolts securing the upper cover (A, **Figure 50**) and side cover (B, **Figure 50**). Remove both covers and gaskets.

3. Remove the adjuster bolt locknut (9, **Figure 51**), valve lever locknut (6, **Figure 51**) and adjuster lever collar (5, **Figure 51**).

4. Pull the pinion shaft (3, **Figure 51**) up and out of the cylinder and remove the adjuster lever (4, **Figure 51**), valve lever (7, **Figure 51**) and valve lever washer (8, **Figure 51**).

5. Withdraw the exhaust valve (11, **Figure 51**) from the valve guide (14, **Figure 51**).

6. Remove the bolt and washer (**Figure 52**) securing the valve guide and remove the valve guide (14, **Figure 51**) from the cylinder.

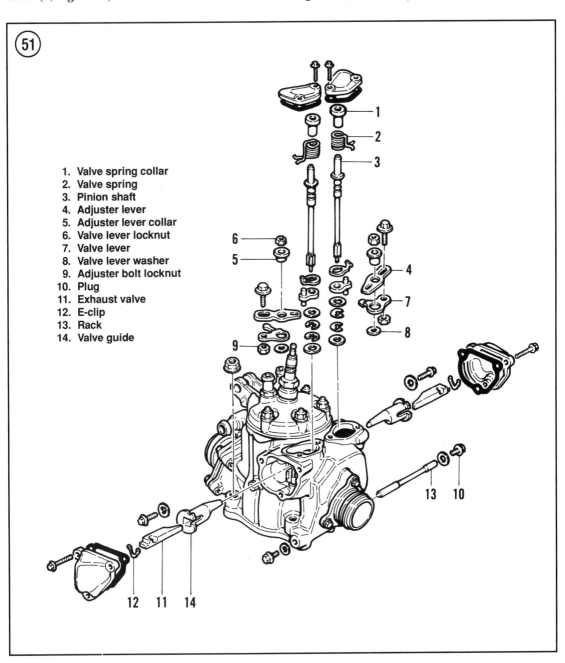

(51)

1. Valve spring collar
2. Valve spring
3. Pinion shaft
4. Adjuster lever
5. Adjuster lever collar
6. Valve lever locknut
7. Valve lever
8. Valve lever washer
9. Adjuster bolt locknut
10. Plug
11. Exhaust valve
12. E-clip
13. Rack
14. Valve guide

6

7. Following removal of components, inspect the cylinder and the threaded stud for damage or wear (**Figure 53**).

8. Clean all carbon deposits from the exhaust valve and guide (**Figure 54**). Thoroughly clean with solvent and dry with compressed air.

9. Inspect the exhaust valve and guide (**Figure 55**) for wear or damage. Check for any abrasion marks on the sliding surfaces of both parts. The exhaust valve must slide smoothly within the guide. Replace both parts as a set, if necessary.

10. If removed, install the E-clip (**Figure 56**) onto the exhaust valve.

11. Install the valve guide by aligning the cutout in the valve guide with the locating pin (**Figure 57**) in the cylinder.

12. Insert the exhaust valve (11, **Figure 51**) (with groove facing up) into the valve guide until the E-clip touches the valve guide surface (A, **Figure 58**).

13. Install the washer and tighten the valve guide stopper bolt (B, **Figure 58**) securely.

14. Make sure the valve lever washer (8, **Figure 51**) is in place on the valve lever threaded stud bolt (**Figure 59**).

15. Perform the following:

a. Install the valve lever (7, **Figure 51**) and align the groove in the valve with the boss on the valve lever (**Figure 60**). On some models, the valve lever is marked with a "L" or "R." Install the valve lever with the mark facing *down.*

b. Install the adjuster lever (4, **Figure 51**) onto the stud bolt, above the valve lever (7, **Figure 51**). On some models, the adjuster lever is marked with a "L" or "R." Install the adjuster lever with the mark facing *up.* Install the adjuster lever collar (5, **Figure 51**) through the adjuster lever and valve lever, then install the locknut (6, **Figure 51**), but don't tighten the locknut yet.

c. Vertically align the adjust bolt holes on the valve lever and adjuster lever, but don't install the adjust bolt yet.

d. Push the valve into the valve guide until the E-clip is touching the valve guide surface (valve fully closed) and install the pinion shaft (3, **Figure 51**). The pinion shaft cam lug should slide into the oval slot on the adjuster lever.

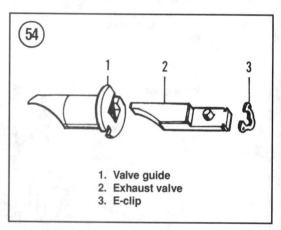

1. Valve guide
2. Exhaust valve
3. E-clip

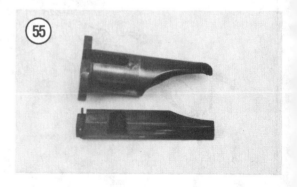

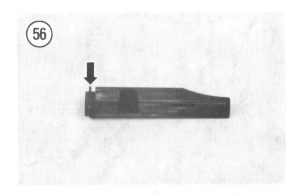

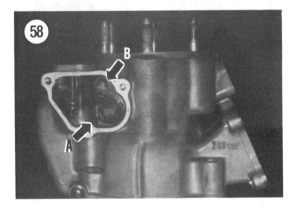

16. Install the adjust bolt and locknut (9, **Figure 51**). Tighten to 5-7 N•m (4-5 ft.-lb.).

17. Repeat Steps 2-16 for the other exhaust valve.

18. Adjust the valves as described in this chapter.

19. Install a new gasket on each cover and install all covers. Tighten the bolts to 10-14 N•m (7-10 ft.-lb.).

20. Install the expansion chamber as described in this chapter.

Exhaust Valve Linkage and Rack Removal

Be sure to keep the parts from the right-hand side of the cylinder separated from the parts from the left-hand side of the cylinder. Place the parts in different boxes that are identified as either right- or left-hand side of the cylinder.

Refer to **Figure 51** for this procedure.

1. Remove the cylinder as described in Chapter Four.

2. Remove the upper (A, **Figure 50**) and side (exhaust valve) (B, **Figure 50**) covers. Remove the cover gaskets.

3. Remove the valve lever locknut (6, **Figure 51**) and adjuster bolt locknut (9, **Figure 51**).

4. Remove the collar (5, **Figure 51**), adjuster lever (4, **Figure 51**), valve lever (7, **Figure 51**) and washer (8, **Figure 51**).

5. Withdraw the exhaust valve (11, **Figure 51**) from the valve guide.

6. Remove the bolt and washer (**Figure 52**) securing the valve guide and remove the valve guide (14, **Figure 51**) from the cylinder.

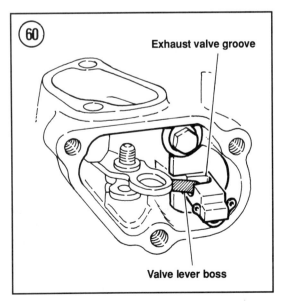

Exhaust valve groove

Valve lever boss

7. Pull the pinion shaft assembly up and out of the cylinder.

8. Remove the rack hole plugs (10, **Figure 51**) and sealing washers from both sides of the cylinder (**Figure 61**).

9. Withdraw the rack from the left-hand side of the cylinder.

Exhaust Valve Linkage and Rack Inspection

1. Inspect the pinion shaft gear (A, **Figure 62**) for wear or damage. If damaged, the pinion shaft must be replaced.

2. Inspect the pinion shaft for straightness (B, **Figure 62**). If bent or warped, replace the pinion shaft.

3. Inspect the locating pin (C, **Figure 62**) on the pinion for wear or damage. If damaged, the pinion shaft must be replaced.

4. Inspect the collar and valve spring (D, **Figure 62**) for wear, damage or spring fatigue; replace if necessary.

5. Inspect the adjuster lever (**Figure 63**) and valve lever (**Figure 64**) for wear or damage; replace if necessary.

6. Inspect the rack for straightness. If bent or warped, replace the rack. Also check the gears on the rack for wear or damage. If damaged, the rack must be replaced.

7. Inspect the exhaust valve and guide (**Figure 65**) for wear or damage. Check for any abrasion marks on the sliding surfaces of both parts. The exhaust valve must slide smoothly within the guide. Replace both parts as a set, if necessary.

Exhaust Valve Linkage and Rack Installation

If both sets of linkage are removed, install the left-hand side first, then the right-hand side. This is necessary to align the rack-to-cylinder-to-pinion shafts properly.

1. Install the right rack hole plug and sealing washer in the cylinder. This is to help locate the rack within the cylinder.

2. Position the rack with the gear teeth facing toward the *rear* on the right-hand side and the gear teeth facing toward the *front* on the left-hand side of the cylinder. Install the rack into the left rack hole plug orientated in this manner. The gear teeth must be straight up and down so that the pinion shaft teeth can mesh properly with the rack gear teeth.

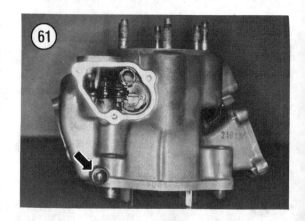

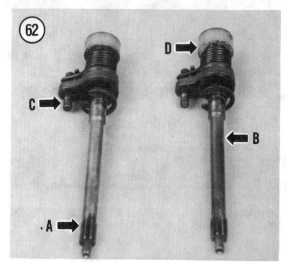

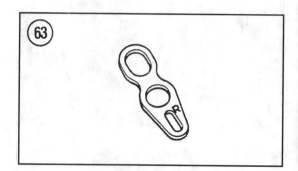

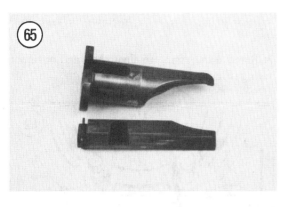

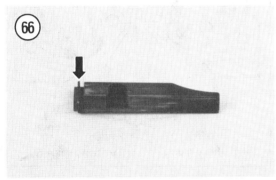

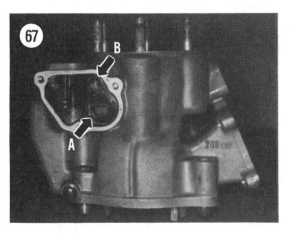

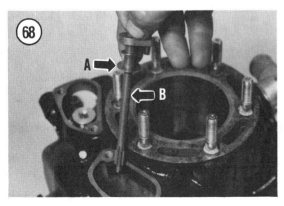

3. Make sure that the pinion shaft assembly is complete (**Figure 62**) and the valve spring, if removed, is installed as shown.

4. If removed, install the E-clip (**Figure 66**) onto the exhaust valve.

5. Install the valve guide by aligning the cutout in the valve guide with the locating pin (**Figure 57**) in the cylinder.

6. Insert the exhaust valve (11, **Figure 51**), with groove facing up, into the valve guide until the E-clip touches the valve guide surface (A, **Figure 67**).

7. Install the washer and tighten the valve guide stopper bolt (B, **Figure 67**) securely.

8. Make sure the valve lever washer is in place on the valve lever threaded stud bolt (**Figure 59**).

9. Perform the following:

   a. Install the valve lever (7, **Figure 51**) and align the groove in the valve with the boss on the valve lever (**Figure 60**). On some models, the valve lever is marked with a "L" or "R." Install the valve lever with the mark facing *down*.

   b. Install the adjuster lever (4, **Figure 51**) onto the stud bolt, above the valve lever (7, **Figure 51**). On some models, the adjuster lever is marked with a "L" or "R." Install the adjuster lever with the mark facing *up*.

   c. Install the adjuster lever collar (5, **Figure 51**) through the adjuster lever and valve lever, then install the locknut (6, **Figure 51**), but don't tighten the locknut yet.

   d. Vertically align the adjuster bolt holes with the holes in the valve lever, but don't install the adjuster bolt yet.

   e. Make sure the washer is installed on the pinion shaft (A, **Figure 68**) and the lug on the pinion shaft cam is facing toward the rear of the cylinder prior to performing sub-step f.

   f. Push the valve into the valve guide until the E-clip is touching the valve guide surface (valve fully closed) and install the pinion shaft (B, **Figure 68**). The pinion shaft cam lug should slide into the oval slot on the adjuster lever.

10. Tighten the valve lever and adjuster locknuts to 5-7 N•m (4-5 ft.-lb.).

11. Install a sealing washer on the left rack hole plug and install the plug. Tighten the plug to the torque specifications in **Table 3**.

12. Repeat Steps 2-10 for the other exhaust valve while noting the following. When the right-hand pinion shaft (A, **Figure 69**) is installed, it must be symmetrical (mirror image) to the left-hand pinion shaft (B, **Figure 70**). They must be aligned as shown so both exhaust valves will operate at the same time and at the same amount of movement.

13. Install the cylinder as described in Chapter Four.

14. Adjust the exhaust valves as described in this chapter.

15. Install a new gasket on each cover and install all covers. Tighten the bolts to 10-14 N•m (7-10 ft.-lb.).

Governor Disassembly

Refer to **Figure 70** for this procedure.

1. Remove the right-hand crankcase cover as described in Chapter Five.

2. While pressing down on the spring end of the governor rocker arm, loosen the screws securing the rocker arm (**Figure 71**). An impact driver might be necessary for this procedure as these screws may be extremely tight. Remove the screws and the rocker arm.

3. Remove the spring retainer shaft and governor spring (**Figure 72**).

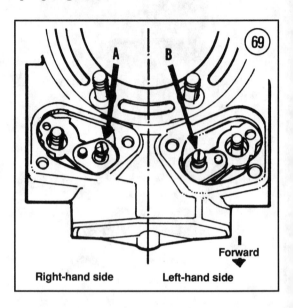

Right-hand side   Left-hand side

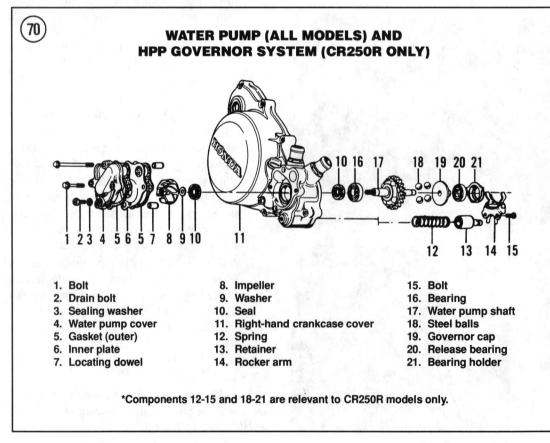

WATER PUMP (ALL MODELS) AND HPP GOVERNOR SYSTEM (CR250R ONLY)

1. Bolt	8. Impeller	15. Bolt
2. Drain bolt	9. Washer	16. Bearing
3. Sealing washer	10. Seal	17. Water pump shaft
4. Water pump cover	11. Right-hand crankcase cover	18. Steel balls
5. Gasket (outer)	12. Spring	19. Governor cap
6. Inner plate	13. Retainer	20. Release bearing
7. Locating dowel	14. Rocker arm	21. Bearing holder

*Components 12-15 and 18-21 are relevant to CR250R models only.

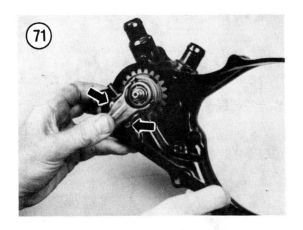

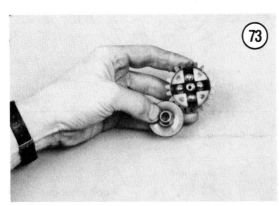

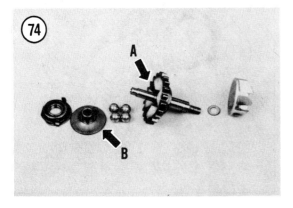

NOTE
For clarification purposes, the water pump shaft and impeller are shown removed from the right crankcase cover. Unless damage to these components is suspected, removal of the impeller and water pump shaft is not necessary for governor inspection.

4. Remove the governor cap and steel balls (**Figure 73**).

Governor Inspection

1. Check the bearing ramps (A, **Figure 74**) on the water pump shaft assembly for wear or gouging. If replacement is necessary, refer to Chapter Eight.

2. Check the inside surface of the governor (B, **Figure 74**) for wear or gouging; replace if necessary.

3. Inspect the spring retainer shaft and the governor spring (**Figure 72**) for wear or damage. Replace as a set if any parts are defective.

Governor Assembly

1. Install the steel balls into the ramps in the water pump shaft assembly (**Figure 73**).

NOTE
Do not apply any type of grease to the steel balls before installing them. They will be lubricated by the transmission/clutch oil.

2. Install the governor cap (B, **Figure 74**) onto the shaft.

3. Install the governor spring and spring retainer shaft (**Figure 72**).

4. Install the rocker arm assembly (**Figure 71**) and align the big end of the rocker arm with the bosses in the governor. Start the screws slowly; be careful not to strip the threads in the crankcase cover.

5. Have an assistant push down on the rocker arm assembly and tighten the screws in 2-3 steps. Tighten the screws to 6-8 N•m (4-6 ft.-lb.).

6. Install the right-hand crankcase cover (clutch cover) as described in Chapter Five.

Exhaust Valve Adjustment

NOTE
The engine and cylinder are shown re-
moved for clarification only.

1. Remove the expansion chamber as described in this chapter.

2. Remove the bolts securing the upper covers (A, **Figure 75**) and the exhaust valve side covers (B, **Figure 75**). Remove both covers and gaskets.

3. Check that the E-clip on the exhaust valve is completely against the surface of the valve guide (**Figure 76**). This means that the valve is closing completely. If this is the case, no adjustment is necessary. If these 2 parts do not touch or there is a gap between them, continue with this procedure.

4. To adjust the valve, perform the following:

    a. Loosen the adjusting bolt locknut (B, **Figure 77**). Then close the right valve fully by turning the adjuster bolt (A, **Figure 77**) *clockwise*. To close the left valve fully, turn the adjuster bolt *counterclockwise*.

    b. While holding the valve fully closed (E-clip against valve guide surface; C, **Figure 77**), tighten the adjusting bolt locknut (B, **Figure 77**) to 5-7 N•m (4-5 ft.-lb.).

5. Repeat Steps 2-4 for the other side of the cylinder.

NOTE
Before proceeding with Step 6, make
sure the E-clips contact the valve guides
(valves fully closed).

6. Using a feeler gauge, check the air gap between the adjuster lever pin (A, **Figure 78**) and the pinion shaft arm spring (B, **Figure 78**). The specified air

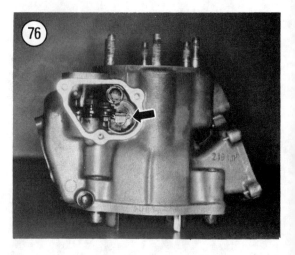

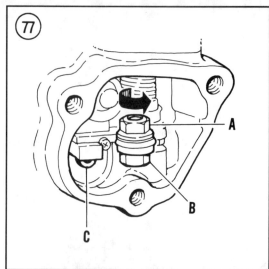

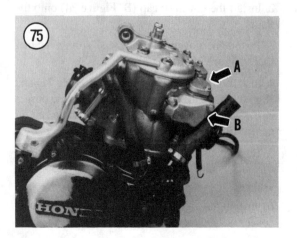

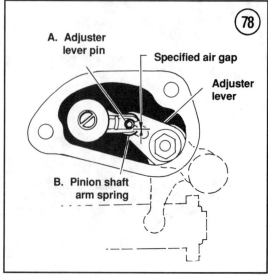

A. Adjuster lever pin

Specified air gap

Adjuster lever

B. Pinion shaft arm spring

gap is 0-0.5 mm (0-0.02 in.). If the gap between the shaft arm spring and adjuster lever pin exceeds 0.5 mm (0.02 in.), the valve mechanism must be disassembled and inspected.

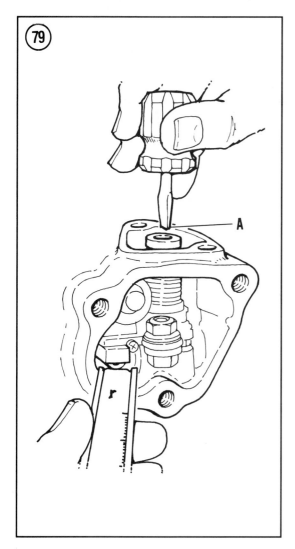

NOTE
Before proceeding with Step 7, make sure the E-clips contact the valve guides (valves fully closed).

7. Using a screwdriver (A, **Figure 79**), insert the blade onto the left-hand pinion shaft, and rotate the left-hand pinion shaft *counterclockwise* until the exhaust valve is completely open. For the right exhaust valve, rotate the right-hand pinion shaft *clockwise* until the exhaust valve is completely open.

8. Measure the distance between the outer surface of the E-clip and valve guide surface (Dimension A, **Figure 80**) on each exhaust valve. The specified distance is 24.5 mm (0.96 in.) minimum. If the valve is not within the specified distance, check for carbon buildup. If carbon buildup is not the problem, the valve actuating mechanism will have to be disassembled and inspected for wear or damage.

9. Tighten the valve adjuster locknut to 5-7 N•m (4-5 ft.-lb.).

10. Install new gaskets and install all 4 covers. Tighten the bolts to 10-14 N•m (7-10 ft.-lb.).

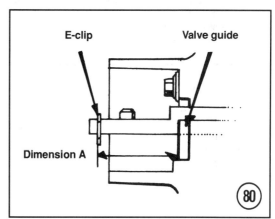

Tables are on the following pages.

Table 1 CARBURETOR SPECIFICATIONS

Item	1988 CR250R	1989 CR250R
Carburetor model No.	PJ26B	PJ26C
Venturi diameter	38.0 mm (1.50 in.)	38.0 mm (1.50 in.)
Float level	16.0 mm (0.63 in.)	16.0 mm (0.63 in.)
Air screw opening	2 turns out	2 turns out
Standard jet needle No.	R1367N	R1369PS
Needle clip position	4th groove	4th groove
Standard main jet No.	185	178
Standard slow jet No.	62	58
Item	**1990 CR250R**	**1991 CR250R**
Carburetor model No.	PJ28A	PJ28C
Venturi diameter	38.0 mm (1.50 in.)	38.0 mm (1.50 in.)
Float level	16.0 mm (0.63 in.)	16.0 mm (0.63 in.)
Air screw opening	2 turns out	2 turns out
Standard jet needle No.	R137ONS	R1369NS
Needle clip position	3rd groove	3rd groove
Standard main jet No.	175	175
Standard slow jet No.	55	55
Item	**1988 CR500R**	**1989 CR500R**
Carburetor model No.	PJ27B	PJ27C
Venturi diameter	38 mm (1.50 in.)	38 mm (1.50 in.)
Float level	16 mm (0.63 in.)	16 mm (0.63 in.)
Air screw opening	1 1/2 turns out	2 turns out
Standard jet needle No.	R1370N	R1370NS
Needle clip position	4th groove	3rd groove
Standard main jet No.	175	170
Standard slow jet No.	55	55
Item	**1990 CR500R**	**1991 CR500R**
Carburetor model No.	PJ27E	PJ27H
Venturi diameter	38 mm (1.50 in.)	38 mm (1.50 in.)
Float level	16 mm (0.63 in.)	16 mm (0.63 in.)
Air screw opening	2 turns out	1 1/2 turns out
Standard jet needle No.	R1369NS	R1368NS
Needle clip position	3rd groove	4th groove
Standard main jet No.	170	170
Standard slow jet No.	55	55

Table 2 TEMPERATURE AND ELEVATION CORRECTION SETTINGS

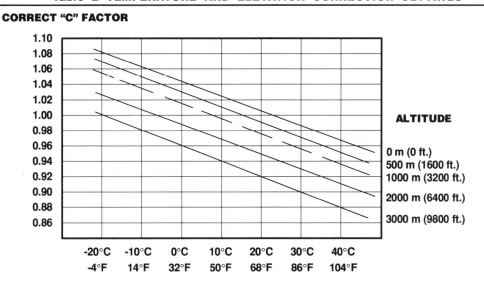

Use the information in this table to determine what carburetor adjustments are necessary for proper engine operation in various areas.

The main chart in the table is divided in 2 directions:

Horizontal—for various ambient temperatures.
Vertical (right-hand side)—various elevations.
Vertical (left-hand side)—for the "C" factor.

Determine the approximate elevation and surrounding air temperature of the area where you are going to race or ride. Locate these 2 factors on the main chart. Where the 2 factors intersect (vertical and horizontal), closest to one of the angled lines, will establish the "C" factor. Use this "C" factor for the following steps:

"C" FACTOR	1.06 or above	1.06-1.02	1.02-0.98	0.98-0.94	0.94 or below
JET NEEDLE	+1	—	—	—	−1
AIR SCREW	−1	−1/2	—	+1/2	+1

To determine main jet size
Multiply the standard main jet number (i.e., 138) by the "C" factor. Use the main jet number closest to the number in the answer.
EXAMPLE: 138 × 0.94 = 129.72. Use main jet number 130.

To determine jet needle clip position
Use the secondary chart. Move the jet needle clip to the next groove as indicated in the chart.
EXAMPLE: 3 − 1 = 2. Move the jet needle clip to the No. 2 position on the jet needle.

To determine air screw position
Use the secondary chart. Turn the air screw in or out as indicated in the chart.
EXAMPLE: 1 1/2 + 1/2 = 2. Turn the air screw out 2 turns from the *lightly seated position.*

Optional Honda factory main jets and needles are available from Honda dealers.

Table 3 HPP SYSTEM TORQUE SPECIFICATIONS

Item	N•m	ft.-lb.
Rack hole plug	8-12	6-8
Rack adjusting bolt locknut	5-7	4-5

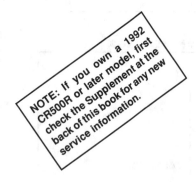

NOTE: If you own a 1992 CR500R or later model, first check the Supplement at the back of this book for any new service information.

CHAPTER SEVEN

ELECTRICAL SYSTEM

The electrical system consists of an ignition system and the alternator which powers it. The capacitor discharge ignition system (CDI) is a sealed component that regulates timing advance, timing retard and other ignition circuits. Although the ignition timing is essentially non-adjustable, replacement of certain electrical components will dictate that an initial timing setting be made. See Chapter Three for spark plug service. **Table 1** and **Table 2** at the end of the chapter provide electrical and tightening torque specifications respectively. Wiring diagrams are at the end of the book.

ALTERNATOR

An alternator is a form of electrical generator in which a magnetized field (called a rotor) revolves within or around a set of stationary coils (called a stator). As the rotor revolves, alternating current is induced in the stator. The current is then rectified to direct current and used to operate the ignition system. The rotor on all models is permanently magnetized.

If the alternator rotor or stator assembly are tested and found to be faulty, they must be replaced. Ignition timing depends on these 2 components; if they are replaced as a matched set the ignition timing will automatically be correct. On all models, if only the rotor or stator assembly is replaced, the ignition timing must be reset as described in this chapter.

> *NOTE*
> *The engine is shown removed in some of the following procedures for clarity only.*

Rotor Removal/Installation

Refer to **Figure 1**.

All models covered in this manual use the outer rotor type of alternator.

1. Place a metal or wood stand under the frame to support the bike securely.

2. Remove the seat.

3. If you know you will want to remove the alternator wiring or stator assembly for service, remove the fuel tank as described under *Fuel Tank Removal/Installation* in Chapter Six.

4. Remove the bolts securing the alternator cover and remove the cover and the gasket (**Figure 2**).

5. Remove the nut and washer securing the rotor (**Figure 3**).

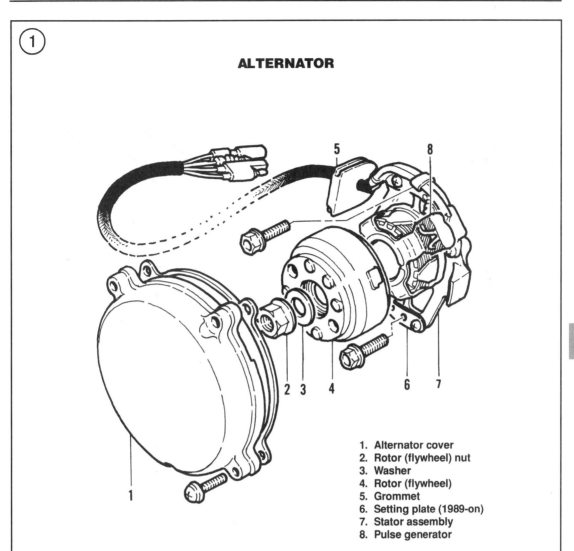

ALTERNATOR

1. Alternator cover
2. Rotor (flywheel) nut
3. Washer
4. Rotor (flywheel)
5. Grommet
6. Setting plate (1989-on)
7. Stator assembly
8. Pulse generator

7

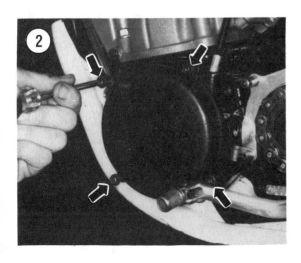

NOTE
*If necessary, use a universal holder (**Figure 4**) to keep the rotor from turning while removing the nut. Or simply shift the transmission into fifth gear and hold the rear brake on.*

6. At this time, you will need a rotor (flywheel) puller. Use the Honda rotor puller part No. 07733-0010000, 07933-0010000, K & N rotor puller part No. 82-015 or equivalent. Screw the rotor puller onto the threads within the rotor center until it stops (**Figure 5**).

CAUTION
Don't try to remove the rotor without a puller. Any attempt to do so will ultimately lead to some form of damage to the engine and rotor. Many aftermarket pullers are available from motorcycle dealers or mail order houses. If you can't buy or borrow one, have a dealer remove the rotor.

7. Turn the outer bolt on the rotor puller clockwise while holding the puller with a wrench until the rotor is free (**Figure 6**).

NOTE
If the rotor is difficult to remove, strike the puller with a hammer a few times. This will usually break it loose.

CAUTION
If normal rotor removal attempts fail, do not force the puller as the threads may be stripped out of the rotor causing expensive damage. Take the bike to a dealer and have the rotor removed.

8. Remove the rotor from the crankshaft and unscrew the puller from the rotor.

CAUTION
*Carefully inspect the inside of the rotor (**Figure 7**) for small bolts, washers or other metal "trash" that may have been picked up by the magnets. These small metal bits can cause severe damage to the alternator stator assembly.*

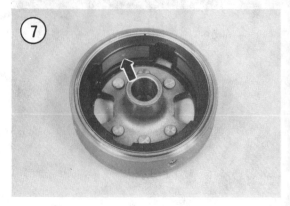

9. Install by reversing these removal steps while noting the following.
10. Make sure the Woodruff key (**Figure 8**) is in place on the crankshaft.

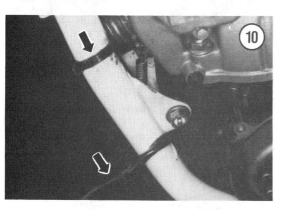

11. Install the washer and tighten the rotor nut to the torque specification listed in **Table 2**.

Rotor Testing

The rotor is permanently magnetized and cannot be tested except by replacement with a rotor known to be good. A rotor can lose magnetism from old age or a sharp blow. If defective, the rotor must be replaced; it cannot be remagnetized.

On all models, if only the rotor is replaced the ignition timing must be reset as described in this chapter. If the rotor, stator assembly and CDI unit are replaced as a matched set, the ignition timing does not have to be reset.

Stator Assembly Removal/Installation

1. Remove the alternator rotor as described in this chapter.
2. Remove the fuel tank as described in Chapter Six, if not previously removed.
3. Disconnect the alternator wires from the CDI unit. On 1988 CR250R models, the wiring consists of a two-pin plug and 3 free connectors. On all other CR250R and CR500R models, the wiring consists of a two-pin plug and 2 free connectors (**Figure 9**).
4. Loosen or remove the plastic clamp securing the electrical harness to the lower front section of the frame and carefully pull the harness free (**Figure 10**). Note the path of the harness, so it can be routed up the frame in the same way.
5. Remove the mounting bolts (**Figure 11**) securing the alternator stator assembly to the crankcase.
6. Carefully pull the rubber grommet and electrical wire harness (A, **Figure 12**) from the crankcase and remove the stator assembly (B, **Figure 12**). Note the

path of the wire harness as it must be routed in the same way during installation.

7. Install by reversing these removal steps while noting the following.

8. Make sure that the electrical wire harness is routed through the frame exactly as before.

9. Connect the alternator wiring to the CDI unit.

10. When installing the stator base assembly, align the index mark on the stator base (or lower stator plate) with the stationary mark on the left crankcase as shown in **Figure 13**. This must be done to maintain proper ignition timing.

11. On 1988 CR500R models, the pulse generator has an adjustable mounting on the stator assembly (**Figure 14**). If the mounting was loosened or removed, the air gap between the retractor and pulse generator must be adjusted following installation of the rotor. Using a feeler gauge as shown in **Figure 15**, adjust the air gap to 0.7 mm (0.03 in.), then tighten the pulse generator mounting screws to 2 N•m (17 in.-lb.).

Stator Assembly Testing

1. Remove the seat and the fuel tank, if not previously removed.

2. Disconnect the electrical connector from the CDI unit.

3. Using an ohmmeter, measure between the terminals indicated in **Table 1** and compare the measurements to the specifications.

4. If the readings do not agree, check the electrical wires to and within the terminal connector for any opens or poor connections.

5. If the connections are okay, but the readings still do not match, replace the stator assembly.

> *NOTE*
> *On 1988-on CR500R and 1989-on CR250R models, replace the stator and pulse generator as a set, if either one tests faulty.*

IGNITION SYSTEM

The ignition system consists of an ignition coil, a CDI unit, a pulse generator coil and a spark plug.

> *NOTE*
> *On the 1988 CR250R, the pulse generator coil is treated as an individual unit.*

On all other CR250R and CR500R models, both (pulse generator and stator) should be replaced, even if only one tests faulty.

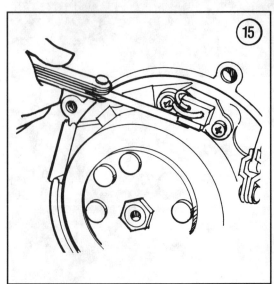

The Honda CR is equipped with a solid state capacitor discharge ignition (CDI) system that uses no breaker points. This system provides a longer life for components and delivers a more efficient spark throughout the entire speed range of the engine.

Direct current charges the capacitor. As the piston approaches the firing position, a pulse from the pulse generator coil triggers the silicone controlled rectifier. The rectifier in turn allows the capacitor to discharge quickly into the primary circuit of the ignition coil, where the voltage is stepped up in the secondary circuit to a value sufficient to fire the spark plug.

Ignition timing is fixed with no means of adjustment. If the alternator stator and rotor are replaced as a matched set, ignition timing is preset. If only one of these parts is replaced, ignition timing must be reset as described in this chapter.

CDI Precautions

Certain measures must be taken to protect the capacitor discharge system. Damage to the semicon-

ductors in the system could occur if the following precautions are not observed.

1. Keep all connections between the various units clean and tight. Be sure that the wiring connections are pushed together firmly to help keep out moisture.
2. Do not substitute another type of ignition coil.
3. Each component is mounted within a rubber vibration isolator. Always be sure that the isolator is in place when installing any units of the system.

CDI Troubleshooting

Problems with the capacitor discharge system are usually the result of a weak spark or no spark at all.
1. Check all connections to make sure they are tight and free of corrosion.
2. Check the ignition coil as described in this chapter.
3. If the ignition coil and ignition pulse generator check out okay, make sure that neither the alternator rotor or the stator assembly has been replaced separately. If replaced separately, the ignition timing must be reset as described in this chapter. If the resetting procedure was followed or if neither part has been replaced (and timing is off) then the CDI unit is at fault and must be replaced.

CDI Unit
Replacement

1. Remove the seat and fuel tank as described in Chapter Six, if not previously removed.
2. Disconnect the electrical connectors going to the CDI unit.
3. Remove the screws securing the CDI unit to the frame and remove the CDI unit from the frame. The CDI mounting location varies with model and year. **Figure 16** shows location of CDI unit on 1988 models. For 1989 and later models, refer to **Figure 17** for CDI location.
4. Install by reversing these removal steps. Make sure all electrical connections are tight and free of corrosion.

CDI Unit
Testing

If the ignition coil, the pulse generator, alternator stator assembly and the wiring harness are good and the ignition timing is not within specifications, replace the CDI unit with a known good unit.

7

PULSE GENERATOR

On the 1988 CR250R, the pulse generator (A, **Figure 18**) is treated as an individual unit. On all other models, it should be considered as part of the alternator stator assembly and should *not* be removed. If either one tests faulty, both (pulse generator and stator assembly) should be removed and replaced.

Replacement (1988 CR250R Models)

1. Remove the seat and fuel tank if not previously removed.

2. Disconnect the two-pin connector that leads to the CDI unit from the pulse generator.

3. Remove the bolts securing the alternator cover (**Figure 2**) and remove the cover and the gasket.

4. Remove the screws (B, **Figure 18**) securing the pulse generator to the stator assembly.

5. Install by reversing these removal steps while noting the following.

6. Make sure all electrical connectors are tight.

Testing (All Models)

In order to get correct test readings, the pulse generator must be warm—at least 20° C (68° F).

1. Remove the seat and fuel tank, if not previously removed.

2. Disconnect the two-pin electrical connector that leads from the pulse generator to the CDI unit. Refer to **Figure 8**.

3. Using an ohmmeter, check resistance between the terminals indicated in **Table 1**. Compare the measurement to the specification. On 1989-on CR250R and all CR500R models, if the ignition pulse generator does not meet this specification, replace the pulse generator and stator assembly together as described in this chapter. It cannot be serviced.

IGNITION COIL

The ignition coil is a transformer which develops the high voltage required to jump the spark plug gap. The only maintenance required is that of keeping the electrical connections clean and tight and occasionally checking to see that the coil is mounted securely.

Removal/Installation

The ignition coil is mounted to the upper frame rail, but minor location variations on the rail exist among the different models.

1. Remove the seat and fuel tank, if not previously removed.

2. Disconnect the spark plug lead (A, **Figure 19**).

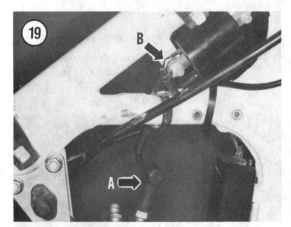

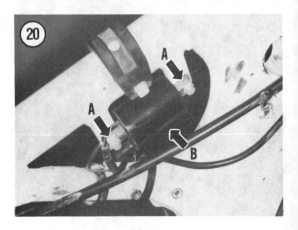

3. Disconnect the primary wire connectors and ground leads (B, **Figure 19**).

4. Remove the bolts(s) securing the ignition coil to the frame (A, **Figure 20**). Remove the ignition coil (B, **Figure 20**).

5. Install by reversing these removal steps. Make sure all electrical connectors are tight and free of corrosion.

Dynamic Test

1. Disconnect the high voltage lead from the spark plug. Remove the spark plug from the cylinder head.

2. Connect a new or known good spark plug to the high voltage lead and place the spark plug base on a good ground such as the engine cylinder head. Have a helper position the spark plug so you can see the electrode.

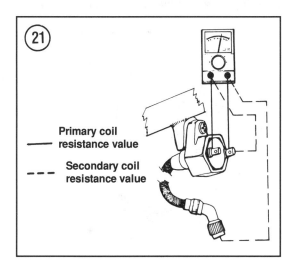

Primary coil resistance value

Secondary coil resistance value

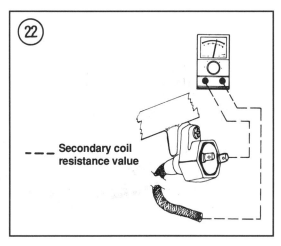

Secondary coil resistance value

WARNING
If it is necessary to hold the high voltage lead in Step 3, do so with an insulated pair of pliers. The high voltage generated could produce serious or fatal shocks.

3. Turn the engine over with the kickstarter a couple of times. If a fat blue spark occurs, the coil is in good condition; if not, it must be replaced. Make sure that you are using a known good spark plug for this test. If the spark plug used is defective, the test results will be incorrect.

4. Reinstall the spark plug in the cylinder head and reconnect the lead.

Continuity Test

1. Remove the seat and fuel tank, if not previously removed.

2. Disconnect the primary and secondary leads from the ignition coil.

3. To test the primary coil, using an ohmmeter set at R × 1, measure between the primary and ground terminals on the ignition coil (**Figure 21**). Compare resistance to **Table 1**.

4. Turn the spark plug cap counterclockwise and disconnect the spark plug cap from the spark plug lead.

5. To test the secondary coil, use an ohmmeter set at R × 1,000 and measure between the spark plug lead and ground terminal on the ignition coil (**Figure 22**). Compare resistance to **Table 1**.

6. If the ignition coil fails to pass any of these tests, it should be replaced.

IGNITION TIMING

The CDI ignition timing for the models covered in this manual is factory preset, and generally requires checking or adjusting only when an electrical system component has been replaced. If either the alternator rotor, stator assembly or pulse generator (on 1988 CR250R) are replaced separately, the ignition timing has to be reset. Setting the ignition timing is accomplished via the alternator rotor and stator assembly.

Timing Adjustment (All Models)

1. Place a metal or wood stand under the frame to support the bike securely.

2. Remove the screws securing the alternator cover and remove the cover and the gasket (**Figure 2**).

3. On 1988 CR500R models, check the air gap between the pulse generator and the retractor as described in Step 11 of *Stator Assembly Removal/Installation* in this chapter. Adjust to specifications before proceeding to Step 4.

NOTE
On 1989 and later models, a setting plate (which can be removed) is mounted to the stator assembly.

4. Refer to **Figure 23**. If the index marks are not aligned, loosen the stator base and align the index mark on the stator base (or setting plate) with the index mark on the crankcase.

5. Connect a portable tachometer and timing light following the manufacturer's instructions.

6. Start and warm up the engine, then hold the throttle so the engine is operated at the following speed:

    a. 1988-on CR250R—5,000 rpm.

    b. 1988-on CR500R—4,000 rpm.

7. Aim the timing light at the rotor and pull the trigger.

8. Have an assistant make a temporary mark on the stator base (or setting plate) that aligns between the "F" marks on the rotor.

9. Shut off the engine.

10. If the stator's (or setting plate's) original mark and the temporary new mark are in the same location, the engine is timed correctly. Remove the portable tachometer and timing light and install all components removed.

11. If the index marks are in 2 different locations, the engine has to be re-timed as described in the following steps.

12. Remove the rotor as described in this chapter and remove the stator assembly.

13. Using a 6.5 mm or size F drill bit, elongate the bolt hole in the stator base (1988 models) or the setting plate (1989-on), so the stator base can be rotated (**Figure 24**).

14. Install the stator assembly and rotor and rotate the stator assembly slightly from the original position to the position where the temporary index mark

will align with the index mark on the crankcase (**Figure 25**).

15. Tighten the stator assembly securely. On 1989 and later models, make sure the setting plate bolt (**Figure 25**) is tightened securely.

16. Start the engine and hold the throttle so the engine is operated at the speed specified in Step 6.

17. Aim the timing light at the rotor and pull the trigger.

18. The new index mark and crankcase index mark should align between the "F" marks on the rotor.

19. Shut off the engine and disconnect the portable tachometer and timing light.

20. Use a scribe to scratch final index marks over the temporary index marks on the stator assembly (or setting plate). These are the new timing marks.

21. Grind off the original index marks on the stator assembly (or setting plate). Refer to **Figure 26**.

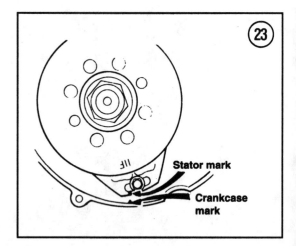

Stator mark

Crankcase mark

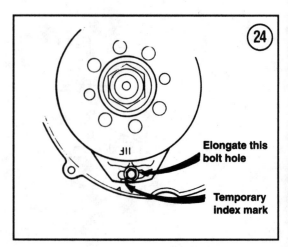

Elongate this bolt hole

Temporary index mark

25

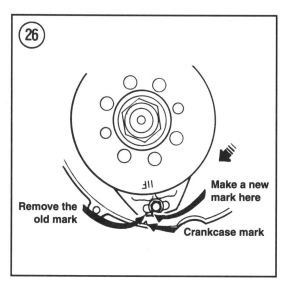

26

Make a new
mark here

Remove the
old mark

Crankcase mark

22. Install the alternator cover and gasket. Tighten the screws securely.

ENGINE KILL SWITCH

Removal/Installation

1. Place a metal or wood stand under the frame to support the bike securely.
2. Remove the seat.
3. Remove the fuel tank as described in Chapter Six.
4. Disconnect the electrical connectors going to the CDI unit from the engine kill switch.
5. Remove the clamping screw and remove engine kill switch from the handlebar.
6. Remove the switch and the electrical wires from the frame.
7. Install by reversing these removal steps.

Testing

1. Check the kill switch connectors with an ohmmeter.
2. With the engine kill switch button depressed, the ohmmeter should read continuity.
3. With the engine kill button released, the ohmmeter should read infinity.
4. Replace the kill switch if the readings indicate it is faulty.

7

Tables are on the following page.

Table 1 ELECTRICAL SPECIFICATIONS

Item	Resistance (ohms)*
Alternator stator	
CR250R	
1988	
Brown-white	360-440
Brown-blue	90-130
1989-1991	
Blue-white	40-140
CR500R	
Blue-white	1-40
Pulse generator	
CR250	
1988	
Blue/yellow-Green/white	94-120
1989	
Blue/yellow-Green/white	50-180
1990-1991	
Blue/yellow-Green/white	180-280
CR500R	
1988-1989	
Blue/yellow-Green/white	50-180
1990-1991	
Blue/yellow-Green/white	180-280
Ignition coil	
Primary coil	0.4-0.6
Secondary coil (without plug cap)	10-16K
Secondary coil (with plug cap)	
CR250R	14-23K
CR500R	
1988-1989	13-23K
1990-1991	14-23K
*All values at 20° C (68° F)	

Table 2 ALTERNATOR ASSEMBLY TORQUE SPECIFICATIONS

Item	N•m	ft.-lb.
Rotor nut	50-60	36-43
Alternator cover screws	3-5	2-4
Pulse generator mounting screw (1988 CR500R)	2	17 in.-lb.

CHAPTER EIGHT

NOTE: If you own a 1992 CR500R or later model, first check the Supplement at the back of this book for any new service information.

LIQUID COOLING SYSTEM

The cooling system consists of two separate radiators, a water pump and interconnecting hoses. The water pump requires no routine maintenance and can be overhauled (replacement parts are available) after removing the right crankcase cover. There is no thermostat or cooling fan and all cooling system services can be performed with the engine in the frame.

This chapter describes repair and replacement of cooling system components. Chapter Three describes routine maintenance of the system. **Table 1** at the end of this chapter provides coolant refill capacity. Note that more coolant is required after disassembly of the system than for just a coolant change.

SAFETY PRECAUTIONS

Certain safety precautions must be kept in mind to protect yourself from injury and the engine from damage. For your own safety, the cooling system must be cool before removing any part of the system including the radiator fill cap.

WARNING
The coolant is very hot and under pressure. Severe scalding could result if the coolant comes in contact with your skin.

To protect the engine and cooling system, drain and flush the cooling system at least every 2 years. Refer to *Coolant Change* in Chapter Three. Refill with a mixture of ethylene-glycol antifreeze (formulated for aluminum engines) and distilled water. Do not reuse the old coolant as it deteriorates with age.

CAUTION
Never operate the cooling system with water only, even in climates where antifreeze protection is not required. The all-aluminum engine will oxidize internally and require costly replacement.

WARNING
Antifreeze has been classified as an environmental toxic waste by the EPA. Dispose of it according to local regulations. Antifreeze is poisonous and may attract animals. Do not store coolant where it is accessible to children or pets.

COOLING SYSTEM CHECK

Two checks should be made before disassembly if a cooling system fault is suspected.
1. Start the engine and let it idle. While the engine is running, a pressure surge should be felt when the radiator hose(s) is squeezed.

8

2. If a substantial coolant loss is noted, the head gasket may have blown. In extreme cases, enough coolant can leak into a cylinder so that the engine cannot be turned over with the kickstarter. White smoke (steam) might also be observed at the muffler when the engine is running. If so, correct the cooling system problem immediately.

WATER PUMP (WATER SEAL AND OIL SEAL INSPECTION)

An inspection hole located at the lower right crankcase cover (**Figure 1**) enables you to determine the condition of the water seal and oil seal located within the water pump assembly. If water or oil is leaking from this hole, further inspection for coolant or transmission oil leakage is necessary. If the hole is blocked or packed with dirt, carefully clean it by twisting a small drill bit between your fingers while moving it into the hole.

RADIATORS

Removal/Installation

1. Remove the seat.
2. Remove the fuel tank and shrouds (**Figure 2**) as described under *Fuel Tank Removal/Installation* in Chapter Six.
3. Drain the cooling system as described in Chapter Three.
4. Disconnect the overflow hose (**Figure 3**) from the filler neck on the radiator.
5. Loosen the water hose clamps (**Figure 4**) on the radiator's inlet hoses.
6. Loosen the hose clamps (**Figure 5**) on the radiator's outlet (lower) hoses.

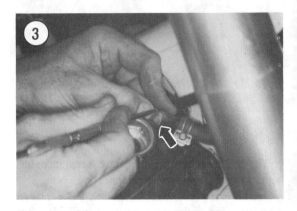

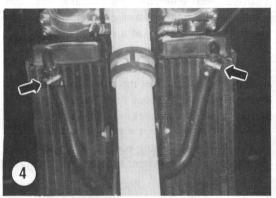

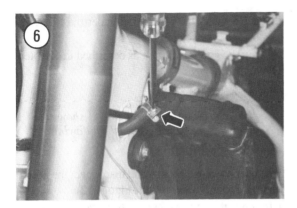

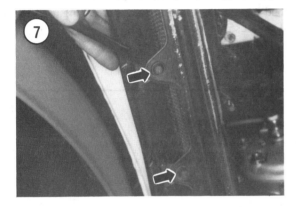

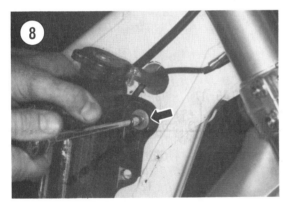

7. Loosen the hose clamps on the interconnecting hose running through the frame between the 2 radiators (**Figure 6**). Remove the hose from one of the radiators.

8. Remove the plastic grille on the front of each radiator by carefully prying the rubber inserts from their mounts with a screwdriver (**Figure 7**).

9. Remove the upper (**Figure 8**) and lower radiator (**Figure 9**) mounting bolts on each radiator.

10. Pull each radiator slightly forward while working the radiator hoses loose from the radiator. Remove both radiators.

11. Install by reversing these removal steps while noting the following.

12. Replace both radiator hoses if either is starting to deteriorate or is damaged.

13. Refill the cooling system with the recommended type and quantity of coolant. Refer to Chapter Three.

Inspection

1. Flush off the exterior of the radiator with a low-pressure stream from a garden hose. Spray both the front and the back to remove all dirt and bugs. Carefully use a whisk broom or stiff paint brush to remove any stubborn dirt.

CAUTION
Do not press too hard or the cooling fins
and tubes may be damaged.

2. Carefully straighten out any bent cooling fins (A, **Figure 10**) with a broad-tipped screwdriver or putty knife. If the radiators have been damaged across approximately 20 percent or more of the frontal area, the radiators should be recored or replaced.

3. Check for cracks or leakage (usually a moss-green colored residue) at the filler neck, the inlet and outlet

hose fittings and the upper and lower tank seams (B, **Figure 10**).

4. Check the hose clamps for excessive rust or damage and replace if necessary.

WATER PUMP

Removal/Installation

For service of the water pump impeller or water pump gaskets, only the water pump cover needs to be removed and only Steps 1-7 need to be followed. For access to governor components or other water pump components, the right crankcase cover must be removed. See **Figure 11** for a breakdown of the components.

1. Place a metal or wood stand under the frame to support the bike securely.

2. Drain the cooling system as described in Chapter Three.

NOTE
For clarification, the engine is shown removed from the frame in the following procedures.

3. Loosen the hose clamps and disconnect the hoses leading into the water pump (**Figure 12**).

4. Remove the 4 bolts securing the water pump cover and remove the cover and the gasket (**Figure 13**). Don't lose the locating dowels.

5. Remove the inner plate and the inner gasket (**Figure 14**).

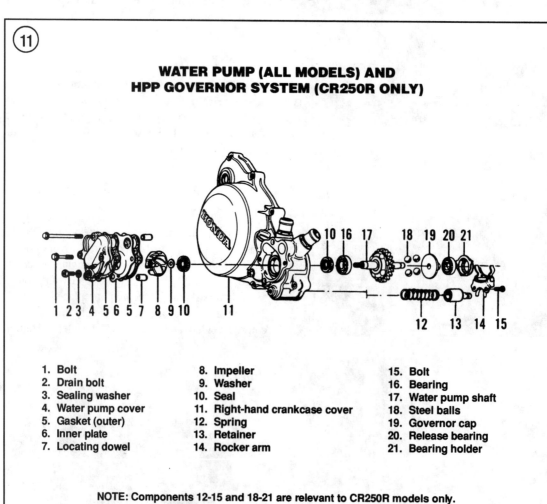

(11)

**WATER PUMP (ALL MODELS) AND
HPP GOVERNOR SYSTEM (CR250R ONLY)**

1. Bolt	8. Impeller	15. Bolt
2. Drain bolt	9. Washer	16. Bearing
3. Sealing washer	10. Seal	17. Water pump shaft
4. Water pump cover	11. Right-hand crankcase cover	18. Steel balls
5. Gasket (outer)	12. Spring	19. Governor cap
6. Inner plate	13. Retainer	20. Release bearing
7. Locating dowel	14. Rocker arm	21. Bearing holder

NOTE: Components 12-15 and 18-21 are relevant to CR250R models only.

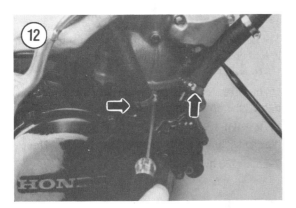

6. To hold the shaft while removing the impeller, shift the transmission into gear and have an assistant hold the rear brake on.

7. Unscrew the impeller (A, **Figure 15**) *counterclockwise* and remove the washer (B, **Figure 15**) from the water pump shaft.

8. Remove the right crankcase cover as described under *Right Crankcase Cover Removal/Installation* in Chapter Four.

9. On CR500R models, the water pump gear and shaft can be removed, at this time, by sliding it out of the water pump bearing.

10. On CR250R models, the governor assembly must be removed prior to removing the water pump shaft. Perform the following:

   a. While pressing against the spring tension of the governor rocker arm (A, **Figure 16**), loosen and remove the rocker arm screws (B, **Figure 16**) and rocker arm. These screws may be extremely tight, and might require the use of an impact driver. Be careful not to damage the screws during removal.

   b. Remove the spring retainer shaft and governor spring (**Figure 17**).

8

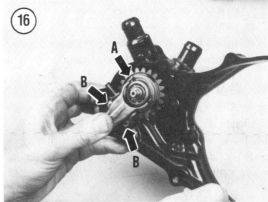

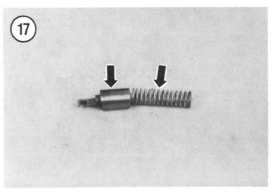

c. Withdraw the water pump shaft from the crankcase cover. Remove the governor cap covering the steel balls (B, **Figure 18**), being careful not to lose the steel balls (A, **Figure 18**).

11. On CR500R models, installation is the reverse of Steps 1 through 9. Tighten the water pump impeller to specifications listed in **Table 2**.

12. On CR250R models, reinstall the governor assembly by performing the following:

    a. Install the water pump shaft and insert the steel balls into the water pump drive gear (A, **Figure 18**). Do not apply grease, they will be oiled by the transmission oil.

    b. Install the governor cap covering the steel balls (B, **Figure 18**) onto the water pump shaft.

    c. Install the governor spring and spring retainer shaft (**Figure 17**).

    d. Position the governor rocker arm and align the big end with the bosses on the governor.

    e. While pushing down on the rocker arm, install and tighten the rocker arm screws (B, **Figure 16**).

    f. Align the notch in retainer shaft (**Figure 17**) so it will engage the HPP follower cam when turned 90°.

    g. Install the impeller washer and impeller and tighten the impeller to specifications listed in **Table 2**.

13. Install the right crankcase cover as described under *Right Crankcase Cover Removal/Installation* in Chapter Four.

14. Install a new gasket on each side of the inner plate and, if removed, install the dowel pins on the water pump cover.

15. Install the water pump cover and 4 cover bolts. The bolt at the lower right of the water pump cover is longer than the other three. Tighten the bolts to 10-14 N•m (7-10 ft.-lb.).

16. Install the coolant hoses onto the water pump and tighten the hose clamps securely.

17. Refill the cooling system with the recommended type and quantity of coolant. Refer to Chapter Three.

18. Start the bike and check for leaks.

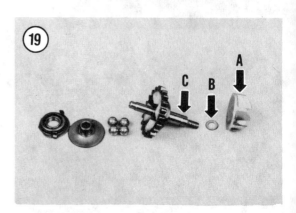

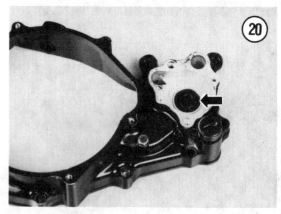

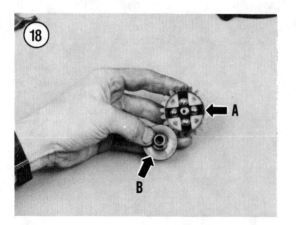

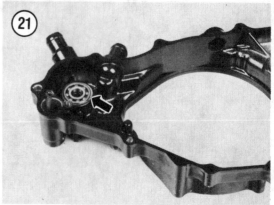

Inspection

1. Inspect the water pump shaft (C, **Figure 19**) for wear or damage. Replace the shaft if necessary.

2. Inspect the pump shaft gear (C, **Figure 19**) for broken or worn teeth. Replace the shaft if necessary.

3. Check the condition of the impeller blades (A, **Figure 19**).

4. Inspect the water seal (outer side) and the oil seal (on inner side of water seal) of the right crankcase cover (**Figure 20**).

5. Inspect the bearing in the right crankcase cover (**Figure 21**).

6. Inspect the shaft bearing in the right crankcase.

7. Inspect the threads on the inside of the impeller (A, **Figure 15**) and on the water pump shaft. If worn or damaged, the shaft and/or impeller must be replaced.

8. Inspect the impeller washer (B, **Figure 19**) for damage or deterioration. Replace if necessary.

9. Make sure the drain hole located at the bottom of the crankcase cover is clear. Clean out with a small piece of wire if clogged.

COOLANT HOSES

Whenever any component of the cooling system is removed, the hoses should be inspected for deterioration, and replaced accordingly. Hoses deteriorate with age and should be replaced periodically or whenever they show signs of cracking or leakage. To be safe, replace the hoses every 2 years. The spray of hot coolant from a cracked hose can cause injury. Loss of coolant can also cause the engine to overheat.

Table 1 COOLING SYSTEM SPECIFICATIONS

CR250R	
Coolant change	0.81 liters (0.856 U.S. qt.)
Disassembly	0.84 liters (0.888 U.S. qt.)
CR500R	
Coolant change	1.08 liters (1.141 U.S. qt.)
Disassembly	1.22 liters (1.289 U.S. qt.)
Freezing point (hydrometer test)	
Water-to-antifreeze ratio	
55:45	-32° C (-25° F)
50:50	-37° C (-34° F)
45:55	-44.5° C (-48° F)

Table 2 TORQUE SPECIFICATIONS

Item	N•m	ft.-lb.
Drain bolts (all)	8-12	6-9
Water pump cover bolts		
1988 CR250R, All CR500R	8-12	6-9
1989-on CR250R	10-14	7-10
Water pump impeller	10-14	7-10

NOTE: If you own a 1992 CR500R or later model, first check the Supplement at the back of this book for any new service information.

FRONT SUSPENSION AND STEERING

This chapter describes repair and maintenance procedures for the front wheel, forks and steering components. Due to the competitive characteristics of the CR models, Honda is constantly refining the handling and suspension qualities. This has led to many changes in the front suspension and steering of these off-road/competition bikes through the various years and models. **Tables 1-4** at the end of this chapter provide specifications and tightening torques.

FRONT WHEEL

Removal

1. Place a metal or wood stand under the frame to support the bike securely with the front wheel off of the ground.
2. On 1988 and 1989 models, perform the following:
   a. Loosen the front axle clamp nuts from the right front fork slider (**Figure 1**).
   b. Unscrew the axle from the right-hand side of the fork assembly.
   c. Pull the wheel down and forward and slide the brake disc out of the caliper assembly. Remove the axle by pulling it through, from the right side.

3. On 1990 and 1991 models, perform the following:
   a. Remove the axle clamp nuts from the holders on both sliders (**Figure 2**). Remove the front wheel and axle shaft as an assembly (**Figure 3**). Use care when pulling the disc from the caliper assembly.
   b. Remove the axle nut (A, **Figure 4**) from the axle shaft.
   c. Remove the side collar (B, **Figure 4**) and pull the axle through the front wheel.

NOTE
Insert a piece of wood or vinyl tube in the caliper in place of the disc. This will keep the pistons from being forced out of the cylinder if the brake lever is inadvertently squeezed. If this does happen, the caliper might have to be disassembled to reseat the pistons and the system will have to be bled.

CAUTION
Do not set disc brake wheels on the disc surface as the disc may get scratched or warped. Set the wheel between 2 blocks of wood.

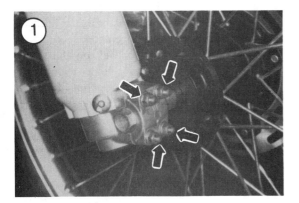

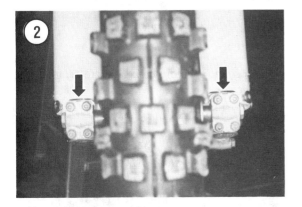

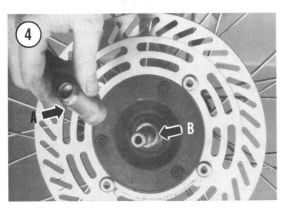

Inspection

Measure the axial and radial runout of the wheel with a dial indicator as shown in **Figure 5**. The maximum axial and radial runout is 2.0 mm (0.08 in.). If the runout exceeds this dimension, check the wheel bearing condition.

If the wheel bearings are okay, some of this condition can be corrected by either tightening or replacing any loose or bent spokes as described in this chapter.

Check axle runout as described under *Front Hub Inspection* in this chapter.

Installation

1. Make sure the axle bearing surfaces of the fork slider (**Figure 6**) and the axle holder(s) are free from dirt or small burrs.

2. Clean the axle in solvent and dry thoroughly. Make sure all surfaces that the axle comes in contact with are clean before installation.

3. Remove the piece of wood or vinyl tubing from the caliper assembly.

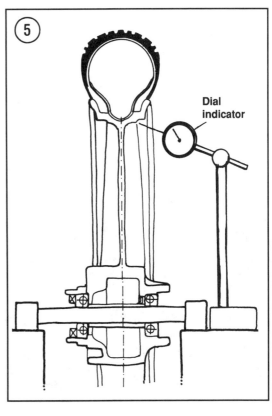

Dial indicator

4. On 1988 and 1989 models, perform the following:

   a. Make sure the collars are in place and position the wheel taking care to align the disc so it will slide in between the brake pads.

   b. Rub a small amount of grease onto the axle shaft and insert the axle through the wheel.

   c. Install the axle holder clamp with the "UP" mark facing up (**Figure 7**).

   d. Install the axle holder clamp nuts finger-tight.

   e. Tighten the front axle to the torque specifications in **Table 1**.

   f. Remove the motorcycle from the stand. While applying the front brake, push the fork up and down several times to seat the axle. Check the brake for proper operation.

   g. Place the motorcycle back on the stand. Tighten the top two axle holder clamp nuts, then tighten the lower two nuts. The torque specifications are listed in **Table 1**.

5. On 1990 and 1991 models, perform the following:

   a. Rub a small amount of grease onto the axle shaft and insert the shaft into the wheel.

   b. Slide the left side collar onto the axle and install the axle nut. Tighten the nut to specifications in **Table 1**.

   c. Position the front wheel and axle shaft in place as an assembly, carefully inserting the disc between the brake pads.

   d. Install the axle holder clamps making sure the "UP" mark is facing up (**Figure 7**).

   e. Using a wrench, *snugly* tighten both axle holder clamps (**Figure 2**), the upper nuts first, then the lower.

   f. Remove the motorcycle from the stand. While applying the front brake, push the fork up and

down several times to seat the axle. Check the front brake for proper operation.

   g. Place the motorcycle back on the stand. Tighten the top two axle holder clamp nuts, then tighten the lower two nuts for each holder. The torque specifications are listed in **Table 1**.

6. After the wheel is completely installed, rotate it several times and apply the brake a couple of times to make sure that the wheel rotates freely and that the brake is operating correctly.

FRONT HUB

Inspection

Inspect each wheel bearing before removing it from the wheel hub.

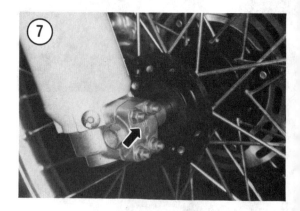

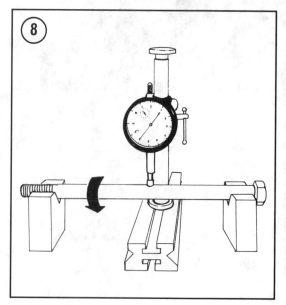

CAUTION
CAUTION
Do not remove the wheel bearings for inspection purposes as they will be damaged during the removal process. Remove the wheel bearings only if they are to be replaced.

1. Perform Steps 1-6 of *Disassembly* in this chapter.

2. Turn each bearing by hand. Make sure the bearings turn smoothly.

3. On non-sealed bearings, check the balls for evidence of wear, pitting or excessive heat (bluish tint). Replace the bearings if necessary; always replace as a complete set. When replacing the bearings, be sure to take your old bearings along to ensure a perfect match.

NOTE
Fully sealed bearings are available from many bearing specialty shops. Fully sealed bearings provide better protection from dirt and moisture that may get into the hub.

4. Check the axle for wear and straightness. Use V-blocks and a dial indicator as shown in **Figure 8**. If the runout is 0.2 mm (0.008 in.) or greater, the axle should be replaced.

Disassembly

Refer to **Figure 9** for the following procedures.

1. Remove the front wheel as described in this chapter.

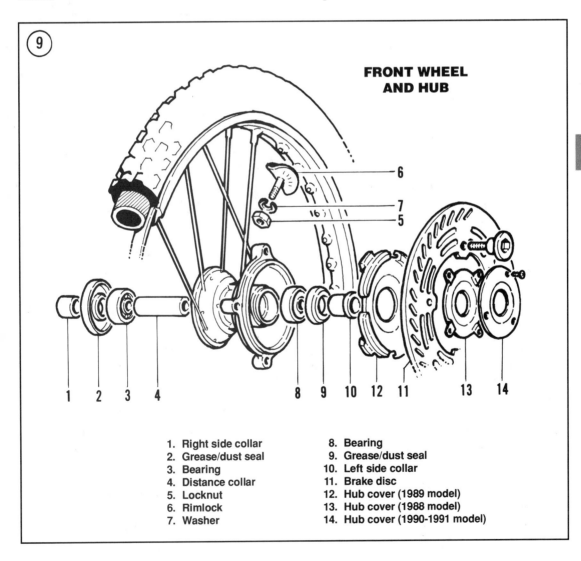

FRONT WHEEL AND HUB

1. Right side collar
2. Grease/dust seal
3. Bearing
4. Distance collar
5. Locknut
6. Rimlock
7. Washer
8. Bearing
9. Grease/dust seal
10. Left side collar
11. Brake disc
12. Hub cover (1989 model)
13. Hub cover (1988 model)
14. Hub cover (1990-1991 model)

2. Remove the side collar and grease seal from the right-hand side.

3. Remove the side collar from the left-hand side (A, **Figure 10**).

4A. On 1988 models, remove the screws securing the hub cover to the disc. On 1990 and 1991 models, remove the screws securing the hub cover and remove the cover (A, **Figure 11**). Then remove the screws securing the brake disc (B, **Figure 11**) and remove the disc from the hub.

4B. On 1989 models, remove the screws securing the brake disc and remove the disc from the hub. Then remove the hub cover from the disc.

5. Remove the grease seal (B, **Figure 10**) from the left-hand side.

6. Before proceeding further, inspect the wheel bearings as described in this chapter. If they must be replaced, proceed as follows.

7. To remove the right- and left-hand bearings and distance collar, insert a soft aluminum or brass drift into one side of the hub. Push the distance collar over to one side and place the drift on the inner race of the lower bearing. Tap the bearing out of the hub with a hammer, working around the perimeter of the inner race. See **Figure 12**.

8. Remove the distance collar.

9. Turn the wheel over and remove the other bearing in the same manner.

Assembly

> *CAUTION*
> *Always reinstall new bearings, as the removal process will generally damage them. Purchase and replace the wheel bearings in pairs.*

1. On non-sealed bearings, pack the bearings with a good-quality bearing grease. Work the grease in between the balls thoroughly. Turn the bearing by hand a couple of times to make sure the grease is distributed evenly inside the bearing.

2. Blow any dirt or foreign matter out of the hub before installing the bearings.

3. Install non-sealed bearings with the single sealed side facing outward (**Figure 13**).

> *CAUTION*
> *Tap the bearings squarely into place and tap on the outer race only. Use a socket (**Figure 14**) that matches the*

outer race diameter. Do not tap on the inner race or the bearing might be damaged. Be sure that the bearings are completely seated.

4. Install the right-hand bearing and press the distance collar into place.

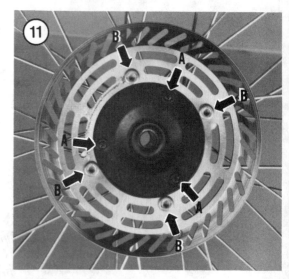

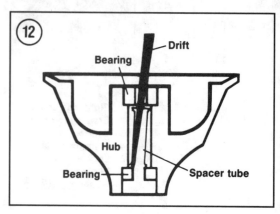

5. Install the left-hand bearing.

6. Check to make sure the bearings are installed squarely and the bearing outer race fits tightly in the hub.

7A. On 1988, 1990 and 1991 models, perform the following:

    a. Install the brake disc and screws (B, **Figure 11**). Tighten the screws to specifications listed in **Table 1**.

    b. Coat the lips of the grease seal with grease and install the grease seal on the left-hand side.

    c. Install the wheel hub cover and hub cover screws (A, **Figure 11**). Tighten the screws to the specifications listed in **Table 1**.

7B. On 1989 models, perform the following:

    a. Install the wheel hub cover to the disc.

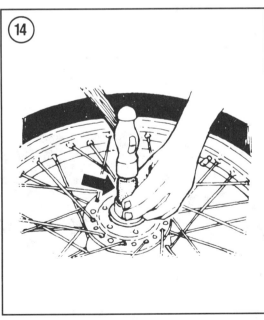

    b. Install the brake disc and brake disc screws. Make sure the disc is installed with the "DRIVE" markings facing outward. Tighten the screws to the specifications listed in **Table 1**.

    c. Coat the lips of the grease seal with grease and install the grease seal on the left-hand side (B, **Figure 10**).

8. Install the collar (A, **Figure 10**) into the left-hand side.

9. Coat the lips of the grease seal with grease and install the grease seal on the right-hand side.

10. Install the side collar to the right-hand side.

WHEEL SPOKES

Inspection and Replacement

Spokes will loosen with use and should be checked periodically. The "tuning fork" method for checking spoke tightness is simple and works well. Tap each spoke with a spoke wrench or the shank of a screwdriver and listen for a tone. A tightened spoke will emit a clear, ringing tone and a loose spoke will sound flat. All the spokes in a correctly tightened wheel will emit tones of similar pitch but not necessarily the same precise tone.

Bent or stripped spokes should be replaced as soon as they are detected, as they can destroy an expensive hub.

1. Unscrew the nipple from the spoke and depress the nipple into the rim far enough to free the end of the spoke; take care not to push the nipple all the way in.

2. Remove the damaged spoke from the hub and use it to match a new spoke of identical length. If necessary, trim the new spoke to match the original and dress the end of the thread with a thread die.

3. Install the new spoke in the hub and screw on the nipple. Tighten (**Figure 15**) until the spoke's tone is similar to the tone of the other spokes in the wheel.

4. Periodically check the new spoke. It will stretch and must be retightened several times before it takes a final set.

5. If the wheels are re-laced, perform the following:

    a. After the front wheel is re-laced, adjust the wheel-to-hub relationship so that dimension "A" (**Figure 16**) is 23.25 mm (0.915 in.) on all models.

9

b. After the rear wheel is re-laced, refer to **Figure 17** and adjust the hub position as follows:
1988-1990-1991 CR250R models and 1988-1989 CR500R models—The distance from the left end surface of the hub to the side of the rim (dimension "A") should be 47 mm (1.85 in.).
1989 CR250R models and 1990-1991 CR500R models—The distance from the left end surface of the hub to the side of the rim (dimension "A") should be 46 mm (1.81 in.).

c. Tighten the spoke nipples and rim locks to the specifications listed in **Table 1**.

Adjustment

Inspect the rims for cracks, warpage or dents (**Figure 18**). Replace a damaged rim.

If all spokes appear loose, tighten all on one side of the hub, then tighten all on the other side. One-half to one turn should be sufficient; do not overtighten.

After tightening the spokes, check rim runout to be sure you haven't pulled the rim out of shape.

One way to check rim runout is to mount a dial indicator on the front fork or swing arm so that it bears against the rim. If you don't have a dial indicator, improvise one as shown in **Figure 19**. Adjust the position of the bolt until it just clears the rim. Rotate the rim and note whether the clearance increases or decreases. Mark the tire with chalk or light crayon at areas that produce significantly large or small clearance. Clearance must not change by more than 2.0 mm (0.08 in.). With the wheel off the motorcycle, check runout using a truing stand (**Figure 20**).

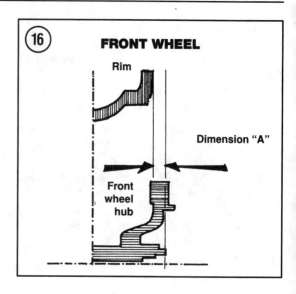

FRONT WHEEL

Rim

Dimension "A"

Front wheel hub

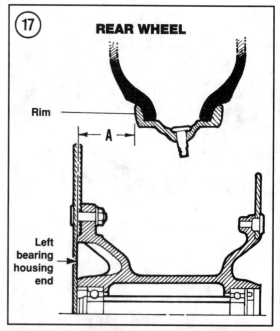

REAR WHEEL

Rim

A

Left bearing housing end

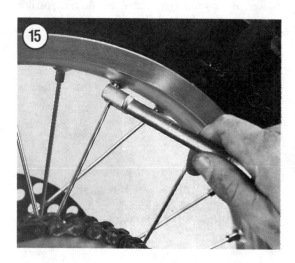

To pull the rim out, tighten spokes which terminate on the same side of the hub and loosen spokes which terminate on the opposite side of the hub (**Figure 21**). In most cases, only a slight amount of adjustment is necessary to true a rim. After adjustment, rotate the rim and make sure another area has not been pulled out of true. Continue adjustment and checking until runout is less than 2.0 mm (0.08 in.).

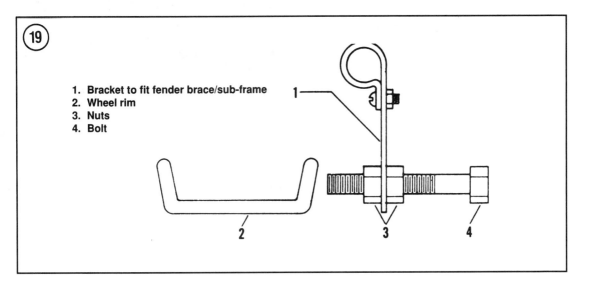

1. Bracket to fit fender brace/sub-frame
2. Wheel rim
3. Nuts
4. Bolt

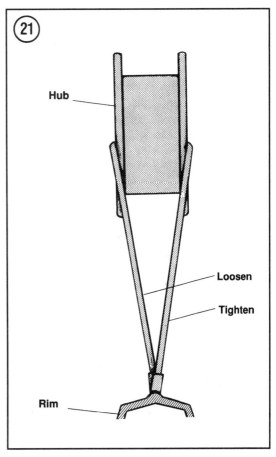

Hub

Loosen

Tighten

Rim

TIRE CHANGING

Removal

1. Remove the valve core (B, **Figure 22**) and deflate the tire.

2. Loosen the rim locknuts (A, **Figure 22**) fully, but don't remove them.

3. Press the entire bead on both sides of the tire into the center of the rim.

4. Lubricate the beads with soapy water.

5. Insert the tire iron under the bead next to the valve (**Figure 23**). Force the bead on the opposite side of the tire into the center of the rim and pry the bead over the rim with the tire iron.

6. Insert a second tire iron next to the first to hold the bead over the rim. Then work around the tire with the first tire iron, prying the bead over the rim. Be careful not to pinch the inner tube with the tire irons.

7. Remove the valve from the hole in the rim and remove the tube from the tire.

NOTE
Step 8 is required only if it is necessary to remove the tire completely from the rim for tire replacement.

8. Stand the tire upright. Insert the tire iron between the second bead and the side of the rim that the first bead was pried over (**Figure 24**). Force the bead on the opposite side from the tire iron into the center of the rim. Pry the second bead off of the rim, working around the wheel with 2 tire irons as with the first bead. Remove the tire from the rim.

Installation

1. Carefully check the tire for any damage, especially inside. On the front tire, carefully check the sidewall as it is vulnerable to damage from rocks, and other rider's footpegs.

2. A new tire may have balancing rubbers inside. These are not patches and should not be disturbed. A colored spot near the bead indicates a lighter point on the tire. This should be placed next to the valve or midway between the 2 rim locks.

3. Check that the spoke ends do not protrude through the nipples into the center of the rim where they can puncture the tube. File off any protruding spoke ends. Be sure the rim rubber tape is in place with the rough side toward the rim.

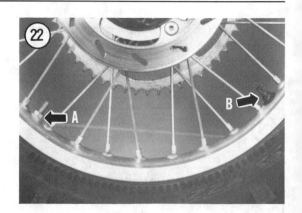

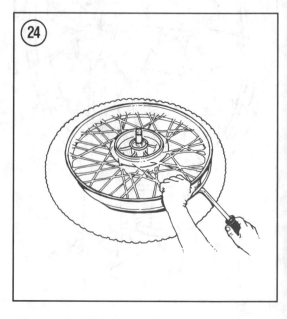

4. Install the valve stem core and tighten securely.

5. Inflate the tube just enough to round it out. Too much air will make it difficult to install it in the tire and too little will increase the chances of pinching the tube with the tire irons. Install the tube into the tire.

6. Lubricate the tire beads and rim with soapy water.

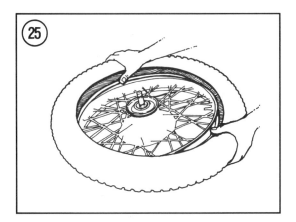

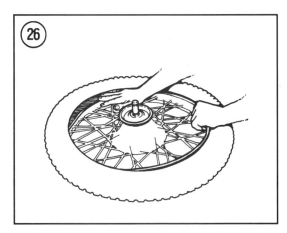

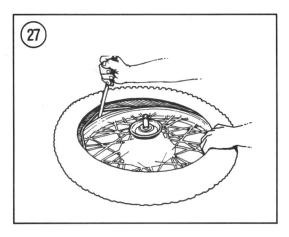

7. Pull the tube partly out of the tire at the valve. Squeeze the beads together to hold the tube and insert the valve into the hole in the rim. The lower bead should go into the center of the rim with the upper bead outside it.

8. Press the lower bead into the rim center on each side of the valve, working around the tire in both directions (**Figure 25**). Use a tire iron for the last few inches of the bead.

9. Press the upper bead into the rim opposite the valve (**Figure 26**). Pry the bead into the rim on both sides of the initial point with a tire iron, working around the rim to the valve (**Figure 27**).

10. Wiggle the valve to be sure the tube is not trapped under the bead. Set the valve squarely in its hole before screwing on the valve nut to hold it against the rim.

11. Check the bead on both sides of the tire for even fit around the rim.

12. Inflate the tire slowly to seat the beads in the rim. It may be necessary to bounce the tire to complete the seating. Inflate to the required pressure as described in Chapter Three. Balance the wheel as described in this chapter.

13. Tighten the rim locknuts.

TIRE REPAIRS

This procedure is included in this chapter for the riders who do not race their bike but use it for off-road fun only. Racers should not try to salvage a punctured tube.

Every rider will eventually experience trouble with a tire or tube. Repairs and replacement are fairly simple and every rider should know the techniques.

Patching a motorcycle tube is only a temporary fix, especially on a dirt bike. The tire flexes too much and the patch could rub right off. However, a patched tire will get you back to camp where you can replace the tube with the extra one that should be carried in your tool box or tow vehicle.

Tire Repair Kits

Tire repair kits can be purchased from motorcycle dealers and some auto supply stores. When buying, specify that the kit you want is for motorcycles.

There are 2 types of tire repair kits:
   a. Hot patch.
   b. Cold patch.

Hot patches are stronger because they actually vulcanize to the tube, becoming part of it. However, they are far too bulky to carry for roadside repairs and the strength is unnecessary for a temporary repair.

Cold patches are not vulcanized to the tube; they are simply glued to it. Though not as strong as hot patches, cold patches are still very durable. Cold patch kits are less bulky than hot and more easily applied under adverse conditions. A cold patch kit contains everything necessary and tucks easily into your emergency tool kit.

Tube Inspection

1. Remove the inner tube as described in this chapter.
2. Install the valve core into the valve stem (**Figure 28**) and inflate the tube slightly. Do not overinflate.
3. Immerse the tube in water a section at a time (**Figure 29**). Look carefully for bubbles indicating a hole. Mark each hole and continue checking until you are certain that all holes are discovered and marked. Also make sure that the valve core is not leaking; tighten if necessary.

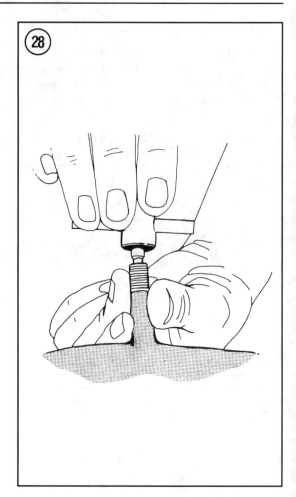

> *NOTE*
> *If you do not have enough water to immerse sections of the tube, try running your hand over the tube slowly and very close to the surface. If your hand is damp, it works even better. If you suspect a hole anywhere, apply some saliva to the area to verify it (**Figure 30**).*

4. Apply a cold patch using the techniques described in this chapter.
5. Dust the patch area with talcum powder to prevent it from sticking to the tire.
6. Carefully check the inside of the tire casing for small rocks or sand which may have damaged the tube. If the inside of the tire is split, apply a patch to the area to prevent it from pinching and damaging the tube again.
7. Check the inside of the rim. Make sure the rim band is in place, with no spoke ends protruding which could puncture the tube.
8. Deflate the tube before installation in the tire.

Cold Patch Repairs

1. Remove the tube from the tire as described in this chapter.

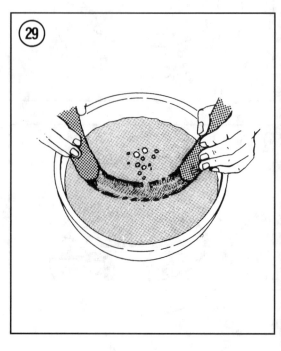

2. Roughen an area around the hole slightly larger than the patch, using a cap from the tire repair kit or a pocket knife. Do not scrape too vigorously or you may cause additional damage.

3. Apply a small quantity of special cement to the puncture and spread it evenly with your finger (**Figure 31**).

4. Allow the cement to dry until tacky—usually 30 seconds or so is sufficient.

5. Remove the backing from the patch.

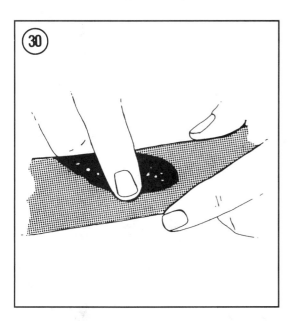

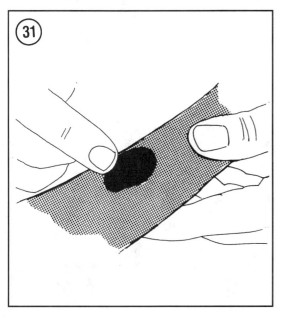

CAUTION
Do not touch the newly exposed rubber with your fingers or the patch will not stick firmly.

6. Center the patch over the hole. Hold the patch firmly in place for about 30 seconds to allow the cement to set (**Figure 32**).

7. Dust the patched area with talcum powder to prevent sticking.

8. Install the tube as described in this chapter.

HANDLEBAR

Removal/Installation

1. Remove the number plate mounting bolt (A, **Figure 33**), then unhook the plastic snap (B, **Figure 33**) and remove the plate.

2. Remove the screw securing the clamp on the engine kill switch (A, **Figure 34**) and remove the switch assembly.

3. Turn the adjusting nut to obtain slack in the clutch cable (B, **Figure 34**) and disconnect the cable from the clutch hand lever.

4. Perform the following:

   a. Remove the screws (A, **Figure 35**) securing the throttle assembly halves.

   b. Remove the assembly and carefully lay the throttle assembly and cable over the fender or back over the fuel tank. Be careful that the cable does not get crimped or damaged.

   c. Remove the clamping screws (B, **Figure 35**) securing the front master cylinder to the

9

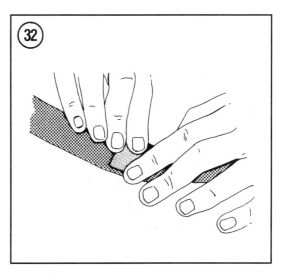

handlebar. Keep the master cylinder in an upright position while removing the assembly. This will minimize the loss of brake fluid and prevent air from entering the brake system.

d. Tie the master cylinder up to the frame, keeping the reservoir in an upright position. It is not necessary to remove the hydraulic brake line from the master cylinder.

5. Remove the bolts (**Figure 36**) securing the handlebar upper holders and remove the holders and the handlebar.

6. To prevent the handlebar from slipping after it has been tightened, clean the knurled section of the handlebar with a wire brush. It should be kept rough so it will be held securely by the holders. The upper and lower holders should also be kept clean and free of any metal that may have been gouged loose by handlebar slippage.

7. Install by reversing these removal steps while noting the following.

8. Position the handlebar in the lower holders on the fork bridge.

9. Position the handlebar upper holders with the punch marks toward the front.

10. Install the bolts. Align the punch mark on the handlebar with the split on the mounting bracket (**Figure 37**). Tighten the front bolts first, then the rear to the torque specifications listed in **Table 1**. After installation is complete, recheck the alignment of the punch mark.

11. Install the throttle grip and align the upper split of the throttle housing with the punch mark in the handlebar.

12. Install the master cylinder holder bracket with the UP arrow (**Figure 38**) facing up. Also align the upper split end of the holder with the punch mark on the handlebar. Tighten the upper holder bolt first, then the lower bolt. The torque specifications are listed in **Table 1**.

13. Adjust the clutch and throttle operation as described in Chapter Three.

STEERING HEAD

The steering head consists of a steering stem that rotates within upper and lower assembled roller bearings. Refer to **Figure 39** for the following procedures.

Disassembly

1. Remove the front wheel as described in this chapter.

2. Remove the handlebar as described in this chapter.

3. Remove the bolts and washers securing the front fender and remove the fender.

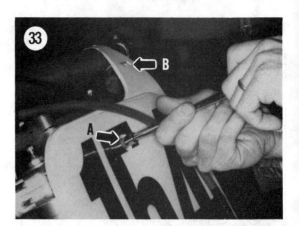

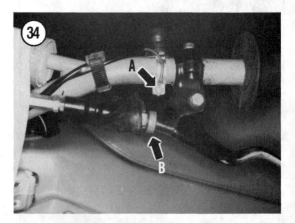

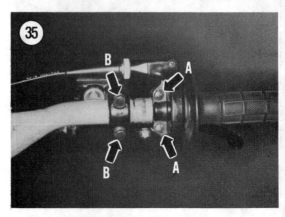

4. Remove the bolt securing the front number plate. Remove the plastic snap and remove the number plate.

5. Remove the brake line guide attached to the front fork lower bridge.

6. Remove the front forks as described in this chapter.

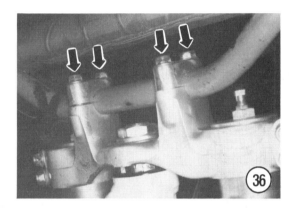

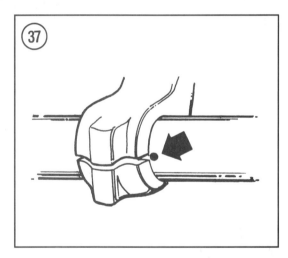

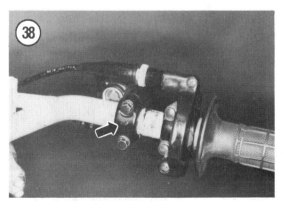

7. Loosen and remove the steering stem nut and washer.

8. Remove the steering head adjusting nut and washer. A special socket (Honda part No. 07916-KA50100) is made for removing the adjusting nut, but a large drift and hammer also can be used. If frequent steering stem maintenance is anticipated, you can easily improvise a tool like the one shown in **Figure 40**.

9. Lower the steering stem assembly down and out of the steering head (**Figure 41**).

Inspection

1. Clean the bearing races and tapered roller bearings with solvent.

2. Check the welds around the steering head for cracks and fractures. If any are found, have them repaired by a competent frame shop or welding service.

3. Check the rollers for pitting, scratches or discoloration indicating wear or corrosion. Replace the tapered roller bearings in sets if any are bad.

4. Check the races for pitting, galling and corrosion. If any of these conditions exist, replace the bearings and races as a set as described in this chapter.

5. Check the steering stem for cracks and check the upper and lower race for damage or wear. If any of the bearing races are damaged, the bearings and races should be replaced as a set. Take the old races and bearings to your dealer to ensure accurate replacement.

Steering Stem Bearing Race Removal/Installation

The steering stem bearing is pressed into place. If removed, proper reinstallation may require the use of a hydraulic press. For this reason, do not remove the bearing unless it is worn and requires replacement.

1. To remove the lower bearing and internal race on the steering stem, try twisting and pulling it up by hand. If it will not come off, carefully pry it up with a screwdriver. Work around in a circle, prying a little more at a time.

2. Remove the lower bearing and internal race.

3. Install the lower bearing and internal race. Special tools (part No. 07946-4300101 for 1988-1989 models and part No. 07946-MAB00000 for 1990 and

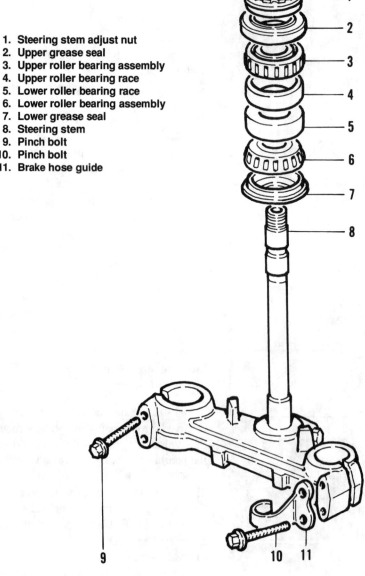

**STEERING STEM
(ROLLER BEARINGS)**

1. Steering stem adjust nut
2. Upper grease seal
3. Upper roller bearing assembly
4. Upper roller bearing race
5. Lower roller bearing race
6. Lower roller bearing assembly
7. Lower grease seal
8. Steering stem
9. Pinch bolt
10. Pinch bolt
11. Brake hose guide

later models) are recommended. If these tools are not available, tap the bearing and race down with a piece of hardwood. Work around in a circle so the bearing will not be damaged. Make sure it is seated squarely and is all the way down.

Headset Bearing Race Removal/Installation

The headset bearing races are pressed into place. Because they are easily bent, do not remove them unless they are worn and require replacement.

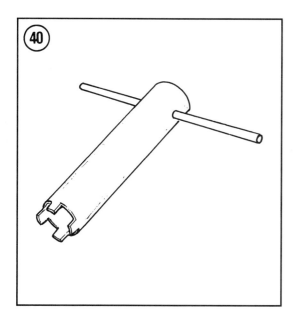

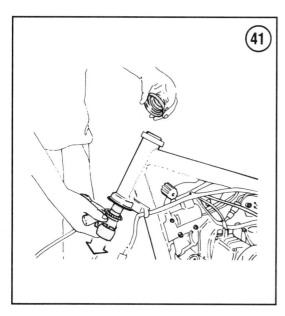

To remove the headset race, use the special tool (Honda part No. 07948-4630100) or insert a hardwood stick or soft punch into the head tube (**Figure 42**) and carefully tap the race out from the inside. After it is started, tap around the race so that neither the race nor the head tube is damaged.

To install the headset race, use special driver (Honda part No. 07749-0010000) and attachment (Honda part No. 07746-0010300) for the upper race. Use the same driver and attachment for the lower race on 1988 and 1989 models. On 1990 and later models, you will need attachment part No. 07746-0010400. If the special tools are not available, tap it

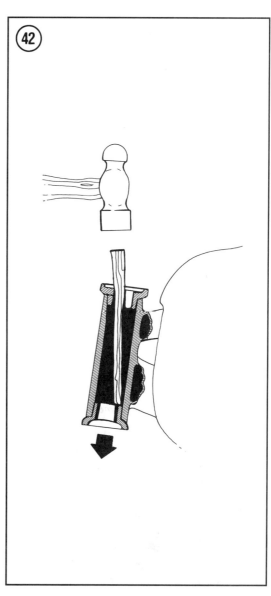

in slowly with a block of wood, a suitable size socket or piece of pipe (**Figure 43**). Make sure that the race is squarely seated in the headset race bore before tapping it into place. Tap the race in until it is flush with the steering head surface.

Assembly

Refer to **Figure 39** for this procedure.

1. Check the steering head and stem races to be sure they are aligned and properly seated.

2. Pack the upper and lower roller bearing assemblies in grease.

3. Install the upper roller bearing assembly and seal into the steering head.

4. Install the steering stem into the head tube and hold it firmly in place.

5. Install the steering stem adjusting nut. Tighten it to the following torque specifications:

    a. 1988-1989—1-2 N•m (0.7-1.4 ft.-lb.).

    b. 1990-1991—8-12 N•m (6-9 ft.-lb.).

6. Turn the steering stem from full left to full right a few times to seat the bearings. Tighten the adjusting nut again.

NOTE
*The adjusting nut should be just tight enough to remove both horizontal and vertical play (**Figure 44**), yet loose enough so that the assembly will turn to both left and right lock positions under its own weight after a light push.*

7. Install the upper fork bridge, washer and steering stem nut. Tighten the steering stem nut to 95-140 N•m (69-101 ft.-lb.).

CAUTION
Steps 8-12 must be performed in this order to assure proper upper and lower fork bridge-to-fork alignment.

8. Slide the fork tubes into position as follows:

    a. On 1988 models—Align the top of the fork tube with the top surface of the upper fork bridge (**Figure 45**).

    b. On 1989 and 1990 models—Align the *index groove* on the fork tube with the top surface of the upper fork bridge (**Figure 46**).

    c. On 1991 models—Align the top surface of the bridge with the groove 10 mm (0.40 in.) below the top of the fork tube (**Figure 47**).

9. On 1988, 1989 and 1990 models, perform the following:

    a. Tighten the lower fork bridge bolts to the torque specified in **Table 1**.

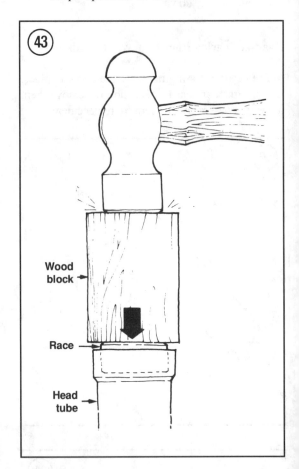

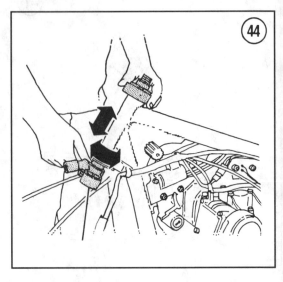

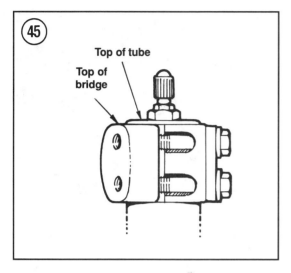

Top of tube

Top of bridge

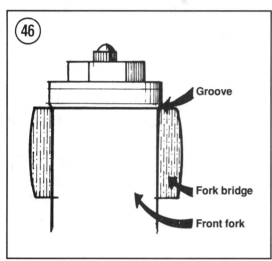

Groove

Fork bridge

Front fork

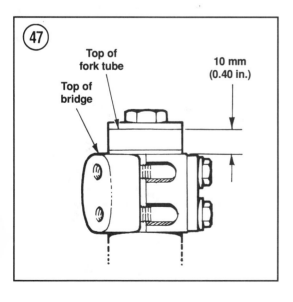

Top of fork tube

Top of bridge

10 mm (0.40 in.)

b. Tighten the upper fork bridge bolts to the torque specified in **Table 1**.

10. On 1991 models, perform the following:

a. Tighten the upper fork bridge bolts to the torque specified in **Table 1**.

b. Tighten the lower fork bridge bolts to the torque specified in **Table 1**.

11. Install the handlebar assembly as described in this chapter.

12. Install the front wheel as described in this chapter.

13. Install the brake line guide to the lower fork bridge.

14. After a few hours of riding, the bearings have had a chance to seat. Readjust the free play in the steering stem with the steering stem adjusting nut. Refer to Step 5.

Adjustment

If play develops in the steering system, it may only require adjustment. Check for a gritty or grinding feeling when turning the stem lock-to-lock. If the stem is noisy, exceptionally loose or feels like it is binding, don't take a chance on it. Disassemble the stem and look for possible damage. Then reassemble and adjust as described in the *Assembly* procedure.

FRONT FORK

The front suspension on all models covered in this manual consists of spring-controlled, hydraulically-damped, telescopic forks.

Removal, installation, disassembly and overhaul procedures vary between year and model. To simplify this material, the forks are divided into groups. Be sure to use the correct procedure for your specific year and model.

Before suspecting major trouble, drain the front fork oil and refill with the proper type and quantity; refer to *Front Fork Oil Change* in Chapter Three.

If you still have trouble, such as poor damping, a tendency to bottom or top out or leakage around the rubber seals, follow the service procedures in this chapter.

The *Removal/Installation* procedures describe instructions for removing the fork legs as a pair. However, to simplify fork service and to prevent the mixing of parts, the legs should be disassembled and serviced *individually*.

9

Front Fork Oil Change

Refer to Chapter Three for fork oil changing procedures.

Front Fork Removal/Installation
(1988-1990 Models)

1. Remove the bolt and collar on the front number plate. Unhook the plastic snap and remove the plate.

2. Remove the air valve bleeder caps and release the air from the fork tubes (**Figure 48**).

> *WARNING*
> *Always bleed off all air pressure. Failure to do so may cause fork oil to spurt out with the air. Protect your eyes and clothing accordingly.*

3. Loosen the upper fork bridge bolts (A, **Figure 49**).

4. If the fork tubes are to be disassembled, loosen, but do not remove, the fork cap/air valve assembly at this time (B, **Figure 49**).

5. Remove the front wheel as described in this chapter.

6. On 1988 models, remove the clamp bolts securing the brake hose to the fork leg. Remove the clamp and move the brake hose to one side.

7. On 1989 and 1990 models, loosen the clamp bolts securing the brake hose to the fork protector. Then remove the bolts securing the plastic fork protectors (**Figure 50**) and remove the protectors.

8. Remove the mounting bolts securing the brake caliper (**Figure 51**) and remove the caliper from the left fork leg. Support the brake caliper by using a coat hanger or other device that will secure it to the upper part of the bike. Do *not* allow the caliper to hang by the brake hose.

9. If the forks are to be completely disassembled, loosen, but do not remove, the damper adjust bolts at the bottom of the fork sliders.

10. Loosen the lower fork bridge bolts.

11. Pull the fork tubes down and out to remove. You may need to rotate the tubes slightly.

12. Installation is the reverse of these steps while noting the following.

13. Unless you are changing the oil per instructions in Chapter Three, follow the *Fork Oil Refilling* procedures pertaining to your model prior to installation.

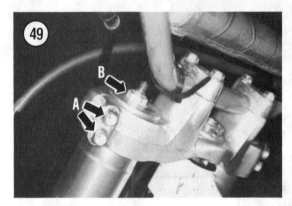

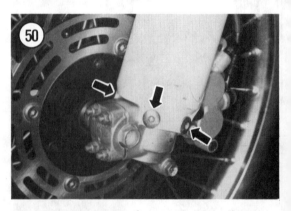

14A. On 1988 models, align the tops of the fork tubes with the top surface of the upper fork bridge (**Figure 45**).

14B. On 1989 and 1990 models, align the index groove on each upper fork leg with the top surface of the upper fork bridge (**Figure 46**).

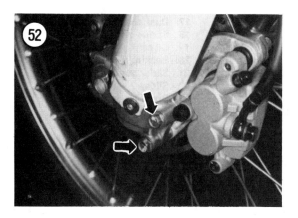

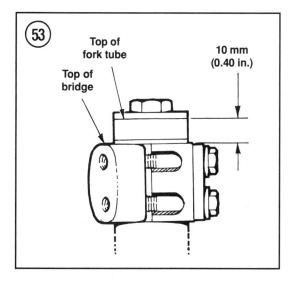

Top of fork tube

10 mm (0.40 in.)

Top of bridge

15. Tighten the lower fork bridge bolts to specifications, then tighten the upper fork bridge bolts to specifications in **Table 1**.

16. On 1988 models, tighten the fork cap/air valve assembly to 15-30 N•m (11-22 ft.-lb.). On 1989 and 1990 models, tighten the fork cap/air valve assembly to 30-40 N•m (22-29 ft.-lb.).

Front Fork Removal/Installation (1991 Models)

1. Remove the bolt on the front number plate. Unhook the snap and remove the number plate.
2. Remove the front wheel as described in this chapter.
3. Remove the clamp bolts securing the brake hose to the fork protector.
4. Remove the bolts securing the fork protectors (**Figure 50**) and remove the protectors.
5. Remove the mounting bolts securing the brake caliper (**Figure 52**) and remove the caliper. Support the caliper by using a coat hanger or other device that will secure it to the upper part of the bike. Do *not* allow the caliper to hang by the brake hose.
6. Loosen the upper and lower fork bridge bolts.
7. If the fork tubes are to be disassembled, perform the following at this time:
   a. Pull the fork tubes down approximately 100 mm (3.9 in.) and tighten the lower bridge bolts.
   b. Loosen, but do not remove, the fork cap assemblies (B, **Figure 49**).
8. Loosen the lower bridge bolts.
9. Pull the fork tubes down and out to remove. You may need to rotate the tubes slightly to ease removal.
10. Installation is the reverse of these steps while noting the following.
11. Insert the fork tubes into the lower fork bridge and clamp into position at approximately 100 mm (3.9 in.) below the normal clamping position.
12. Tighten the fork caps to 30-40 N•m (22-29 ft.-lb.).
13. Loosen the lower fork bridge bolts, slide the tubes up, then align the top surface of the upper fork bridge with the groove 10 mm (0.40 in.) below the top of the fork tube (**Figure 53**).
14. Tighten the upper fork bridge bolts to specifications in **Table 1**.
15. Tighten the lower fork bridge bolts (**Figure 54**) to specifications in **Table 1**.

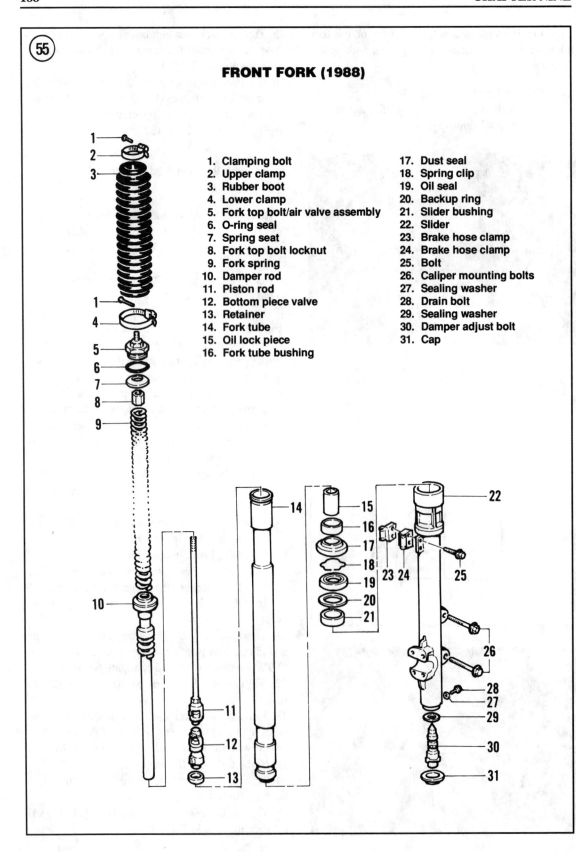

FRONT FORK (1988)

1. Clamping bolt
2. Upper clamp
3. Rubber boot
4. Lower clamp
5. Fork top bolt/air valve assembly
6. O-ring seal
7. Spring seat
8. Fork top bolt locknut
9. Fork spring
10. Damper rod
11. Piston rod
12. Bottom piece valve
13. Retainer
14. Fork tube
15. Oil lock piece
16. Fork tube bushing

17. Dust seal
18. Spring clip
19. Oil seal
20. Backup ring
21. Slider bushing
22. Slider
23. Brake hose clamp
24. Brake hose clamp
25. Bolt
26. Caliper mounting bolts
27. Sealing washer
28. Drain bolt
29. Sealing washer
30. Damper adjust bolt
31. Cap

16. When installing the brake caliper, insert the longer of the caliper bolts into the upper caliper bolt hole.

Front Fork Disassembly (1988 Models)

Refer to **Figure 55** during disassembly and assembly procedures.

1. Remove the clamping screws and clamps (**Figure 56**) at the top and bottom of the rubber boot. Remove the rubber boot from the groove in the top of the slider and slide the boot off of the fork tube.

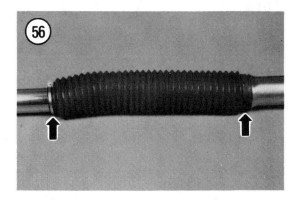

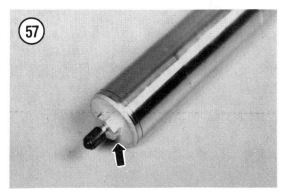

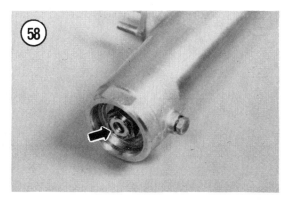

2. The fork cap should have been loosened in Step 4 of *Fork Removal/Installation*. If not, clamp the slider portion of the fork in a vise with soft jaws and loosen the fork cap by unthreading it (**Figure 57**).

> *WARNING*
> *Be careful when removing the fork cap/air valve assembly as the spring is under pressure.*

3. Remove the fork cap and, while holding the fork over a drain pan, expel the fork oil by pumping the fork up and down several times.

4. The damper adjust bolt at the bottom of the fork should have been loosened in *Front Fork Removal/Installation*, Step 9. If not, clamp the slider in a vise with soft jaws, then loosen and remove the bolt (**Figure 58**) and sealing washer. Discard the sealing washer; it should be replaced every time the damper adjust bolt is removed.

5. Remove the fork piston/piston rod/fork spring assembly by withdrawing it from the fork tube.

6. To remove the fork cap from the piston rod, perform the following:

    a. Hold (compress) the spring back to gain access to the fork cap locknut.

    b. Place a wrench (A, **Figure 59**) on the fork cap locknut (B, **Figure 59**).

    c. Place a wrench (C, **Figure 59**) on the fork cap/air valve assembly (D, **Figure 59**) and loosen the fork top bolt/air valve assembly.

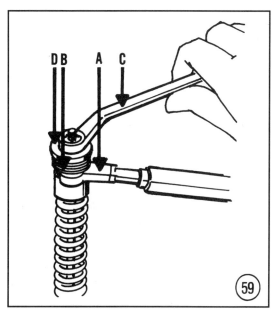

d. Remove the fork cap/air valve, spring seat and the fork spring.

e. Unscrew the fork top bolt locknut and withdraw the piston rod from the piston.

7. Install the fork slider in a vise with soft jaws.

8. Remove the dust seal from the fork slider (**Figure 60**).

9. Carefully pry out the stopper ring (**Figure 61**).

NOTE
Force is needed to remove the fork tube from the slider. It won't simply slide apart like many forks.

10. There is an interference fit between the bushing in the fork slider and the bushing on the fork tube. In order to remove the fork tube from the fork slider, pull hard on the fork tube using quick in and out strokes. Doing this will withdraw the fork tube with the bushing, backup ring and oil seal from the slider.

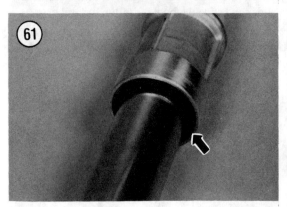

NOTE
It may be necessary to heat the area on the slider around the oil seal slightly before removal. Use a rag soaked in hot water. Do not apply a flame directly to the fork slider.

11. Withdraw the fork tube from the fork slider.

12. Turn the fork tube upside down and slide off the oil seal, backup ring and slider bushing from the fork tube (**Figure 62**). Leave the fork tube bushing on the fork tube at this time.

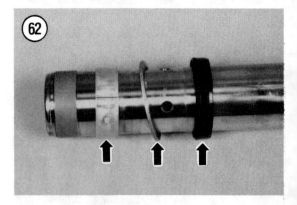

13. Remove the oil lock piece from the fork slider.

14. If necessary, use Honda special tool (part No. 07GMA-KS70100) and remove the retainer and bottom piece valve (**Figure 63**) from the piston. It is not necessary to remove these 2 parts unless you suspect that they are damaged.

Front Fork Inspection (1988 Models)

1. Thoroughly clean all parts in solvent and dry them. Check the fork tube for signs of wear or scratches.

2. Check the fork piston rebound spring (A, **Figure 64**) for wear or damage; replace if worn or sagged.

3. Check the piston ring (B, **Figure 64**) for wear or damage; replace if necessary.

4. Check the fork tube, fork piston, piston rod and fork slider for score marks, scratches, excessive or abnormal wear; replace any damaged parts.

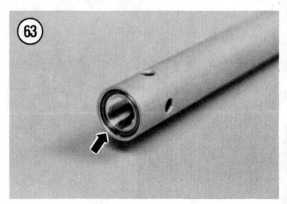

5. Check the slider for dents or exterior damage that may cause the upper fork tube to hang up during riding; replace if necessary.

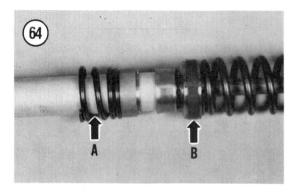

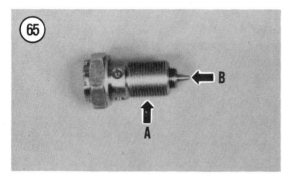

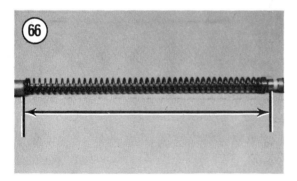

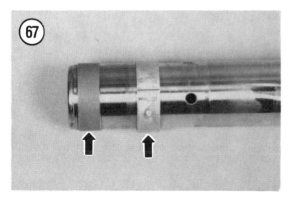

6. Inspect the threads (A, **Figure 65**) and the needle edge (B, **Figure 65**) of the damper adjust bolt for damage; replace if necessary.

7. Measure the uncompressed length of the fork spring (not rebound spring) as shown in **Figure 66**. If the spring has sagged to the service limit dimension listed in **Table 3** or less, the spring must be replaced.

8. Inspect the slider and fork tube bushings (**Figure 67**). If either is scratched or scored, they must be replaced. If the Teflon coating is worn off so that the copper base material is showing on approximately 3/4 of the total surface, the bushing must be replaced. Also check for distortion on the check points on the backup ring; replace as necessary. Refer to **Figure 68**.

9. Any parts that are worn or damaged should be replaced. Simply cleaning and reinstalling unserviceable components will not improve the performance of the front suspension.

Front Fork Assembly (1988 Models)

1. Coat all parts with the recommended fork oil before installation.

2. If removed, install a new fork tube bushing (**Figure 69**).

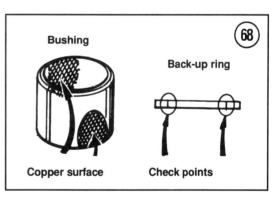

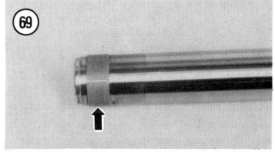

3. Assemble the fork piston/fork spring assembly as follows:

CAUTION
Be careful not to damage the guide bushing inside the fork piston with the threads on the piston rod during installation.

a. Carefully install the piston rod into the fork piston from the bottom.

b. Screw the fork top bolt locknut onto the piston rod and thread it down all the way.

c. Install the fork spring, spring seat and the fork top bolt/air valve assembly.

d. Hold the spring back slightly. Tighten the fork top bolt/air valve assembly only finger-tight at this time.

4. If the bottom piece valve was removed, oil and install a new sealing washer, then install the bottom piece valve and retainer into the fork piston (**Figure 63**). Tighten the retainer to the torque specified in **Table 1**. Use the same special tool used during removal.

5. Install the fork piston/piston rod/fork spring assembly into the fork tube (**Figure 70**). Temporarily tighten the fork cap/air valve assembly to the torque specification listed in **Table 1**.

6. Install the oil lock piece onto the end of the fork piston (**Figure 71**).

7. Install the fork tube assembly into the slider (**Figure 72**).

8. Prior to installing the damper adjust bolt, turn the damping adjuster *counterclockwise* until it stops. Install a new sealing washer and the damper adjust bolt into the base of the slider (**Figure 58**).

9. Place the fork slider in a vise with soft jaws and tighten the damper adjust bolt to the torque specification listed in **Table 1**.

NOTE
Following disassembly and inspection of both fork legs, make sure the damping adjuster is at the same adjustment position on both forks.

10. Slide a new fork slider bushing (A, **Figure 73**) down the fork tube and rest it on the slider.

11. Drive the bushing into the fork slider with Honda special tool Fork Seal Driver (part No. 07947-KA50100) and attachment (part No. 07947-

KA40200). Drive the bushing into place until it seats completely in the recess in the slider.

12. Install the backup ring (B, **Figure 73**) with the flat side facing toward the slider bushing.

NOTE
A homemade tool like a piece of galvanized pipe (of appropriate size) can work as an installation tool. If both ends are threaded, wrap one end with duct tape to prevent the threads from damaging the interior of the slider.

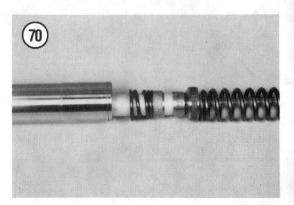

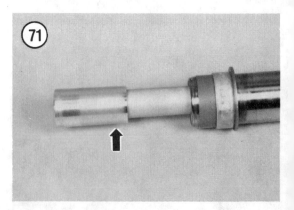

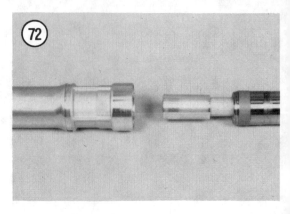

13. To prevent damage to the inner surface of the new oil seal, wrap the groove in the upper end of the fork tube with a piece of smooth tape (i.e., 3M Magic Transparent Tape). Do not use masking or duct tape as they are rough and may damage the inner rubber surface of the oil seal.

14. Coat the new oil seal with fork oil. Position the seal with the marking facing upward and slide it down onto the fork tube (C, **Figure 73**). Drive the seal into the fork slider (**Figure 74**) with Honda special tool Fork Seal Driver (part No. 07947-KA50100) and attachment (part No. 07947-KA40200). Drive the oil seal in until the stopper ring

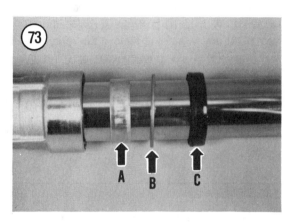

73

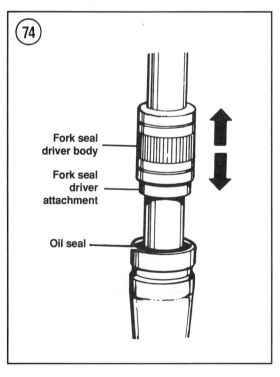

74

Fork seal
driver body

Fork seal
driver
attachment

Oil seal

groove in the slider can be seen above the top surface of the oil seal.

NOTE
The oil seal can be driven in with a homemade tool as described in the NOTE following Step 12.

15. Install the stopper ring (**Figure 61**). Make sure the stopper ring is completely seated in the groove in the fork slider.

16. Install the dust seal (**Figure 60**).

Fork Oil Refilling (1988 Models)

1. Unscrew the fork cap/air valve assembly from the fork tube.

2. Remove the fork spring by performing the following: sub-steps a through d will not be necessary, if the fork cap locknut was only hand-tightened.

    a. Hold the spring back to allow access to the fork cap locknut.

    b. Place a wrench (A, **Figure 59**) on the fork cap locknut (B, **Figure 59**).

    c. Place a wrench (C, **Figure 59**) on the fork cap/air valve assembly (D, **Figure 59**) and loosen the fork top bolt/air valve assembly.

    d. Remove the fork top bolt/air valve assembly, spring seat and the fork spring.

3. If removed, install the sealing washer and drain bolt in the fork slider. Tighten the bolt securely.

4. Fill the fork tube with the recommended fork oil. Refer to **Table 4** for the specific quantity for each fork leg.

5. Hold the fork assembly vertical and slowly pump the fork tube several times. Slowly pump the piston rod at least 10 times.

6. Compress the fork completely and measure the fluid level from the top of the fork tube (**Figure 75**) after the fork fluid settles. Refer to **Table 5** for specified fork oil level.

7. Wipe off the fork spring with a lint-free cloth.

8. Install the fork spring and spring seat.

9. Make sure the O-ring seal is in place on the fork cap/air valve assembly and in good condition; replace if necessary.

10. To tighten the fork top bolt/air valve assembly, perform the following.

    a. Hold (compress) the spring back to allow access to the fork cap locknut.

9

b. Place a wrench (A, **Figure 59**) on the fork cap locknut (B, **Figure 59**).

c. Place a wrench (C, **Figure 59**) on the fork cap/air valve assembly (D, **Figure 59**) and tighten the fork top bolt locknut against the fork cap/air valve assembly. Tighten the fork top bolt locknut to 17.5-22.5 N•m (13-16 ft.-lb.).

11. Screw the fork cap/air valve assembly into the fork tube while pushing down on the spring. Start the bolt slowly; don't crossthread it.

12. Place the slider in a vise with soft jaws and tighten the fork cap/air valve assembly to 15-30 N•m (11-22 ft.-lb.).

13. Slide the rubber boot and clamps onto the fork tube. Install the rubber boot into the groove in the top of the slider. Do not tighten the clamp screws at this time.

14. Install the fork assemblies as described in this chapter.

15. After the fork assembly and front wheel are installed, rotate the rubber boot so the breather holes are facing toward the rear.

16. Push the rubber boot up until it touches the bottom surface of the lower fork bridge. Tighten the clamp screws on each clamp.

Front Fork Disassembly (1989-1990 Models)

Refer to **Figure 76** for the following procedures.

Some fork disassembly/reassembly procedures on 1989 and 1990 models require the use of special tools. A special fork slider spacer (Honda part No. 07KMZ-KZ30101) is a relatively inexpensive tool, but will be needed during disassembly, reassembly and refilling procedures. A seal case holder (Honda part No. 07KMB-KZ30200) and oil seal driver (Honda part No. 07KMD-KZ30100) are necessary when installing the guide bushing and oil seal during fork reassembly. Other special tools may be required as indicated. Read this section carefully before starting work and make sure these tools are available prior to performing these procedures.

1. Make sure the sliding surfaces and the dust seal of the fork slider are clean.

2. Unthread the fork cap/air valve assembly (1, **Figure 76**) from the fork tube.

NOTE
To avoid damage to the dust seal, use the special slider spacer.

If damage occurs, oil may leak from the slider.

3. Install the special slider spacer (**Figure 77**) tool onto the lower end of the slider and carefully lower the fork tube onto the tool.

4. Remove the fork cap/air valve assembly from the piston rod by performing the following:

a. Place a wrench on the fork cap/air valve assembly (A, **Figure 78**).

b. While holding the locknut (B, **Figure 78**) with a wrench, loosen and remove the fork cap/air valve assembly from the piston rod.

5A. On 1989 models, push the spring collar (C, **Figure 78**) downward and remove the spring seat (D, **Figure 78**). Then remove the spring collar and locknut.

5B. On 1990 models, push the spring collar (C, **Figure 78**) downward and remove the locknut (B, **Figure 78**). Then remove the spring seat and spring collar.

6. Remove the special slider spacer from the slider.

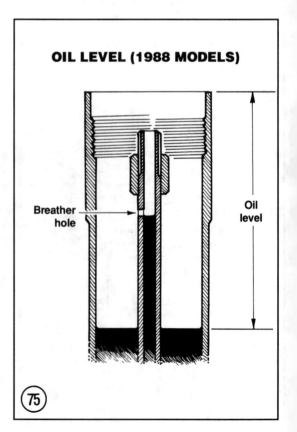

OIL LEVEL (1988 MODELS)

Breather hole

Oil level

⑦⑤

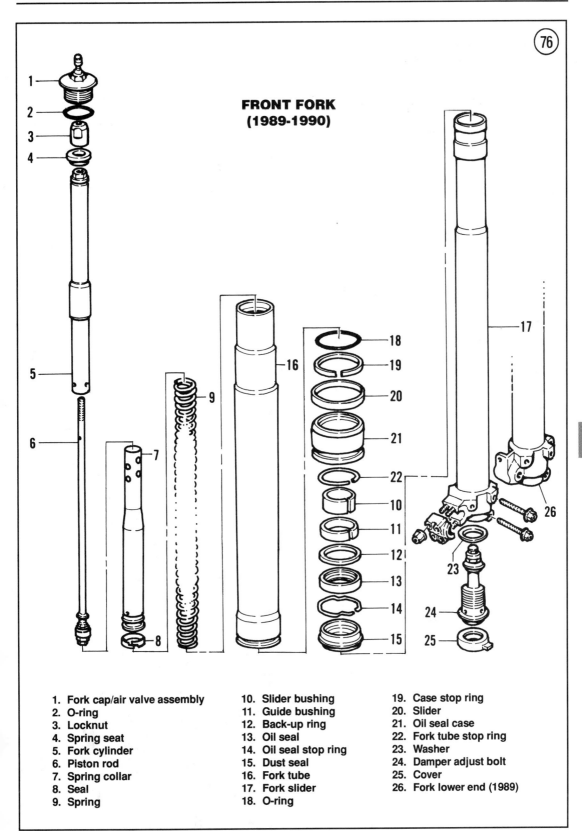

**FRONT FORK
(1989-1990)**

76

1. Fork cap/air valve assembly
2. O-ring
3. Locknut
4. Spring seat
5. Fork cylinder
6. Piston rod
7. Spring collar
8. Seal
9. Spring
10. Slider bushing
11. Guide bushing
12. Back-up ring
13. Oil seal
14. Oil seal stop ring
15. Dust seal
16. Fork tube
17. Fork slider
18. O-ring
19. Case stop ring
20. Slider
21. Oil seal case
22. Fork tube stop ring
23. Washer
24. Damper adjust bolt
25. Cover
26. Fork lower end (1989)

9

CAUTION
Following removal of the fork cap from the piston rod, you will note that the tube can move up and down freely in the slider. Hold both the fork tube and slider with your hands to keep from damaging the guide and slide bushing. If damage occurs, fork oil may leak from the slider.

7. Remove the fork spring.

8. Hold the fork leg over a drain pan with one hand. With the other hand, hold the piston rod and pump the rod in and out of the leg to expel the fork oil. Do this about 8-10 times or until all the oil is expelled.

9. The damper adjust bolt (24, **Figure 76**) should have been loosened during the *Front Fork Removal* steps. If not, clamp the fork slider in a vise with soft jaws. Loosen and remove the damper adjust bolt and washer (23, **Figure 76**). You may need to use a cylinder holder (Honda part No. 07KMB-KZ30100) to hold the cylinder during this step. Discard the washer as it must be replaced during assembly. Do not disassemble the damper adjust bolt.

10. Withdraw the fork piston rod (6, **Figure 76**) and cylinder (5, **Figure 76**) from the fork slider.

11. Remove the piston rod from the fork cylinder.

NOTE
Do not damage the guide bushing inside the fork cylinder with the threads of the piston rod.

12. Remove the dust seal (**Figure 79**).

13. Remove the stop ring (**Figure 80**) from the stop ring groove.

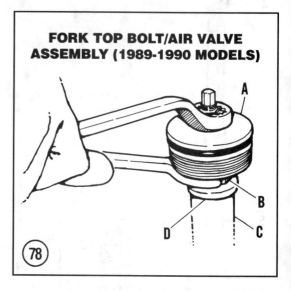

FORK TOP BOLT/AIR VALVE ASSEMBLY (1989-1990 MODELS)

⑦⑧

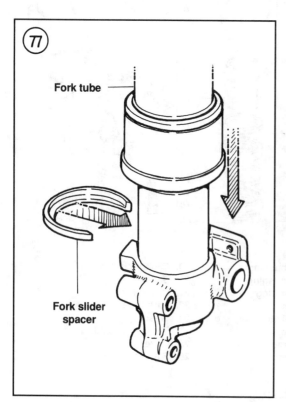

⑦⑦

Fork tube

Fork slider spacer

⑦⑨

⑧⓪

14. There is an interference fit between the bushing in the fork slider and the bushing on the fork tube. In order to remove the fork tube from the slider, pull hard on the fork tube using quick in and out strokes.

15. Withdraw the fork tube (16, **Figure 76**) from the slider (17, **Figure 76**).

16. Gently pry open the end of the slider bushing (F, **Figure 81**) with a screwdriver and remove the slider bushing. Do not open the end too far, or a loss of tension will occur.

17. Slide off the guide bushing (C, **Figure 81**), backup ring (E, **Figure 81**), oil seal (B, **Figure 81**),

stop ring (D, **Figure 81**) and dust seal (A, **Figure 81**).

Front Fork Inspection (1989-1990 Models)

1. Thoroughly clean all parts in solvent and dry them. Check the fork tube for wear or scratches.

2. Inspect the oil case slider (B, **Figure 82**). If it is worn, perform the following, but do not remove the oil seal case unless absolutely necessary.

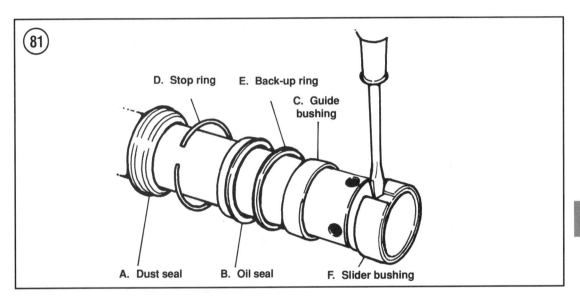

D. Stop ring   E. Back-up ring   C. Guide bushing
A. Dust seal   B. Oil seal   F. Slider bushing

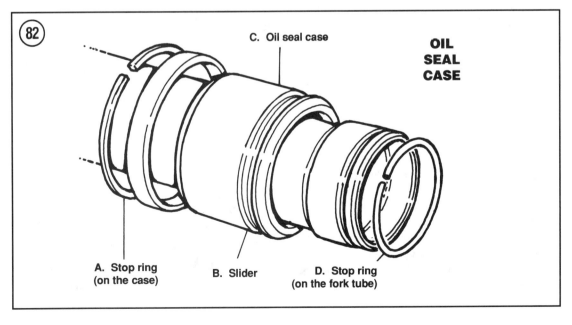

C. Oil seal case   OIL SEAL CASE
A. Stop ring (on the case)   B. Slider   D. Stop ring (on the fork tube)

a. Slide the oil seal case (C, **Figure 82**) down, away from the fork tube stop ring (D, **Figure 82**).

b. Remove and replace the oil case slider (B, **Figure 82**). Replace the case stop ring (A, **Figure 82**), if it is worn or damaged.

c. Remove the O-ring (C, **Figure 83**) in the oil seal case groove.

d. Assemble by reversing these steps.

3. Check the piston ring on the end of the piston rod for wear or damage; replace if necessary.

4. Check the fork tube (16, **Figure 76**), fork cylinder (5, **Figure 76**), piston rod (6, **Figure 76**) and fork slider (17, **Figure 76**) for score marks, scratches, excessive or abnormal wear; replace any damaged parts.

5. Check the slider for dents or exterior damage that may cause the upper fork tube to hang up during riding; replace if necessary.

6. Inspect the spring collar (C, **Figure 78**) for wear or damage; replace if necessary.

7. Inspect the threads on the damper adjust bolt (24, **Figure 76**). Replace the washer (23, **Figure 76**) and O-ring with new ones prior to reassembly.

8. Measure the uncompressed length of the fork spring as shown in **Figure 84**. If the spring has sagged to the service limit dimension listed in **Table 3** or less, the spring must be replaced.

9. Inspect the slider (F, **Figure 81**) and guide bushings (C, **Figure 81**). If either is scratched or scored, they must be replaced. If the Teflon coating is worn off so that the copper base material is showing on approximately 3/4 of the total surface, the bushing must be replaced. Also check for distortion on the check points of the back-up ring; replace as necessary. Refer to **Figure 85**.

10. Any parts that are worn or damaged should be replaced. Simply cleaning and reinstalling unserviced components will not improve front suspension performance.

Front Fork Assembly (1989-1990 Models)

1. Coat all parts with the recommended fork oil before installation.

2. If the oil seal case (A, **Figure 83**) was removed, install a new O-ring (C, **Figure 83**) in the case groove (B, **Figure 83**). Install the oil seal case as described in *Front Fork Inspection* and make sure it is seated against the stop ring.

3. Wrap the end of the fork slider with tape. This will ease installation of the components in the next few steps.

4. Install the dust seal (**Figure 79**) and stop ring (**Figure 80**).

5. Coat the oil seal lips with oil and install it with its marked side facing the dust seal.

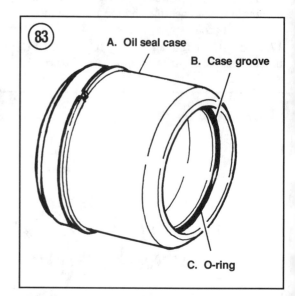

83

A. Oil seal case

B. Case groove

C. O-ring

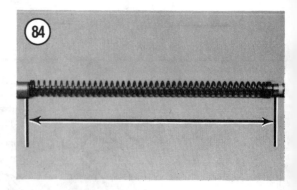

84

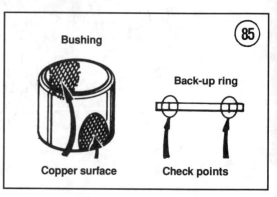

85

Bushing

Back-up ring

Copper surface   Check points

6. Remove the tape from the end of the slider and install the back-up ring with the chamfered side facing the bushings.

7. Install the guide bushing (C, **Figure 81**) and slider bushing (F, **Figure 81**).

8. Put some tape on the dust seal and stop ring to secure them while performing the rest of the steps.

9. Install the fork slider into the fork tube.

NOTE
For installation of the guide bushing and oil seal, use oil seal driver (Honda part No. 07KMD-KZ30100) and seal case holder (Honda part No. 07KMB-KZ30200).

10. Using the seal case holder (B, **Figure 86**) and a vise, hold the oil seal case as shown.

11. Position the guide bushing (G, **Figure 86**) and back-up ring (F, **Figure 86**) and drive them into the fork tube with the oil seal driver (A, **Figure 86**).

12. Coat the lips of the oil seal with fork oil and drive the oil seal (E, **Figure 86**) into the oil seal case using the oil seal driver (A, **Figure 86**).

13. Remove the tape from the stop ring and dust seal and install them into place.

CAUTION
Since the fork tube will move up and down freely on the fork slider, hold both the slider and fork tube with your hands. This will avoid damage to the guide, slider bushings and dust seal.

14. Install the special fork slider spacer (**Figure 77**) used in disassembly to avoid damage to the dust seal.

15. Install the piston rod (6, **Figure 76**) into the fork cylinder (5, **Figure 76**) from the bottom. Be careful not to damage the guide bushing inside of the fork cylinder with the piston rod threads.

16. Install the fork cylinder and piston rod into the slider.

17. Install the damper adjust bolt (24, **Figure 76**) and washer (23, **Figure 76**).

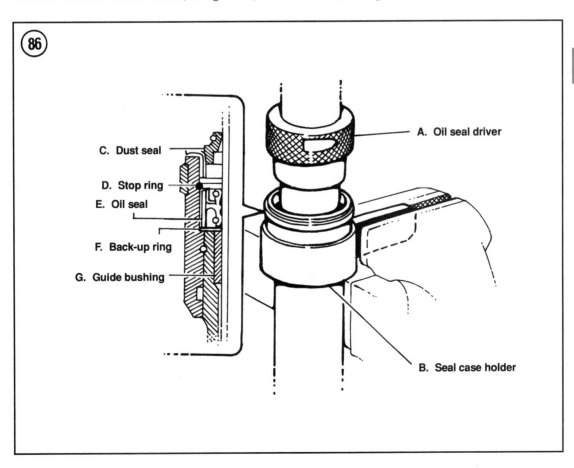

86

A. Oil seal driver

C. Dust seal
D. Stop ring
E. Oil seal
F. Back-up ring
G. Guide bushing

B. Seal case holder

9

18. Clamp the slider in a vise with soft jaws.

19. Tighten the fork damper adjust bolt to the specification listed in **Table 1**. You may need to hold the fork cylinder with the special cylinder holder (Honda part No. 07KMB-KZ30100 or -KZ3010A).

> *NOTE*
> *Make a note of the position of the damping adjuster. Following reassembly of the opposite fork leg, make sure both damping adjusters are in the same adjustment position.*

20. Remove the slider from the vise.

21. Refill the fork leg with oil as described in *Front Fork Refilling* for your specific model.

22. Install the fork assemblies as described in this chapter.

Fork Oil

The procedure for refilling the forks varies between 1989 and 1990 models. However, the special fork slider spacer (Honda part No. 07KMZ-KZ30101) is necessary for obtaining an accurate oil level measurement on both models (**Figure 77**). Make sure to perform the specific refilling procedures for your model. The factory recommended fork oil for 1989 models is Pro Honda Suspension Fluid SS-7 or equivalent. The factory recommended fork oil for 1990 models is Pro Honda Suspension Fluid SS-7M or equivalent.

Front Fork Refilling (1989 Models)

1. Install the special fork slider spacer at the lower end of the slider as shown in **Figure 77**.

2. Support the fork leg vertically and pour the fork oil into the piston rod until a small amount can be seen flowing from the side breather hole (**Figure 87**).

3. Pump the piston rod 8-10 times, then hold the piston rod at its full bottomed position.

4. Measure the fork oil level (**Table 5**) from the top of the fork tube (**Figure 87**) with the fork leg secure and vertical.

> *NOTE*
> *Make a note of the oil level, so the opposite fork leg can be refilled to the same capacity.*

5. Install the fork cap locknut so that its inner threads are facing upward.

6. Thread the locknut, by hand, all the way down until it seats.

7. Install the spring into the fork tube.

8. Perform the following:
   a. Cut a piece of stiff wire to approximately 12 in.
   b. Wrap one end of the wire around the piston rod, below the locknut.
   c. Feed the other end of the wire through the spring collar, and pull the piston rod up through it.
   d. Remove the wire from the piston rod.

9. Measure the distance between the nut and the top of the piston rod. It should measure at least 14 mm (0.55 in.). Adjust if necessary.

10. While pushing the collar down against the tension of the fork spring, install the seat stopper between the locknut and collar.

11. Lubricate and install a new O-ring onto the fork cap.

12. Thread the fork cap onto the piston rod until it makes contact with the locknut.

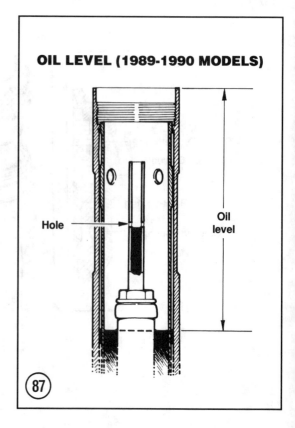

OIL LEVEL (1989-1990 MODELS)

Hole

Oil level

87

13. Using a wrench to hold the fork cap (A, **Figure 78**), place a wrench on the piston rod locknut (B, **Figure 78**) and tighten to 17.5-22.5 N•m (12.7-16.3 ft.-lb.).

14. Thread the fork cap into the fork tube, but do not tighten completely. It will be tightened to specifications during installation.

15. Remove the special fork slider spacer.

Front Fork Refilling (1990 Models)

1. Install the locknut to the piston rod with the cutout facing upward. This is a temporary installation to prevent the piston rod from falling into the cylinder. Tighten the locknut securely with your hand.

2. Install the special fork slider spacer (**Figure 77**) at the lower end of the slider.

3. While securing the fork leg vertically, pour half of the recommended amount of fork oil into the slider and fork tube.

4. Position the piston rod at its minimum stroke. Pour fork oil into the piston rod until a small amount can be seen flowing out of the side breather hole (**Figure 87**).

5. Slowly pump the piston rod and fork tube, about 8-10 times.

6. Compress the fork leg fully.

7. Measure the oil level from the top of the tube, with the fork leg secure and vertical. See the oil level specifications in **Table 5**.

NOTE
Make a note of the oil level, so the opposite fork leg can be refilled to the same capacity.

8. Install the spring with the tapered side facing upward. Only the tapered end will fit into the fork cap, so use the cap as a guide.

9. Perform the following:
   a. Cut a piece of stiff wire to 24 in.
   b. Secure one end of the wire around the threaded area of the piston rod, below the locknut.
   c. Feed the other end of the wire through the spring collar.
   d. While holding the wire, rock the collar until it slides down into the fork leg.

10. Remove the wire and the piston locknut.

11. Push the spring collar downward, against the tension of the spring.

12. Install the spring seat and locknut. Thread the locknut, by hand, until it stops.

NOTE
Make sure the spring seat is seated in its groove within the collar. If not installed properly, the seat will be damaged and damping performance will be altered.

13. The distance between the locknut and the top of the piston should be at least 14 mm (0.55 in.). Adjust if necessary.

14. Lubricate and install a new O-ring onto the fork cap.

15. Tighten the fork cap bolt, by hand, until it makes contact with the locknut.

16. Using a wrench to hold the fork cap bolt (A, **Figure 78**), place a wrench on the piston rod locknut (B, **Figure 78**) and tighten to 17.5-22.5 N•m (12.7-16.3 ft.-lb.).

17. Thread the fork cap into the fork tube, but do not tighten completely. The fork cap will be tightened to specifications during fork installation.

18. Remove the special slider spacer from the slider.

19. Install the fork as described in this chapter.

Front Fork Disassembly (1991 Models)

Refer to **Figure 88**.

Some of the disassembly, reassembly and fork oil refilling procedures on the 1991 models require the use of special tools. A special fork slider spacer (Honda part No. 07KMZ-KZ30101) is a relatively inexpensive tool, but will be necessary during disassembly, reassembly and refilling procedures. If the oil seal case is to be removed and reinstalled, a seal case holder (Honda part No. 07KMB-KZ30200), oil seal driver (Honda part No. 07749-0010000) and attachment (Honda part No. 07746-0010400) will be necessary. The same seal case holder and oil seal driver are also necessary for installing the guide bushing, back-up ring and oil seal during fork reassembly. Read this entire section carefully before starting work and make sure these tools are available prior to performing these procedures.

1. Make sure the fork is clean, especially the sliding surfaces and the damper adjust bolt, located at the bottom of the slider.

FRONT FORK (1991)

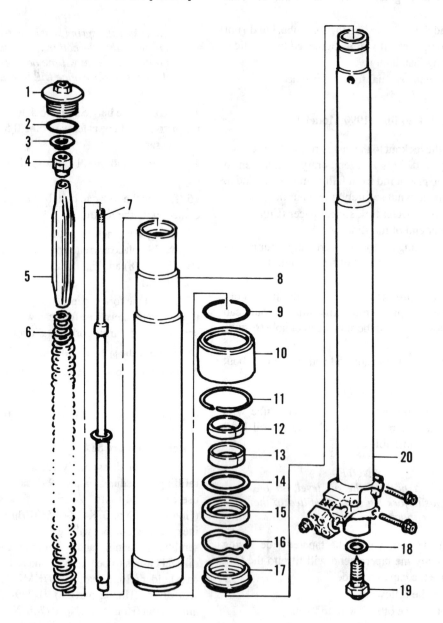

1. Fork cap
2. O-ring
3. Spring seat
4. Locknut
5. Spring guide
6. Spring
7. Damper assembly
8. Fork tube
9. O-ring
10. Oil seal case
11. Stop ring
12. Slider bushing
13. Guide bushing
14. Back-up ring
15. Oil seal
16. Stop ring
17. Dust seal
18. Washer
19. Damper adjust bolt
20. Fork slider

2. Install the special slider spacer to the fork slider, just above the axle holder (**Figure 77**). This will prevent damage to the dust seal and guide bushing.

3. While holding the fork tube, unscrew the fork cap (1, **Figure 88**) from the fork tube and gently lower the fork tube down onto the slider spacer.

4. Hold the fork cap with a wrench (A, **Figure 89**). Insert a wrench onto the piston rod locknut (B, **Figure 89**) and remove the fork cap from the piston rod.

5. Remove the spring seat from the fork cap.

6. Remove the fork spring (C, **Figure 89**).

CAUTION
After the fork cap is removed, you will notice that the fork slider can move up and down freely within the fork tube. Hold both the fork tube and slider with your hands to prevent movement or guide and slide bushings can be damaged. If damage occurs, fork oil may leak from the fork slider.

7. Remove the locknut and spring guide (D, **Figure 89**) from the piston rod. Inspect the spring guide for damage; replace if necessary.

8. Hold the fork leg over a drain pan and pour until all of the oil appears to have been expelled.

9. Clamp the lower end of the slider into a vise with soft jaws.

10. If not already loosened during fork removal, loosen and remove the damper adjust bolt and sealing washer. Handle the bolt carefully, as the bolt has a needle in the center, which is easily bent or damaged.

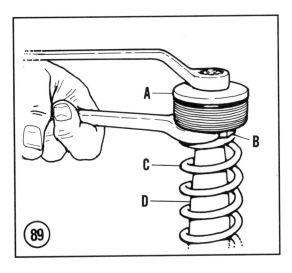

11. Remove the fork from the vise and remove the special slider spacer from the slider.

12. Pull the fork piston assembly from the fork slider.

13. While holding the piston with one hand, pump the piston rod 8-10 times with the other, to expel oil from the damper.

14. Remove the dust seal (**Figure 79**) and stop ring (**Figure 80**).

15. Check the fork slider at this time, to make sure it moves smoothly in the fork tube. If it is less than smooth, check the slider and fork tube for damage or bends. Also, check the bushings for wear or damage.

16. There is an interference fit between the bushing in the fork slider and the bushing on the fork tube. In order to remove the fork tube from the fork slider, pull hard on the tube using quick in and out strokes. Doing this will withdraw the bushing, back-up ring and oil seal from the slider.

17. Carefully pry open the end of the slider bushing (F, **Figure 81**) with a screwdriver. Do not pry the opening more than necessary for removal or tension on the bushing will be lost.

18. Remove the guide bushing (C, **Figure 81**), back-up ring (E, **Figure 81**), oil seal (B, **Figure 81**), stop ring (D, **Figure 81**) and dust seal (A, **Figure 81**).

19. If the oil seal case (10, **Figure 88**) shows signs of wear or oil leakage, the O-ring must be replaced. Perform the following, but do not remove the oil seal case unless it is absolutely necessary. Special Driver (Honda part No. 07749-0010000), seal case holder (part No. 07KMB-KZ30200) and attachment (part No. 07746-0010400) are needed for this procedure.

  a. Move the case (C, **Figure 82**) away from the fork tube stop ring (D, **Figure 82**) and remove the stop ring from the fork tube.

  b. Hold the oil seal case with the special seal case holder (C, **Figure 90**). Using the driver (A, **Figure 90**) and attachment (B, **Figure 90**), force the fork tube out of the oil seal case.

  c. Remove the O-ring and discard.

Front Fork Inspection (1991 Models)

1. Thoroughly clean all parts in solvent and dry them.

2. Check the fork tube and fork slider for dents, score marks, scratches and excessive or abnormal wear.

3. Check the piston rod (A, **Figure 91**) for bends, abnormal wear or damage.

4. Check the oil lock valve (B, **Figure 91**) for damage or wear.

5. Check the slider (F, **Figure 81**) and guide bushing (C, **Figure 81**) for excessive wear or scratches. Remove any metal powder with fork oil and a nylon brush. If either is scratched or scored, they must be replaced. If the Teflon coating is worn to the point where copper appears, replace the bushing. If burrs are present on the slider bushing, remove them carefully to avoid removing the Teflon coating.

6. Check for distortion on the check points on the back-up ring; replace as necessary. See **Figure 85**.

7. Measure the uncompressed length of the fork spring (**Figure 84**). If the spring has sagged to the service limit dimension in **Table 3** or less, the spring must be replaced.

8. Inspect the threads of the damper adjust bolt (19, **Figure 88**) and needle edge for damage; replace if necessary.

9. Any parts that are worn or damaged should be replaced. Simply cleaning and reinstalling unserviced components will not improve the performance of the front suspension.

Front Fork Assembly (1991 Models)

1. If the oil seal case was removed, a hydraulic press and special tools (Honda part Nos. 07749-0010000 and 07KMB-KZ30200 with attachment part No. 07746-0010400) are needed for reassembly. Perform the following:

    a. Lubricate and install a new O-ring (C, **Figure 83**) in the groove (B, **Figure 83**) in the seal case.

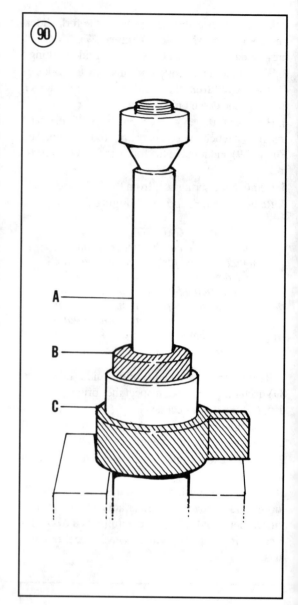

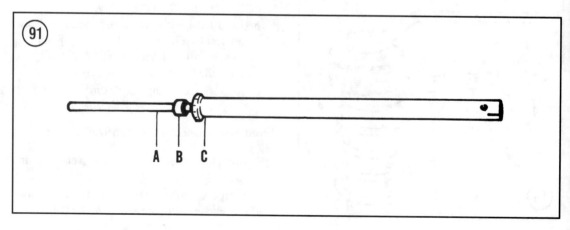

b. Lubricate the end of the fork tube and install the oil seal case onto the fork tube.

c. Install the stop ring (D, **Figure 82**) into the groove in the fork tube.

d. Position the oil seal case over the stopper ring and hold it with the special seal case holder (C, **Figure 90**).

e. Press the fork tube with the special driver (A, **Figure 90**) and attachment (B, **Figure 90**) until the stopper ring makes contact with the oil seal case.

2. Wrap the end of the fork tube with tape to ease installation, and slide on a new dust seal and slide on the stop ring.

3. Lubricate the lips of the oil seal and install it with the markings facing the dust seal.

4. Install the backup ring and guide bushing.

5. Remove the tape and install the slider bushing.

6. Lubricate the guide bushings and slider and install the fork slider into the fork tube.

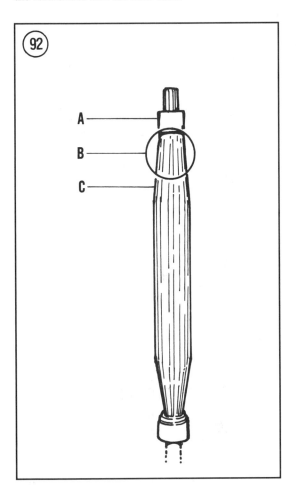

7. Using a vise with soft jaws and the special seal case holder to hold the oil seal case (B, **Figure 86**), position the guide bushing (G, **Figure 86**) and back-up ring (F, **Figure 86**). Drive the guide bushing with the back-up ring into the fork tube using the special driver (A, **Figure 86**).

8. Using the special driver, drive on the new oil seal (E, **Figure 86**) until the stop ring groove is visible.

9. Install the stop ring into the groove in the oil seal case (D, **Figure 86**).

10. Slide the dust seal into position (C, **Figure 86**).

NOTE
*Install the special slider spacer (**Figure 77**) in the lower end of the slider. This will avoid damage to the fork dust seal and guide bushing. If damage does occur, oil may leak from the slider.*

11. Install the fork damper assembly (7, **Figure 88**) into the fork slider.

12. Clamp the axle holder portion of the fork slider into a vise with soft jaws.

13. Install a new sealing washer (18, **Figure 88**) and damper adjust bolt (19, **Figure 88**). Tighten the damper adjust bolt to specifications listed in **Table 3**. If the fork damper assembly rotates while tightening the center bolt, install the fork spring and fork cap. This will secure the piston assembly and allow tightening of the damper adjust bolt.

14. Clean the spring guide thoroughly and install the spring guide (C, **Figure 92**) onto the piston rod with the oil hole facing upward (B, **Figure 92**).

15. Install the locknut (A, **Figure 92**) with the flange side facing upward. This is a temporary installation to hold the spring guide during the refilling procedure.

16. Refill the fork with fork oil as described under *Fork Oil Refilling*.

17. Install the fork assembly as described in this chapter.

Fork Oil Refilling (1991 Models)

The recommended fork oil for 1991 models is Pro Honda Suspension Fluid SS-7M or equivalent.

1. Make sure the special slider spacer (**Figure 77**) is in place at the lower end of the slider. This spacer is necessary for obtaining a correct oil level measurement and to prevent damage to the dust seal during refilling.

9

2. Pour half of the recommended amount of fork oil into the fork leg.

3. Bleed the air from the fork leg by performing the following:

CAUTION
*See **Figure 93**. On CR250R models, do not extend the fork tube more than 300 mm (11.8 in.) at dimension "A." On CR500R models, do not extend the fork tube more than 250 mm (9.8 in.) at dimension "A." If the tubes are extended farther than these dimensions, fork oil will spill out of the oil hole in the fork slider.*

a. Extend the fork tube. While covering the top of the fork tube with your hand, compress the leg slowly. Hold the leg vertical and use the floor or a tabletop to push against.

b. Perform this procedure 2-3 times.

4. With the piston rod at its bottomed-out position, pour the fork oil into the piston rod until a small amount can be seen flowing out from the piston rod end.

5. Slowly pump the piston rod and fork tube, 8-10 times.

6. Again, pour in fork oil, this time to the recommended capacity. Measure the fork oil level (**Table 5**), from the top of the fork tube, with the fork leg in a secured vertical position. Repeat Step 5.

7. Compress the fork tube fully and set it aside for 5 minutes. This will allow the air bubbles in the oil to settle.

8. With the fork leg in a secure vertical position, measure the fork oil level again, from the top of the fork tube (**Figure 94**).

NOTE
Make a note of the fork oil level, so the opposite fork leg can be refilled to the same capacity.

9. Install the spring and fork cap by performing the following:

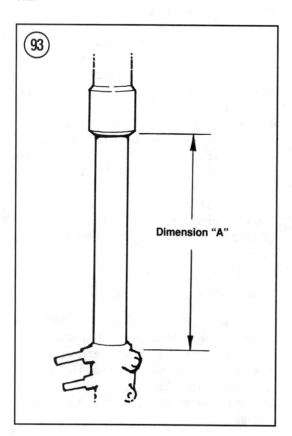

(93) Dimension "A"

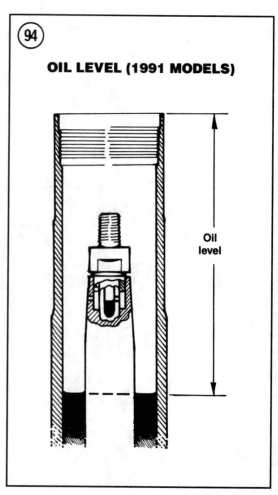

(94) OIL LEVEL (1991 MODELS)

Oil level

a. Cut a piece of stiff wire to 24 in.

b. Attach one end of the wire around the locknut on the piston rod.

c. Hold the fork spring with the tapered end up. The tapered end is the only end that will fit inside the fork cap.

d. Feed the other end of the wire through the fork spring and hold the oil lock valve.

e. Remove the wire and thread the locknut (correctly) onto the piston rod, by hand, until it seats.

10. Lubricate and install a new O-ring on the fork cap.

11. Install the spring seat onto the fork spring and thread the fork cap onto the piston rod. Make sure the spring seat is seated correctly between the fork spring and fork cap.

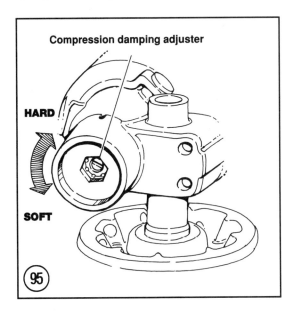

Compression damping adjuster

HARD

SOFT

95

12. While holding the locknut with a wrench (B, **Figure 89**), tighten the fork cap bolt (A, **Figure 89**) with a wrench to 20-24 N•m (14-17 ft.-lb.).

13. Thread the fork cap into the fork tube, but do not tighten. It will be tightened to specifications during fork installation.

FRONT FORK ADJUSTMENT

Compression Damping Adjustment

The compression damping adjuster is mounted in the center of the compression bolt installed in the bottom of the fork tube (**Figure 95**). The compression damping adjustment affects how quickly the front fork compresses. Turning the compression adjuster clockwise increases (stiffer) the compression damping; turning the compression adjuster counterclockwise decreases (softer) the compression damping. **Table 6** lists the standard compression adjustment position. Turning the compression adjuster 1 full turn changes the adjuster by 4 positions.

To adjust the compression damping adjuster to its standard position, perform the following:

1. Remove the plug from the bottom of each fork tube.

2. Turn the compression damping adjuster *clockwise* until it stops (**Figure 95**).

3. Turn the compression damping adjuster *counterclockwise* the standard number of turns listed in **Table 6** for your model.

4. Set the compression adjustment on both fork tubes to the same adjustment setting.

NOTE
Make sure the compression adjuster screw is located in one of the detent positions and not in between any 2 settings.

9

Tables are on the following pages.

Table 1 FRONT SUSPENSION TORQUE SPECIFICATIONS

Item	N·m	ft.-lb.	in.-lb.
Front axle			
1988-1989	55-70	40-51	
1990-1991	80-93	59-68	
Front axle holder nuts	10-12	7-9	
Handlebar holder bolts	18-25	13-18	
Fork bridge bolts			
Upper			
1988-1989	18-25	13-18	
1990-1991	30-34	22-25	
Lower			
1988-1989	18-25	13-18	
1990-1991	24-30	17-22	
Upper steering stem locknut	95-140	70-103	
Steering stem adjust nut			
1988-1989	1-2	–	9-17
1990-1991	8-12	–	71-106
Fork top bolt			
1988	15-30	11-22	
1989-1991	30-40	22-29	
Fork cap/air valve assembly	30-40	22-29	
Fork bottom piece valve			
1988 CR250R and CR500R	3-6	–	26-53
Fork damper adjust (center) bolt			
CR250R			
1988	30-40	22-29	
1989	40-45	29-33	
1990	50-55	36-40	
1991	40-50	29-36	
CR500R			
1988	30-40	22-29	
1989-1990	40-45	29-33	
1991	40-50	29-36	
Fork top bolt locknut			
1988-1990	17-22	12-16	
1991	20-24	14-17	
Spoke nipples	2.5-5.0	–	22-44
Rim locks	10-15	7-11	
Brake disc screws			
1988-1989	14-16	10-12	
1990-1991	40-45	29-33	

Table 2 FRONT FORK STANDARD AIR PRESSURE

| Model | Air pressure | |
	psi	kg/cm^2
All models	0	0

Table 3 FRONT FORK SPRING FREE LENGTH (STANDARD SPRING)

	Standard	Service limit
CR250R and CR500R		
1988	562.8 mm (22.15 in.)	557.2 mm (21.94 in.)
1989-1990	510.0 mm (20.08 in.)	504.9 mm (19.88 in.)
1991	509.0 mm (20.04 in.)	503.9 mm (19.84 in.)

Table 4 FRONT FORK OIL CAPACITY

	ml	U.S. oz.	Imp. oz
CR250R			
1988			
Standard	564	19.1	19.9
Minimum	516	17.5	18.2
Maximum	573	19.4	20.2
1989			
Standard	657	22.2	23.1
Minimum	636	21.5	22.4
Maximum	671	22.7	23.7
1990			
Standard	640	21.6	22.5
Minimum	617	20.8	21.7
Maximum	650	22.0	22.9
1991			
Standard	651	22.0	22.9
Minimum	631	21.3	22.7
Maximum	665	22.5	23.4
CR500R			
1988			
Standard	575	19.4	20.2
Minimum	527	17.8	18.5
Maximum	584	19.8	20.5
1989			
Standard	641	21.7	22.6
Minimum	620	21.0	21.9
Maximum	655	22.1	23.0
1990			
Standard	612	20.7	21.6
Minimum	605	20.5	21.4
Maximum	639	21.6	22.5
1991			
Standard	657	22.2	23.1
Minimum	631	21.3	22.2
Maximum	665	22.5	23.4

9

Table 5 FRONT FORK OIL LEVEL

	mm	in.
CR250R		
1988		
Standard	124	4.88
Maximum	115	4.53
Minimum	170	6.69
1989		
Standard	115	4.53
Maximum	105	4.13
Minimum	132	5.20
1990		
Standard	124	4.88
Maximum	114	5.67
Minimum	144	5.67
1991		
Standard	107	4.21
Maximum	95	3.74
Minimum	124	4.88

(continued)

Table 5 FRONT FORK OIL LEVEL (continued)

	mm	in.
CR500R		
1988		
Standard	123	4.84
Maximum	114	4.49
Minimum	169	6.65
1989		
Standard	127	4.99
Maximum	116	4.6
Minimum	146	5.8
1990		
Standard	158	6.22
Maximum	133	5.2
Minimum	164	6.5
1991		
Standard	102	4.02
Maximum	95	3.74
Minimum	124	4.88

Table 6 FRONT FORK COMPRESSION DAMPING ADJUSTMENT

Model	Standard adjustment
CR250	
1988	
1989	
1990	11 clicks from hardest position
1991	5 clicks from hardest position
CR500R	
1988	
1989	
1990	5 clicks from hardest position
1991	4 clicks from hardest position

CHAPTER TEN

NOTE: If you own a 1992 CR500R or later model, first check the Supplement at the back of this book for any new service information.

REAR SUSPENSION

This chapter includes repair and replacement procedures for the rear wheel and rear suspension components.

Tables 1-3 at the end of this chapter provide specifications and tightening torque recommendations.

REAR WHEEL

Removal/Installation

It is not necessary to remove the disc brake or any disc brake components when removing the rear wheel.

1. Place the bike's skidplate on a metal or wood stand so the rear wheel will clear the ground.

2. If the drive chain will be removed for cleaning or other service, rotate the wheel until the master link is visible. Using a pair of needle-nose pliers, remove the clip at the master link (**Figure 1**) and remove the master link and chain.

3. If the drive chain will not be completely removed, perform Step 4, then slide the wheel forward enough to remove the chain from the rear sprocket.

4. Loosen the axle nut (**Figure 2**), drive chain adjuster locknuts (A, **Figure 3**) and drive chain adjusting bolts (B, **Figure 3**).

5. Remove the axle nut and pull the axle through the wheel and swing arm from the left side (**Figure 4**).

6. Remove the wheel.

7. Installation is the reverse of these steps while noting the following.

8. When sliding the wheel into position, make sure the brake disc slides between the brake pads. Be careful not to damage the pads.

9. If the chain retaining clip and master link were removed, install the master link, then install a new clip with the closed end in the direction of wheel rotation (**Figure 5**).

10. If the rear chain was not completely removed, slide the wheel forward enough to install the drive chain on the rear sprocket.

11. Adjust the chain tension as described in Chapter Three.

12. Tighten the axle nut to the torque specified in **Table 1**.

10

Inspection

Measure the axial and radial runout of the wheel with a dial indicator as shown in **Figure 6**. The maximum axial and radial runout is 2.0 mm (0.08 in.). If the runout exceeds this dimension, check the wheel bearing condition.

Some of this condition can be corrected as described under *Spoke Inspection and Replacement* in Chapter Nine.

Check axle runout as described under *Rear Hub Inspection* in this chapter.

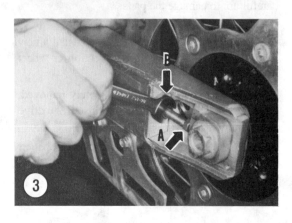

Master link clip

Direction of travel

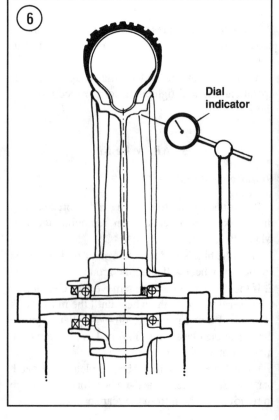

Dial indicator

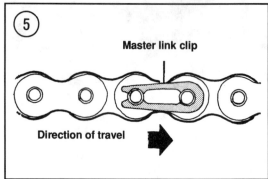

REAR HUB

The rear hub varies from year to year. 1988 CR250R models have a bearing retainer located on the left side while CR500R models have the bearing retainer on the right side. On all 1989 and later models, the bearing retainer is located on the right side. All 1990 and 1991 models have 2 sets of bearings, an inner and outer bearing, in the left side of the hub.

Refer to **Figure 7** for 1988 CR250R models and **Figure 8** for 1988 CR500R models. **Figure 9** illustrates 1989-1991 CR250R and CR500R models.

Inspection

Inspect each wheel bearing prior to removing it from the wheel hub.

CAUTION
Do not remove the wheel bearings for inspection purposes as they will be damaged during the removal process. Remove the wheel bearings only if they are to be replaced.

1. Perform Steps 1-6 of *Disassembly* in this chapter.

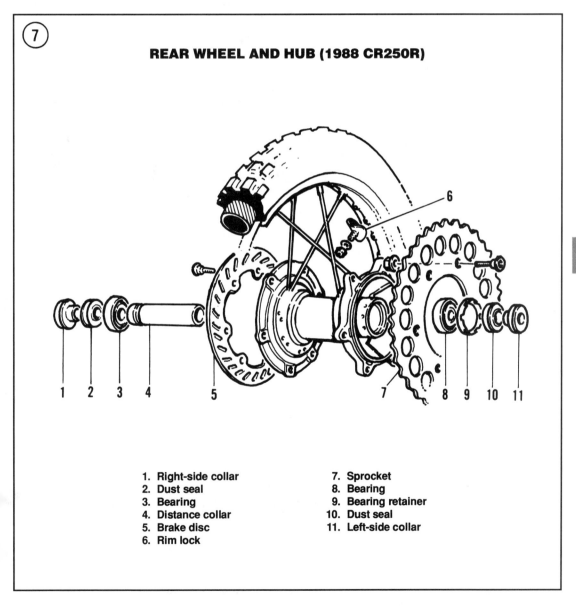

7

REAR WHEEL AND HUB (1988 CR250R)

1 2 3 4 5 6 7 8 9 10 11

1. Right-side collar
2. Dust seal
3. Bearing
4. Distance collar
5. Brake disc
6. Rim lock
7. Sprocket
8. Bearing
9. Bearing retainer
10. Dust seal
11. Left-side collar

10

REAR WHEEL AND HUB
(1988 CR500R)

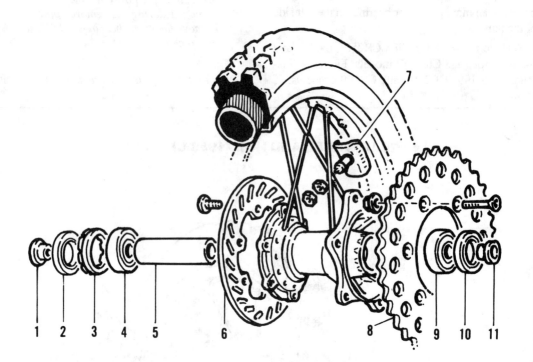

1. Right-side collar
2. Dust seal
3. Bearing retainer
4. Bearing
5. Distance collar
6. Brake disc
7. Rim lock
8. Sprocket
9. Bearing
10. Dust seal
11. Left-side collar

⑨

**REAR WHEEL AND HUB
(1989-1991)**

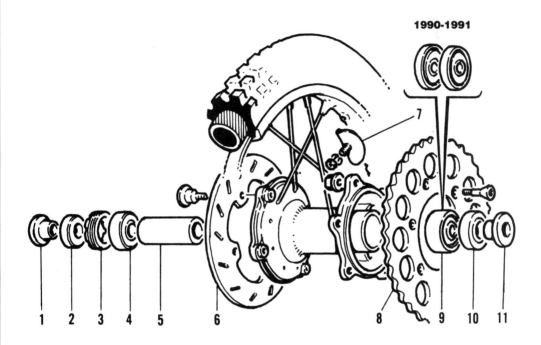

1990-1991

1. Right-side collar
2. Dust seal
3. Bearing retainer
4. Bearing
5. Distance collar
6. Brake disc
7. Rim lock
8. Sprocket
9. Bearing (s)
10. Dust seal
11. Left-side collar

10

2. Turn each bearing by hand. Make sure bearings turn smoothly.

3. On non-sealed bearings, check the balls for evidence of wear, pitting or excessive heat (bluish tint). Replace the bearings if necessary; always replace as a complete set. When replacing the bearings, take your old bearings along to ensure a perfect matchup.

NOTE
Fully sealed bearings are available from many bearing specialty shops. Fully sealed bearings provide better protection from dirt and moisture that may get into the hub.

4. Check the axle for wear and straightness. Use V-blocks and a dial indicator as shown in **Figure 10**. If the runout is 0.2 mm (0.01 in.) or greater, the axle should be replaced.

Disassembly

1. Remove the rear wheel as described in this chapter.

2. Remove the collars from both sides of the wheel hub (A, **Figure 11**).

3. Remove the dust seals (B, **Figure 11**) from both sides of the wheel hub.

4. Remove the nuts and bolts securing the sprocket and remove the sprocket (**Figure 12**).

5. Remove the bolts securing the brake disc and remove the disc. There are 6 brake disc bolts on 1988 models and 4 brake disc bolts on 1989 and later models.

6A. On CR500R models, use a small drift and hammer or special bearing retainer wrench (Honda part No. 07HMA-KS70100) and attachment (part No. 07710-0010401) and unscrew bearing retainer from the right side.

6B. On 1988 CR250R models, use a small drift and hammer or special bearing retainer wrench (Honda part No. 07HMA-KS70100) and attachment (part No. 07710-0010401) and unscrew the retainer from the left side.

6C. On 1989 and later CR250R models, use a small drift and hammer or special bearing retainer wrench (Honda part No. 07710-0010200) and attachment (part No. 07710-0010401) and unscrew the retainer from the right side (**Figure 13**).

7. Before proceeding further, inspect the wheel bearings as described in this chapter.

8. If the bearings require removal, perform the following:

   a. Insert a soft-aluminum or brass drift into the left-hand side of the hub.

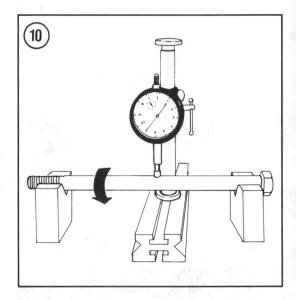

b. Push the distance collar over to one side and place the drift on the inner race of the right-hand bearing.

c. Tap the bearing out of the hub with a hammer, working around the perimeter of the inner race.

d. Remove the distance collar.

e. Turn the wheel over and tap the left-hand bearing out of the hub in the same manner. On 1990 and 1991 models, remove the inner and outer left-hand bearings using the same method.

9. Clean the inside and outside of the hub with solvent. Dry with compressed air or a shop cloth.

Assembly

1. On non-sealed bearings, pack the bearings thoroughly with a good-quality bearing grease. Work the grease in between the balls thoroughly; turn the

bearing by hand a couple of times to make sure the grease is distributed evenly inside the bearing.

2. Blow any dirt or foreign matter out of the hub before installing the bearings.

3. Pack the hub with multipurpose grease.

4. If you are using standard bearings that are sealed on one side, install them with the sealed side facing out.

5. Tap the bearings squarely into place and tap only on the outer race. Use a socket (**Figure 14**) that matches the outer race diameter. Do not tap on the inner race or the bearing will be damaged. Be sure to tap the bearings in until they seat completely.

6A. On 1988 CR250R and CR500R models, perform the following:

a. Lubricate and install the left-hand bearing.

b. Insert the distance collar from the right side, then lubricate and install the right-hand bearing.

c. Lubricate and install the bearing retainer using the same tools used during removal.

6B. On 1989 and later CR250R and CR500R models, perform the following:

a. Lubricate and install the right-hand bearing.

> *CAUTION*
> *On 1990 and 1991 models, install both inner and outer left-hand bearings with the sealed sides facing out.*

b. Insert the distance collar into the hub from the left-hand side, then install the left-hand bearing(s).

c. Lubricate and install the bearing retainer using the same tools used during removal.

7. After the bearing retainer has been screwed in securely, lock it in place by staking it with a center punch and hammer.

8. Lubricate and install new dust seals (B, **Figure 11**) and tap the seals into place.

9. Install the driven sprocket and its bolts and nuts (**Figure 12**), and tighten to the torque specification in **Table 1**.

10. Install the left and right side collars (A, **Figure 11**).

11. Install the rear wheel as described in this chapter.

DRIVE CHAIN

Removal/Installation

1. Place a metal or wood stand under the frame to support the bike securely with the rear wheel off the ground.

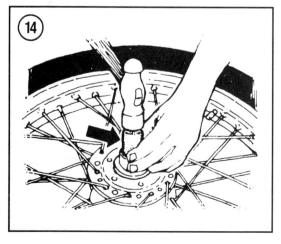

10

2. Remove the bolts (**Figure 15**) securing the drive sprocket guard and remove the guard.

3. Loosen the drive chain adjuster locknuts (A, **Figure 3**) and adjuster bolts (B, **Figure 3**) on each end of the swing arm.

4. Loosen the rear axle nut (**Figure 2**).

5. Push the rear wheel forward to obtain maximum chain slack.

6. Rotate the rear wheel until the drive chain master link is visible.

7. Remove the clip on the master link (**Figure 1**) and remove the master link from the chain.

8. Remove the drive chain and inspect it as described in Chapter Three.

9. Install by reversing these removal steps while noting the following.

10. Install a new drive chain master link clip with the closed end facing in the direction of chain travel (**Figure 16**).

11. Adjust the drive chain tension as described in Chapter Three.

12. Tighten the axle nut to the torque specification in **Table 1**.

13. After the wheel is completely installed, rotate it several times to make sure it rotates smoothly. Apply the brake several times to make sure it operates correctly.

SWING ARM

Worn pivot bushings and needle bearings can produce erratic and dangerous handling. Common symptoms are wheel hop, pulling to one side during acceleration and pulling to the other side during braking.

Swing arm designs vary slightly according to year and model. Refer to **Figure 17** for 1988 CR500R swing arm design. Refer to **Figure 18** for 1988-on CR250R models and 1989-on CR500R models.

Removal

1. Place a metal or wood stand under the frame to support the bike securely with the rear wheel off the ground.

2. Remove the rear wheel as described in this chapter.

3. Remove the rear brake pedal as described in Chapter Eleven. This will allow access to the swing arm pivot bolt.

4. Remove the brake line hose guides from the swing arm.

5. Remove the rear brake caliper assembly by sliding it backward and out of the swing arm slide track. Tie the caliper assembly to the mid-frame section to support it. Do *not* allow the caliper assembly to hang by the brake hose.

6A. On CR250R and all 1989 and later CR500R models, perform the following:

    a. Remove the shock absorber lower bolt (A, **Figure 19**). This will take some the tension off of the shock arm and allow easier removal.

    b. Remove the cover on each side of the swing arm (B, **Figure 19**).

    c. Loosen and remove the nut from the shock arm bolt on the right side. Pull the shock arm bolt through the swing arm and shock arm. This will separate the shock arm and linkage from the swing arm.

6B. On 1988 CR500R models, perform the following:

    a. Loosen and remove the lower shock absorber bolt.

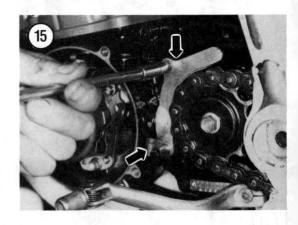

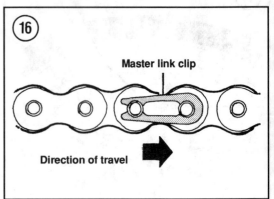

Master link clip

Direction of travel

(17)

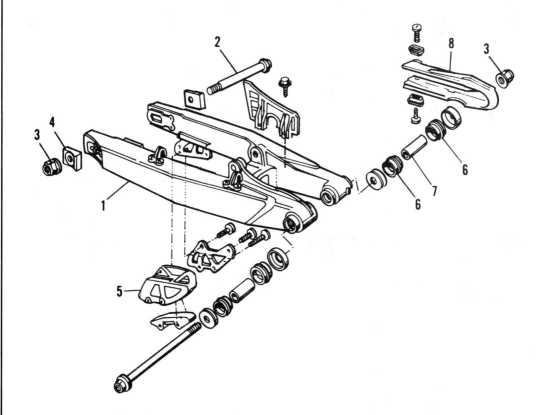

**SWING ARM
(1988 CR500R)**

10

1. Swing arm
2. Axle bolt
3. Axle nut
4. Adjuster plate
5. Chain guide
6. Dust seal
7. Spacer
8. Chain slider

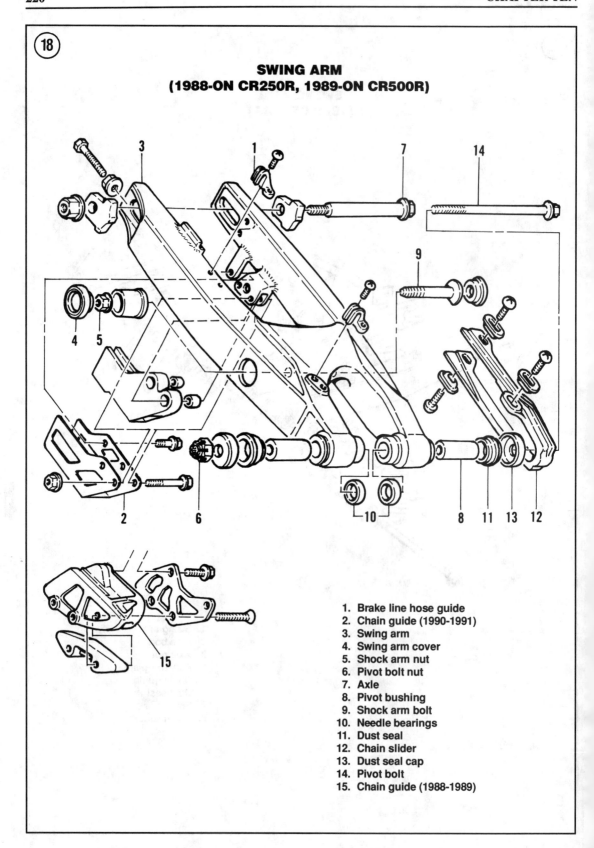

⑱

**SWING ARM
(1988-ON CR250R, 1989-ON CR500R)**

1. Brake line hose guide
2. Chain guide (1990-1991)
3. Swing arm
4. Swing arm cover
5. Shock arm nut
6. Pivot bolt nut
7. Axle
8. Pivot bushing
9. Shock arm bolt
10. Needle bearings
11. Dust seal
12. Chain slider
13. Dust seal cap
14. Pivot bolt
15. Chain guide (1988-1989)

b. Remove the nut and bolt linking the shock arm to the swing arm (**Figure 20**). This will separate the shock arm and linkage from the swing arm.

7. Grasp the rear end of the swing arm and try to move it from side to side in a horizontal arc. There should be no noticeable side play. If play is evident and the pivot bolt nut is tightened correctly, the swing arm bushings and/or needle bearings should be inspected and replaced.

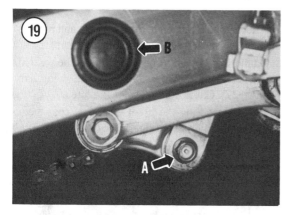

8. Place a wood block under the rear of the swing arm to hold it in the raised-up position.

9. Remove the pivot bolt nut. On 1988 CR500R models, the nut is located on the left-hand side of the frame. On all other models, the nut is located on the right-hand side (**Figure 21**).

10. Remove the pivot bolt. On 1988 CR500R models, remove the bolt from the right-hand side. On all other models remove the bolt from the left-hand side (**Figure 22**).

11. Pull back on the swing arm, free it from the frame and remove it from the frame.

Installation

1. Position the swing arm into the mounting area of the frame. Align the holes in the swing arm with the holes in the frame.

2. Apply a light coat of multipurpose grease to the pivot bolt.

3. Make sure the dust seals and dust seal caps (**Figure 23**) are installed to the swing arm.

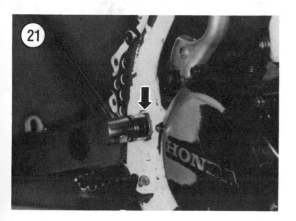

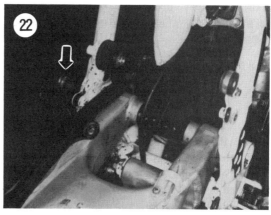

10

4. Make sure the bushings located at the rear of the engine case (**Figure 24**) are in place and install the pivot bolt. On 1988 CR500R models, install the pivot bolt from the right-hand side. On all other models, install the pivot bolt from the left-hand side.

5. Check to make sure the swing arm is properly located in the frame and then tighten the pivot bolt nut to the torque specified in **Table 1**.

6. Align the swing arm with the shock arm and install the shock arm bolt through both, then install the nut. This will connect the swing arm to the shock linkage.

7. Install the shock absorber lower bolt. Tighten the bolt to specifications in **Table 1**.

8. Tighten the shock arm nut to specifications in **Table 1**.

9. On 1988 CR250R and 1989 and later CR500R models, install the swing arm rubber covers.

10. Install the brake pedal as described in Chapter Eleven.

11. Install the rear brake line guides.

12. Install the rear brake caliper assembly by sliding it forward on the swing arm slide track.

13. Move the swing arm up and down several times to make sure all components are properly seated.

14. Install the rear wheel as described in this chapter.

Disassembly/Inspection/Assembly

The swing arm is equipped with pivot bushings and needle bearings secured with thrust collars. The pivot bushings (A, **Figure 25**) will come right out after the dust seal caps are removed (B, **Figure 25**). The needle bearings and thrust collars are pressed into place. Both have to be removed with force as described in this chapter.

1. Remove the swing arm as described in this chapter.

2. Inspect the chain slider (A, **Figure 26**) and chain guide (B, **Figure 26**) for wear or deterioration. 1988 models are equipped with a chain guard located on the upper left swing arm. If necessary, remove the screws securing the guide, slider and guard (if equipped) and replace, if necessary.

3. Remove the dust seal caps (B, **Figure 21**) and dust seals, if they have not already fallen off during the removal sequence.

4. Push out the pivot bushings (A, **Figure 21**).

5. Clean the pivot bushings in solvent and dry thoroughly.

6. Wipe off any excess grease from the needle bearings at each end of the swing arm. The needle bearings wear very slowly and wear is very difficult to measure. Turn each bearing with your fingers. Make sure it rotates smoothly. Check the rollers for evidence of wear, pitting or color change (bluish tint) indicating heat from lack of lubrication.

NOTE
Always replace both needle bearing assemblies even though only one may be worn.

7. If necessary, remove the thrust collars and replace the needle bearings as described in this chapter.

8. On the 1988 CR500R models, inspect the welded area where the shock arm attaches to the swing arm (**Figure 27**). Check for cracks or fractures.

9. Before installing the pivot bushings, coat them with molybdenum disulfide grease (NLGI No. 2).

10. Coat the dust seals with molybdenum disulfide grease (NLGI No. 2) and install.

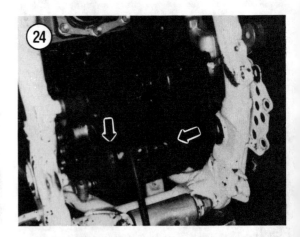

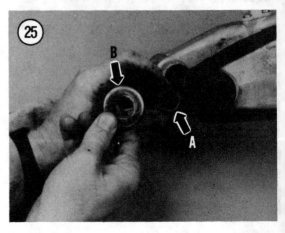

11. Install the dust seal caps.

12. Install the swing arm as described in this chapter.

Needle Bearing Replacement

The thrust collars and needle bearings are pressed into place and have to be removed with force. The bearing race will get distorted when removed, so don't remove it unless absolutely necessary.

On 1988 CR500R models, the needle bearings can be removed with a hammer and drift or special tool (Honda part No. 0796-KA50000). On all other models, the needle bearings should be removed with a hydraulic press and special tools available from a Honda dealer (part Nos. 07946-MJ00100 and 0796-KM40701).

1. Remove the swing arm as described in this chapter.

2. On 1988 CR500R models, perform the following:

   a. Secure the swing arm in a vise with soft jaws.

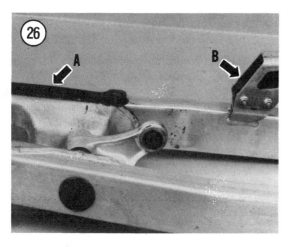

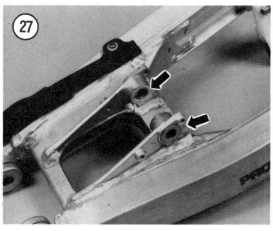

   b. If the special tool isn't available, remove the thrust collars, then carefully tap out the needle bearing(s) using a suitable size drift or socket and extension. Drive them out from the opposite end.

CAUTION
Do not remove the bearings just for inspection as they will be damaged during removal and new bearings must be installed.

3. On all other models, use a hydraulic press and the special tools. Install the driver head to the driver shaft and drive the bearings and thrust collar out of the swing arm.

4. For 1988 CR500R models, turn the swing arm over in the vise and repeat Step 2 for the other side.

5. For all other models, turn the swing arm over and repeat Step 3 for the other side.

6. Thoroughly clean out the inside of the swing arm with solvent and dry with compressed air.

7. Apply a light coat of molybdenum disulfide grease (NLGI No. 2) to all parts before installation.

NOTE
Either the right- or left-hand needle bearing(s) can be installed first. 1988 CR500R models have thrust collars on both the inside and outside of the swing arm.

8. Insert the bearings with the marks on the bearing facing outward.

9A. On 1988 CR500R models, use the same tool setup used in Step 2. Be careful not to damage the bearing race.

9B. On all other models, use a hydraulic press and install the inside needle bearing with special tools, Honda part Nos. 07946-KM40701 and 07946-MJ00100. Install the second bearing and outside thrust collar with special tools, Honda part Nos. 07749-0010000, 07746-0010100 and 07746-0041000.

10. Drive the needle bearings and thrust collars into place slowly and squarely. Make sure the bearings seat properly.

11. Install the new dust seals on each end of the swing arm.

12. Install the swing arm as described in this chapter.

10

PRO-LINK SYSTEM

The single shock absorber and linkage of the Pro-Link suspension system (**Figure 28**) are attached to the swing arm, just behind the swing arm pivot point and to the lower rear portion of the frame. All of these items are located forward of the rear wheel.

The shock link and shock arms working together with the matched spring rate and damping rates of the shock absorber combine to achieve a "progressive rising rate" rear suspension. This system provides the rider with the best of both worlds—greater rider comfort and better transfer of power to the ground over rough terrain.

As the rear suspension is moved upward by bumps, the shock absorber is compressed by the movement of the shock arm.

As rear suspension travel increases, the portion of the shock link where the shock absorber is attached rises above the swing arm, thus increasing shock absorber travel (compression). This provides a progressive rise rate in which the shock eventually moves at a faster rate than the wheel. At about halfway through the wheel travel the shock begins to move at a faster rate than it did in the beginning.

> *WARNING*
> *All bolts and nuts used in the Pro-Link*
> *suspension must be replaced with parts*

*of the same type. **Never** use a replacement part of lesser quality or substitute design, as this may affect the performance of the system or result in failure of the part which will lead to loss of control of the bike. Torque values listed in **Table 1** must be used during assembly and installation to ensure proper retention of these parts.*

SHOCK ABSORBER

The single shock absorber (A, **Figure 29**) is a spring-loaded hydraulically-damped unit that has an integral oil/nitrogen reservoir.

Spring Preload Adjustment

There must be pre-load on the spring at all times. Never ride the bike without spring pre-load as loss of control could result.

The spring pre-load must be maintained within the dimensions listed in **Table 3**.

1. Place a metal or wood stand under the frame to support the bike securely with the rear wheel off the ground.

2. Remove the sub-frame as described in this chapter.

> *CAUTION*
> *After the air cleaner air box is removed,*
> *the carburetor throat is exposed. Close*

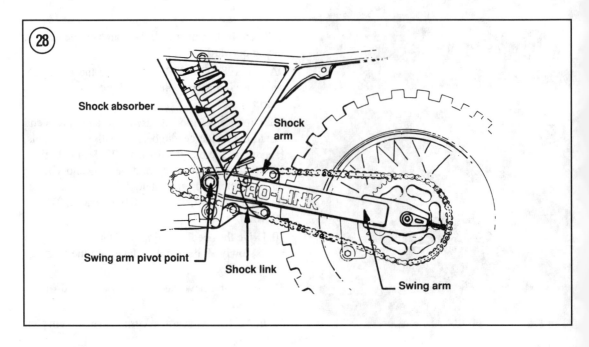

Figure 28

Shock absorber
Shock arm
Swing arm pivot point
Shock link
Swing arm

off the opening with a clean shop cloth or plastic bag so dirt or foreign matter will not enter into the carburetor.

3. Measure the existing spring length (**Figure 30**).

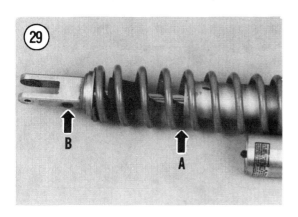

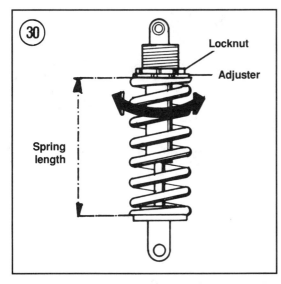

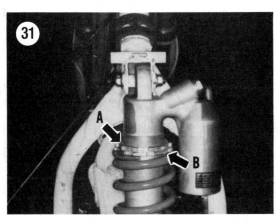

4. To adjust, loosen the locknut (A, **Figure 31**) and turn the adjuster (B, **Figure 31**) in the desired direction. Tightening the adjuster increases spring pre-load and loosening it decreases pre-load.

NOTE
Special tools (pin spanners, Honda part No. 89201-KS6-810) are required to turn the locknut and the adjuster on the shock absorber.

5. One complete turn (360°) of the adjuster moves the spring 1.5 mm (1/16 in.).

CAUTION
Remember, the spring length (pre-load) must be maintained between the minimum and maximum dimensions listed in **Table 2**.

6. After the desired spring length is achieved, tighten the locknut to the torque specifications listed in **Table 1**.

7. Install all parts that were removed.

Rebound Damping Adjustment

The rebound damping adjuster is located at the base of the shock absorber (B, **Figure 29**). The rebound damping adjustment affects how quickly the rear shock absorber extends after compression. Turning the rebound adjuster clockwise increases (stiffens) the rebound damping; turning the adjuster counterclockwise decreases (softens) the rebound damping. **Table 4** lists the number of damping adjustments available while also listing the standard position. Turning the rebound damping adjuster 1 full turn changes the adjuster by 4 positions.

To adjust the rebound damping adjuster to its standard setting, perform the following:

1. Turn the rebound damping adjuster clockwise until it stops (B, **Figure 29**).

2. Turn the rebound damping adjuster counterclockwise the standard number of turns listed in **Table 4** for your model. The punch marks on the shock absorber and adjuster will align when the standard setting is obtained.

NOTE
Make sure the rebound adjuster is located in one of the detent positions and not in between any 2 settings.

Compression Damping Adjustment

The compression damping adjuster is located at the top of the shock absorber (**Figure 32**). The compression damping adjustment affects how quickly the rear shock absorber compresses. Turning the compression adjuster clockwise increases (stiffens) the compression damping; turning the adjuster counterclockwise decreases (softens) the compression damping. **Table 5** lists the number of damping adjustments available while also listing the standard position. Turning the compression damping adjuster 1 full turn changes the adjuster by 4 positions.

To adjust the compression damping adjuster to its standard setting, perform the following:

1. Turn the compression damping adjuster clockwise until it stops (**Figure 32**).

2. Turn the compression damping adjuster counterclockwise the standard number of turns listed in **Table 5** for your model. The punch marks on the shock absorber and adjuster will align when the standard setting is obtained.

> *NOTE*
> *Make sure the compression adjuster is located in one of the detent positions and not in between any 2 settings.*

Removal/Installation

1. Place a metal or wood stand under the frame to support the bike securely with the rear wheel off the ground.

2. Remove the sub-frame as described in this chapter.

> *CAUTION*
> *After the sub-frame and the air cleaner air box are removed, the carburetor throat is exposed. Close off the opening with a clean shop cloth or plastic bag so dirt or foreign matter will not enter into the carburetor.*

3. Remove the upper shock absorber mounting bolt and nut (**Figure 33**).

4. Raise the rear wheel and swing arm.

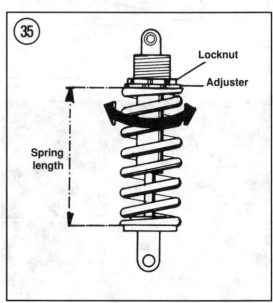

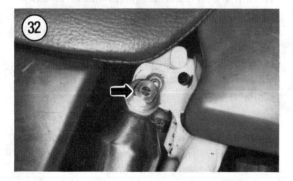

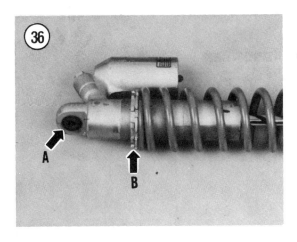

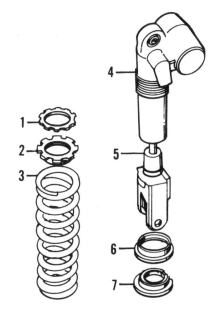

REAR SHOCK ABSORBER
(1988 CR250R, CR500R)

1. Locknut
2. Adjusting nut
3. Spring
4. Damper unit
5. Rubber stopper
6. Spring seat
7. Spring seat stopper

5. Remove the lower shock absorber bolt (**Figure 34**) which secures the shock absorber to the shock arm.

6. Carefully remove the shock absorber from the frame.

7. Install by reversing these removal steps while noting the following.

8. Apply a light coat of molybdenum disulfide grease to all pivot and mounting areas of the shock absorber and the shock arm.

9. Make sure the shock absorber rebound adjuster is facing the right side.

10. Install the upper and lower mounting bolts from the left.

11. Tighten the shock absorber bolts to the torque specified in **Table 1**.

12. Install the sub-frame as described in this chapter.

Disassembly/Assembly

Service by the home mechanic is limited to removal and installation of the spring. Under no circumstances should you attempt to disassemble the shock absorber unit or reservoir due to the high internal pressure of the nitrogen.

If you are satisfied with the existing spring preload setting and want to maintain it, measure and record the spring length (**Figure 35**) before disassembly.

1. Hold the shock absorber upside down and secure the upper mounting portion of the shock and reservoir (A, **Figure 36**) in a vise with soft jaws. Use pieces of wood to protect the reservoir tank from the vise jaws.

NOTE
Special pin spanners (Honda part No.
89201-KS6-810) are required to loosen
the locknut and the adjuster.

2. Using pin spanners, loosen the locknut and the spring adjuster all the way (B, **Figure 36**).

3. Remove the shock absorber assembly from the vise.

4. On 1988 CR250R and CR500R models, refer to **Figure 37**. Slide out the spring seat stopper (7) from the lower portion of the shock absorber assembly. Slide off the spring seat (6) and the spring. On 1988 CR500R models, remove the spacer between the spring stopper and spring seat.

10

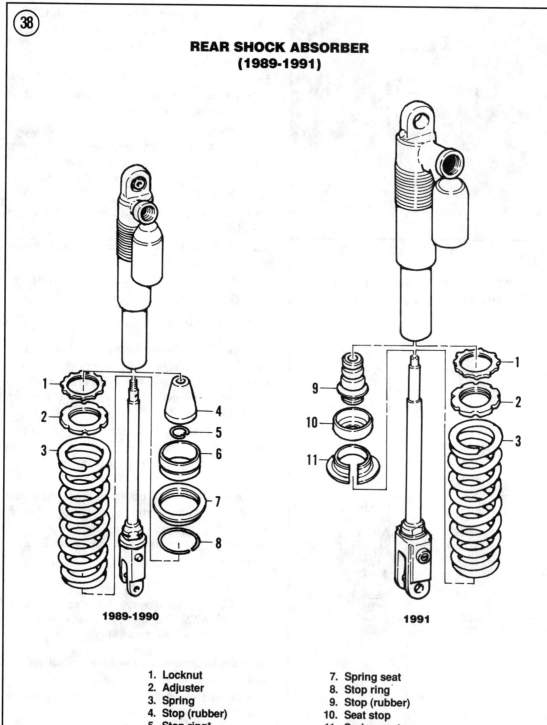

**REAR SHOCK ABSORBER
(1989-1991)**

1989-1990

1991

1. Locknut
2. Adjuster
3. Spring
4. Stop (rubber)
5. Stop ring*
6. Stopper seat
7. Spring seat
8. Stop ring
9. Stop (rubber)
10. Seat stop
11. Spring seat

*All 1989 models and 1990 CR500R models.

5. On 1989 and 1990 models, refer to **Figure 38**. Remove the stop ring (8). Slide off the spring seat (7) and spring (3).

6. On 1991 models, refer to **Figure 38**. Remove the spring seat (11) and spring (3).

7. Measure the free length of the spring (**Figure 39**). Replace the spring if it has sagged to the service limit listed in **Table 3**.

8. Inspect the condition of the upper mounting bushing; replace if necessary.

9. Check the damper unit for dents, oil leakage or other damage. Make sure the damper rod is straight.

NOTE
The damper unit cannot be rebuilt; it must be replaced as a unit.

WARNING
The shock absorber body and reservoir contain nitrogen gas compressed to 20 kg/cm² (284 psi). Do not tamper with or attempt to open the damper and reservoir unit. Do not place it near an open flame or other extreme heat. Do not dispose of the damper assembly your-

self. Take it to a dealer where it can be deactivated and disposed of properly. Never attempt to remove the valve core in the base of the reservoir.

10. On 1988 models, refer to **Figure 37** and perform the following:

   a. Install spring (3), spring seat (6) (raised inner flange facing up toward the spring) and seat stopper (7).

   b. Make sure the rebound adjuster screw is on the reservoir side.

   c. Slide on the spring stopper.

NOTE
On models with tapered spring coils, install the tapered end of the coil downward.

11. On 1989-1990 models, refer to **Figure 38** and perform the following:

   a. Install spring (3) and spring seat (7). Make sure the rebound adjuster screw is on the same side as the reservoir.

   b. Install stop ring (8) into the groove.

12. On 1991 models, refer to **Figure 38**. Install the spring (3) and spring seat (11).

13. Hold the shock absorber upside down and secure the upper mounting portion of the shock and reservoir in a vise with soft jaws. Use wood pieces to protect the reservoir tank from the vise jaws.

14. Screw the adjuster and locknut (B, **Figure 36**) on by hand until they contact the spring.

15. Use pin spanners to tighten the adjuster to the standard spring length or the length measured before disassembly. The standard spring pre-load length is listed in **Table 3**. Refer to **Figure 35**.

16. Tighten the locknut securely.

17. Remove the shock absorber assembly from the vise.

PIVOT ARM ASSEMBLY

Removal

Refer to **Figure 40** for 1988 CR500R models, **Figure 41** for 1988 CR250R models, **Figure 42** for all 1989 and 1990 models and **Figure 43** for all 1991 models.

1. Remove the lower shock absorber mounting bolt (A, **Figure 44**).

2. On 1989 and later models, remove the bottom chain tensioner roller by removing the bolt. This is

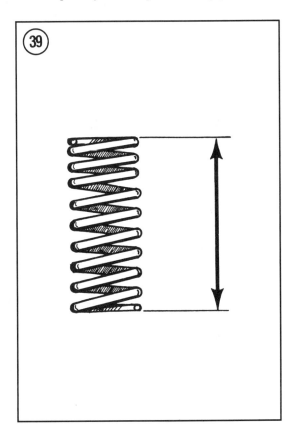

(40)

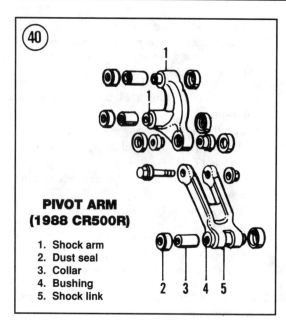

PIVOT ARM
(1988 CR500R)

1. Shock arm
2. Dust seal
3. Collar
4. Bushing
5. Shock link

(41)

PIVOT ARM
(1988 CR250R)

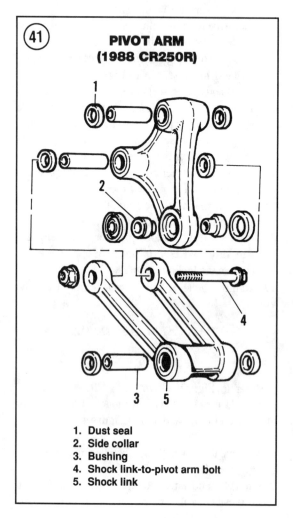

1. Dust seal
2. Side collar
3. Bushing
4. Shock link-to-pivot arm bolt
5. Shock link

(42)

PIVOT ARM
(1989-1990 CR250R
AND CR500R)

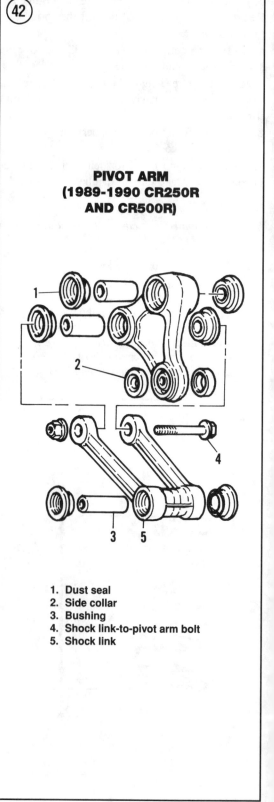

1. Dust seal
2. Side collar
3. Bushing
4. Shock link-to-pivot arm bolt
5. Shock link

not absolutely necessary, but it provides easier access to the lower linkage bolts.

3. On CR250R models and 1989-on CR500R models, remove the rubber covers located on the sides of the swing arm.

4A. On 1988 CR500R models, remove the bolt securing the pivot arm to the swing arm (**Figure 45**).

4B. On all other models, remove the pivot arm bolt by removing the nut and pulling the bolt through the swing arm and pivot arm from the left side.

5. Remove the bolt and nut securing the shock link to the frame (B, **Figure 44**).

6. Remove the pivot arm assembly and shock link for inspection.

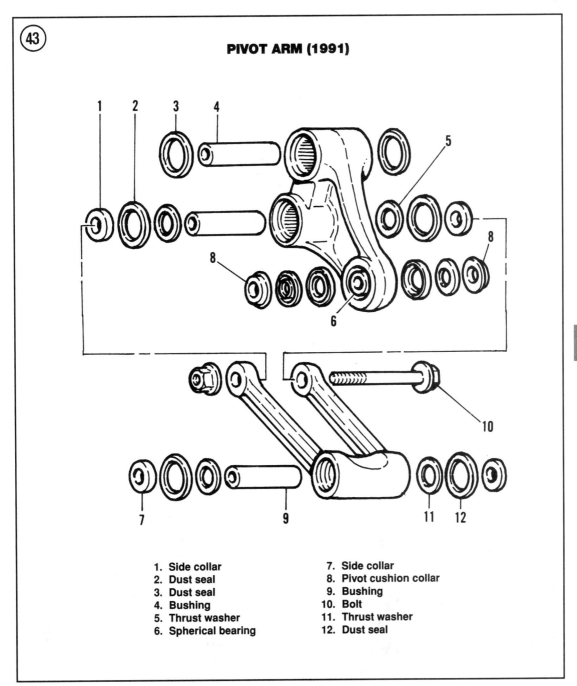

43 **PIVOT ARM (1991)**

1. Side collar
2. Dust seal
3. Dust seal
4. Bushing
5. Thrust washer
6. Spherical bearing
7. Side collar
8. Pivot cushion collar
9. Bushing
10. Bolt
11. Thrust washer
12. Dust seal

10

7. Inspect the shock link arms (**Figure 46**) and the pivot arm for cracks or damage; replace as necessary.

8. Remove the bolt and nut (A, **Figure 47**) securing the shock link to the pivot arm.

9. Remove the dust seals (B, **Figure 47**), if equipped, at all pivot points.

10. On 1988-1990 models, remove the dust seals, side collars and bushings. Refer to **Figures 40-42**.

11. On 1991 models, refer to **Figure 43** and remove the pivot cushion collars (8) on the sides of the shock mount bearing. Remove the side collars (1 and 7) and thrust washers (5 and 11) located on the shock link arm and the pivot arm.

12. Clean all parts in solvent and dry thoroughly with compressed air.

13. Inspect the bushings for scratches, abrasion or abnormal wear; replace as necessary.

14. Inspect the needle bearings in the shock link and the pivot arm for wear or damage. Replace the bearings, if necessary.

15. Inspect the spherical bearing for wear or damage. Replace the bearing, if necessary.

16. On 1991 models, inspect the pivot cushion collars and thrust bearings. Replace them as sets, if wear or damage is present.

17. Inspect the dust seals. Replace all of them as a set if any are worn or starting to deteriorate. If the dust seals are in poor condition, they will allow dirt to enter into the pivot areas and cause the bushings to wear.

Installation

1. Coat all surfaces of the pivot receptacle, the bushings and the inside of the dust seals with molybdenum disulfide paste grease.

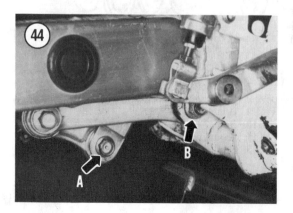

2. On 1988-1990 models, refer to **Figures 40-42**. Insert the bushings into the bearings, then install the side collars and dust seals.

3. On 1991 models, refer to **Figure 43** and install the bushings, thrust washers, pivot cushion collars and side collars. Install the dust seals.

CAUTION
Make sure the dust seal lips seat correctly. If not, they will allow dirt and

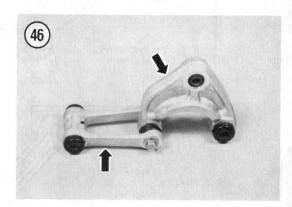
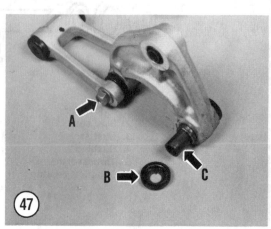

moisture into the bushing areas leading to wear.

4. Make sure the dust seals are installed on the frame shock link. On 1991 models, make sure the thrust washers are in place.

5. Assemble the shock link to the frame and install the pivot bolt from the left-hand side (**Figure 48**).

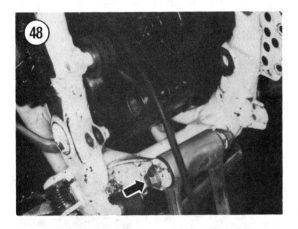

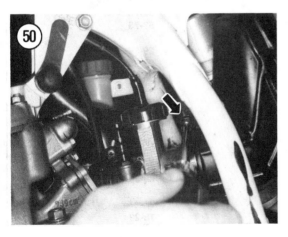

Install the nut and tighten to the torque specifications listed in **Table 1**.

6. Assemble the shock link to the pivot arm by inserting the shock link bolt from the left side (A, **Figure 47**). Install the nut and tighten to specification listed in **Table 1** after completing Step 7A or Step 7B.

7A. On 1988 CR500R models, line up the pivot arm and swing arm and install the pivot bolt from the left-hand side (**Figure 45**). Tighten the nut to the torque specification listed in **Table 1**.

7B. On all other models, center the pivot arm within the swing arm and insert the bolt from the left-hand side through the swing arm and pivot arm. Install the nut and tighten to the torque specification listed in **Table 1**.

8. Install the shock absorber by inserting the mounting bolt from the right side (**Figure 49**). On 1991 models, make sure pivot cushion collars on the spherical bearing are in place. Tighten the nut to the torque specification listed in **Table 1**.

9. On 1989 and later models, install the bottom chain tensioner and tighten the tensioner bolt.

10. On CR250R and 1989-on CR500R models, install the rubber covers into the sides of the swing arm.

PIVOT ARM AND SHOCK LINK NEEDLE BEARING REPLACEMENT

The tools and steps for removal and replacement of the needle bearings in the pivot arm and shock link are similar to those used in swing arm bearing replacement. However, a hydraulic press and a variety of special bearing tools are needed for spherical bearing removal and replacement. You can save a considerable amount of time and money by removing the pivot arm and shock link and taking them to your Honda dealer for bearing replacement.

SUB-FRAME

Removal/Installation

1. Place a metal or wood stand under the frame to support the bike securely.

2. Remove the seat and right side cover.

3. Loosen the clamping band screw (**Figure 50**) securing the air cleaner boot to the carburetor throat.

4. Remove the upper bolt (**Figure 51**) securing the sub-frame to the main frame.

5. Remove the lower bolts (one on each side) securing the sub-frame to the main frame (**Figure 52**).

6. Pull the sub-frame toward the back, being careful not to damage the mud guard.

7. Install by positioning the sub-frame so the mud guard fits in between the rear tire and Pro-Link linkage.

8. Align the lower bolt holes and install the lower bolts only finger-tight.

9. Slowly move the sub-frame up while aligning the exhaust system connection and the air cleaner boot. Install the upper bolt only finger-tight.

10. Engage the expansion chamber to the muffler and make sure the rubber connection is sealing the pipes.

11. Install the air cleaner rubber boot onto the carburetor throat and tighten the clamping band screw.

12. Tighten the mounting bolts to the torque specification listed in **Table 1**.

13. Install the seat and side cover.

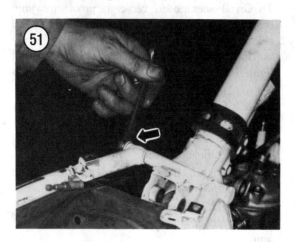

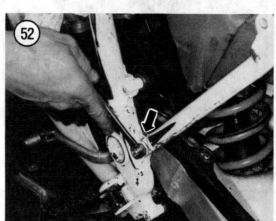

Table 1 REAR SUSPENSION TORQUE SPECIFICATIONS

	N·m	ft.-lb.
Rear axle nut	85-105	62-77
Swing arm pivot shaft nut	80-100	59-73
Shock absorber locknut	80-100	59-73
Shock absorber mounting		
Upper bolt	40-50	29-36
Lower bolt	38-48	28-35
Pro-link mounting bolts		
Shock link-to-frame		
1988	40-50	29-36
1989-1991	55-70	40-51
Shock link-to-shock arm		
1988	40-50	29-36
1989-1991	55-70	40-51
Shock arm-to-swing arm	55-70	40-51
Shock arm-to-shock	38-48	28-35
Driven sprocket nut		
1988-1989	32-37	23-27
1990-1991	25-31	18-22

Table 2 REAR SHOCK ABSORBER INSTALLED SPRING LENGTH (STANDARD)

Model	mm	in.
CR250R		
1988	267.5	10.53
1989	267	10.51
1990	267	10.51
1991	250	9.84
CR500R		
1988	275	10.8
1989	267	10.5
1990	267	10.5
1991	254	10.0

Table 3 REAR SHOCK ABSORBER SPRING FREE LENGTH

Model	Standard		Service limit	
	mm	in.	mm	in.
CR250R and CR500R				
1988-1990	280	11.0	277	10.9
1991	265	10.4	262	10.3

Table 4 REAR SHOCK ABSORBER REBOUND DAMPING ADJUSTMENT

Model	Number of adjustment positions	Standard position
CR250R		
1988		
1989		
1990	21 or more	12-15 clicks out from full in
1991	20 or more	6-9 clicks out from full in
CR500R		
1988		
1989		
1990	21 or more	10-13 clicks out from full in
1991	20 or more	10-13 clicks out from full in

Table 5 REAR SHOCK ABSORBER COMPRESSION DAMPING ADJUSTMENT

Model	Adjustment positions	Standard position
CR250R		
1988		
1989		
1990	22 or more	12-15 clicks out from full in
1991	22 or more	11-14 clicks out from full in
CR500R		
1988		
1989		
1990	22 or more	10-13 clicks out from full in
1991	22 or more	4-7 clicks out from full in

10

NOTE: If you own a 1992 CR500R or later model, first check the Supplement at the back of this book for any new service information.

CHAPTER ELEVEN

BRAKES

All CR250R and CR500R models covered in this manual are equipped with front and rear hydraulic disc brakes. Both front and rear systems are similar, the main difference being that the front is controlled by a hand lever and the rear by a foot pedal.

Table 1 contains specifications for the hydraulic disc brakes. **Table 2** provides tightening torque specifications. Both tables are located at the end of this chapter.

HYDRAULIC DISC BRAKE

When working on hydraulic brake systems, it is necessary that the work area and all tools be absolutely clean. Any tiny particles of foreign matter and grit in the caliper assembly or the master cylinder can damage the components. Also, sharp tools must not be used inside the caliper or on the pistons. If there is any doubt about your ability to correctly and safely carry out major service on the brake components, take the job to a dealer or brake specialist.

DRAINING BRAKE FLUID

1. Remove the dust cap from the bleed valve (**Figure 1**).

2. Connect a rubber hose to the caliper bleed valve and place the other end of the hose into a suitable container (**Figure 2**).

3. Loosen the caliper bleed valve. Pump the brake lever until all of the brake fluid has been forced out of the bleed valve.

4. Tighten the bleed valve to specifications in **Table 2**.

> *CAUTION*
> *Never reuse brake fluid. Contaminated brake fluid can cause brake failure. Dispose of brake fluid according to local EPA regulations.*

FRONT MASTER CYLINDER

Removal/Installation

> *CAUTION*
> *Cover the fuel tank and front fender with a heavy cloth or plastic tarp to protect them from accidental brake fluid spills. Wash brake fluid off any painted or plated surfaces immediately, as it will destroy the finish. Use soapy water and rinse completely.*

1. Drain the brake fluid as described in this chapter.

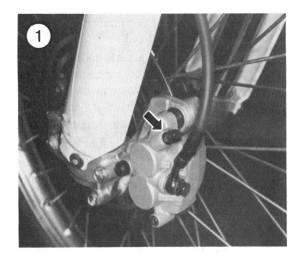

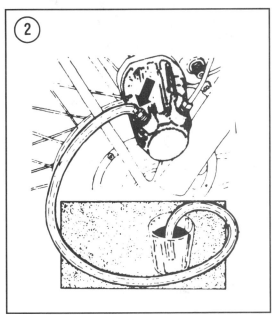

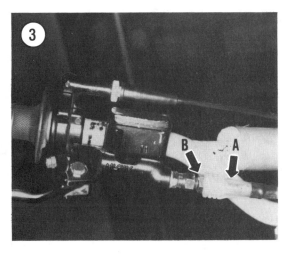

2. Unscrew the brake hose (A, **Figure 3**), brake hose joint (B, **Figure 3**) and sealing washer from the master cylinder. Tie the brake hose up and cover the end to prevent the entry of foreign matter.

3. Remove the clamping bolts (**Figure 4**) and clamp securing the master cylinder to the handlebar and remove the master cylinder.

4. Install by reversing these removal steps while noting the following.

5. Install the clamp with the "UP" arrow (**Figure 5**) facing up.

6. Tighten the upper clamping bolt and then the lower bolt to the specification listed in **Table 2**.

7. Install the sealing washer, brake hose joint and brake hose onto the master cylinder. Make sure the path of the brake hose from the caliper to the master cylinder is smooth with no sharp bends or kinks. Tighten the brake hose joint and brake hose to the torque specifications listed in **Table 2**.

8. Fill the brake system with fluid and bleed the brake as described in this chapter.

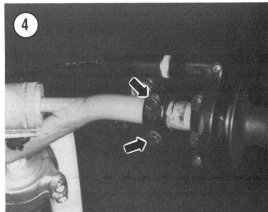

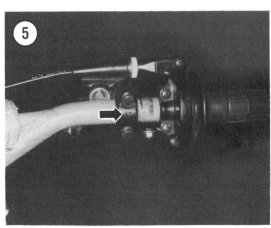

11

Disassembly

Refer to **Figure 6** for the following procedure.

1. Slide back the rubber boot and remove the pivot bolt and nut (**Figure 7**) securing the brake lever. Remove the brake lever. Do *not* lose the small coil return spring.

2. Remove the screws securing the cover and remove the cover and diaphragm (**Figure 8**). Pour out the brake fluid and discard it. *Never* reuse brake fluid.

3. Remove the rubber piston boot from the area where the hand lever actuates the internal piston.

4. Using circlip pliers, remove the internal circlip from the cylinder body.

5. Remove the stopper plate and the piston assembly.

6. Remove the spring.

Inspection

1. Clean all parts in denatured alcohol or fresh brake fluid. Inspect the cylinder bore and piston contact surfaces for signs of wear and damage. If either part is worn or damaged, replace the cylinder body.

2. Check the end of the piston for wear caused by the hand lever. Replace the piston assembly if either cup is worn or damaged.

3. Inspect the pivot hole in the hand lever. If worn or elongated, it must be replaced.

4. Make sure the passages in the bottom of the brake fluid reservoir are clear. Check the reservoir cap and diaphragm for damage and deterioration and replace as necessary.

5. Inspect the brake line threads in the reservoir bore.

6. Check the hand lever pivot lug for cracks.

7. Measure the cylinder bore (**Figure 9**). Replace the master cylinder if the bore exceeds the service limit listed in **Table 1**.

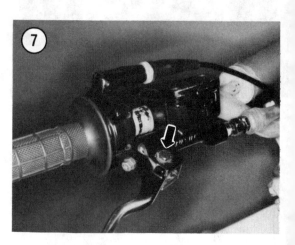

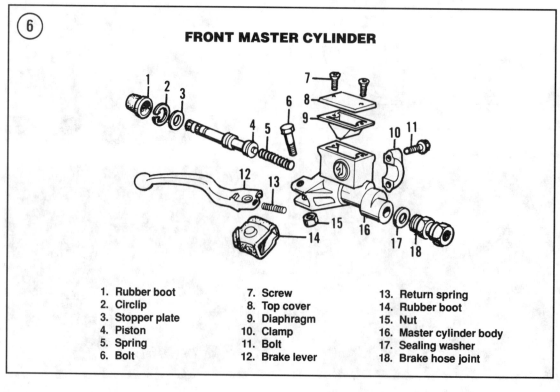

FRONT MASTER CYLINDER

1. Rubber boot	7. Screw	13. Return spring
2. Circlip	8. Top cover	14. Rubber boot
3. Stopper plate	9. Diaphragm	15. Nut
4. Piston	10. Clamp	16. Master cylinder body
5. Spring	11. Bolt	17. Sealing washer
6. Bolt	12. Brake lever	18. Brake hose joint

8. Measure the outside diameter of the piston assembly with a micrometer as shown in **Figure 10**. Replace the piston assembly if it is less than the service limit listed in **Table 1**.

Assembly

Refer to **Figure 6** for the following procedure.

1. Soak the new piston assembly in fresh brake fluid for at least 15 minutes to make the cups pliable. Coat the inside of the cylinder with fresh brake fluid before assembly.

> *CAUTION*
> *When installing the piston assembly, do not allow the cups to turn inside out as they will be damaged and allow brake fluid leakage within the cylinder bore.*

2. Install the spring and the piston assembly into the cylinder together.

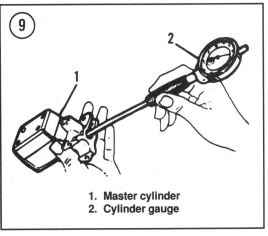

1. Master cylinder
2. Cylinder gauge

3. Install the stopper plate and circlip. Make sure the circlip is correctly seated in the circlip groove in the master cylinder. Slide in the rubber boot.

4. Install the diaphragm and cover. Do not tighten the cover screws at this time as fluid will have to be added later.

5. Install the master cylinder as described in this chapter.

6. Install the brake lever onto the master cylinder body. Slide the rubber boot back into position.

REAR MASTER CYLINDER

Removal/Installation

1. If the master cylinder is to be rebuilt, drain the brake fluid as described in this chapter.

2. Remove the brake lever pivot bolt.

3A. On 1988 CR500R models, perform the following:

    a. Loosen the locknut at the brake adjuster on the master cylinder pushrod.

    b. Remove the pin securing the brake arm to the master cylinder.

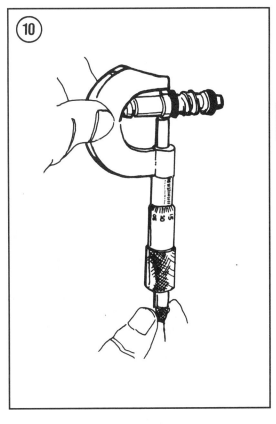

11

3B. On all other models, remove the pivot link (A, **Figure 11**) between the master cylinder pushrod and brake arm by removing the cotter pin and washer and pulling the pin through the pivot link (B, **Figure 11**).

4. Remove the brake line banjo bolt (**Figure 12**) and disconnect the brake line and remove the two sealing washers. Plug the brake line to prevent entry of moisture and dirt, and tie the end up out of the way.

5. Remove the 2 Allen bolts mounting the master cylinder (**Figure 13**) to the frame and remove the cylinder.

6. Unbolt the master cylinder reservoir from the frame (**Figure 14**). Keep the top cap on the reservoir until the master cylinder will be disassembled to prevent entry of moisture and dirt.

7. Install the master cylinder with the 2 Allen bolts.

8. Install the reservoir.

9. Connect the brake line with the banjo bolt and 2 new sealing washers. On 1988 models, make sure the brake line fitting is against the boss on the master cylinder (**Figure 15**), then tighten the bolt to the torque specified in **Table 2**. On 1989 and later models, make sure the brake line fitting fits snugly within the bosses (**Figure 16**), then tighten the bolt to the torque specified in **Table 2**. Make sure that the brake line clears the rear shock absorber and all other moving suspension parts.

10. Install the brake arm with the brake arm pivot bolt. Tighten the bolt to 24-28 N•m (17-20 ft.-lb.).

11A. On 1988 CR500R models, connect the brake arm to the master cylinder with the pin.

11B. On all other models, connect the brake arm to the master cylinder pushrod by installing the pivot link and pin, then installing the washer and cotter pin (**Figure 11**).

12. Refill the reservoir with brake fluid and bleed the brake as described in this chapter.

Disassembly

Refer to **Figure 17** for the following procedure.

1. Remove the snap ring from the side of the master cylinder and pull the reservoir hose out of the body.

2. Remove the rubber piston boot.

3. Remove the snap ring, pushrod and washer from the end of the master cylinder body.

WARNING
The pushrod is under spring pressure and could fly out when the snap ring is

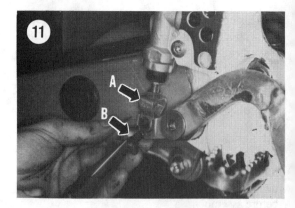

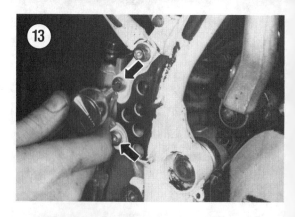

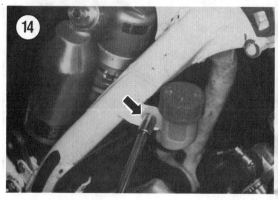

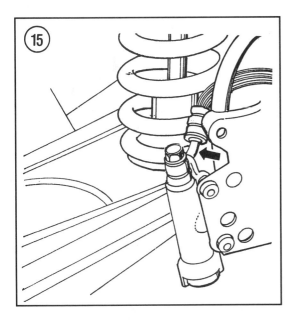

free. Take care not to let brake fluid splash into your eyes.

4. Remove the piston and spring.

NOTE
If the piston won't come out easily, apply air pressure to the brake hose connection to force it out.

Inspection

1. Clean all parts in denatured alcohol or fresh brake fluid.
2. Make sure the passages in the bottom of the brake fluid reservoir are clear. Check the reservoir cap and diaphragm for damage and deterioration and replace as necessary.
3. Inspect the brake line threads in the cylinder bore.
4. Inspect the cylinder bore and piston contact surfaces for signs of wear and damage. If either part is worn or damaged, replace the cylinder.
5. Check the end of the piston for wear caused by the pushrod. Replace the piston assembly if either of the rubber cups is worn or damaged.
6. Measure the cylinder bore (**Figure 18**). Replace the master cylinder if the bore exceeds the service limit listed in **Table 1**.
7. Measure the outside diameter of the piston assembly with a micrometer as shown in **Figure 19**. Replace the piston assembly if it is less than the service limit listed in **Table 1**.

Assembly

Refer to **Figure 17** for the following procedure.

11

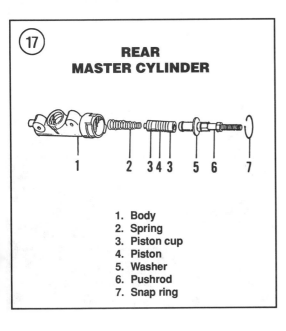

REAR MASTER CYLINDER

1. Body
2. Spring
3. Piston cup
4. Piston
5. Washer
6. Pushrod
7. Snap ring

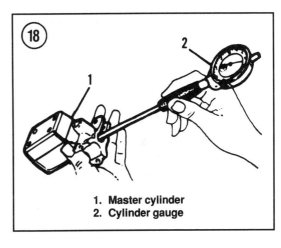

1. Master cylinder
2. Cylinder gauge

1. Lubricate all internal parts liberally with clean brake fluid. Soak the primary and secondary cups in brake fluid to make them pliable.

2. Install the spring and piston. Be careful not to cut the rubber cups on the body when inserting them, and make sure that they do not turn inside out.

3. Slide the washer onto the pushrod and insert the pushrod onto the master cylinder body.

4. Secure the pushrod with the snap ring. Make sure that the snap ring seats firmly in the groove in the body.

5. Install the rubber boot.

6. Lubricate the O-ring on the cylinder reservoir hose connection.

7. Install the reservoir hose connection in the body and secure it with the snap ring.

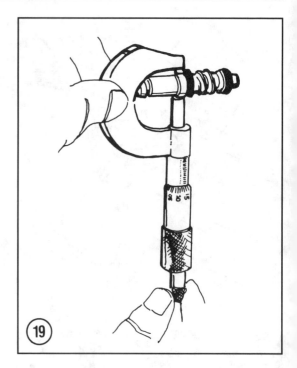

BRAKE PAD REPLACEMENT

There is no recommended milage interval for changing the friction pads in the disc brake. Pad wear depends greatly on riding habits and conditions. The pads should be checked for wear every 6 months and replaced when the wear indicator reaches the edge of the brake disc.

When purchasing new pads, check with your dealer to make sure the friction compound of the new pads is compatible with the disc material. Also, replace pads in pairs to maintain even brake pressure.

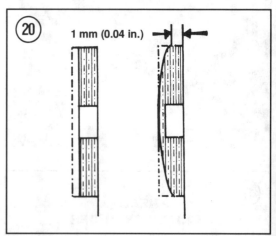

CAUTION
*Watch the pads more closely as the pads wear close to the bottom of the groove (**Figure 20**). If pad wear happens to be uneven for some reason, the backing plate may come in contact with the disc and cause damage.*

Front and Rear Brake Pad Replacement

Replacement is the same for both front and rear brakes. It is not necessary to remove the caliper bracket when replacing the brake pads.

1. Remove the slotted plug for the brake pad pin shown in **Figure 21** for the front brake and **Figure 22** for the rear brake.

2. Unscrew the brake pad pin with a 5 mm Allen wrench (**Figure 23**).

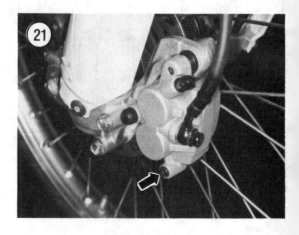

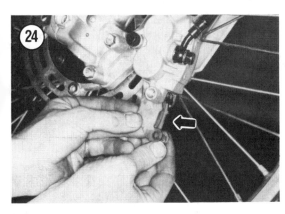

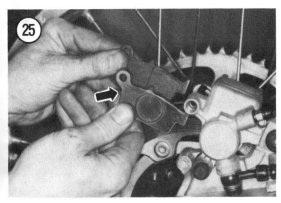

3. Slide the two pads out from the bottom of the front caliper (**Figure 24**) or from the rear (**Figure 25**) of the rear caliper.

4. Remove the anti-chatter shim. Replace it if broken or cracked.

NOTE
The rear wheel is shown removed for clarification only. It is not necessary to remove the wheel for these procedures.

5. Separate the caliper body from the caliper bracket (A, **Figure 26**).

6. Clean the pad recess and the end of the piston (rear) or both pistons (front) with a soft brush. Do not use solvent, a wire brush or any hard tool which would damage the cylinders or the pistons.

7. Lightly coat the ends of the piston (rear) or pistons (front) and the *backs* (not the friction material) of the new pads with disc brake lubricant.

WARNING
Disc brake lubricant is specially formulated for high temperatures generated by disc brakes. Do not use any other type of lubricant, or the brakes may fail.

8. Clean the top of the master cylinder of all dirt and foreign matter, and remove the cap and diaphragm from the master cylinder.

9. *Slowly* push the piston (rear) or pistons (front) back into the caliper. The caliper piston(s) should move freely. If the piston(s) does not and there is evidence of it sticking in the cylinder, the caliper should be removed and serviced as described in this chapter.

11

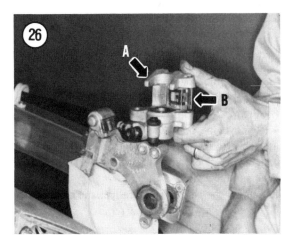

CAUTION
Do not let the reservoir overflow. Re-move fluid, if necessary.

10. Install the anti-chatter shim. Clip it on the caliper as shown in B, **Figure 26** for the rear caliper or A, **Figure 27** for the front caliper.

11. Lubricate the caliper pin with disc brake lubricant. See B, **Figure 27**.

12. Install the caliper body onto the mounting bracket.

13. Slide the new brake pads into place in the caliper.

14. Secure the pads with the brake pad pin.

15. Install the slotted plug.

FRONT CALIPER

Removal/Installation

It is not necessary to remove the front wheel in order to remove the caliper assembly.

CAUTION
Do not spill any brake fluid on the painted portion of the fork or wheel. Wash off any spilled brake fluid imme-diately, as it will destroy the finish. Use soapy water and rinse completely.

1. Place a metal or wood stand under the skid plate to support the bike with the front wheel off the ground.

2. Place a container under the brake line at the caliper and perform the following:

   a. Remove the union bolt and sealing washers (A, **Figure 28**) securing the brake line to the caliper assembly.

   b. Remove the brake line and let the brake fluid drain out into the container. Dispose of this brake fluid. *Never* reuse brake fluid.

   c. To prevent the entry of moisture and dirt, cap the end of the brake line and tie the loose end up to the front fork.

3. Remove the pad pin plug and loosen the pad pin (B, **Figure 28**).

4. Remove the bolts securing the caliper bracket assembly to the front fork (**Figure 29**). Push on the caliper while loosening the bolts to push the pistons back into the caliper.

5. Remove the caliper bolts, caliper and bracket.

6. Install by reversing these removal steps while noting the following.

7. Carefully install the caliper assembly onto the disc. Be careful not to damage the leading edge of the pads during installation.

8. Install the longer of the caliper bolts into the upper caliper bolt hole.

9. Tighten the caliper mounting bolts to the torque specification listed in **Table 2**.

10. Install the brake hose, with a sealing washer on each side of the fitting, onto the caliper. Install the union bolt and tighten to the torque specification listed in **Table 2**.

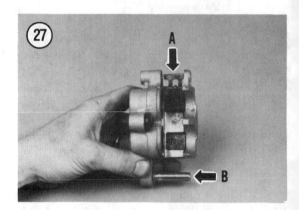

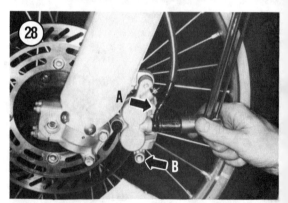

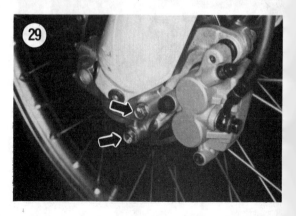

11. Tighten the pad pin and install the pad pin plug.

12. Spin the front wheel and activate the brake lever as many times as it takes to refill the cylinder in the caliper and correctly locate the pads.

> *WARNING*
> *Use brake fluid clearly marked DOT 4 from a sealed container. Other types may vaporize and cause brake failure. Always use the same brand name; do not intermix as many brands are not compatible.*

13. Refill the master cylinder reservoir, if necessary, to maintain the correct fluid level. Install the diaphragm and top cap.

> *WARNING*
> *Do not ride the bike until you are sure the brake is operating correctly with full hydraulic advantage.*

14. Bleed the brake system as described in this chapter.

Disassembly

Refer to **Figure 30**.

1. Remove the brake pads as described in this chapter.

2. Remove the caliper as described in this chapter.

3. Pull the caliper bracket out of the caliper. Remove the pad retainer from the bracket.

4. Remove the pad spring from the caliper housing.

5. Remove the pivot boots from the caliper housing.

> *WARNING*
> *In Step 6, the pistons will be forced out of the caliper with considerable force. Do not cushion the pistons with your fingers, as injury could result.*

6. Cushion the caliper pistons with a shop rag, making sure to keep your fingers and hand away from the piston area. Then apply compressed air through the brake line port (**Figure 31**) to remove the pistons.

7. Remove the dust (A, **Figure 32**) and piston seals (B, **Figure 32**) from the grooves inside the cylinders. Discard the seals as new ones must be installed.

8. Remove the bleed valve and its cover from the caliper.

Inspection

1. Clean the caliper housing in solvent and dry with compressed air.

2. Clean the pistons with DOT 4 brake fluid.

3. Check each piston and cylinder for deep scratches or other obvious wear marks. Do not hone the cylinder.

4. Measure each cylinder bore diameter with a bore gauge (**Figure 33**) and compare with the wear limit in **Table 1**. If any one cylinder bore is too large, replace the caliper and pistons as an assembly.

5. Measure each piston diameter with a micrometer and compare with the wear limit in **Table 1**. If any one of the pistons is too small, replace the caliper and pistons as an assembly.

6. Clean the bleed valve with compressed air.

7. Replace the caliper pivot boots if excessively worn or damaged.

8. Replace the pad spring if damaged.

9. Replace the pad retainer if damaged.

Assembly

Refer to **Figure 30**.

> *NOTE*
> *Use new DOT 4 brake fluid when brake fluid is called for in the following steps.*

1. Soak the new piston and dust seals in brake fluid for approximately 5 minutes.

2. Lightly coat the pistons and cylinder bores with brake fluid.

3. Install a new piston seal (A, **Figure 34**) into the rear cylinder bore groove. See B, **Figure 32**.

4. Install a new dust seal (B, **Figure 34**) into the front cylinder bore groove. See A, **Figure 32**.

5. Repeat Steps 3 and 4 for the other cylinder bore.

> *NOTE*
> *Check that each seal fits squarely into its respective cylinder bore groove.*

6. Install each piston into its cylinder with its plate side facing out (toward brake pads).

7. Repeat Step 6 for the other piston.

8. Install the bleed valve into the caliper.

9. Install the pivot boots into the caliper groove.

10. Install the pad retainer onto the caliper bracket.

11. Install the pad spring into the caliper.

11

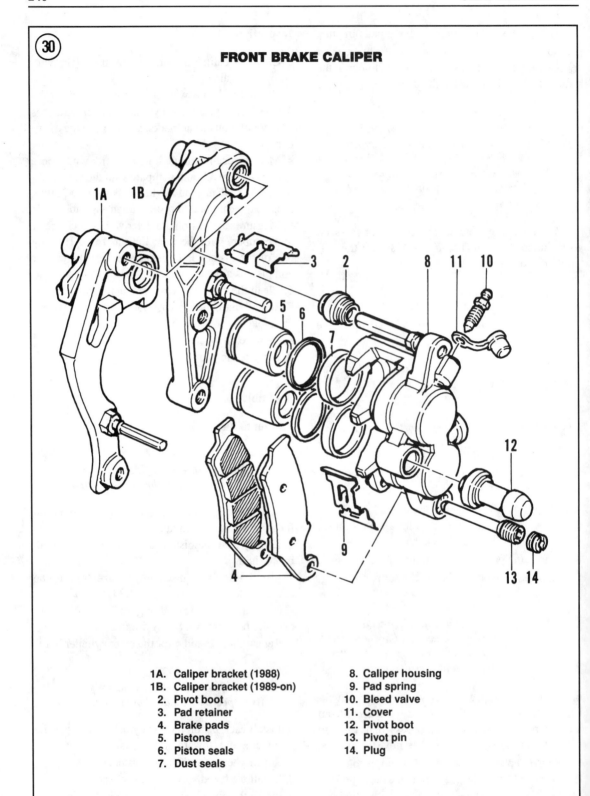

FRONT BRAKE CALIPER

1A. Caliper bracket (1988)
1B. Caliper bracket (1989-on)
2. Pivot boot
3. Pad retainer
4. Brake pads
5. Pistons
6. Piston seals
7. Dust seals
8. Caliper housing
9. Pad spring
10. Bleed valve
11. Cover
12. Pivot boot
13. Pivot pin
14. Plug

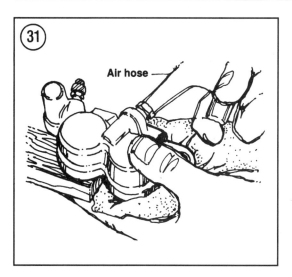

Air hose

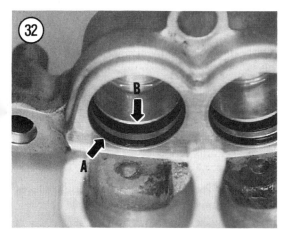

B

A

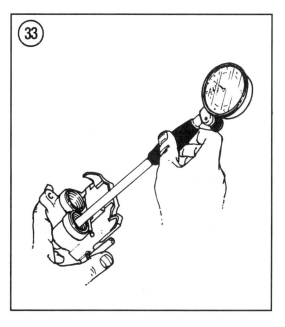

12. Apply a silicone grease onto the caliper bracket shafts and install the bracket into the caliper.

13. Install the brake pads and caliper as described in this chapter.

REAR CALIPER

Removal/Installation

1. Place a metal or wooden stand under the skid plate to support the bike with the rear wheel off the ground.

2. Remove the 2 bolts securing the caliper guard plate (**Figure 35**).

3. Place a container under the brake line at the caliper.

4. Remove the union bolt (**Figure 36**) and sealing washers securing the brake line to the caliper assembly.

A

B

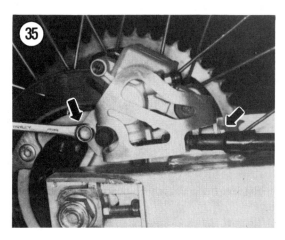

11

5. Remove the brake line and let the brake fluid drain into the container. Dispose of this brake fluid. *Never reuse brake fluid.*

6. Cap the end of the brake line to prevent the entry of moisture and dirt, and tie the loose end up out of the way.

7. Remove the pad pin plug and loosen the pad pin.

8. Remove the rear wheel as described in Chapter Ten.

9. Slide the caliper backward and out of the swing arm slide track.

10. Remove the brake disc guard from the caliper assembly.

11. Install by reversing these removal steps while noting the following.

12. Install the brake hose, with a new sealing washer on each side of the fitting, onto the caliper. Install the union bolt (**Figure 36**) and tighten to the torque specification listed in **Table 2**.

13. Install the rear wheel as described in Chapter Ten. Be careful not to damage the leading edge of the pads during installation.

14. Tighten the pad pin and install the pad pin plug.

15. Spin the wheel and activate the rear brake pedal as many times as it takes to refill the cylinder in the caliper and correctly locate the pads.

> *WARNING*
> *Use only brake fluid clearly marked DOT 4 from a sealed container. Other types may vaporize and cause brake failure. Always use the same brand name; do not intermix as some brands are not compatible.*

16. Refill the master cylinder reservoir, if necessary, to maintain the correct fluid level. Install the top cap and tighten securely.

> *WARNING*
> *Do not ride the bike until you are sure the brake is operating correctly with full hydraulic advantage.*

17. Bleed the brake as described in this chapter.

Disassembly

Refer to **Figure 37**.

1. Remove the brake pads as described in this chapter.

2. Remove the caliper as described in this chapter.

3. Pull the caliper bracket out of the caliper. Remove the pad retainer from the bracket.

4. Remove the pad spring from the caliper housing.

5. Remove the pivot boots from the caliper housing and caliper bracket.

> *WARNING*
> *In Step 6, the piston will be forced out of the caliper with considerable force. Do not cushion the piston with your fingers, as injury could result.*

6. Cushion the caliper piston with a shop rag, making sure to keep your fingers and hand away from the piston area. Then apply compressed air through the brake line port (**Figure 31**) to remove the piston.

7. Remove the dust (A, **Figure 38**) and piston seals (B, **Figure 38**) from the grooves inside the cylinder. Discard the seals as new ones must be installed.

8. Remove the bleed valve and its cover from the caliper.

Inspection

1. Clean the caliper housing in solvent and dry with compressed air.

2. Clean the pistons with DOT 4 brake fluid.

3. Check each piston and cylinder for deep scratches or other obvious wear marks. Do not hone the cylinder.

4. Measure the cylinder bore I.D. with a bore gauge (**Figure 33**) and compare with the wear limit in **Table 1**. If the bore diameter is too large, replace the caliper and piston as an assembly.

5. Measure the piston diameter with a micrometer and compare with the wear limit in **Table 1**. If the

piston diameter is too small, replace the caliper and piston as an assembly.

6. Clean the bleed valve with compressed air.

7. Replace the caliper pivot boots if excessively worn or damaged.

8. Replace the pad spring if damaged.

Assembly

Refer to **Figure 37**.

NOTE
Use new DOT 4 brake fluid when brake fluid is called for in the following steps.

1. Soak the new piston and dust seals in brake fluid for approximately 5 minutes.

2. Lightly coat the piston and cylinder bore with brake fluid.

3. Install a new piston seal (A, **Figure 39**) into the rear cylinder bore groove. See B, **Figure 38**.

4. Install a new dust seal (B, **Figure 39**) into the front cylinder bore groove. See A, **Figure 38**.

NOTE
Check that each seal fits squarely into its respective cylinder bore groove.

5. Install the piston into its cylinder with its open side facing out (toward brake pads).

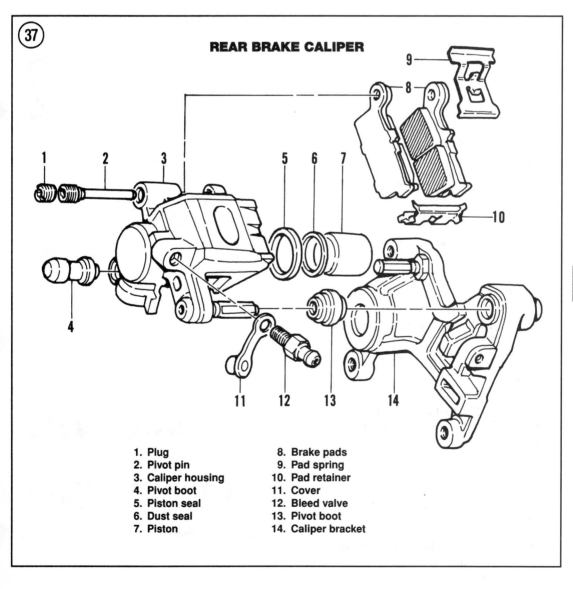

REAR BRAKE CALIPER

1. Plug
2. Pivot pin
3. Caliper housing
4. Pivot boot
5. Piston seal
6. Dust seal
7. Piston
8. Brake pads
9. Pad spring
10. Pad retainer
11. Cover
12. Bleed valve
13. Pivot boot
14. Caliper bracket

6. Install the bleed valve into the caliper.

7. Install the pivot boots into the caliper and support bracket.

8. Install the pad spring into the caliper.

9. Apply a silicone grease to the caliper bracket shafts and install the bracket into the caliper. Make sure the pivot boots seat in the caliper bracket pin grooves as shown in **Figure 40**.

10. Install the brake pads and caliper as described in this chapter.

BRAKE HOSE REPLACEMENT

There is no factory-recommended replacement interval but it is a good idea to replace the brake hose every 2 years or if it shows signs of cracking or damage.

Front Brake Hose Replacement

CAUTION
Cover the front wheel, fender and fuel tank with a heavy cloth or plastic tarp to protect it from accidental spilling of brake fluid. Wash any brake fluid off of any painted or plated surface immediately, as it will destroy the finish. Use soapy water and rinse completely.

1. Place a metal or wood stand under the skid plate to support the bike with the front wheel off the ground.

2. Remove the bolt and plastic snap securing the number plate and remove the plate.

3. Place a container under the brake line at the caliper.

4. Remove the union bolt and sealing washers (A, **Figure 28**) securing the brake line to the caliper assembly.

5. Allow brake fluid to drain out into the container. Cap the opening in the caliper to prevent entry of dirt and moisture.

WARNING
*Dispose of this brake fluid. **Never** reuse brake fluid. Contaminated brake fluid can cause brake failure.*

6. Remove the bolts and lower bracket (**Figure 41**) securing the brake hose to the front fork.

7. Remove the bolt securing the brake hose guide (**Figure 42**) to the lower fork bridge.

8. Loosen the brake hose joint nut, then unscrew the brake hose (A, **Figure 43**) from the brake hose joint (B, **Figure 43**).

9. Route the new hose in the same way as the old hose.

10. Connect the new brake hose to the brake hose joint, then tighten the brake hose joint nut. Make sure

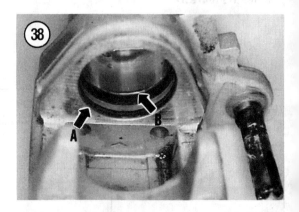

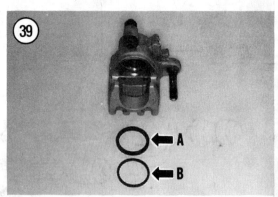

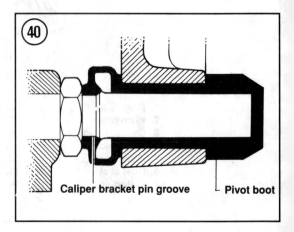

Caliper bracket pin groove   Pivot boot

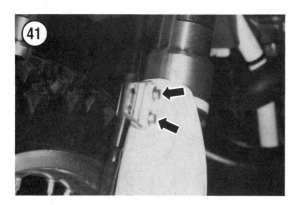

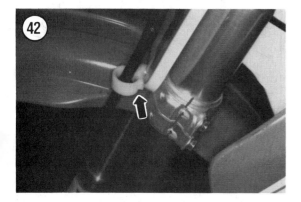

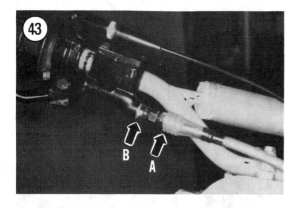

the path of the brake hose from the caliper to the master cylinder is smooth with no sharp bends or kinks.

11. Connect the brake hose to the caliper assembly with the union bolt and 2 new sealing washers. Tighten the bolt to the torque specified in **Table 2**.

12. Tighten the hose guide bolt on the lower fork bridge (**Figure 42**) and the hose clamp bolts on the fork (**Figure 41**) to the torque specifications listed in **Table 2**.

13. Refill the master cylinder with fresh brake fluid clearly marked DOT 4 only.

14. Bleed the brake as described in this chapter.

> *WARNING*
> *Do not ride the bike until you are sure that the brakes are operating properly.*

Rear Hose Replacement

> *CAUTION*
> *Cover the swing arm and frame with a heavy cloth or plastic tarp to protect it from accidental spilling of brake fluid. Wash any brake fluid off any painted or plated surface, as it will destroy the finish. Use soapy water and rinse completely.*

1. Place a metal or wood stand under the skid plate to support the bike with the rear wheel off the ground.

2. Remove the caliper guard (**Figure 35**).

3. Place a container under the brake line at the caliper.

4. Remove the union bolt and sealing washers (**Figure 36**) securing the brake line to the caliper assembly.

5. Allow brake fluid to drain out into the container. Plug the opening in the caliper to prevent entry of dirt and moisture.

> *WARNING*
> *Dispose of this brake fluid. **Never** reuse brake fluid. Contaminated brake fluid can cause brake failure.*

6. Place the container under the brake line at the rear master cylinder.

7. Remove the union bolt and sealing washers securing the brake line to the rear master cylinder (A, **Figure 44**).

8. Remove the plastic brake line clips (B, **Figure 44**) from the swing arm.

9. Carefully note the routing of the old brake line, then remove it.

10. Route the new brake line the same way as the old one.

11. Connect the brake line to the caliper with the union bolt and 2 new sealing washers. Tighten the bolt to the torque specified in **Table 2**.

12. Connect the other end of the brake line to the master cylinder with the union bolt and 2 new sealing washers. On 1988 models, turn the fitting until it contacts the boss on the master cylinder body (**Figure 45**), then tighten the bolt to the torque specified in **Table 2**. On 1989 and later models, position the fitting snugly between the 2 bosses, then tighten the bolt to the torque specified in **Table 2**.

13. Refill the system with new brake fluid and bleed the brake as described in this chapter.

BRAKE DISC

Inspection

It is not necessary to remove the disc from the wheel to inspect it. Small marks on the disc are not important, but radial scratches deep enough to snag a fingernail reduce braking effectiveness and increase brake pad wear. If these grooves are found, the disc should be replaced.

1. Measure the thickness of the disc at several locations around the disc with vernier calipers or a micrometer (**Figure 46**). If the thickness, in any area, is less than the service limit listed in **Table 1**, the disc must be replaced.

2. Clean the disc of any rust or corrosion and wipe clean with lacquer thinner. Never use an oil based solvent that may leave an oil residue on the disc.

Front Disc Removal/Installation

1. Remove the front wheel as described in Chapter Nine.

> *NOTE*
> *Place a piece of wood or vinyl tube in the caliper in place of the disc. This way, if the brake lever is squeezed inadvertently, the pistons will not be forced out of the cylinders. If this does happen, the caliper must be disassembled to reseat*

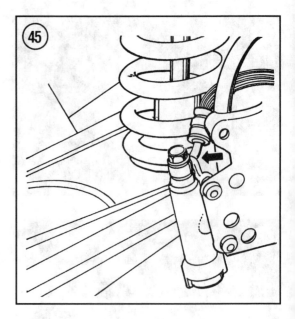
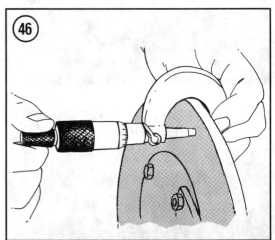
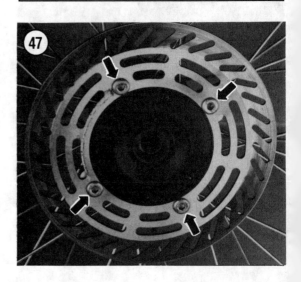

the pistons and the system will have to be bled.

2A. On 1988 models, remove the screws securing the hub cover to the disc and remove the cover. Then remove the screws securing the brake disc and remove the disc from the hub.

2B. On 1989 and later models, remove the screws securing the brake disc (**Figure 47**) and remove the disc from the hub. On 1989 models, you will need to remove the hub cover at this time.

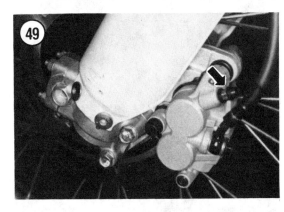

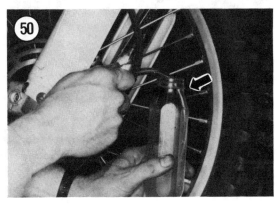

3. Install by reversing these removal steps while noting the following.

4. Install and tighten the disc mounting screw to the torque specification listed in **Table 2**.

Rear Disc Removal/Installation

1. Remove the rear wheel as described in Chapter Ten.

> *NOTE*
> *Place a piece of wood or vinyl tube in the caliper in place of the disc to prevent pistons from being forced out of the cylinders.*

2. Remove the bolts (**Figure 48**) securing the brake disc to the hub assembly.

3. Install by reversing these steps. Tighten the disc mounting bolts to the torque specified in **Table 2**.

BLEEDING THE SYSTEM

This procedure is not necessary unless the brakes feel spongy, there has been a fluid or air leak in the system or a component of the brake system has been replaced.

1. Remove the dust cap from the bleed valve (**Figure 49**).

2. Connect a length of clear tubing to the bleed valve on the caliper. Place the other end of the tube into a clean container (**Figure 50**).

3. Fill the container with enough fresh brake fluid to keep the end submerged. The tube should be long enough so that a loop can be made higher than the bleed valve to prevent air from being drawn into the caliper during bleeding.

> *CAUTION*
> *Cover the front rim or the swing arm area with a heavy cloth or plastic tarp to protect it from the accidental spilling of brake fluid. Wash any brake fluid off of any painted or plated surface immediately, as it will destroy the finish. Use soapy water and rinse completely.*

4. Clean the top of the master cylinder of all dirt and foreign matter.

11

5A. At the master cylinder on the front brake, remove the screws securing the top cover. Remove the top cover and diaphragm (**Figure 51**).

5B. On the rear brake, unscrew the reservoir cap. See **Figure 52**.

6. Fill the reservoir almost to the top lip. Loosely install the diaphragm and top cover or reservoir cap. Leave the top cover or reservoir cap in place during this procedure to prevent the entry of dirt.

> *NOTE*
> *Use brake fluid clearly marked DOT 4 only. Others may vaporize and cause brake failure. Always use the same brand name. Do not intermix as many brands are not compatible.*

7. Slowly apply the brakes several times, then hold them on. Open the bleed valve about one-half turn. Allow the lever or pedal to travel to its limit. When this limit is reached, tighten the bleed screw.

8. As the fluid enters the system, the level will drop in the reservoir. Maintain the level at about 3/8 inch from the top of the reservoir to prevent air from being drawn into the system.

9. Continue to pump the brake and fill the reservoir until the fluid emerging from the hose is completely free of bubbles.

> *NOTE*
> *Do not allow the reservoir to empty during the bleeding operation or more air will enter the system. If this occurs, the entire procedure must be repeated.*

10. Hold the brake on and tighten the bleed valve to the torque specification listed in **Table 2**.

11. Remove the bleed tube and install the bleed valve dust cap.

12. If necessary, add fluid to correct the level in the reservoir. It should be to the upper level line.

13. For the front master cylinder, install the diaphragm and reservoir top cover. Tighten the screws securely. For the rear master cylinder, install the reservoir cap.

14. Test the feel of the brake. It should be firm and should offer the same resistance each time it's operated. If it feels spongy, it is likely that there is still air in the system and it must be bled again. When all air has been bled from the system and the fluid level is correct in the reservoir, double-check for leaks and tighten all fittings and connections.

> *WARNING*
> *Before riding the bike, make certain that the brake is operating correctly by operating the lever several times.*

15. Test ride the bike slowly at first to make sure that the brake is operating properly.

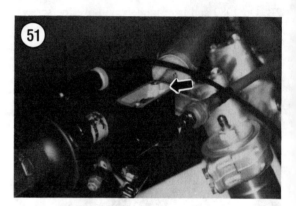

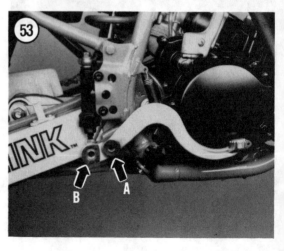

REAR BRAKE PEDAL ASSEMBLY

Removal/Installation

1A. On 1988 models, perform the following:

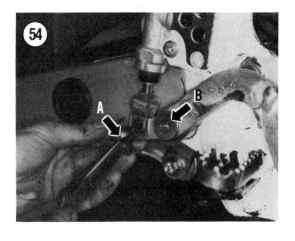

a. Remove the brake arm pivot bolt (A, **Figure 53**).

b. Back off the locknut on the master cylinder pushrod at the brake linkage.

c. Remove the pin securing the brake arm to the master cylinder (B, **Figure 53**).

1B. On 1989 and later models, remove the pivot link by removing the cotter pin and washer and pulling the pin out (A, **Figure 54**).

2. Remove the rear brake arm pivot bolt (B, **Figure 54**).

3. Inspect the O-rings on the brake arm. If damaged, replace them.

4. Lightly grease the brake arm pivot bolt.

5. Install by reversing the removal steps while noting the following:

a. On 1989 and later models, make sure the washer and cotter pin are secure.

b. Adjust the pushrod and tighten the locknut.

Table 1 BRAKE SPECIFICATIONS

Item	Specification	Wear limit
Front master cylinder		
Cylinder bore diameter	11.000-11.043 mm	11.05 mm
	(0.4331-0.4346 in.)	(0.435 in.)
Piston diameter	10.957-10.984 mm	10.84 mm
	(0.4314-0.4324 in.)	(0.427 in.)
Front caliper		
Cylinder bore diameter	27.00-27.05 mm	27.06 mm
	(1.0630-1.0650 in.)	(1.065 in.)
Piston diameter	26.90-26.95 mm	26.89 mm
	(1.0591-1.0610 in.)	(1.059 in.)
Rear master cylinder		
Cylinder bore diameter	12.700-12.743 mm	12.76 mm
	(0.5000-0.5017 in.)	(0.502 in.)
Piston diameter	12.657-12.684 mm	12.64 mm
	(0.4983-0.4994 in.)	(0.498 in.)
Rear caliper		
Cylinder bore diameter	27.00-27.05 mm	27.06 mm
	(1.0630-1.0650 in.)	(1.065 in.)
Piston diameter	26.935-26.968 mm	26.89 mm
	(1.0604-1.0617 in.)	(1.059 in.)
Front disc thickness	3.0 mm (0.12 in.)	2.5 mm (0.10 in.)
Rear disc thickness	4.5 mm (0.18 in.)	4.0 mm (0.16 in.)
Front and rear disc warpage	—	0.15 mm (0.006 in.)
Brake pad thickness		
Front	4.4 mm (0.17 in.)	1.0 mm (0.04 in.)
Rear	6.4 mm (0.25 in.)	1.0 mm (0.04 in.)
Brake fluid		
Front	DOT 3 or 4	
Rear	DOT 4	

11

Table 2 BRAKE TORQUE SPECIFICATIONS

Item	N·m	ft.-lb.	in.-lb.
Front master cylinder			
Clamping bolts	8-12	6-9	
Adjuster locknut	5-7	–	44-62
Lever bolt	8-12	6-9	
Caliper mounting bolt			
1988	20-30	14-22	
1989	32-36	23-26	
1990	24-30	17-22	
1991	28-34	20-25	
Caliper bleed valve	4-7	–	35-62
Brake hose union bolt			
1988	25-35	18-25	
1989-1991	30-40	22-29	
Brake hose joint			
To master cylinder	30-40	22-29	
To brake hose	12-15	9-11	
Brake pad pin bolts			
Upper	20-25	14-18	
Lower	10-15	7-11	
Brake disc bolts			
1988-1989	14-16	10-12	
1990-1991	40-45	29-33	
Brake pedal pivot bolt	24-28	17-20	
Lower fork bridge bolts			
1988	18-25	13-18	
1989-1991	24-30	17-22	

SUPPLEMENT

CR500R 1992-1996 SERVICE INFORMATION

This chapter contains all procedures and specifications unique to 1992-1996 CR500R models. If this supplement does not include a specific procedure, refer to the CR500R procedure in prior chapters.

The headings in this chapter correspond to those in the other chapters of this book.

12

CHAPTER ONE

GENERAL INFORMATION

Table 1 lists engine and chassis numbers for 1992-on CR500R models.

Table 1 ENGINE AND CHASSIS NUMBERS

Model	Year	Engine serial no. start to end	Frame serial no. start to end
CR500R	1992	PE02E-5100009-5102184	PE020-NM100006-MM101487
	1993	PE02E-5200006-on	PE020-PM200005-on
	1994	PE02E-5300005-5301886	PE020-RM300005-RM301209
	1995	PE02E-5400008-on	PE020-SM400001-on
	1996	PE02E-5500001-on	PE020-TM500001-on

CHAPTER THREE

LUBRICATION, MAINTENANCE AND TUNE-UP

PERIODIC LUBRICATION

Table 2 lists the fork oil capacity for 1992-on CR500R models.

Table 3 lists the fork oil level measurements for 1992-on CR500R models.

Fork Oil Change (1992-1994)

Procedures used to change the fork oil remain the same as for 1991 models in the main book, except the following:

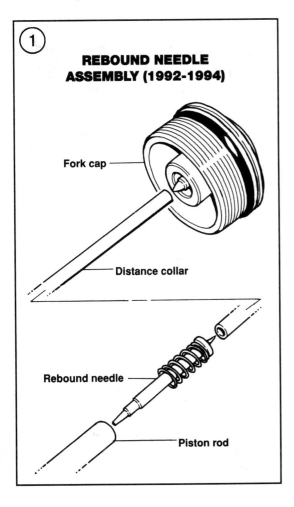

REBOUND NEEDLE ASSEMBLY (1992-1994)

Fork cap

Distance collar

Rebound needle

Piston rod

a. When changing the fork oil, first refer to *Fork Oil Change (1991 Models)* in Chapter Three of the main book.

b. The 1992-1994 CR500R fork tubes are equipped with a distance collar, rebound needle and spring. All 3 parts are installed inside the piston rod. See **Figure 1**. The piston rod is mounted on the damper rod.

c. After removing the fork cap, spring seat and fork spring as described in Chapter Three of the main book, next remove the distance collar, rebound needle and spring (**Figure 1**). Then pump the piston rod to drain as much oil from the damper rod assembly (cartridge) as possible.

d. After draining the oil, install the spring, rebound needle and distance collar. Then add fork oil as described in Chapter Three of the main book.

Fork Oil Change (1995-on)

1. Clean both fork tubes to prevent dirt from entering the fork tubes.

2. Loosen the upper fork tube pinch bolts and loosen the fork cap. Do not unscrew the fork cap from the fork tube.

3. Remove the fork assembly as described under *Front Fork Removal/Installation (1991)* in Chapter Nine of the main book.

4. Loosen the fork cap air screw (**Figure 2**) to release air from the fork tube.

CAUTION
Turning the rebound adjuster as described in Step 5 will prevent the adjuster from being damaged when you remove the fork cap.

5. Turn the rebound adjuster (**Figure 2**) counterclockwise to its softest setting.

6. Turn the compression damper adjuster (**Figure 3**) counterclockwise to its softest setting.

12

7. Unscrew the fork cap and slide the fork tube down until it seats against the axle holder (**Figure 4**).

8. Hold the fork cap (A, **Figure 5**) and loosen the piston rod locknut (B, **Figure 5**). Unscrew the fork cap and remove it from the piston rod.

9. Remove the spring seat and fork spring (C, **Figure 5**).

10. Remove the adjuster rod (**Figure 6**) from the piston rod.

11. Tie a long piece of wire to the piston rod locknut. This will allow you to retrieve the piston rod when it slides into the fork tube.

12. Hold the piston rod and turn the fork tube over to drain the oil into a drain pan. Pump the fork tube to drain as much oil as possible. Then, with the fork tube collapsed, pump the piston rod and pump oil out of the damper rod (cartridge). Repeat until you have removed as much oil as possible.

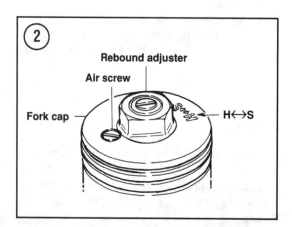

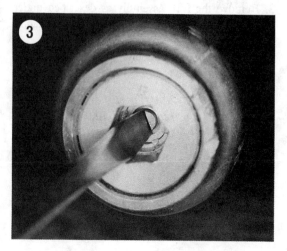

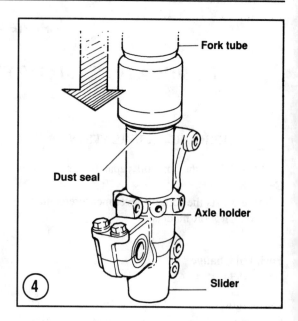

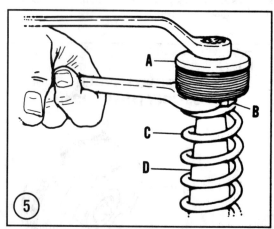

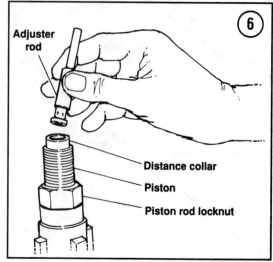

13. Clean the fork cap, spring seat, fork spring and adjuster rod in solvent and dry thoroughly.

14. Replace the fork cap O-ring if leaking or damaged.

15. Install the adjuster rod into the piston rod with the adjuster rod's oil hole facing down (**Figure 6**).

NOTE
*Refer to **Table 2** (fork oil capacity) and **Table 3** (oil level) when refilling the fork tubes with oil.*

16. Bottom the fork tube dust seal against the axle holder on the slider (**Figure 4**).

17. Pour half the recommended amount of fork oil into the fork tube.

18. To bleed air from the fork tube, do the following:

a. Extend the fork tube.

b. Cover the fork tube with your hand and compress the fork slowly.

c. Repeat until the fork's movement feels consistent throughout its complete range.

d. Bottom the fork tube dust seal against the axle holder on the slider (**Figure 4**).

e. With the piston rod bottomed out, slowly add more fork oil until the oil starts to flow out of the end of the piston rod.

f. Slowly pump the piston rod and fork tube together 8 to 10 times.

g. Pour the remaining amount of fork oil into the fork tube and repeat substep f.

19. To set the oil level, do the following:

a. Bottom the fork tube dust seal against the axle holder on the slider (**Figure 4**).

b. Place the fork tube in a vertical position.

c. Using an oil level gauge, set the oil level (**Figure 7**) to the specification listed in **Table 3**.

d. Remove the oil level gauge.

20. Turn the piston rod locknut (**Figure 8**) until it bottoms on the piston rod.

21. Install the fork spring into the fork tube with its tapered end facing up. Feed the wire up through the spring while installing the spring.

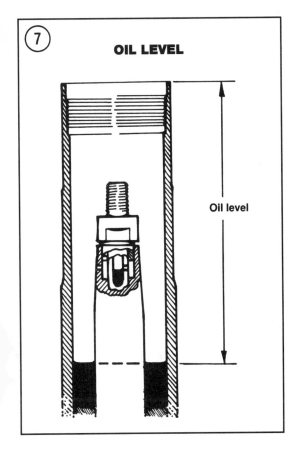

OIL LEVEL

Oil level

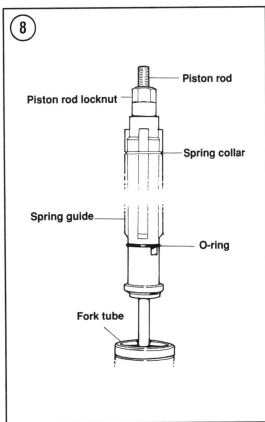

Piston rod
Piston rod locknut
Spring collar
Spring guide
O-ring
Fork tube

12

22. Slowly pull the piston rod up, then remove the wire. Do not let go of the piston rod.

23. Install the spring seat onto the fork spring.

24. Screw the fork cap onto the end of the piston rod.

25. Hold the locknut (B, **Figure 5**) and tighten the fork cap (A, **Figure 5**) against the locknut to 28 N•m (20 ft.-lb.).

26. Check that the spring seat is centered correctly against the fork cap and spring.

27. Pull the fork tube up and thread the fork cap into the fork tube.

28. Install the front fork into the steering stem. Tighten the lower pinch bolts to 22 N•m (16 ft.-lb.).

CAUTION
Overtightening the fork tube pinch bolts can distort the outer fork tube. Doing so will reduce fork performance and damage the outer fork tube.

29. Tighten the fork cap to 30 N•m (22 ft.-lb.).

30. Loosen the lower pinch bolts and install the fork tube as described under *Front Fork Removal/Installation (1991)* in Chapter Nine of the main book.

31. Repeat for the opposite fork tube.

PERIODIC MAINTENANCE

Drive Chain Adjustment

Table 4 lists the new drive chain slack specification for 1992-on models.

Table 5 lists the rear axle torque specification for 1992-on models.

Disc Brake Pad Wear

Procedures used to inspect the brake pads remain the same for 1991 models, except the following:

   a. Honda replaced the single wear limit groove on the front brake pads with 3 wear limit grooves.

   b. If the pads are worn to the bottom of any wear limit groove, replace both front pads as a set.

Front Disc Brake Lever Free Play

Procedures used to set the front disc brake lever play are the same as for 1991 and earlier models, but the free play specification has changed. If the free play amount exceeds 20 mm (0.8 in.), there is probably air in the brake line and you must bleed the brake. See *Bleeding the System* in Chapter Eleven of the main book.

Rear Brake Pedal Height Adjustment

Procedures used to adjust the rear brake pedal height remain the same as for 1991 and earlier models. However, if the brake pedal height free play exceeds 30 mm (1.2 in.), there is probably air in the brake line and you must bleed the brake. See *Bleeding the System* in Chapter Eleven of the main book.

Table 2 FRONT FORK OIL CAPACITY

	ml	U.S. oz.	Imp. oz
1992			
Standard	582	19.7	20.5
Minimum	552	18.7	19.5
Maximum	584	19.8	20.6
1993			
Standard	572	19.3	20.1
Minimum	541	18.3	19.1
Maximum	584	19.8	20.6
1994			
Standard	567	19.2	20.0
Minimum	534	18.1	18.9
Maximum	576	19.5	20.3
1995			
Standard	525	17.8	18.5
Minimum	499	16.9	17.6
Maximum	539	18.2	19.0
1996			
Standard	636	21.5	22.4
Minimum	613	20.7	21.6
Maximum	658	22.3	23.2

Table 3 FRONT FORK OIL LEVEL

	mm	in.
1992		
Standard	95	3.74
Maximum	93	3.66
Minimum	124	4.88
1993		
Standard	105	4.13
Maximum	93	3.66
Minimum	136	5.35
1994		
Standard	110	4.33
Maximum	101	3.98
Minimum	143	5.63
1995		
Standard	98	3.86
Maximum	84	3.31
Minimum	124	4.88
1996		
Standard	92	3.62
Maximum	73	2.87
Minimum	112	4.41

Table 4 DRIVE CHAIN SLACK

	mm	in.
CR500R 1992-on	35-45	1 3/8-1 49/64

Table 5 REAR AXLE NUT TORUE SPECIFICATIONS

	N·m	ft.-lb.
CR500R 1992-on	95	70

12

CHAPTER FOUR

ENGINE

Table 6 lists engine service specifications for 1992-on CR500R models that differ from 1991 and earlier models.

Table 7 lists all of the engine torque specifications for 1992-on CR500R models.

RIGHT CRANKCASE COVER

Installation

Tighten the right crankcase mounting bolts to 10 N•m (88 in.-lb.).

PRIMARY DRIVE GEAR

Removal/Installation

On 1992-on models, Honda replaced the conical spring washer with a plain lockwasher (**Figure 9**). The new lockwasher is not marked with an OUT mark. You can install the plain lockwasher with either side facing out.

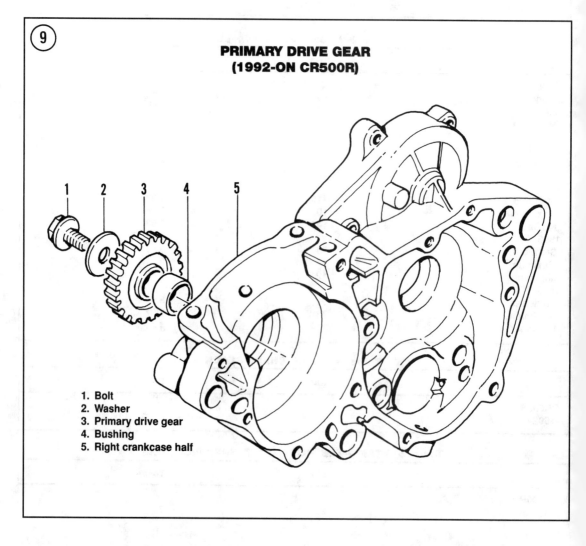

⑨

PRIMARY DRIVE GEAR (1992-ON CR500R)

1. Bolt
2. Washer
3. Primary drive gear
4. Bushing
5. Right crankcase half

Table 6 ENGINE SPECIFICATIONS

	Specification	Wear limit
Kickstarter idler gear Bushing outer diameter	19.979-20.000 mm (0.7866-0.7874)	19.94 mm (0.785 in.)

Table 7 ENGINE TORQUE SPECIFICATIONS

	N·m	ft.-lb.
Engine mounting bolts		
Lower/front	65	47
Upper engine mounting bolt		
1992	43	31
1993-on	40	29
Hanger plate bolts	27	20
Shock absorber lower bolt		
1992	43	31
1993-on	45	33
Brake arm pivot bolt	26	19
Swing arm pivot bolt	90	66
Cylinder head nuts	27	20
Cylinder nuts	40	29
Cylinder stud bolts	12	9
Alternator rotor	55	40
Primary drive gear bolt	45	33
Drive sprocket bolt	27	20

12

CHAPTER FIVE

CLUTCH AND TRANSMISSION

Table 8 lists transmission specifications for 1992-on CR500R models that differ from 1991 and earlier models.

Table 9 lists clutch torque specifications for 1992-on CR500R models that differ from 1991 and earlier models.

5-SPEED TRANSMISSION AND INTERNAL SHIFT MECHANISM

Removal/Installation

1. On 1992-on CR500R models, install the shift forks (**Figure 10**) as follows:

a. Install the right and left shift forks with the R and L marks facing up (away from right crank-case).

b. Install the center shift fork with the C mark facing down (toward the right crankcase).

Mainshaft Disassembly/Assembly

Mainshaft disassembly and reassembly procedures remain the same for 1991 and earlier CR500R models. However, the mainshaft fourth and fifth gears (**Figure 11**) were changed as follows:

a. On 1992 models, fourth gear has 24 teeth. On 1993-on models, fourth gear has 22 teeth.

b. On 1992 models, fifth gear has 23 teeth. On 1993-on models, fifth gear has 24 teeth.

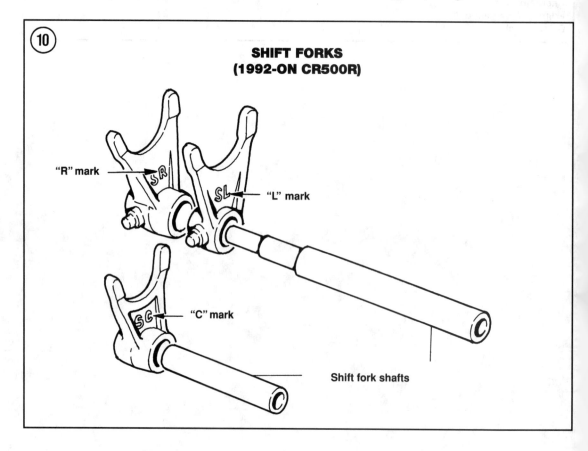

**SHIFT FORKS
(1992-ON CR500R)**

"R" mark

"L" mark

"C" mark

Shift fork shafts

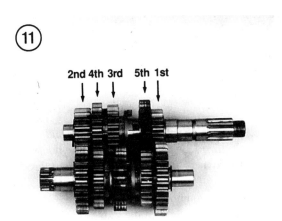

2nd 4th 3rd   5th 1st

While these changes will not affect the mainshaft's service procedures, make sure you install the correct gears for your Honda's model year.

Countershaft Disassembly/Assembly

Countershaft disassembly and reassembly procedures remain the same for 1991 and earlier CR500R models. However, the countershaft fourth and fifth gears (**Figure 11**) were changed as follows:

    a. On 1992 models, fourth gear has 24 teeth. On 1993-on models, fourth gear has 21 teeth.

    b. On 1992 models, fifth gear has 19 teeth. On 1993-on models, fifth gear has 20 teeth.

While these changes will not affect the countershaft's service procedures, make sure you install the correct gears for your Honda's model year.

Table 8 TRANSMISSION SPECIFICATIONS

	Wear limit
Gear inner diameter mainshaft 5th	25.07 mm (0.987 in.)

Gear inner diameter countershaft
  1st
  2nd
  3rd
	22.07 mm (0.869 in.)
	27.07 mm (1.066 in.)
	25.07 mm (0.987 in.)

Countershaft
  2nd gear bushing
    outer diameter
	26.95 mm (1.061 in.)

Table 9 CLUTCH TORQUE SPECIFICATIONS

	N·m	ft.-lb.
Clutch center nut	82	60

12

CHAPTER SIX

FUEL AND EXHAUST SYSTEMS

Table 10 lists carburetor specifications for 1992-on CR500R models.

THROTTLE CABLE

Removal/Installation

1. On 1993-on models, do the following:
   a. On 1994-on models, remove the dust cover from the throttle housing.
   b. Remove the throttle cable housing cover screws and remove the cover (**Figure 12**).
   c. Remove the throttle cable roller and collar (**Figure 13**) from the throttle cable housing.
   d. Disconnect the throttle cable from the throttle grip.
2. On 1993-on models, do the following:
   a. Reconnect the throttle cable to the throttle grip.
   b. Fit the throttle cable to the outside of the roller and install the roller and collar (**Figure 13**).
   c. Install the throttle cable housing cover (**Figure 12**) and its mounting screws.
   d. On 1994-on models, install the dust cover.

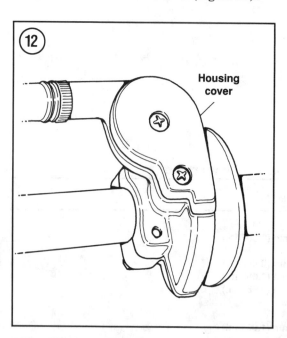

(12) Housing cover

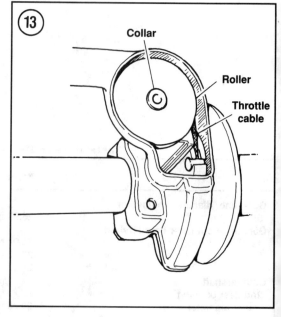

(13) Collar / Roller / Throttle cable

Table 10 CARBURETOR SPECIFICATIONS

Item	1992-on CR500R
Carburetor model No.	
1992	PJ27J
1993	PJ27L
1994	PJ27M
1995	PJ27N
1996	PJ27P
Venturi diameter	38 mm (1.50 in.)
Float level	16.0 mm (0.63 in.)
Air screw opening	1 1/2 turns out
Standard jet needle setting	4th groove
Standard main jet No.	170
Standard slow jet No.	55

CHAPTER SEVEN

ELECTRICAL SYSTEM

Table 11 lists electrical specifications for 1992-on CR500R models that differ from 1991 and earlier models.

Table 12 lists alternator torque specifications for 1992-on CR500R models that differ from 1991 and earlier models.

12

Table 11 ELECTRICAL SPECIFICATIONS

Item	Resistance (ohms)*
Ignition coil	
Secondary coil (with plug cap)	13-23K
* All values at 20° C (68° F)	

Table 12 ALTERNATOR ASSEMBLY TORQUE SPECIFICATIONS

	N·m	ft.-lb.	in.-lb.
Rotor nut	55	40	
Alternator cover screws	4	–	35

CHAPTER EIGHT

LIQUID COOLING SYSTEM

Table 13 lists cooling system torque specifications 1992-on CR500R models that differ from 1991 and earlier models.

Table 13 COOLING SYSTEM TORQUE SPECIFICATIONS

	N·m	in.-lb.
Drain bolts	10	88
Water pump cover bolts	12	106
Water pump impeller	12	106

CHAPTER NINE

FRONT SUSPENSION AND STEERING

Table 2 lists front fork oil capacity specifications for 1992-on CR500R models.

Table 3 lists front fork oil level specifications for 1992-on CR500R models.

Table 14 lists front suspension torque specifications for 1992-on CR500R models.

Table 15 lists front fork spring specifications for 1992-on CR500R models.

Table 16 lists front fork compression damping specifications for 1992-on CR500R models.

Table 17 lists front fork rebound damping specifications for 1992-on CR500R models.

FRONT WHEEL
(1992-ON)

Removal

1. Support the bike with the front wheel off the ground.
2. On 1995-on models, remove the front brake disc cover bolts and the disc cover.
3. Remove the axle nut (**Figure 14**).
4. Loosen the axle pinch bolts (**Figure 15**) and remove the front axle from the right side.
5. Remove the front wheel.

NOTE
Identify the collars as you remove them in Step 6.

6. Remove the left and right side collars from the wheel.

7. Insert a spacer in the caliper in place of the disc.

NOTE
The spacer used in Step 7 will keep the pistons from being forced out of the cylinder if you inadvertently squeeze the brake lever. If this does happen, you

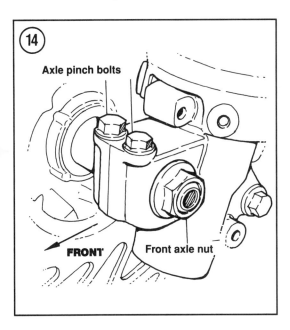

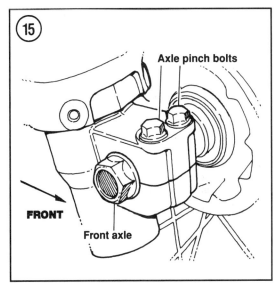

must disassemble the caliper to reseat the pistons.

CAUTION
Handle the wheel carefully to prevent damaging the brake disc.

Inspection

Inspection procedures are the same for 1991 and earlier models. Refer to *Front Wheel Inspection* in Chapter Nine in the main book.

Installation

1. Clean the front axle and axle nut in solvent and dry thoroughly. Check that the axle holders and pinch bolts in the sliders are free from dirt; clean if necessary.

2. Remove all burrs from the front axle and axle holders.

3. Remove the spacer from the caliper assembly.

4. Apply a thin coat of grease to the axle.

5. If removed, install the left and right side collars into the wheel.

6. Install the front wheel between the fork tubes. Also, carefully insert the disc between the brake pads.

7. Install the front axle (**Figure 15**) from the right side. Then check that the axle seats firmly in the left fork tube axle holder.

8. Install the axle nut (**Figure 14**) and tighten to the torque specification in **Table 14**.

9. Tighten the left axle holder pinch bolts (**Figure 14**) to the torque specification in **Table 14**.

10. Remove the stand from underneath the bike so that the front wheel contacts the ground.

11. Apply the front brake and pump the forks up and down to help seat the front axle in the axle holders.

12. Turn the handlebar so that the front wheel faces straight ahead and tighten the right axle holder pinch bolts (**Figure 15**) to the torque specification in **Table 14**.

13. On 1995-on models, install the brake disc cover. Then apply ThreeBond medium strength threadlock to the disc cover bolts. Install these bolts and tighten to the torque specification in **Table 14**.

14. After you completely install the wheel, rotate it several times and then apply the brake a couple of

12

times to make sure that the wheel rotates freely and that the brake is operating correctly.

FRONT HUB

Procedures used to service the front hub bearings remain the same for 1991 and earlier models, except that Honda changed the shape and size of the outer

spacers. Refer to **Figure 16** (1992-1994) or **Figure 17** (1995-on) when servicing the front hub.

WHEEL SPOKES

Inspection and Replacement

Procedures used to service the wheel spokes remain the same as for 1991 and earlier models, except

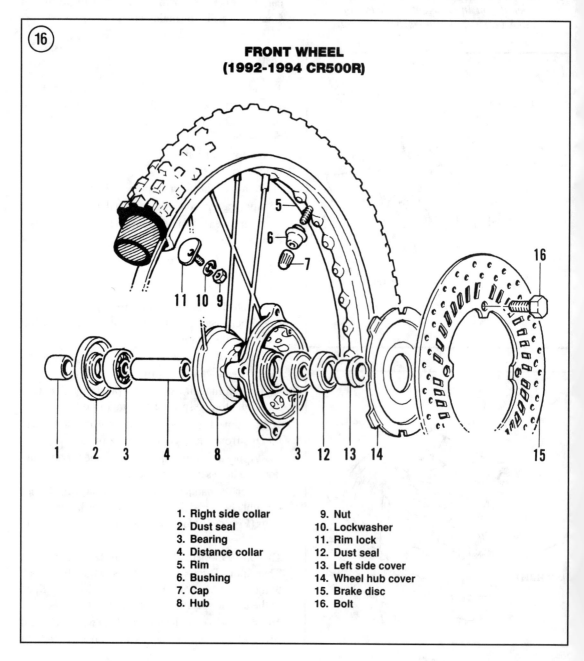

(16)

**FRONT WHEEL
(1992-1994 CR500R)**

1. Right side collar
2. Dust seal
3. Bearing
4. Distance collar
5. Rim
6. Bushing
7. Cap
8. Hub
9. Nut
10. Lockwasher
11. Rim lock
12. Dust seal
13. Left side cover
14. Wheel hub cover
15. Brake disc
16. Bolt

that the distance from the hub to the rim has changed. You must maintain the following dimensions when respoking and truing a wheel.

a. When truing a front wheel on 1992-1994 models, position the hub so that its left side is 20.0 mm (0.79 in.) higher than the left rim surface as shown in **Figure 18**.

b. When truing a front wheel on 1994 models, position the hub so that its left side is 23.25 mm (0.915 in.) higher than the left rim surface as shown in **Figure 18**.

c. When truing a front wheel on 1995-on models, position the hub so that its disc brake mounting surface (without a brake disc installed) is 27.25 mm (1.073 in.) higher than the adjacent rim surface as shown in **Figure 19**.

d. When truing a rear wheel on 1992-1994 models, position the hub so that the distance from

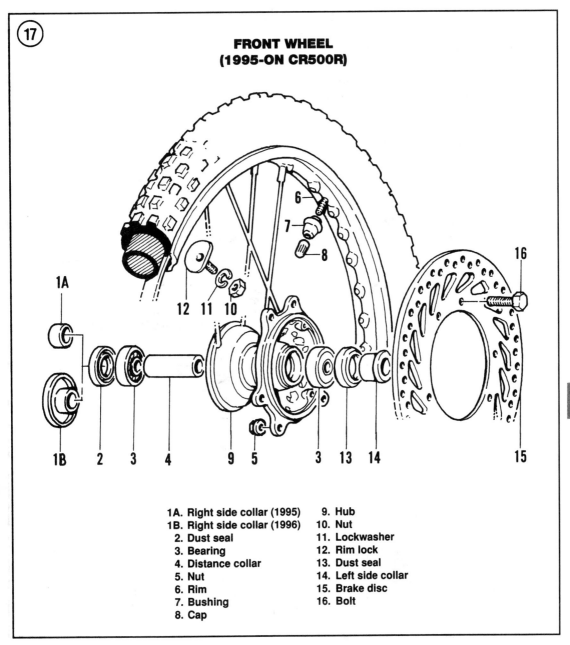

(17)

**FRONT WHEEL
(1995-ON CR500R)**

1A. **Right side collar (1995)**
1B. **Right side collar (1996)**
2. **Dust seal**
3. **Bearing**
4. **Distance collar**
5. **Nut**
6. **Rim**
7. **Bushing**
8. **Cap**
9. **Hub**
10. **Nut**
11. **Lockwasher**
12. **Rim lock**
13. **Dust seal**
14. **Left side collar**
15. **Brake disc**
16. **Bolt**

12

its left side to the rim side is 43.25 mm (1.703 in.); see **Figure 20**.

e. When truing a rear wheel on 1995-on models, position the hub so that the distance from its left side to the rim side is 47.0 mm (1.85 in.); see **Figure 20**.

HANDLEBAR

Removal/Installation

Procedures used to remove and install the handle-bar remain the same as for 1992 and earlier models, except when you install the throttle housing. Note the following:

a. On 1993-on models, align the mark on the throttle housing with the punch mark on the handlebar (**Figure 21**).

b. On 1993-on models, tighten the throttle housing bolts to the torque specification in **Table 14**.

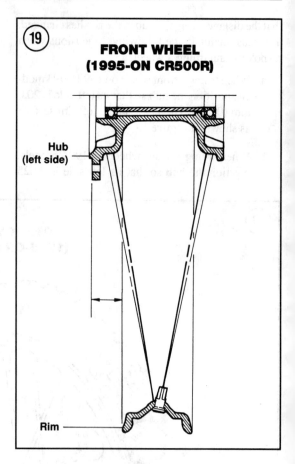

(19) FRONT WHEEL
(1995-ON CR500R)

Hub
(left side)

Rim

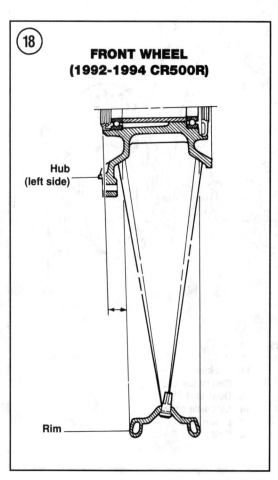

(18) FRONT WHEEL
(1992-1994 CR500R)

Hub
(left side)

Rim

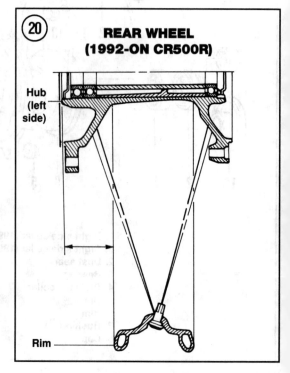

(20) REAR WHEEL
(1992-ON CR500R)

Hub
(left side)

Rim

STEERING HEAD

Assembly

1. Slide the fork tubes into position as follows:

    d. On 1992-on models—align the top surface of the bridge with the groove 9 mm (0.35 in.) below the top for the fork tube (**Figure 22**).

2. On 1992-on models, do the following:

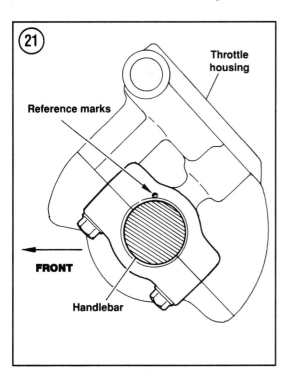

21

Throttle housing

Reference marks

FRONT

Handlebar

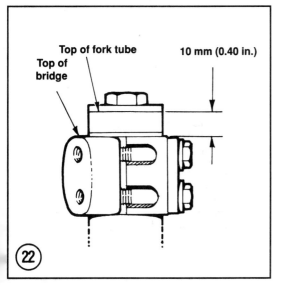

22

Top of fork tube   10 mm (0.40 in.)

Top of bridge

CAUTION
Overtightening the fork tube pinch bolts can distort the outer fork tube. Doing so will reduce fork performance and damage the outer fork tube.

    a. Tighten the lower fork bridge bolts to the torque specified in **Table 14**.

    b. Tighten the upper fork bridge bolts to the torque specified in **Table 14**.

FRONT FORKS

**Front Fork Disassembly
(1992-1994 Models)**

    Refer to **Figure 23**.

    When disassembling the front fork forks in this section, you need the following Honda tools (or equivalent):

    a. Honda fork slider spacer (part No. 07KMZ-KZ3010A) or equivalent.

    b. Honda damper rod holder (part No. 07PMB-KZ4010A).

1. Clean the fork tubes and the bottom the compression bolt before disassembling the fork tube.

2. Loosen the fork cap air release screw (**Figure 24**) to release air from the fork tube.

CAUTION
Turning the rebound adjuster as described in Step 3 will prevent the adjuster from being damaged when you remove the fork cap.

3. Turn the rebound adjuster (**Figure 24**) counterclockwise to its softest setting.

4. Turn the compression adjuster (**Figure 25**) counterclockwise to its softest setting.

5. Install the fork slider spacer on the lower fork axle holder (**Figure 26**).

6. Hold the upper fork tube and unscrew the fork cap. Then slowly lower the upper fork tube down onto the fork slider spacer (**Figure 26**).

7. Hold the fork cap with a wrench (A, **Figure 27**). Then insert another wrench onto the piston rod locknut (B, **Figure 27**) and unscrew the fork cap from the piston rod.

8. Remove the spring seat.

9. Remove the fork spring (C, **Figure 27**).

10. Remove the locknut and slide the spring guide off the piston rod.

12

FRONT FORK
(1992-1994 CR500R)

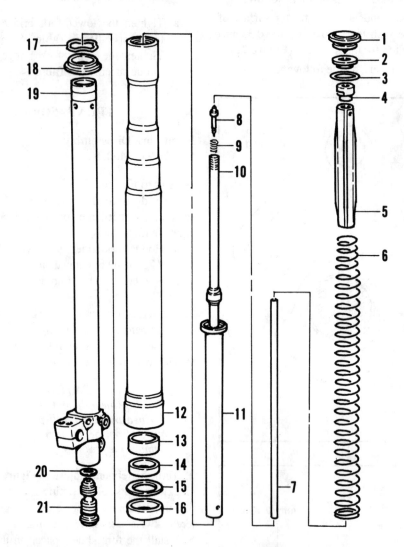

1. Fork cap/rebound adjuster
2. Spring seat
3. O-ring
4. Locknut
5. Spring guide
6. Fork spring
7. Distance collar
8. Rebound needle
9. Spring
10. Piston rod
11. Damper rod
12. Upper fork tube
13. Slider bushing
14. Guide bushing
15. Backup ring
16. Oil seal
17. Stopper ring
18. Dust seal
19. Slider
20. Washer
21. Compression bolt

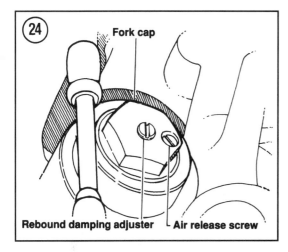

Fork cap

Rebound damping adjuster — Air release screw

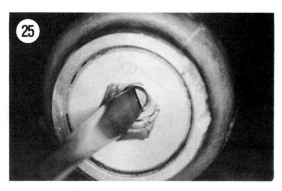

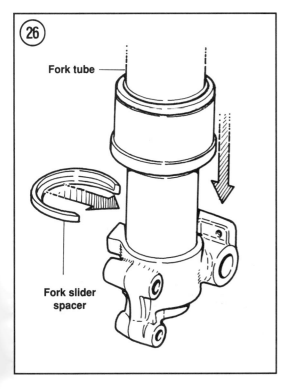

Fork tube

Fork slider spacer

11. Remove the distance collar, rebound needle and spring from the piston rod (**Figure 28**).

CAUTION
Handle the rebound needle carefully to avoid damaging its tip.

12. Turn the fork tube over and drain the oil into a clean pan.

13. Perform the following steps to remove the compression bolt assembly:

    a. Clamp the slider (axle holder) in a vise with soft jaws.

    b. Insert the damper rod holder into the fork tube and engage it with the piston rod (**Figure 29**).

    c. Hold the damper rod holder securely and loosen the compression bolt.

    d. Remove the compression bolt and its washer from the slider.

    e. Remove the damper rod holder from the upper fork tube.

    f. Remove the fork tube from the vise.

14. Turn the fork over and remove the damper rod assembly.

15. Hold the damper rod over the drain pan and pump the piston rod to help empty oil from the damper rod.

16. Remove the fork slider spacer from the fork tube.

17. Carefully pry the dust seal (**Figure 30**) out of the upper fork tube.

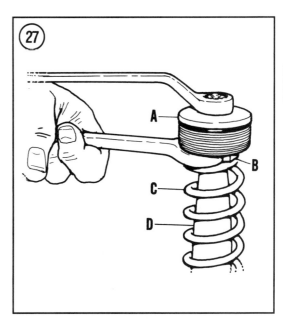

A
B
C
D

12

18. Pry the stop ring out of the groove in the upper fork tube.

19. Hold the upper tube and slowly move the slider up and down. The slider must move smoothly. If there is any noticeable binding or roughness, check the upper tube for any dents or other damage.

20. There is an interference fit between the upper fork tube and slider bushings. To separate the fork tubes, hold the upper tube and pull hard on the slider using quick in and out strokes (**Figure 31**). This action withdraws the bushing, backup ring and oil seal from the upper fork tube. See **Figure 32**.

21. Carefully open the end of the fork tube bushing and slide it off the fork tube. Do not pry the opening more than necessary or you may damage the bushing.

22. Remove the following parts from the slider bushing (F, **Figure 32**):

   a. Guide bushing (C, **Figure 32**).

   b. Stop ring (E, **Figure 32**).

   c. Oil seal (B, **Figure 32**).

   d. Backup ring (D, **Figure 32**) and dust seal (A, **Figure 32**).

23. Inspect the fork assembly as described under *Front Fork Inspection (1991 Models)* in Chapter Nine of the main book.

**Front Fork Assembly
(1992-1994)**

Refer to **Figure 23**.

When assembling the front forks in this section, you will need the following Honda tools (or equivalent):

   a. Honda fork slider spacer (part No. 07KMZ-KZ3010A).

   b. Honda damper rod holder (part No. 07PMB-KZ4010A).

   c. Honda oil seal driver (part No. 07KMB-KZ30100).

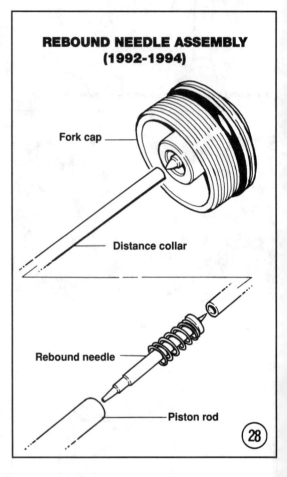

**REBOUND NEEDLE ASSEMBLY
(1992-1994)**

Fork cap

Distance collar

Rebound needle

Piston rod

28

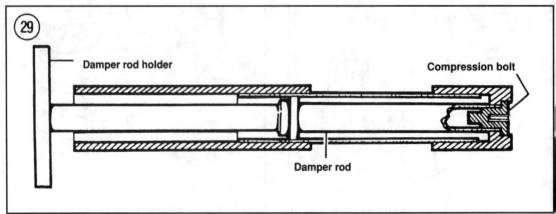

29

Damper rod holder

Compression bolt

Damper rod

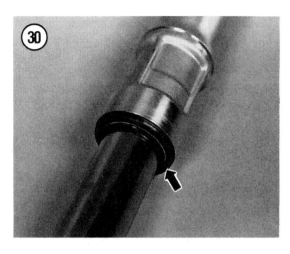

d. Honda oil seal driver attachment (part No. 07NMD-KZ30100).

1. Before assembly, make sure you have repaired or replaced all worn or defective parts. All parts must be clean before assembly.

2. Lubricate the parts with Pro Honda Suspension Fluid SS-7M or an equivalent fork oil.

3. Wrap the end of the upper fork tube with tape or cover it with a thin plastic bag. Coat the tape or bag with fork oil.

NOTE
Covering the upper fork tube as described in Step 3 will prevent the fork

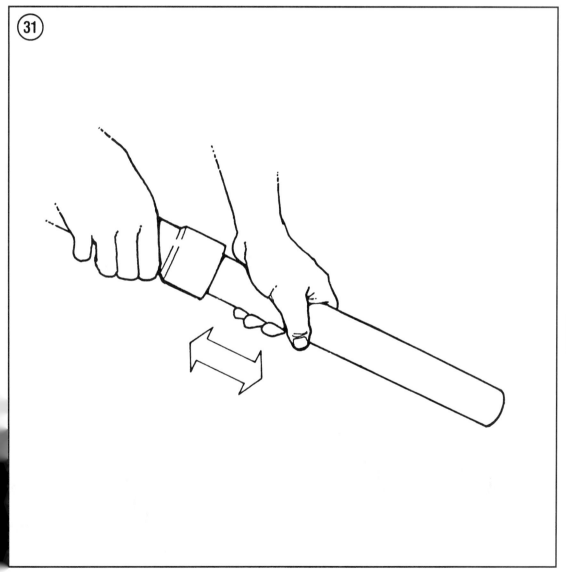

12

tube from tearing the dust and oil seals when you install them in Step 4.

4. Install the following parts (**Figure 33**) onto the slider as follows:

    a. Dust seal (A). Install the dust seal (**Figure 34**) so that its open side faces up (toward top of slider).

    b. Stop ring (B).

    c. Oil seal (C). Install the oil seal so that its open side faces up (toward top of slider). See **Figure 35**.

    d. Backup ring (D).

    e. Guide bushing (E).

    f. Slider bushing. Seat the bushing into the groove in the top of the slider. See **Figure 36**.

5. Coat the slider and the slider bushing with fork oil and install the slider into the fork tube.

6. Install the guide bushing (E, **Figure 33**) as follows:

    a. Support the fork assembly so that the slider is facing up.

    b. Position the guide bushing so that it rests against the fork tube.

    c. Position the backup ring against the guide bushing.

    d. Drive the guide bushing (with the backup ring on top of it) into the fork tube until it bottoms

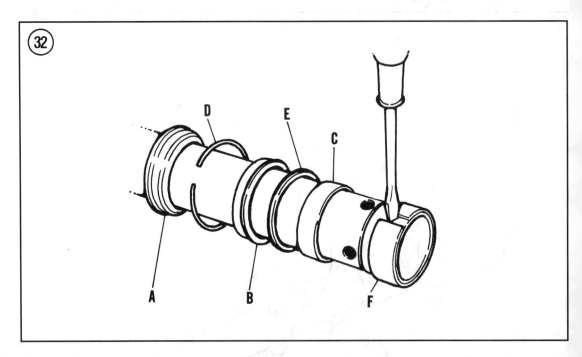

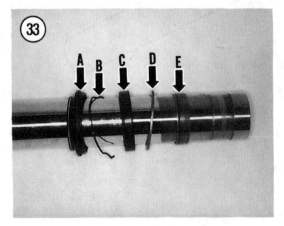

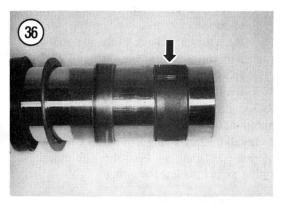

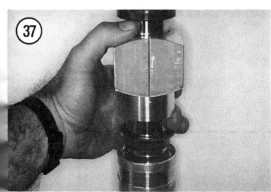

out. Use the Honda oil seal driver and attachment (or an equivalent tool) to install the bushing. See **Figure 37**.

7. Install the oil seal (C, **Figure 33**) as follows:

  a. Drive the oil seal (**Figure 38**) into the fork tube with the same tool used in Step 6.

  b. Drive the oil seal into place until the stop ring groove is visible above the oil seal.

8. Install the stop ring into the fork tube groove. Make sure the stop ring is completely seated in the groove.

9. Seat the dust seal (A, **Figure 33**) into the fork tube.

10. Install the fork slider spacer (**Figure 26**) onto the slider to avoid damaging the dust seal.

11. Perform the following steps to install the damper rod and compression bolt assembly:

  a. Clamp the slider (axle holder) in a vise with soft jaws.

  b. Insert the damper rod holder into the fork tube and engage it with the piston rod (**Figure 29**).

  c. Install a new washer onto the compression bolt.

  d. Apply fork oil onto the compression bolt O-rings (**Figure 39**).

  e. Apply ThreeBond medium strength threadlock onto the compression bolt threads.

CAUTION
Do not allow the threadlock to contact the O-rings, shim pack, or piston on the compression bolt.

  f. Install the compression bolt through the slider and thread it into the bottom of the damper rod.

12

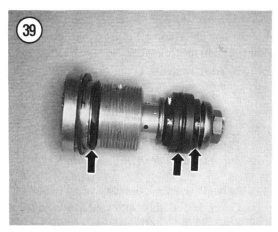

g. Hold the damper rod with the special tool and tighten the compression bolt to the torque specification in **Table 14**.

h. Remove the damper rod holder from the fork tube.

12. Install the spring, rebound needle and distance collar into the piston rod.

13. Wipe off any oil from the spring guide and install it over the piston rod with its oil hole facing up.

14. Install the piston rod locknut with its flange side facing up. This is a temporary installation to hold the spring guide during the refilling procedure.

15. Refill the fork with oil and set the oil level as described under *Fork Oil Refilling (1992-1994 Models)* in this chapter.

Fork Oil Refilling
(1992-1994 Models)

The recommended fork oil for 1992-1994 models is Pro Honda Suspension Fluid SS-7M or equivalent.

1. Install the fork slider spacer (**Figure 26**) over the slider. This spacer is required for obtaining the correct oil level measurement and to prevent the slider from damaging the dust seal when the forks are compressed.

2. Tie a long piece of wire to the piston rod locknut. This will allow you to retrieve the piston rod if it slides into the fork tube.

> *NOTE*
> *Refer to* **Table 2** *fork oil capacity specifications.*

3. Bottom the upper fork tube against the fork slider spacer (**Figure 26**).

4. Pour half the recommended amount of fork oil (**Table 2**) into the fork tube.

5. To bleed air from the fork tube, do the following:

> *CAUTION*
> *Do not extend the fork tube more than 250 mm (9.8 in.) from the axle holder (A,* **Figure 40***). Otherwise, oil will squirt out of the oil hole in the fork slider.*

a. Extend the outer fork tube.

b. Cover the fork tube with your hand and compress the fork slowly.

c. Repeat until the fork's movement feels consistent.

d. Bottom the upper fork tube against the fork slider spacer.

e. With the piston rod bottomed out, slowly add more fork oil until the oil starts to flow out of the end of the piston rod.

f. Slowly pump the piston rod and fork tube 8 to 10 times.

g. Pour in the remaining amount of fork oil (**Table 2**) and repeat substep f.

6. To set the oil level, do the following:

a. Bottom the upper fork tube against the fork slider spacer.

b. Place the fork tube in a vertical position.

c. Using an oil level gauge, set the oil level to the specifications listed in **Table 3**. See **Figure 41**.

d. Remove the oil level gauge.

7. Turn the piston rod locknut until it bottoms on the piston rod.

8. Install the fork spring into the fork tube with its tapered end facing up. Feed the wire thought the spring while installing the spring.

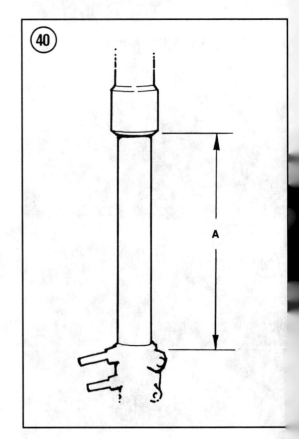

9. Slowly pull the piston rod up, then remove the wire. Do not let go of the piston rod.

10. Install the spring seat onto the fork spring.

11. Screw the fork cap onto the end of the piston rod.

12. Hold the locknut and tighten the fork cap against the locknut to 22 N•m (16 ft.-lb.).

13. Check that the spring seat is positioned correctly against the fork cap and spring.

14. Pull the outer tube up and thread the fork cap into the outer tube.

15. Install the fork tube as described in Chapter Nine of the main book.

**Front Fork Disassembly
(1995-on Models)**

Refer to **Figure 42**.

When disassembling the front fork forks, you need the Honda damper rod holder (part No. 07PMB-KZ40100) or an equivalent tool to hold the damper rod.

1. Clean the fork tubes and the compression bolt before disassembling the fork tube.

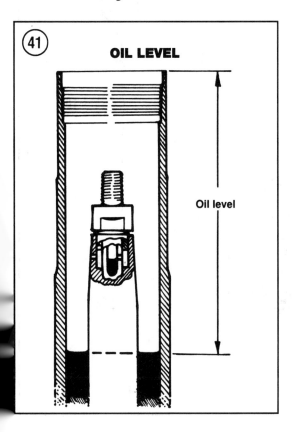

OIL LEVEL

Oil level

2. Loosen the fork cap air screw (**Figure 43**) to release air from the fork tube.

CAUTION
Turning the rebound and compression adjusters as described in Step 3 and Step 4 will prevent the adjuster from being damaged when you remove the fork cap.

3. Turn the rebound damper adjuster (**Figure 43**) counterclockwise to its softest setting.

4. Turn the compression damper adjuster (**Figure 44**) counterclockwise to its softest setting.

5. Unscrew the fork cap and slide the outer tube down until it seats on the axle holder.

6. Hold the fork cap (A, **Figure 45**) and loosen the piston rod locknut (B, **Figure 45**). Unscrew the fork cap and remove it from the piston rod.

7. Remove the spring seat and the fork spring and set them aside.

8. Remove the adjuster rod (**Figure 46**) from the piston rod.

9. Remove the following parts from the piston rod (**Figure 47**):

    a. Piston rod locknut.

    b. Spring collar.

    c. Spring guide.

    d. O-ring.

10. Hold the piston rod and the turn the fork tube over to drain the oil into a clean pan. Pump the fork tube to drain as much oil as possible. Then, with the fork tube collapsed, pump the piston rod to pump oil out of the cartridge. Repeat until you have removed as much oil as possible.

11. Remove the distance collar from inside the piston rod.

12. Perform the following steps to remove the compression bolt assembly:

    a. Clamp the lower fork tube (axle holder) in a vise with soft jaws.

    b. Insert the damper rod holder into the fork tube and engage it with the damper rod (**Figure 48**).

    c. Hold the damper rod holder securely and loosen the compression bolt.

    d. Remove the compression bolt and its washer from the lower fork tube.

    e. Remove the damper rod holder from the upper fork tube.

    f. Remove the fork tube from the vise.

12

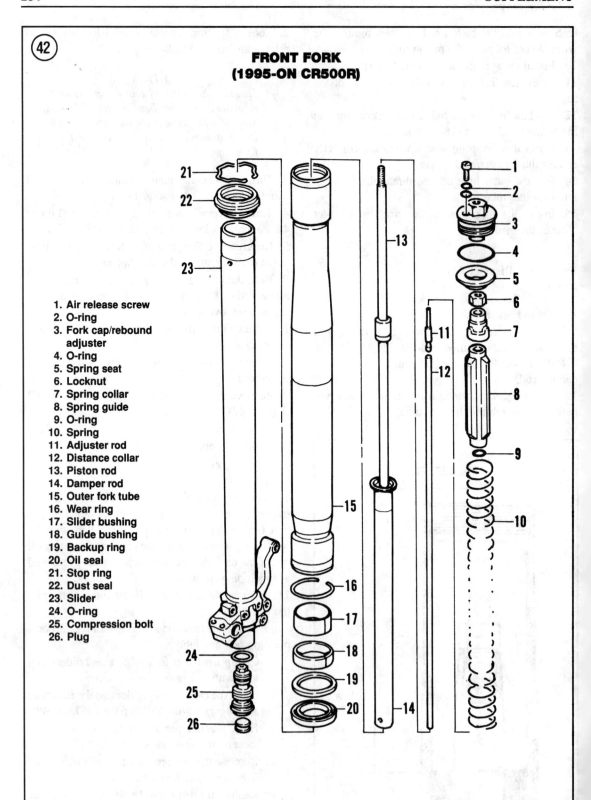

**FRONT FORK
(1995-ON CR500R)**

1. Air release screw
2. O-ring
3. Fork cap/rebound adjuster
4. O-ring
5. Spring seat
6. Locknut
7. Spring collar
8. Spring guide
9. O-ring
10. Spring
11. Adjuster rod
12. Distance collar
13. Piston rod
14. Damper rod
15. Outer fork tube
16. Wear ring
17. Slider bushing
18. Guide bushing
19. Backup ring
20. Oil seal
21. Stop ring
22. Dust seal
23. Slider
24. O-ring
25. Compression bolt
26. Plug

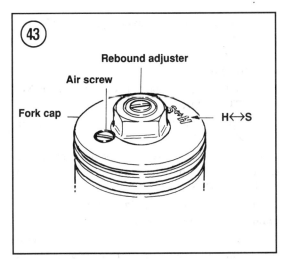

43

Rebound adjuster

Air screw

Fork cap

H↔S

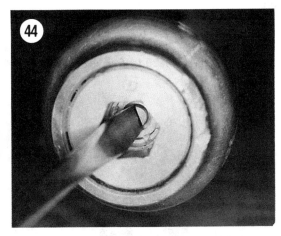

44

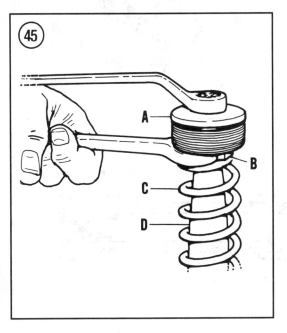

45

A

B

C

D

13. Turn the fork over and remove the damper rod assembly.

14. Hold the damper rod over the drain pan and pump the piston rod to help empty oil from the damper rod unit.

15. Carefully pry the dust seal (**Figure 49**) out of the upper fork tube.

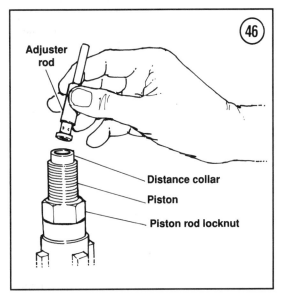

46

Adjuster rod

Distance collar

Piston

Piston rod locknut

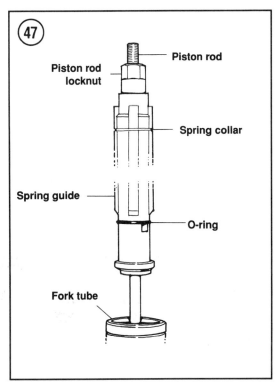

47

Piston rod

Piston rod locknut

Spring collar

Spring guide

O-ring

Fork tube

12

16. Pry the stop ring out of the groove in the upper fork tube.

17. Hold the upper fork tube and slowly move the slider in and out of the upper tube. The slider must move smoothly. If there is any noticeable binding or roughness, check the upper fork tube for any dents or other damage.

18. There is an interference fit between the upper fork tube and slider bushings. To separate the fork tubes, hold the upper tube and pull hard on the lower tube using quick in and out strokes (**Figure 50**). This action withdraws the bushing, backup ring and oil seal from the upper fork tube. See **Figure 51**.

19. Carefully open the end of the fork tube bushing and slide it off the fork tube. Do not pry the opening more than necessary or you may damage the bushing.

20. Remove the following parts from the lower fork tube:

    a. Guide bushing (C, **Figure 51**).

    b. Backup ring (E, **Figure 51**).

    c. Oil seal (B, **Figure 51**).

    d. Stop ring (D, **Figure 51**) and dust seal (A, **Figure 51**).

21. Inspect the fork assembly as described under *Front Fork Inspection (1991 Models)* in Chapter Nine of the main book.

Front Fork Assembly (1995-on)

Refer to **Figure 42**.

When assembling the front fork forks in this section, you need the following Honda tools (or equivalent):

    a. Honda damper rod holder (part No. 07PMB-KZ40100).

    b. 1995 models: Honda oil seal driver (part No. 07KMB-KZ30100).

    c. 1996 models: Honda oil seal driver (part No. 07TMD-MAC0100).

    d. Honda oil seal driver attachment (part No. 07NMD-KZ3010A).

1. Before assembly, make sure you have repaired or replaced all worn or defective parts. All parts must be clean before assembly.

2. Lubricate the parts with Pro Honda Suspension Fluid SS-7M or an equivalent fork oil.

3. Wrap the end of the slider with tape or cover it with a thin plastic bag. Coat the tape or bag with fork oil.

NOTE
Covering the slider as described in Step 3 will prevent the slider from tearing the

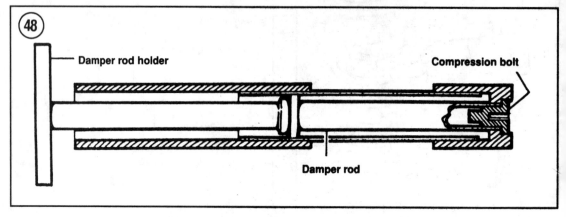

Damper rod holder   Compression bolt

Damper rod

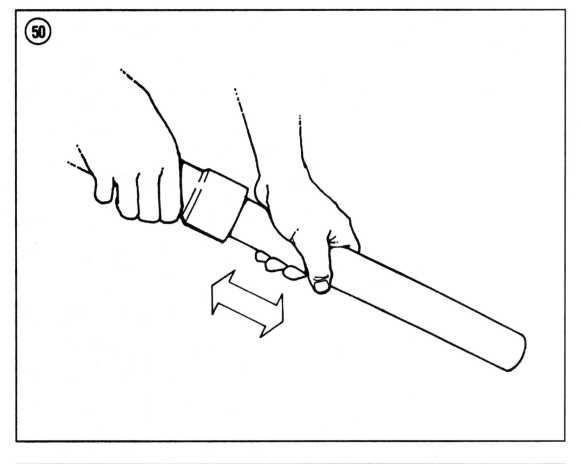

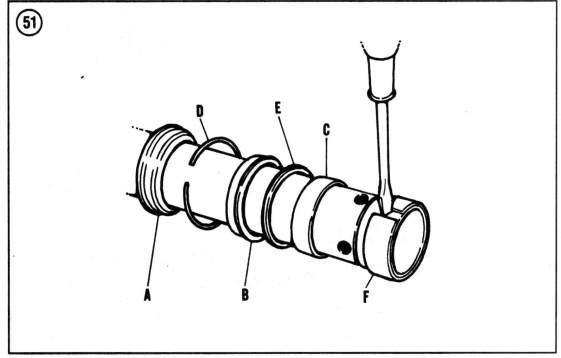

12

oil and dust seals when you install them in Step 4.

4. Install the following parts (**Figure 52**) onto the slider as follows:

   a. Dust seal (A). Install the dust seal (**Figure 53**) so that its open side face up (toward top of the slider).

   b. Stop ring (B).

   c. Oil seal (C). Install the oil seal so that its open side faces up (toward top of slider). See **Figure 54**.

   d. Backup ring (D).

   e. Guide bushing (E).

   f. Slider bushing. Seat the bushing into the groove in the top of the slider. See **Figure 55**.

5. Coat the slider and the slider bushing with fork oil and install the slider into the fork tube.

6. Install the guide bushing (E, **Figure 52**) as follows:

   a. Support the fork assembly so that the slider is facing up.

   b. Position the guide bushing so that rests against the fork tube.

   c. Position the backup ring against the guide bushing.

   d. Drive the guide bushing (with the backup ring on top of it) into the fork tube until it bottoms out. Use the Honda oil seal driver and attachment (or an equivalent tool) to install the bushing. See **Figure 56**.

7. Install the oil seal (C, **Figure 52**) as follows:

   a. Drive the oil seal (**Figure 57**) into the fork tube with the same tools used in Step 6.

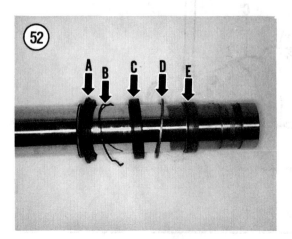

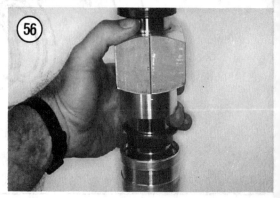

b. Drive the oil seal into place until the stop ring groove is visible above the oil seal.

8. Install the stop ring into the fork tube groove. Make sure the stop ring is completely seated in the groove.

9. Seat the dust seal (A, **Figure 52**) into the fork tube.

10. Perform the following steps to install the damper rod and compression bolt assembly:

   a. Clamp the slider (axle holder) in a vise with soft jaws.

   b. Install the damper rod holder into the fork tube seat it into the bottom of the slider.

   c. Insert the damper rod holder into the fork tube and engage it with the damper rod (**Figure 48**).

   d. Install a new washer onto the compression bolt.

   e. Apply fork oil to the compression bolt O-rings (**Figure 58**).

f. Apply ThreeBond medium strength thread-lock onto the compression bolt threads.

> *CAUTION*
> *Do not allow the threadlock to contact the O-rings, shim pack, or piston on the compression bolt.*

   g. Install the compression bolt through the slider and thread it into the bottom of the damper rod.

   h. Hold the damper holder with the special tool and tighten the compression bolt to the torque specification in **Table 14**.

   i. Remove the damper rod holder from the fork tube.

11. Install the following parts (**Figure 47**) onto the piston rod:

   a. O-ring—coat the O-ring with fork oil before installing it.

   b. Spring guide.

   c. Spring collar.

   d. Piston rod locknut—install locknut with its cut out side facing down. This is a temporary installation to hold the spring guide during the refilling procedure.

12. Install the distance collar (**Figure 46**) into the piston rod.

13. Install the adjuster rod into the piston rod with its oil hole side facing down. See **Figure 46**.

14. Refill the fork with oil and set the oil level as described under *Fork Oil Refilling* in this chapter.

**Fork Oil Refilling
(1995-on Models)**

The recommended fork oil for 1995-on models is Pro Honda Suspension Fluid SS-7M or equivalent.

1. Tie a long piece of wire to the piston rod locknut. This will allow you to retrieve the piston rod when it slides into the fork tubes.

> *NOTE*
> *Refer to **Table 2** fork oil capacity speci-fications.*

2. Bottom the fork tube dust seal against the axle holder on the slider (**Figure 59**).

3. Pour half the recommended amount of fork oil into the fork tube.

4. To bleed air from the fork tube, do the following:

   a. Extend the fork tube.

b. Cover the fork tube with your hand and compress the fork slowly.

c. Repeat until the fork's movement feels consistent.

d. Bottom the fork tube dust seal against the axle holder on the slider (**Figure 59**).

e. With the piston rod bottomed out, slowly add more fork oil until the oil starts to flow out of the end of the piston rod.

f. Slowly pump the piston rod and fork tube 8 to 10 times.

g. Pour the remaining amount of fork oil and repeat substep f.

5. To set the oil level, do the following:

a. Bottom the fork tube dust seal against the axle holder on the slider (**Figure 59**).

b. Place the fork tube in a vertical position.

c. Using an oil level gauge, set the oil level to the specifications listed in **Table 3**. See **Figure 60**.

d. Remove the oil level gauge.

6. Turn the piston rod locknut until it bottoms on the piston rod.

7. Install the fork spring into the fork tube with its tapered end facing up. Feed the wire thought the spring while installing the spring.

8. Slowly pull the piston rod up, then remove the wire. Do not let go of the piston rod.

9. Install the spring seat onto the fork spring.

10. Screw the fork cap onto the end of the piston rod.

11. Hold the locknut and tighten the fork cap against the locknut to 28 N•m (20 ft.-lb.).

12. Check that the spring seat is positioned correctly against the fork cap and spring.

13. Pull the outer tube up and thread the fork cap into the outer tube.

14. Install the fork tubes as described in Chapter Nine of the main book.

FRONT FORK ADJUSTMENT

Compression Damping Adjustment

The compression damping adjuster is mounted in the center of the compression bolt installed in the bottom of the fork tube (**Figure 61**). The compression damping adjustment affects how quickly the front fork compresses. Turning the compression adjuster clockwise increases (stiffens) the compression damping; turning the compression adjuster counter-

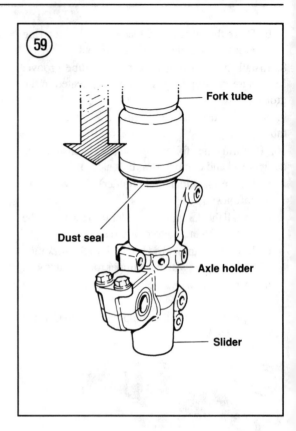

(59)

Fork tube

Dust seal

Axle holder

Slider

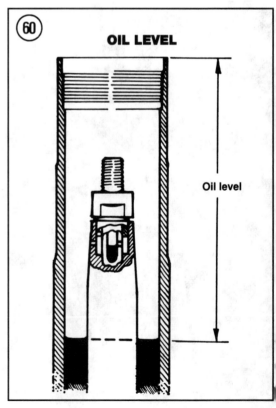

(60)   **OIL LEVEL**

Oil level

clockwise decreases (softens) the compression damping. **Table 16** lists the standard compression damping positions. Turning the compression adjuster 1 full turn changes the adjuster by 4 positions.

To adjust the compression damping adjuster to its standard position, perform the following:

1. Remove the plug from the bottom of each fork tube.

2. Turn the compression damping adjuster (**Figure 61**) *clockwise* until it stops.

3. Turn the compression damping adjuster *counterclockwise* the standard number of turns listed in **Table 16** for your model.

4. Set both fork tubes to the same damping position.

NOTE
Make sure the compression adjuster screw is located in one of the detent positions and not in between any 2 settings.

Rebound Damping Adjustment

The rebound damping adjusters are mounted in the center of each fork cap (**Figure 62**). The rebound damping adjustment affects how quickly the front fork extends after compression. Turning the rebound adjuster clockwise increases (stiffens) the rebound damping; turning the rebound adjuster counterclockwise decreases (softens) the rebound damping. **Table 17** lists the standard rebound damping adjustment position. Turning the rebound damping adjuster 1 full turn changes the adjuster by 4 positions.

To adjust the rebound damping adjuster to its standard position, perform the following:

1. Turn the rebound damping adjuster (**Figure 62**) *clockwise* until it stops.

2. Turn the rebound damping adjuster *counterclockwise* the standard number of turns listed in **Table 17** for your model.

3. Set both fork tubes to the same damping setting.

NOTE
Make sure the rebound adjuster screw is located in one of the detent positions and not in between any 2 settings.

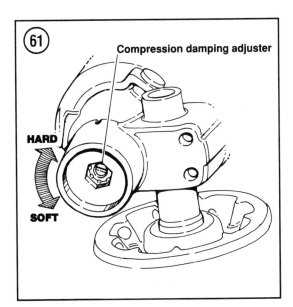

Compression damping adjuster
HARD
SOFT

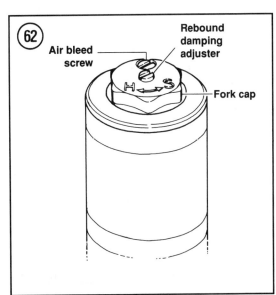

Air bleed screw
Rebound damping adjuster
Fork cap

12

Tables 14-17 are on the following pages.

Table 14 FRONT SUSPENSION TORQUE SPECIFICATONS

	N·m	ft.-lb.	in.-lb.
Front axle			
1992-1994	87	64	
1995-on	88	65	
Front axle holder bolts	20	14	
Fork bridge bolts			
Upper			
1992-1994	22	16	
1995-on	21	15	
Lower	22	16	
Upper steering stem locknut			
1992	118	87	
1993-on	130	95	
Steering stem adjust nut			
1992-1994	2.0	–	18
1995-on	13	–	115
Fork cap			
1992-1994	35	25	
1995-on	30	22	
Fork compression bolt	80	59	
Piston rod locknut			
1992-1994	22	16	
1995-on	28	20	
Spoke nipples	3.8	–	33
Rim locks	13	–	115
Brake disc mounting bolts			
1992-1994	20	14	
1995-on	16	12	
Throttle housing bolts	10	–	88

Table 15 FRONT FORK SPRING FREE LENGTH (STANDARD SPRING)

Model	Standard	Service limit
CR500R		
1992-1994	512 mm	504.4 mm
	(20.2 in.)	(19.86 in.)
1995	490 mm	487 mm
	(19.3 in.)	(19.2 in.)
1996	470 mm	467 mm
	(18.5 in.)	(18.4 in.)

Table 16 FRONT FORK COMPRESSION DAMPING ADJUSTMENT

Model	Number of adjustment positions	Standard adjustment position
CR500R		
1992	14 or more	4
1993	14 or more	6
1994	14 or more	14
1995	20 or more	14
1996	20 or more	8

Table 17 FRONT FORK REBOUND DAMPING ADJUSTMENT

Model	Number of adjustment positions	Standard adjustment position
CR500R		
1992	17 or more	20
1993	17 or more	10
1994	17 or more	12
1995	18 or more	16
1996	18 or more	16

CHAPTER TEN

REAR SUSPENSION

Rear suspension specifications for 1992-on CR500R models are listed in the following tables:

  a. Rear suspension torque specifications: **Table 18**.

  b. Rear shock absorber installed spring length (standard): **Table 19**.

  c. Rear shock absorber spring free length: **Table 20**.

  d. Rear shock absorber rebound damping adjustment: **Figure 21**.

  e. Rear shock absorber rebound damping adjustment: **Figure 22**.

SWING ARM

All procedures related to the swing are the same as for 1989-1991 CR500R models. Refer to the following illustrations for 1992-on CR500R swing arms:

  a. **Figure 63**: 1992 CR500R.

  b. **Figure 64**: 1993-on CR500R.

SHOCK ABSORBER

Procedures used to service the rear shock absorber remain the same as for earlier models, except for the information provided in this section. **Table 18** lists the rear shock absorber tightening torque specifications.

Rebound Damping Adjustment

Procedures used to adjust the rebound damping remain the same as for earlier models, but the standard setting adjustments have changed. **Table 21** lists the standard settings for 1992-on models.

Compression Damping Adjustment (1992-1995)

Procedures used to adjust the compression damping remain the same as for earlier models, but the standard setting adjustments have changed. **Table 22** lists the standard settings for 1992-1995 models.

12

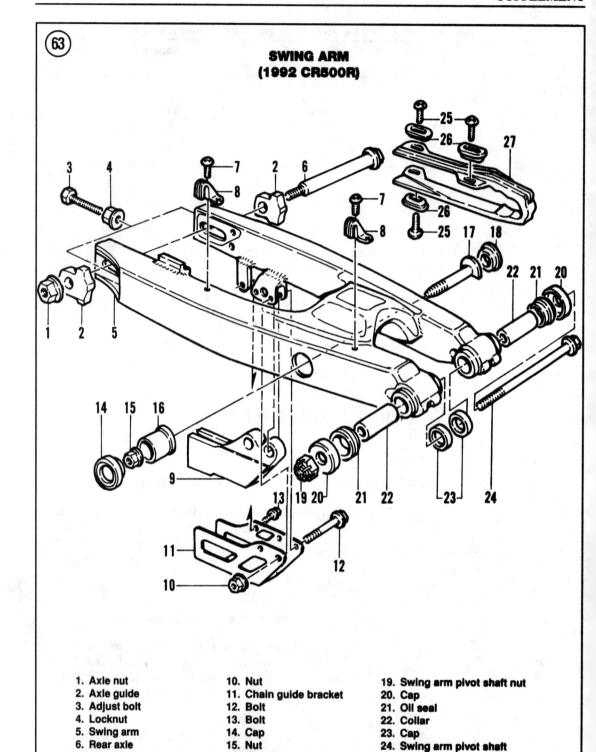

63

SWING ARM
(1992 CR500R)

1. Axle nut
2. Axle guide
3. Adjust bolt
4. Locknut
5. Swing arm
6. Rear axle
7. Screw
8. Brake hose clamp
9. Chain guide
10. Nut
11. Chain guide bracket
12. Bolt
13. Bolt
14. Cap
15. Nut
16. Collar
17. Pivot shaft
18. Cap
19. Swing arm pivot shaft nut
20. Cap
21. Oil seal
22. Collar
23. Cap
24. Swing arm pivot shaft
25. Screw
26. Damper
27. Chain guide

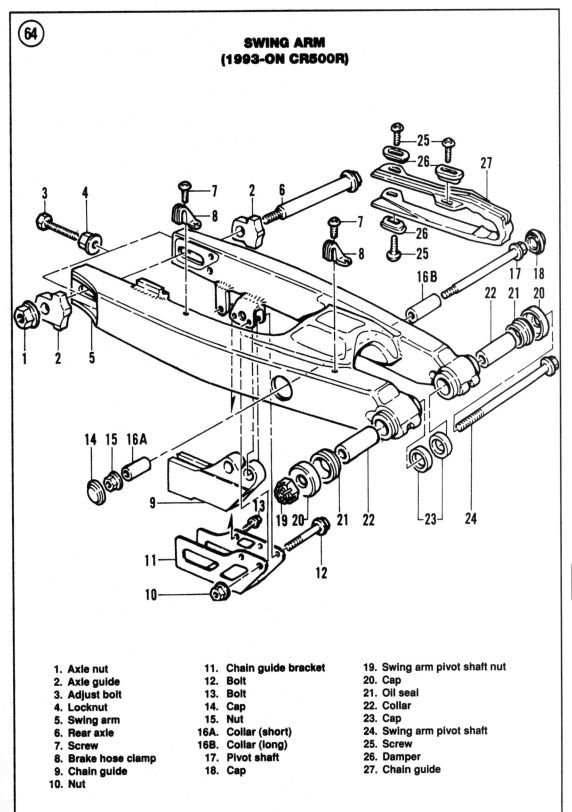

**SWING ARM
(1993-ON CR500R)**

1. Axle nut
2. Axle guide
3. Adjust bolt
4. Locknut
5. Swing arm
6. Rear axle
7. Screw
8. Brake hose clamp
9. Chain guide
10. Nut
11. Chain guide bracket
12. Bolt
13. Bolt
14. Cap
15. Nut
16A. Collar (short)
16B. Collar (long)
17. Pivot shaft
18. Cap
19. Swing arm pivot shaft nut
20. Cap
21. Oil seal
22. Collar
23. Cap
24. Swing arm pivot shaft
25. Screw
26. Damper
27. Chain guide

12

Compression Damping Adjustment (1996)

The rear shock absorber on these models is equipped with low and high speed compression damping adjusters. Both adjusters are located on the right side of the shock. See **Figure 65**.

High speed compression damping adjustment

To adjust the high speed compression damping adjuster to its standard position, perform the following:

1. Turn the high speed compression damping adjuster *clockwise* until it stops (**Figure 65**).

2. Turn the high speed compression damping adjuster one full turn *counterclockwise*. At this position, the 2 adjuster marks should align, indicating that the high speed adjustment is set in the standard position.

NOTE
Adjust the high speed compression damping adjuster in 1/12 turn increments.

Low speed compression damping adjustment

Turning the low speed rebound adjuster clockwise increases (stiffens) the low speed rebound damping; turning the low speed rebound adjuster counterclockwise decreases (softens) the low speed rebound damping. **Table 22** lists the standard low speed rebound damping adjustment positions. Turning the adjuster 1 full turn changes the adjuster by 4 positions.

To adjust the low speed rebound damping adjuster to its standard position, perform the following:

1. Turn the low speed rebound damping adjuster *clockwise* until it stops (**Figure 65**).

2. Turn the low speed rebound damping adjuster *counterclockwise* the standard number of turns listed

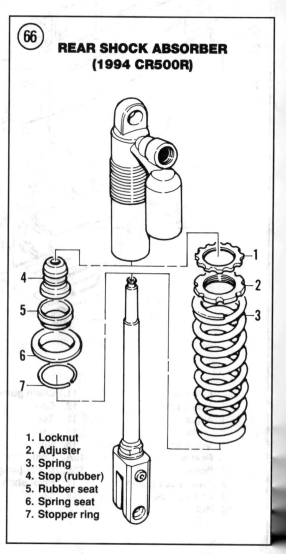

66

REAR SHOCK ABSORBER (1994 CR500R)

1. Locknut
2. Adjuster
3. Spring
4. Stop (rubber)
5. Rubber seat
6. Spring seat
7. Stopper ring

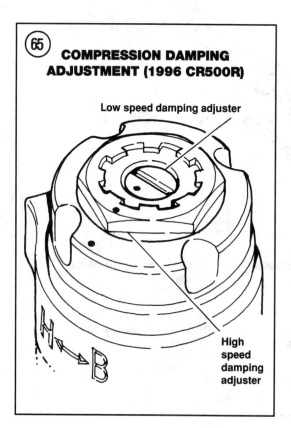

65

COMPRESSION DAMPING ADJUSTMENT (1996 CR500R)

Low speed damping adjuster

High speed damping adjuster

in **Table 22** for your model. The low speed rebound damping adjuster can be adjusted to 8 or more positions.

Disassembly/Assembly (1994)

Procedures used to remove and install the rear shock spring remain the same as for 1991-1993 and 1995-1996 models, except for the spring seat arrangement (**Figure 66**) at the bottom shock mount. To remove and install the spring seat on 1994 models, do the following:

1. Loosen the shock absorber adjusters as described under *Shock Absorber Disassembly/Assembly* in Chapter Ten of the main book.
2. Remove the stopper ring from the rubber seat.
3. Remove the spring seat and spring.
4. Install the spring over the shock with the narrow wound spring coil facing down.
5. Install the spring seat over the shock and seat it against the spring.

6. Install the stopper ring onto the rubber seat.
7. Complete spring assembly by performing the procedures in Chapter Ten of the main book.

Disassembly/Assembly (1992-1993 and 1995-1996)

When installing the rear shock spring on these models, install it so that its narrow wound spring coil faces down.

PIVOT ARM ASSEMBLY

Procedures used to service the pivot arm assembly remain the same as for earlier models, except for the information provided in the following sections. See **Table 18** for pivot arm tightening torque specifications.

Refer to the following illustrations for pivot arm component alignment:
   a. 1992-1995: **Figure 67**.
   b. 1996: **Figure 68**.

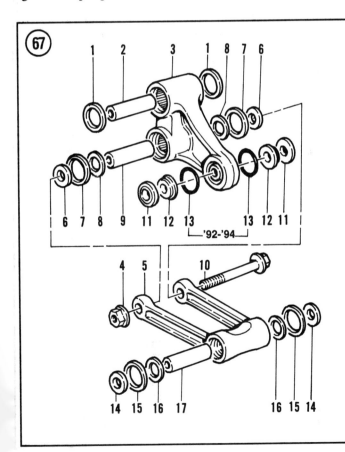

67

PIVOT ARM (1992-1995)

1. Oil seal
2. Collar
3. Pivot arm
4. Nut
5. Shock link
6. Collar
7. Oil seal
8. Thrust washer
9. Collar
10. Pivot bolt
11. Collar
12. Dust seal
13. Stopper ring
14. Side collar
15. Oil seal
16. Thrust washer
17. Collar

12

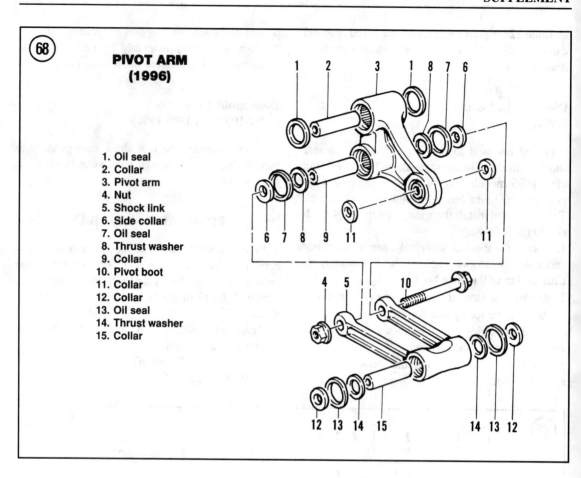

PIVOT ARM (1996)

68

1. Oil seal
2. Collar
3. Pivot arm
4. Nut
5. Shock link
6. Side collar
7. Oil seal
8. Thrust washer
9. Collar
10. Pivot boot
11. Collar
12. Collar
13. Oil seal
14. Thrust washer
15. Collar

Table 18 REAR SUSPENSION TORQUE SPECIFICATONS

	N·m	ft.-lb.
Rear axle nut	95	70
Swing arm pivot bolt nut	90	66
Shock absorber spring locknut		
1992-1994	90	66
1995-on	29	21
Shock absorber mounting bolts		
Upper	45	33
Lower		
1992	43	31
1993-on	45	33
Pro link mounting bolts		
Shock link to frame	63	46
Shock arm to swing arm		
1992	63	46
1993-on	90	66
Shock arm to shock link	63	46
Driven sprocket nuts	33	24
Rear brake disc mounting bolts	43	31
Chain guide bolts	12	9
Chain roller bolt	22	16
Brake pedal pivot bolt	26	19

Table 19 REAR SHOCK ABSORBER INSTALLED SPRING LENGTH (STANDARD)

Model	mm	in.
CR500R		
1992-1993	250	9.8
1994	280	11.0
1995-on	253.5	9.98

Table 20 REAR SHOCK ABSORBER SPRING FREE LENGTH

Model	Standard		Service limit	
	mm	in.	mm	in.
CR500R				
1992-1993	265	10.4	262	10.3
1994	280	11.0	277	10.9
1995-on	265	10.4	*	*

*Not specified.

Table 21 REAR SHOCK ABSORBER REBOUND DAMPING ADJUSTMENT

Model	Number of adjustment positions	Standard adjustment position
CR500R		
1992	20 or more	11-14
1993	22 or more	8-12
1994	22 or more	8-12
1995	20 or more	9-12
1996	20 or more	9-12

Table 22 REAR SHOCK ABSORBER COMPRESSION DAMPING ADJUSTMENT

Model	Number of adjustment positions	Standard adjustment position
CR500R		
1992	22 or more	16-19
1993	20 or more	5-9
1994	20 or more	5-9
1995	20 or more	6-9
1996		
High speed	—	See text
Low speed	8 or more	3-6

12

CHAPTER ELEVEN

BRAKES

The brake specifications listed in **Table 1** in Chapter Eleven of the main book are the same for 1992-on models, except for the brake pad thickness specifications. For 1992-on models, Honda does not list standard brake pad thickness specifications. However, the wear limit specification of 1.0 mm (0.04 in.) for the front and rear brake pads remains the same. To inspect the brake pads on these models, use the information listed under *Disc Brake Pad Wear* in Chapter Three of this supplement and in Chapter Three of the main book.

Table 23 lists brake torque specifications for 1992-on CR500R models.

FRONT MASTER CYLINDER

Procedures used to service the front master cylinder remain the same as for earlier models, except for the following:

a. When installing the master cylinder onto the handlebar, align the end of the master cylinder holder with the punch mark on the handlebar (**Figure 69**).

b. Connect the brake hose to the master cylinder by centering the hose between the 2 hose tabs on the master cylinder housing (**Figure 70**).
c. Secure the hose with the banjo bolt and 2 new washers (**Figure 70**).
d. Tighten the brake hose banjo bolt (**Figure 70**) to the torque specification in **Table 21**.
e. Bleed the front brake as described under *Bleeding the System* in Chapter Eleven of the main book.

> *WARNING*
> *Do not ride the bike until the front and rear brakes work properly.*

BRAKE HOSE REPLACEMENT

Front Brake Hose

Procedures used to replace the front brake hose remain the same as for earlier models, except how the brake hose attaches to the front master cylinder. To service the front brake hose at the master cylinder, refer to *Front Master Cylinder* in this supplement.

(69)

Front master cylinder

Brake hose bolt

Handlebar index mark

Clamp

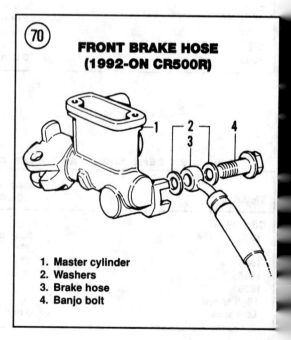

(70)

FRONT BRAKE HOSE (1992-ON CR500R)

1. Master cylinder
2. Washers
3. Brake hose
4. Banjo bolt

Table 23 BRAKE TORQUE SPECIFICATIONS

	N·m	ft.-lb.	in.-lb.
Front master cylinder			
Clamp bolts	10	–	88
Adjuster locknut	6	–	53
Brake lever pivot nut	6	–	53
Front brake caliper mounting bolts	31	22	
Brake caliper bleed valve	6	–	53
Brake hose banjo bolt	35	25	
Front brake caliper pin bolt	23	17	
Pad pin plug	2.5	–	22
Pad pin	18	13	
Bracket pin bolt			
1992-1993	13	10	
1994-on	23	17	
Rear brake master cylinder mounting bolts			
1992-1994	15	11	
1995-on	15	11	
Rear brake disc guard screws	7	–	62
Rear brake caliper pin bolt			
1992-1994	28	20	
1995-on	28	20	
Rear brake caliper bracket pin bolt	13	10	
Brake hose guide	5.3	–	47

12

INDEX

13

13

W

1988 CR250R

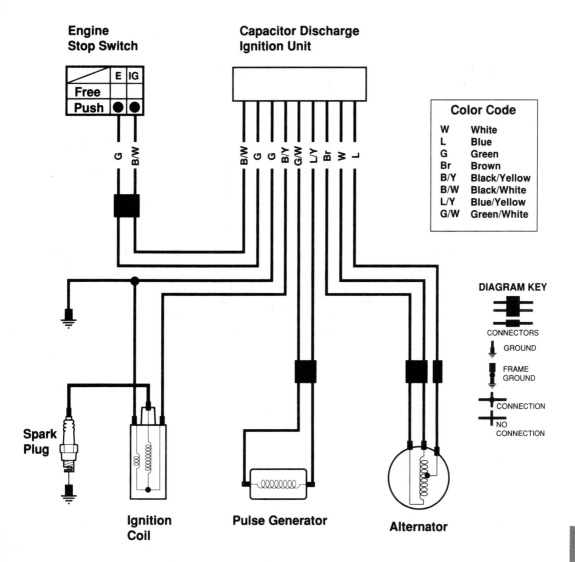

Engine Stop Switch

	E	IG
Free		
Push	●	●

Capacitor Discharge Ignition Unit

Color Code

W	White
L	Blue
G	Green
Br	Brown
B/Y	Black/Yellow
B/W	Black/White
L/Y	Blue/Yellow
G/W	Green/White

DIAGRAM KEY

CONNECTORS
GROUND
FRAME GROUND
CONNECTION
NO CONNECTION

Spark Plug

Ignition Coil

Pulse Generator

Alternator

14

1989-1991 CR250R
1988-1991 CR500R

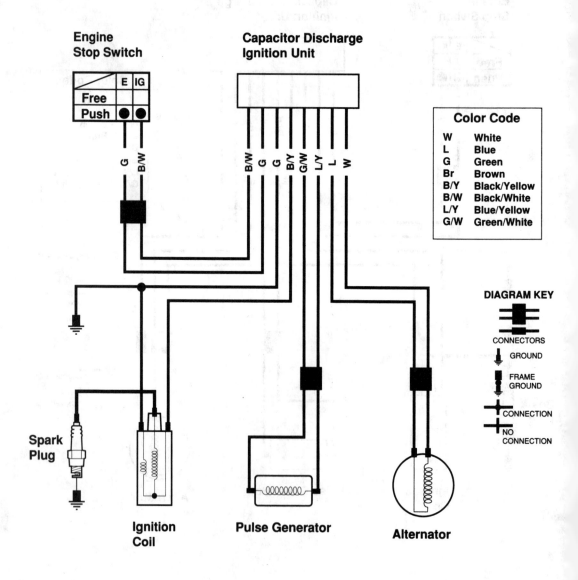

1992-1996 CR500R

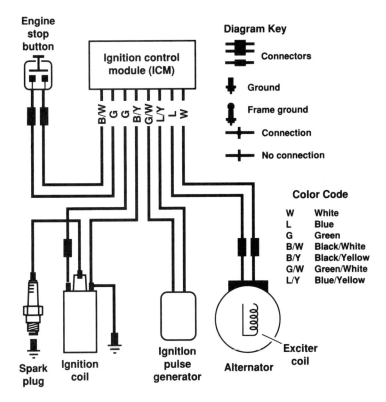

NOTES

NOTES

NOTES

NOTES

MAINTENANCE LOG

Service Performed	Mileage Reading				
Oil change (example)	2,836	5,782	8,601		